Library of
Davidson College

Naval History

Naval History

The Seventh Symposium of the U.S. Naval Academy

William B. Cogar
General Editor

with
Patricia Sine
Assistant Editor

Scholarly Resources Inc.
Wilmington, Delaware

The paper used in this publication meets the minimum requirements of the American National Standard for permanence of paper for printed library materials, Z39.48, 1984.

©1988 Scholarly Resources Inc.
All rights reserved
First published 1988
Printed and bound in the United States of America

Scholarly Resources Inc.
104 Greenhill Avenue
Wilmington, Delaware 19805-1897

Library of Congress Cataloging-in-Publication Data

United States Naval Academy Symposium (7th : 1988)
  Naval history : the Seventh Symposium of the U.S. Naval Academy / William B. Cogar, general editor with Patricia Sine, assistant editor.
    p.   cm.
  ISBN 0-8420-2299-6
  1. Naval art and science—History—Congresses. 2. Naval history—Congresses. I. Cogar, William B., 1949-   . II. Sine, Patricia. III. Title.
V27.U55 1988
359'.009—dc 19   88-11691
                                                            CIP

To My Wife Jackie

Contents

Foreword	xi
Contributors	xiii

RECONSTRUCTING A GREEK TRIREME

Historical Value and Authenticity of the Trireme Replica *John S. Morrison*	2
A Problem in Naval Engineering and Design *John F. Coates*	7
The Value of Sea Trials in Experimental Archaeology *John R. Hale*	13
Convoys and Squadrons: English Naval Strategy and Deterrence, 1674–88 *Sari Hornstein*	18
The French Raid upon the Newfoundland Fishery in 1762: A Study in the Nature and Limits of Eighteenth-Century Sea Power *Olaf Uwe Janzen*	35
The Battle of Grenada and Caribbean Strategy, 1779 *Alan G. Jamieson*	55
Naval Medicine in an Emerging Crisis, 1845–63 *Allen Richman*	63

THE *MONITOR* PROJECT

The USS *Monitor* as a National Marine Sanctuary *Edward M. Miller*	72
The Historical Importance of the USS *Monitor* *William N. Still*	75
The Importance of Understanding the Construction of the USS *Monitor* *Ernest W. Peterkin*	81
The USS *Monitor* Project Research Design *Richard A. Gould*	83

CONTENTS

The Royal Navy and the Projection of British Power, 1863–1900 — 89
Bruce Collins

The Diplomat versus the Sailor: Armed Intervention in Taiwan, 1867 — 107
David F. Long

Tirpitz: Architect of Modern German Naval Power — 117
Gary E. Weir

Choosing among Technologies in the Anglo-German Naval Arms Competition, 1898–1915 — 127
Charles H. Fairbanks, Jr.

Admiral Nelson and the Concept of Patriotism: The Trafalgar Centenary, 1905 — 143
Gerald Jordan

The Imperial Russian Navy's Pioneer Efforts in Arctic Aviation — 156
William Barr

"World Wide Wireless": The U.S. Navy, Big Business, Technology, and Radio Communications, 1919–22 — 170
John P. Rossi

U.S. Naval Air Expeditions in the Arctic in the 1920s — 186
Nancy Fogelson

Admiral Mahan, "Narrative Fidelity," and the Japanese Attack on Pearl Harbor: The Rhetorical Interaction between Discourse and Corroborative Events — 195
Ronald H. Carpenter

Prisoner in the Mediterranean: The Evolution and Execution of Italian Naval Strategy, 1919–42 — 212
Brian R. Sullivan

Erich Raeder and the Coming of the Second World War — 222
Charles S. Thomas

War Plan Orange, 1897–1941: The Blue Thrust through the Pacific — 239
Edward S. Miller

Portrait of an Intelligence Officer: James McHugh in China, 1937–42 — 249
William M. Leary

The Distorted Danger: Winston Churchill and the French Dreadnoughts — 264
Calvin W. Hines

RCN-USN, 1939–45: Some Reflections on the Origins of a New Alliance — 276
Marc Milner

An Antediluvian Monstrosity: The Battleship Revisited — 284
Lawrence C. Allin

General Louis H. Wilson: 26th Commandant of the
   Marine Corps, 1975–79 293
   David H. White, Jr.

Foreword

Sponsored by the History Department of the U.S. Naval Academy, the Naval History Symposium began in 1971 as a limited concept with a small number of invited retired naval officers who lectured on selected topics. In 1977 it was decided to expand the symposium concept and model it more along the lines of such prestigious academic conferences as those sponsored by the American Historical Association and the Organization of American Historians. Since that year, the symposium has been held every two years and has grown steadily in size and registration to become the leading conference of its type, not only in the United States but also in the entire world. The international reputation of the Naval History Symposium is evidenced by the participation of scholars from around the globe.

The Seventh Naval History Symposium, directed by Professor Kenneth J. Hagan and ably assisted by Lieutenant Commander Andrew Koczon, USNR, and Mrs. Connie Grigor, consisted of twenty-three panels with sixty-two papers and over 110 participants. An additional 300 scholars and naval and Marine Corps personnel attended the sessions and heard the very interesting and entertaining banquet speaker, Professor D. Clayton James, who discussed General Douglas MacArthur's relationship with the U.S. Navy.

Well over 200 proposals from the United States and eight countries were considered by the symposium committee for selection into the program. The following essays are a sample of the high quality of proposals made and papers read. The papers are diverse and eclectic and thus range from the reconstruction of a classical Greek trireme to a reassessment of the battleship and its role in modern maritime strategy. As with past symposium publications, the diversity of the essay subjects, both printed here but also indicative of those papers presented at the symposium, show the wide range of topics which loosely fit into the general area or discipline of naval and maritime history. In keeping with the decision to have no central theme for the symposium and elicit instead papers from a broad range of historical eras, nationalities, and themes, the past directors have sought to generate more interest in traditional naval and maritime issues while also suggesting new avenues for the overall discipline of naval history. It is generally thought that this policy has been a great success, and it is hoped that future symposia also will remain broad in their range of subjects.

While directed by a committee, the symposium's existence and overall success was the result of the efforts of a large number of people. Naval Academy Superintendent Rear Admiral Charles R. Larson, Academic Dean Dr. Karl A. Lamb, Vice Dean Dr. Richard Mathieu, and Colonel John W. Ripley, USMC, director of the Division of English and History; Professor Frederick S. Harrod, chairman of the History Department; Lieutenant Commander Don T. Sine, USN; and members of the History Department were all very active in their support, and sincere gratitude is extended to each of them. A special note of thanks goes to my colleagues Professor Jane Good and Professor Phyllis Culham.

The conference was indeed fortunate to have a distinguished group of scholars who served as chairmen or commentators at the sessions. As such, they offered many serious and constructive suggestions. They were: Dean C. Allard, Naval Historical Center; Captain James Barber, USN (Ret.), U.S. Naval Institute; K. Jack Bauer, Rensselaer Polytechnic Institute; Daniel Baugh, Cornell University; Keith Bird, Hesser College; James Bradford, Texas A&M University; William Braisted, University of Texas, Austin; Captain Angelo Collura, USNR; B. Frank Cooling, Office of Air Force History; Philip Crowl, U.S. Naval War College; W. A. B. Douglass, National Defense Headquarters, Canada; James F. Downs, University Research Corporation; Frederick C. Drake, Brock University; Benis Frank, Headquarters, U.S. Marine Corps; Norman Friedman; Thomas C. Gilmer, U.S. Naval Academy (Ret.); John Guilmartin, Rice University; Michael Guyer, University of Michigan; Holger Herwig, U.S. Naval War College; Vice Admiral Edwin B. Hooper, USN (Ret.); Jacob W. Kipp, Miami University, Ohio; Neville Kirk, U.S. Naval Academy, Emeritus; Richard H. Kohn, Office of Air Force History; Harold Langley, Smithsonian Institution; Archibald R. Lewis, University of Massachusetts; John W. Long, Rider College; Philip Lundeberg, Smithsonian Institution; K. S. MacKenzie, Canadian National Railways; Michael MccGwire, Brookings Institution; John McCusker, University of Maryland; Peter Mersky, Naval Safety Center; Rear Admiral George H. Miller, USN (Ret.); Frederick Rainbow, U.S. Naval Institute; Stephen S. Roberts, Ph.D.; Philip Rosen, University of Alaska, Anchorage; Captain Paul Ryan, USN (Ret.), Hoover Institution; Captain Raymond P. Schmidt, USNR; Jack Schulimson, Headquarters, U.S. Marine Corps; Robert Seager II, University of Kentucky; Dennis Showalter, Colorado College; Commander Edward P. Stafford, USN (Ret.); James L. Stokesbury, Acadia University; David Syrett, Queens College, SUNY; Spencer C. Tucker, Texas Christian University; and Rear Admiral Robert Weeks, USN (Ret.). Sincere thanks are extended to each of them and to the numerous attendees who made the symposium such a success.

Finally, there are several people who greatly assisted me in editing the following papers and who must be publicly thanked. Patricia Sine, an instructor in the Naval Academy's English Department, was invaluable by proofreading many of the papers. Editorial assistance also was given by Jimmy Haritos and Tara Gray. Thanks cannot be extended enough to Connie Grigor, who so kindly put up with numerous requests on her time and patience. Finally, the greatest gratitude and appreciation must go to my family and especially to my wife, who endured far beyond the call of duty.

William B. Cogar
General Editor

Contributors

LAWRENCE C. ALLIN received his Ph.D. in 1976 from the University of Maine, where he has been teaching maritime and military history since 1970. He was service historian for the Army Corps of Engineers from 1979 to 1982. He is presently maritime historian at the University of Maine and also teaches at the Bangor Theological Seminary.

WILLIAM BARR is a geographer who studied at the University of Aberdeen and McGill University. Researching into the history of Arctic exploration, with particular emphasis on the Russian Arctic, he is currently head of the Department of Geography, University of Saskatchewan.

RONALD H. CARPENTER, professor of English at the University of Florida, writes about historians as rhetorical stylists and mass persuaders. His publications include *The Eloquence of Frederick Jackson Turner* and numerous essays. He has received a University of Florida President's Scholar Award and a Speech Communication Association Monograph Award.

JOHN F. COATES is the coauthor of *The Athenian Trireme* (with John S. Morrison). His career in the British navy led to an appointment as deputy director of ship design for the Ministry of Defense, a position from which he recently retired.

BRUCE COLLINS received his Ph.D. from Cambridge University. His publications include, among scholarly and review articles, *The Origins of America's Civil War* (1981) and *The Growth of Federal Power in American History*. He is presently a lecturer in modern history at the University of Glasgow.

CHARLES H. FAIRBANKS, JR., is research professor at the Johns Hopkins School of Advanced International Studies and the director of the Program in Soviet and American National Security Policymaking at its Foreign Policy Institute. After teaching at Yale University, he served in the State Department as a member of the Policy Planning Staff and as deputy assistant secretary.

NANCY FOGELSON received her Ph.D. in 1983 from the University of Cincinnati. Presently teaching American history at the University of Kentucky and continuing research on Arctic exploration and international relations, she is working on a biography of Adolphus Washington Greely.

RICHARD A. GOULD is a noted archaeologist whose recent interest is developing the theory and methods for maritime archaeology; he is conducting project work in Bermuda. He is currently chairman of the Department of Anthropology at Brown University.

JOHN R. HALE is an archaeologist at the University of Louisville. His publications include "Plank-built Boats in the Bronze Age" (1980), as well as studies of rowing techniques in ancient warships.

CALVIN W. HINES received his Ph.D. from the University of Texas, where he specialized in U.S. diplomacy with emphasis on World War II, the French navy, and American policy in the Caribbean, on which he has contributed articles and papers. Since 1968, Dr. Hines has been on the faculty of Stephen F. Austin State University.

SARI HORNSTEIN holds a M.Sc. in economic history from the London School of Economics and a Ph.D. in history from the University of Leiden. Besides revising her dissertation for publication, she is also preparing a volume for the Navy Records Society on the English navy's Mediterranean activities in the late seventeenth century.

ALAN G. JAMIESON joined University College, London, in 1980, one year before receiving his D.Phil. degree from Oxford University. Besides writing several articles on maritime history, he was the editor and principal author of *A People of the Sea: The Maritime History of the Channel Islands.*

OLAF UWE JANZEN received his postgraduate education at Queen's University, Kingston, Ontario. Since 1980 he has been with Memorial University of Newfoundland at its Corner Brook campus, where he teaches Canadian and Newfoundland history. His most recent publication appeared in *Acadiensis.*

GERALD JORDAN attended the University of California at Irvine, studying naval history under the late Arthur Marder, and received his Ph.D. in 1974. He has published chapters and journal articles on, among other subjects, popular attitudes toward empire. He is presently an associate professor of history at York University in Toronto.

WILLIAM M. LEARY received his Ph.D. from Princeton University in 1966. A professor of history at the University of Georgia since 1973, he has served as Fulbright-Hays senior lecturer in Taiwan and Thailand. His most recent publications include editing *The Central Intelligence Agency: History and Documents.*

DAVID F. LONG has been a professor of history at the University of New Hampshire since 1948 and specializes in nineteenth-century U.S. diplomatic and naval history. In addition to writing three biographies, he has revised and expanded Charles O. Paullin's *Diplomatic Negotiations of American Naval Officers.*

EDWARD M. MILLER is a sanctuary project manager for the Marine and Estuarine Management Division of the National Oceanic and Atmospheric Administration. A graduate of the Naval Academy, he is responsible for the USS *Monitor* National Marine Sanctuary.

EDWARD S. MILLER is a retired mining executive. A Phi Beta Kappa graduate of Syracuse University, he attended the Harvard Business School. He has lectured at the Naval War College, the National War College, and conducted seminars at Op-60, the current maritime strategy group at the Pentagon.

MARC MILNER is a former historian with the Directorate of History, Canadian Armed Forces. He has worked on official histories of the Canadian air force and navy. Currently professor of military history at the University of New

Brunswick, he has written *North Atlantic Run: The Royal Canadian Navy and the Battle for the Convoys.*

JOHN S. MORRISON is the author of *Greek Oared Ships,* the standard reference work on Hellenic galleys and naval warfare. In a scholarly career spanning five decades, he has published a series of articles which for the first time reconciled the ancient evidence about the design of the trireme with the demands of practical naval design. Professor Morrison became the first president of Wolfson College, Cambridge, in 1966.

ERNEST W. PETERKIN, a retired captain in the U.S. Naval Reserve, is a recognized authority on the construction of the USS *Monitor.* He assisted the Smithsonian Institution during 1968–69 with the evaluation of the Civil War ironclad *Tecumseh,* which sank in Mobile Bay.

ALLEN RICHMAN holds a M.A. degree from Penn State and his Ph.D. in history from the University of Minnesota. He is an associate professor of history at Stephen F. Austin State University, where he has taught since 1965.

JOHN P. ROSSI is a graduate student at Rutgers University, where he is completing under the guidance of Professor Lloyd C. Gardner a doctoral dissertation on the U.S. search for order in East Asia from 1917 to 1928.

WILLIAM N. STILL is a professor of history at East Carolina University and is a well-known authority on the naval side of the Civil War. He has been involved with research on the USS *Monitor* for over a decade.

BRIAN R. SULLIVAN received his Ph.D. from Columbia University and is presently an assistant professor at Yale University. He served as a Marine artillery officer in Vietnam and is a historian officer specialist in the Marine Corps Reserve. He is currently writing a biography of Margherita Sarfatti.

CHARLES S. THOMAS completed his Ph.D. from Vanderbilt University in 1983. An assistant professor of history at Georgia Southern College, he is currently studying the German naval officer corps during both the peacetime regime of Hitler and the war years.

GARY E. WEIR received his Ph.D. from the University of Tennessee. His work on naval-industrial relations in Imperial Germany has appeared in *Military Affairs* and the *International History Review.* He has taught at St. Ann's School in Washington, DC, since 1982. During the academic year 1986–87, he taught and researched at the U.S. Naval Academy.

DAVID H. WHITE, JR., received his doctorate from Tulane University in 1974. Presently professor of history and director of the Conference on War and Diplomacy at The Citadel, Charleston, he also serves as academic associate of the Atlantic Council of the United States and is a lieutenant colonel in the Marine Corps Reserve.

RECONSTRUCTING A GREEK TRIREME

In 1983 the Trireme Trust began building a full-scale replica of a Greek trireme, the most famous and most enigmatic of ancient warships. So promising were the initial small-scale models and mock-ups that the Greek government offered to pay for building the trireme replica, which then will be commissioned into the Hellenic navy. The following three papers present an overview of the problems of historical evidence and naval engineering leading to the reconstruction, now under way at Perama near Athens, along with an analysis of the lessons to be learned from some earlier reconstructions and sea trials.

Historical Value and Authenticity of the Trireme Replica

JOHN S. MORRISON

Practical marine archaeology conserves, reconstructs from a preserved basis, or wholly recreates relevant artifacts of a given historical period. Ships such as the *Constitution* at Boston, the *Victory* at Portsmouth, and the *Cutty Sark* at Greenwich are examples of the conserved category. The Roskilde Viking ships, the *Mary Rose,* and the Kyrenia ship are examples of the partially preserved category, while the *Mayflower* and the *Kon-Tiki* represent the wholly recreated kind.

The replica of an ancient Greek trireme which is now under construction in Athens is also an example of a model wholly recreated from a combination of historical, technological, and archaeological evidence. It is worthwhile considering the reasons for such enterprises in practical archaeology, all of them costly. Why do individuals and governments spend large sums of money on them? What, in fact, can a conserved or recreated artifact of a past age contribute to modern scholarship?

Objects retrieved from ships, such as those recently recovered from the wrecks in the drained Zuyder Zee or from the *Mary Rose,* appeal to us and have a value as providing a tangible link with an earlier age. The *Mayflower* and the *Cutty Sark,* and especially those ships that have taken part in glorious naval actions—the Athenian trireme at Salamis, the *Victory* at Trafalgar, the *Olympia* at Manila—have acquired an added value on that account.

Where such significant events play a part in world history and the development of civilization in which many nations share, then the ships have a significance and emotive value that reaches beyond national boundaries. The trireme will have a significant and emotive value first for Greeks, and then also among the wider circle of peoples in Europe and America for whom Greek history and civilization have been seminal, laying the foundations of the way in which they think, write, and govern themselves. The ships mentioned above will have a value in one or another of these senses, but the trireme in all of them.

More specifically, one may press further the question of what precisely a replica of a sixteenth-century galley, a Roman quinquereme, or an Athenian trireme will offer students of history. In the first place, replicas will furnish the students' mental pictures of the practices and events of a past age, from which they will be able to make useful evaluations and draw probable conclusions. The value of history is much diminished as an educational and scientific pursuit if the imagination cannot be stimulated by true images of the past. The exercise of creative imagination, putting flesh on the dead bones, is the reward and culmination of necessarily plodding historical study, and the creative imagination needs true images if its exercise is to have scholarly value.

The second sense in which the replica of a historical ship (provided that it is a working replica) may be of use to the historian is by its performance. Sea trials of authentic replicas can provide data for the assessment of voyages, naval movements, actions and, more widely, the potentialities of trade and the effectiveness of sea power.

There are some particular historical questions which a working replica of a trireme may answer. First, the 200 Athenian triremes under Themistocles at Salamis helped to win, against great odds, a battle that is traditionally numbered among the most decisive battles in the world. A very large Persian fleet was defeated by a much smaller fleet of Greek allies in which the Athenian triremes, "specially built for speed and maneuverability,"[1] played the decisive role. A replica of one of these triremes will explain how and to what degree this speed and maneuverability were achieved.[2]

Second, in the late fifth century B.C., Athens became the richest and most powerful city in the Mediterranean, largely, it seems, through its ability to dominate a considerable area of sea to its own advantage. This power was attributed by contemporary writers to the preeminent skill of Athenian seamen and commanders in the use of the trireme. Thus, Athens was in a position to develop the civilization which has been so much admired. How was the city able to found a political hegemony on the skill in building and operating a type of warship that its rivals also possessed? This question has been asked by scholars and historians since the Renaissance. Only practical experience with the trireme will provide a satisfactory answer.

It is unfortunately the case with the trireme that the trouble and expense of a full-scale model are required before these questions can be answered. The interpretation of the evidence relating to the oar system, on which the design entirely depends, has been, and to some extent still is, highly controversial.[3] Only a full-scale replica with men pulling it will show whether or not the oar system that the evidence can be claimed to indicate is actually workable in practice.

There is a further reason why in the case of the trireme, and indeed of all wholly recreated artifacts, only a complete full-scale replica will serve the purpose. All the claims that have just been made for the conserved, partially reconstructed, or wholly recreated artifacts rest on their authenticity. There is no doubt about the authenticity of the *Constitution* or the *Victory,* and there is certainly enough surviving of the *Mary Rose* and the Kyrenia ship to provide solid evidence for reconstructing the remainder. For the trireme, however, not only has no wreck been found, but also no wreck is likely ever to be found on the seabed, since if holed or swamped such a light galley would not have sunk to the bottom. The trireme must then be recreated by careful piecing together of the evidence from various sources, and the authenticity of the replica proved by subsequent full-scale experiment. The trireme project thus has more to gain than most enterprises of this kind and also more to lose.

An account of the piecing together of the evidence is out of place and out of scale in this paper. The story of the scholarly controversy, however, is enlightening in this connection and worthy of a brief review.

The first consideration is the name of the ship itself. The Greek term for the vessel, *trieres,* meaning "three-fitted," might have been expected to give a clue to the ship's structure. Literature and vase paintings show oared warships playing an important part in Greek life from the earliest times, as would be expected from the geography of the Hellenic world.[4] In the *Iliad* and the *Odyssey,* believed to have been composed in the eighth century B.C., are twenty-oared ships and (in the "Catalogue of Ships" in the second book of the *Iliad*) fifty-oared ships, both types presumably with one file of oarsmen on each side, as later vase paintings show. Pride of place in Homer's "Catalogue" is taken by fifty Boeotian ships, each manned by 120 young warriors. Thucydides later states specifically that they all pulled oars.[5] Since one file of sixty is a practical impossibility, these ships must have had two files of oarsmen on each side at different levels, the double manning of oars being unknown at this period. Such an arrangement is confirmed for the end of the eighth century by an Attic vase painting found in Thebes and by an Assyrian relief from the palace of Sennacherib.[6]

The larger and more complicated trireme with a crew of 200 appears to have been invented either in Phoenicia (as M. Basch believes) or in Corinth about the beginning of the next century.[7] This new type seems to have been developed from the Boeotian ship, with its two files of oarsmen on each side, by the addition of a third file. The old sixty-per-side arrangement seems to have been discontinued. However, a more satisfactory two-level arrangement does reappear in ships with twenty-five men at two levels on each side. This latter type did not require a new name (the terms *dieres* and *dikrotos* not appearing until much later), since it was in fact a fifty-oared ship and thus already had a Greek name, pentecontor. On the other hand, the new three-level ship did need a new name and was called *trieres,* "three-fitted." This name can be interpreted in two possible ways. It may refer either to oarsmen seated at three levels or to three files of oarsmen on each side of the ship.

There is a general and unfortunate assumption in modern times that the name *trieres* refers to three levels of oarsmen, unfortunate because it creates grave difficulties when the names of later types are considered. In the early fourth century B.C., *tetrereis* (fours), *pentereis* (fives), and *hexereis* (sixes) were built in Syracuse to meet the threat of Carthage. At the end of the same century, the successors of Alexander fought for control of the Mediterranean in fleets which contained *heptereis* (sevens), *octereis* (eights), and so on. That obsessive naval builder, Demetrius Poliorcetes, used up to "elevens" in battle and built even larger ones for show.

Finally, Ptolemy Philopater in Egypt built a monstrosity, the well-documented *tessaraconteres* (forty). The reductio ad absurdum was plain. "The *trieres* is a ship with three levels and the name means that, so a ship called *tessaraconteres* must have forty levels, as its name implies. But this is absurd. Of course the *tessaraconteres* cannot have had forty levels, *and therefore the 'trieres' did not have three.*"[8] This conclusion, which does not in fact follow since it rests on a false premise, has caused a great deal of trouble.

Renaissance scholars were naturally curious about what sort of ship the *trieres* might be, since they had read about them in the Greek historians. They were equally curious about the quadrireme and the quinquereme, which the Roman historians mentioned. Thus the trireme controversy began. The evidence available to these early scholars was scanty. In sixteenth-century Rome they could see Trajan's column, showing the emperor's undecked, three-level flagship; the relief that is the original of the dal Pozzo drawing, showing, with some mistakes, the bow section of a three-level oared ship; and probably also the Aquila relief, showing the stern of a similar ship.

In Italian waters, however, there were also to be seen galleys that the Venetians called *triremi, quadriremi,* and *quinqueremi*, with three, four, and five files of oarsmen on each side *at one level*. Two different arrangements were used in these Venetian galleys. In the *triremi alla sensile*, three oarsmen sat on each of many benches on each side of the ship, each man pulling his own oar. In the later *triremi, quadriremi,* and *quinqueremi a scaloccio*, squads of three, four, and five men together pulled massive oars. These ships were claimed by some to be lineal descendants of the ancient Greek and Roman warships, which accordingly must have been pulled by oarsmen seated at one level. Analogy might have taught these scholars that the names referred to files, not levels, also in ancient times.

Sir Henry Savile, tutor to Queen Elizabeth I, protested against these claims as going against the ancient literature and "the ancient portraytures remaining yet to be seen."[9] In the case of literary evidence he was probably thinking of the passage in Aristophanes' *Frogs* where an oarsman is said to have made wind—and worse—in the face of the *thalamax,* a slang word for the oarsman who sat in the hold of a trireme (*thalamios*).[10] Savile noted too that there could be no direct lineal descent from ancient to modern galleys, since Zosimus in the fifth century A.D. said that the building of *trierika ploika* had long been forgotten in his day.[11]

The view that Savile represented, that of the scholars, was challenged by Lazar de Baïf, the French ambassador to the Venetian Republic, who claimed that a three-level Greek trireme necessarily implies a four-level quadrireme, and so on ad absurdum.[12] The "ancient portraytures" were just wrong. A more formidable challenge was added in the eighteenth century by the commander of Louis XIV's galleys, Barras de la Penne. He stated categorically that any three-level ship must have been pulled by oars that differed in length, and a synchronized stroke in such a ship would have been impossible.[13]

So the battle lines were drawn for the next two centuries. The scholars' case was strengthened in 1853 by the discovery on the Athenian Acropolis of the Lenormant relief. This fragment apparently showed the midships section of an oared galley of which the dal Pozzo drawing and the Aquila relief might well be the depictions of the bow and stern, all three representations being on the same scale.[14] In 1861–62, a full-scale replica of a Roman trireme was built on the Seine on the orders of Napoleon III. It was a disastrous failure and led to a renewal of the arguments for a one-level trireme using one of the Venetian systems.

German excavations at Athens, however, had brought to light the slips of the ship sheds in which the Athenian triremes had been kept when not at sea. These sheds in the naval harbor at Zea revealed the maximum dimensions of the ship, and inscriptions had been discovered which show that the oarsmen numbered 170 and that the oars were no longer than 4.2 meters.[15] These hard facts rule out both Venetian systems in which the oars were very much longer than 4.2 meters. Although it is possible to imagine an *alla sensile* galley with oars of about the right length, the ship would have had a dangerously low freeboard. In any case, 170 oarsmen could not be fitted into an *alla sensile* galley narrow enough to fit inside the ship sheds at Zea.

The stalemate was broken in favor of the scholars by meeting the two classical objections. If *trieres* means not a ship of three levels but rather one with three files of oarsmen on each side (as *triremi* did in Venice), then de Baïf's objection disappears. The ships with higher ratings can be envisaged as having many files of oarsmen pulling large oars *a scaloccio* in squads, but never at more than three levels. The more serious objection of Barras de la Penne also disappears if it can be demonstrated that a ship with oars on three levels does not need oars differing in length according to the level. The Morrison model of a trireme in 1941 showed that such an arrangement was indeed feasible.[16]

The removal of these objections opened the way to the use of the literary, epigraphical, and archaeological evidence in recreating the design of a three-level oared warship. The consistency of such evidence is remarkable, but by itself it does not make a ship for which the claim can be made that it is on the one hand an authentic replica of a fifth- and fourth-century B.C. Athenian trireme, or on the other hand a workable, seaworthy ship. Only when the laws of physics and recent additional evidence about ancient shipbuilding are applied to the problem, and the resulting design is seen to offer only minimal options to the designer, can the resultant ship have a claim to be considered historically authentic and therefore of value to scholarship.

NOTES

1. Plutarch, *Cim.* 12.1.
2. The question of speed is particularly intriguing. It is worth remembering that at the battle of Lepanto the two lines of oared galleys approached each other at a speed of only two knots.
3. J. S. Morrison, "The Greek Trireme," *Mariner's Mirror* 27 (January 1941): 14-44.
4. The evidence is assembled in J. S. Morrison and R. T. Williams, *Greek Oared Ships, 900-322 B.C.* (London, 1968).
5. Thucydides, 1.10.2.
6. R. T. Williams, "Early Greek Ships of Two Levels," *Journal of Hellenic Studies* 78 (1958): 121-30.
7. I believe it was invented in Corinth. J. S. Morrison, "The First Triremes," *Mariner's Mirror* 65 (February, 1979): 53-63.
8. Morrison and Williams, *Greek Oared Ships*, 244-307.
9. Sir Henry Savile, "A View of Certain Military Matters for the Better Understanding of the Ancient Roman Stories," in Morrison, "The Greek Trireme," 20-21.
10. Aristophanes, *Frogs* 1701-4.
11. Morrison, "The Greek Trireme," 20-21.
12. L. de Baïf, *De re navali* (Basel, 1536).
13. Morrison, "The Greek Trireme," 24.
14. Ibid., 27-30.
15. Morrison and Williams, *Greek Oared Ships*, 181-92.
16. Morrison, "The Greek Trireme," 14-44.

A Problem in Naval Engineering and Design

JOHN F. COATES

The trireme controversy traditionally has been the domain of historians and classicists. As soon as the leap is made from scholarly speculation to actual reconstruction, however, it becomes appropriate to describe the design of a Greek trireme as one would that of any other warship today. One starts with the chief of naval operations' requirements for a seaworthy ship and any other constraints on the design. For the trireme, these constraints are simply the three kinds of historical evidence that bear on the vessel: epigraphical, litrary, and archaeological.

In order to accord with the historical evidence, any trireme reconstruction must have an overall beam of less than 5.5 meters and an overall length of less than 37 meters. It must be propelled by 170 oarsmen arranged in three files on each side of the ship, with 31 oarsmen in the top file and 27 in each of the others. The oarsmen in each file must be spaced 0.888 meters apart. Each man pulls an oar 4.2 or 4.0 meters long, the short oars being at the ends of the ship.

The hull and ram structure are required to accord with both the artistic representations of triremes in ancient reliefs and vase paintings and with the evidence of ancient wrecks recovered by underwater archaeologists. The litrary accounts of Greek historians such as Herodotus and Thucydides require a ship that is quick to turn, suitable for coming to Mediterranean beaches stern-to, and capable of being pulled 190 miles in just over twenty-four hours. Finally, the chief of naval operations will insist that the ship be strong enough structurally to survive the most severe seas in which its navigation would be necessary and stable enough to carry a useful spread of canvas rigged in the manner of the time, and that it have the smallest mass consistent with the evidence.

The speed requirement is particularly formidable.[1] Over long distances it would appear that the trireme was faster than a modern eight-oared shell with all its refinements. It is a pity that the statistics are not directly comparable, there being no records of trireme speeds over short distances, nor of modern racing eights over distances of more than 100 miles.

The trireme was plainly fast enough to need oars of the highest practicable gearing, like all the fast-pulling sea boats of the past. Thus of the four-meters length of oar, only one meter would extend inboard of the thole, the pin about which the oar hinges. That measurement has an effect on the arrangement of the oarsmen within the hull and on the practicability of their close longitudinal spacing. In the trireme depicted in profile on the Lenormant relief from the Athenian Acropolis, the top oarsmen, or thranites, are shown seated high in the outrigger.[2] The slope of those thranite oars must be considered. Its practical limit, as our experiments have shown, is about 35 degrees, owing to the limitations in both wrist movement and in the movement of the oar handle required to raise the blade clear of the water between strokes. For these reasons the thranite oarsmen cannot be seated more than about 1.4 meters above the waterline.

No ship design can progress very far without estimates of the ship's weight, its displacement, the position of its center of gravity (especially of its height in the case of narrow vessels), and stability. As naval architects well know, any or all can impose limits on the design.

Evidence obtained in recent decades from ancient wrecks in the Mediterranean has established how the lower parts of ships were built from the Bronze Age onward. For almost two millennia there seems to have been fair uniformity in shape and building methods at any given time over a wide area, changing slowly over the centuries. While the great majority of wrecks investigated by archaeologists have been of round merchant vessels, a few long ships have been found, though not a trireme. The evidence seemed to justify adopting the build and scantlings of the long ships found off Marsala in Sicily for the trireme reconstruction.[3] Since the dimensions of the trireme were already known, the weight of the hull could now be estimated at about 27 metric tonnes. Adding the weight of the crew (200 men), oars, masts, and such brought the weight of the whole ship up to about 50 tonnes.

The limited height of the thranite oarsmen was leading to a low, shallow hull and therefore to possible trouble with longitudinal strength. The bending movements likely to be experienced by our ship—34 meters long on the waterline and weighing 50 tonnes—can be expected to be about 25 tonne-meters hogging in still water and 100 meters hogging on the crest of a wave. In addition, the ship would experience about one quarter of that amount in sagging. A little calculation showed that the draft could be estimated at about 1 meter, so the thranite seats and the gunwales would be only 2.5 meters above the keel. A little more calculation confirmed that a hull so extremely shallow for its length would be very highly stressed when the ship was among waves. It also followed that the middle and lower files of oarsmen must work their oars through the ports in the side of the hull.

The next step was to examine the arrangement of the oarsmen, which was tentatively assumed to have been that proposed by J. S. Morrison,[4] but with more vertical overlap between the files in order to reduce the slope of the thranite oars. These calculations involved checking for fouls, as well as for excessive clearances, between the oars, the rowers, and the structural members of the hull. The effects of the ship heeling as much as 3 degrees also were taken into consideration. As a test of the arrangement, a mock-up was built with room for four oarsmen. Experience with this model made it possible to reduce the height of the thranite seats by 0.2 meters and the slopes of their oars to 32 degrees. The resulting midsection arrangement (Figure 1) includes canting the top and bottom oarsmen, feet inboard, to throw their blades into positions as equally spaced in the water as possible.

The next issue to be considered was the stability of such a design of vessel, linked with the vexed question of whether or not these slender ships, packed as they were with 170 oarsmen in three superimposed files, also carried ballast. Since marines or foot soldiers, as moving weights, could heel the ship enough

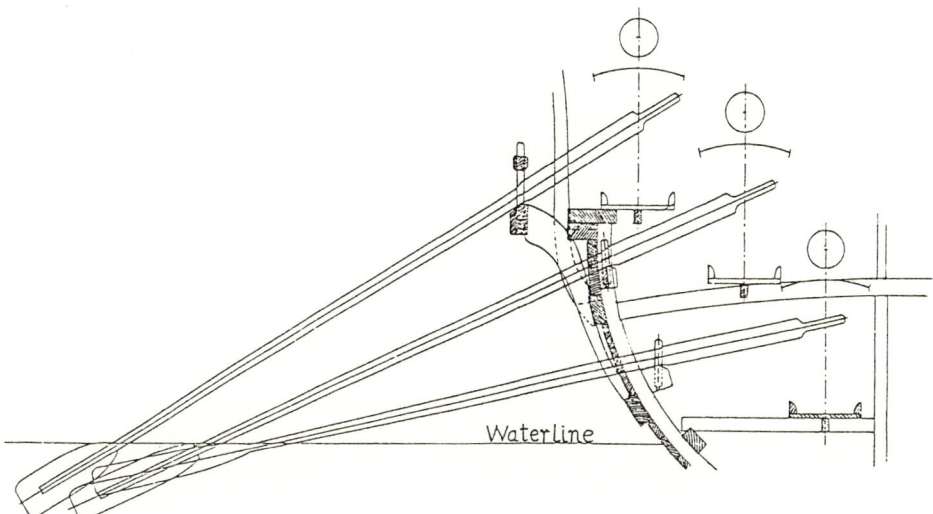

Figure 1. Midsection of the trireme replica: the oar system

to spoil the efforts of the oarsmen if it were insufficiently stiff, a trireme customarily carried very few. It was therefore more likely the capacity to carry sail that determined the required stability. A useful spread of sail, rigged in the manner of the fifth century B.C., would call for a metacentric height of at least half a meter.

Fortunately, such a height was amply provided by the midsection so far developed. This discovery was most encouraging: a light design now looked possible as the need for ballast could be laid aside. Prospects brightened for adequacy of hull strength as well as for speed and agility, the latter being essential for success in a ramming battle. Here too was technical evidence supporting the testimony of ancient historians that triremes did not actually sink after being rammed and were often towed away by the victors. The light hull and absence of ballast also would explain why no wrecks of triremes have yet been found and suggest that there is little gain in waiting for such a discovery before building a replica.

Waterline breadth has a powerful effect on stability. In the design as reconstructed so far, a reduction of waterline breadth by as little as 0.1 meter would reduce sail-carrying capacity to an implausibly low level, so that dimension seems to be fixed within quite close limits. The midsection of the trireme is therefore seen to be fairly closely determined by four factors: 1) the given overall beam, to fit the ship sheds at Piraeus; 2) the arrangement of oarsmen necessary to accord with the evidence in a practical manner; 3) the wineglass hull section of the ships of the period; and 4) the close determination of the waterline beam.

Another physically necessary feature is confirmed by the evidence. In the reconstructed midsection it was found that the tholes of the lowest oarsmen had to be set quite far inboard from the shell. Their oarports must therefore be larger than those above in order to give the oars room to make their stroke. Most ship designers would be loath to accept such large holes so near the water. Ancient literary references, however, confirm that these lowest oarports were so large that a man's head could pass through them. The practical solution to the problem is shown in a painting on the Athenian vase known as the Talos vase.[5] In this depiction of a trireme's stern section, the upper oarports are open, whereas the lower one is closed with a leather sleeve to keep the water out.

The task of reconstructing the trireme is by no means encompassed by the midsection. A general arrangement drawing shows the whole design (Figure 2). The ship may not look so very thin in a plan view, but on the waterline it certainly is, being 8.5 times as long as it is wide.

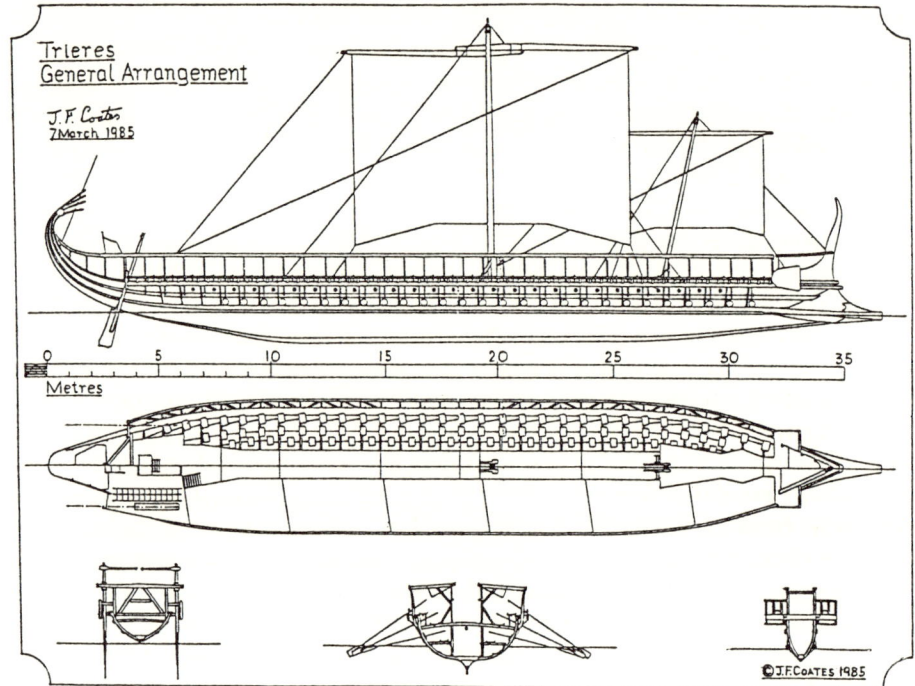

Figure 2. The trireme replica: general arrangement

Fitting the ends of the files of oarsmen into the hull proved to be a challenge. In the model, the heels of the after oarsman in the bottom file (the thalamian) were just clear of the hull timbers. In the middle file (the zygian), two oarports extended aft of the last thalamian, more being prevented by the slope of the ship's side. At the level of the gunwales, two thranites extended aft of the last zygian, the gunwale curving in sharply at this point. This particular progressive ending of the files is due to the rising bottom and increasing flare of the stern, and it accords very well with the evidence.

At the fore end of the ship, the hull narrows laterally, causing fouls between the converging files of thalamian oarsmen and the fore-and-aft gangway, which has to be raised to allow them to come together beneath it. The given numbers in each file were actually found to fit perfectly, because the zygians were squeezed out first by the men of the other two levels. Thus it was determined that, to fit the required shape of hull, the files had to end as the historical and epigraphical evidence required. Such concurrence between evidence and physical need can only be revealed by very detailed reconstruction.

All that the evidence allows and that common sense dictates has been done to make the replica equal the speed of its original. Hull ends are as fine as other demands allow, and thanks to the ram, bow waterlines are also fine. The Hellenic navy arranged for the hull form to be towed in a tank, with the results indicating that at 7.5 knots an effective power of 10 kilowatts will be required. At a somewhat conjectural and, it is to be hoped, pessimistic propulsive efficiency of 60 percent, that figure would call for 100 watts (0.13HP) from each oarsman—a demanding performance.

Up to about 8 knots, total effective power required is nearly all due to friction with the water. In the replica as it stands, little can be done to reduce wetted hull area, so if it proves difficult to repeat the famous dash of 427 B.C. from Athens to Mytilene,[6] it may be necessary to polish the hull. Sprint speeds are likely to be limited by the prismatic hump, as it is called by naval architects, around the Froude Number of 0.3, which will occur in the trireme at a speed of about 10 knots. The reason for developing such long warships in antiquity probably sprang from the need to raise that hump speed to a figure above the speed that could be sustained for a period of hours, rather than minutes.

The shipwrights of ancient Athens were willing to pay a high price to attain the greatest possible length. The length of the trireme is by the standards of the last thousand years phenomenal, being about fifteen times the depth of the hull. Two technical features make this long, slender hull design possible. First, it would have been impossible to build a hull of these proportions sufficiently light and strong unless the hull planks had been joined edge to edge by large numbers of tenons, as was usual in the ancient Mediterranean. There will be about 20,000 tenons in the replica, and in regions of high sheer stress they will be heavily loaded in rough weather. The strength of the tenons has been investigated to ensure their adequacy in this extreme design of ship. Their accurate and tight fit is stressed in the building specifications.

Second, the strength of the trireme's hull was reinforced by the hypozomata, two long loops of heavy rope twisted within the ship. The length of each rope was enough for the loops to stretch the entire length of the hull. Structurally, the hypozomata act simply and effectively as a tight tendon, applying a force of up to 300 kilonewtons (30 tonnes force), compressing the hull longitudinally. In the replica, the hypozomata will reduce maximum tensile stresses in the gunwale by one third, thus greatly contributing to the longevity of the hull.

Although the data presented above have been concerned with the design of the hull only, many other aspects have had to be investigated and reconstructed before the replica could be considered complete. These include the rig, steering, planking, fastenings, and the form of the ram itself, the raison d'être of the trireme. These details also have been reconstructed, using a combination of archaeological and historical evidence.

It is remarkable how the trireme has emerged as a ship whose size and proportions were developed to the technical limit in all main respects: length, slenderness, propulsive power, stability, strength, and weight. The interlocking nature of these attributes in any extreme design makes it difficult to conceive of any fundamentally different design which would conform to the same evidence. The replica, and any competitors stimulated by it, will show how far that conclusion is justified.

NOTES

1. For curves of speed of oared ships and boats against distance traveled see John Guilmartin, *Gunpowder and Galleys: Changing Technology and Mediterranean Warfare at Sea in the Sixteenth Century* (New York, 1974), fig. 10, p. 199.
2. J. S. Morrison, "The Greek Trireme," *Mariner's Mirror* 27 (January 1941): 27–30.
3. H. Frost, "The Punic Wreck in Sicily: I. Second Season of Excavation," *International Journal of Nautical Archaeology* 3 (1974): 35–42.
4. Morrison, "The Greek Trireme," 14–44.
5. Ibid.
6. Thucydides 3.50.

The Value of Sea Trials
In Experimental Archaeology

JOHN R. HALE

The replica of an ancient Greek trireme now being constructed in Athens represents the culmination of a controversy that has engaged the ingenuity of many generations of classicists, but it has also enjoyed the benefit of almost a century of archaeological experience gained from the testing of reconstructed ships and other watercraft. This branch of experimental archaeology was initiated in 1893 when a Norwegian-built replica of the Gokstad ship made a transatlantic crossing from Bergen to Newfoundland.[1] Its captain thus demonstrated the veracity of the Viking sagas and at the same time added a sardonic Scandinavian comment to the 400th-anniversary celebrations of the "discovery" of America by Christopher Columbus.

Since that successful maiden voyage, ship reconstructions and sea trials have remained the most well-publicized, hazardous, and expensive projects in the field of experimental archaeology. The great value of these numerous experiments in demonstrating the unsuspected scope of ancient seafaring and marine technology has more than justified the costs.[2]

In the majority of ship experiments, an ancient watercraft of known design and construction has been recreated by modern builders and then taken to sea by a mixed crew of archaeologists and sailors in order to test its performance and, in most cases, its capacity for long-range voyages. Through experiments of this type it has been demonstrated that the Greek geographer Eratosthenes may have been correct in claiming that ancient reed boats regularly sailed from Egypt to Ceylon; that the account of Leif Eriksson's expedition to North America is fact rather than heroic fancy; and that Polynesian mariners colonized the vast reaches of the Pacific, not through accidental and hapless drift voyages, but through a series of deliberate explorations using sophisticated sailing and navigational techniques.

In the case of the Greek trireme, however, the nature of the experiment is reversed. The mystery does not concern the ship's performance (the details of which are well known to every reader of Thucydides and Xenophon) but the actual design of the ship itself, for which there is almost no direct evidence. Not one author in antiquity thought it necessary to write a description of a trireme, and not so much as a plank of any of the thousands built in the fifth and fourth centuries B.C. has survived. The challenge confronting John Morrison and John Coates has been to derive a seaworthy hull design for a three-level oared galley from the scraps of evidence preserved in such disparate sources as passages from comic playwrights, ancient dictionaries, shards of painted vases, and fragmentary inscriptions of inventories and accounts from the Athenian navy yard.[3]

To have succeeded in reconciling all the conflicting bits of evidence with the demands of physics and naval architecture is in itself an unparalleled achievement. However, the experimenters, in conjunction with the Hellenic navy, have accepted the ultimate challenge of putting their design to the test in a full-scale replica, which will be expected to duplicate some of the most demanding feats ever recorded before the advent of steam-powered vessels.

If it is to satisfy the ancient sources, the trireme replica must prove itself capable of achieving the ultimate in maneuverability, speed, and seaworthiness. An admittedly extreme example of maneuverability is the exploit of an Athenian trireme chased by an enemy fleet into port. Rather than escape to the safety of the harbor, the Athenian executed a racing turn of 270 degrees around a moored merchantman and rammed its closest pursuer amidships.[4] For speed, there are the accounts in the Peloponnesian Wars of triremes covering just under 200 miles in a day and a night. As for seaworthiness, although triremes did not customarily venture out to sea in rough weather, the text of Herodotus proves that a fleet of Phoenician triremes circumnavigated the continent of Africa two thousand years before the epic voyage of Vasco da Gama.[5]

Although the nature of the trial confronting the trireme replica is different from that taken up by such previous reconstructions as the Gokstad ship, the *Kon-Tiki,* and the Brendan ship, some useful guidelines may be derived from these earlier experimenters. In particular, three areas of potential problems stand out in surveys of past sea trials.

First, it has been demonstrated in previous trials that the smallest structural detail, if overlooked or misinterpreted, may make the difference between success and failure. Halfway across the Atlantic in 1969, Thor Heyerdahl discovered that the *Ra I* was sinking because he had omitted a minute but essential part of his reed raft. Ancient Egyptian painters frequently had depicted a thin diagonal line connecting the upswung stern of a reed vessel to a point near the cabin. Since the archaeologist could not see the purpose of the line, he did not include it in the experimental model and learned too late that its function was to prevent the stern from sagging when the reed bundles of the hull became waterlogged.[6]

A similar problem, though with far less drastic consequences, affected the sea trials of the small Viking *faering* reconstructed by the British National Maritime Museum in 1973. The boatwrights followed modern practice in using glue to secure the joints and seams of this small rowing boat. The glue introduced an element of rigidity into a structure whose original design, it was discovered, had called for flexibility and give in handling in rough water.[7]

Second, it has been demonstrated that some ancient techniques and practices fall outside or even contradict the conventional, modern received body of wisdom concerning naval architecture. When the Gokstad ship was prepared for launching in 1893, its recreator and captain, Magnus Anderson, was solemnly informed that an open boat with such a low freeboard could not possibly avoid being swamped amid the rollers of the open Atlantic. Although their pronouncements were correct from the standpoint of nineteenth-century principles, these experts were unaware of the special properties the Viking ships derived from their use of withies to secure the planking of the hull.

Another "lost principle" of boatbuilding was rediscovered by Heyerdahl, who had already demonstrated in 1947 the seaworthiness of the Peruvian balsa raft by sailing his *Kon-Tiki* across the Pacific Ocean. Skeptics were still able to claim that the balsa raft was incapable of sailing into the wind and therefore could never have returned to Peru from Polynesia. Accordingly, in the following decade, Heyerdahl demonstrated with a smaller raft that the South American Indians had, in fact, invented a unique steering system which dispensed entirely with oars and rudders and relied instead on a set of movable centerboards, or "guaras." Manipulating these guaras made it possible to tack upwind with complete success, although by conventional expectations such a log raft should not have been able to make any headway at all.[8]

Third, previous sea trials have taught the hard lesson that success in a trial of seaworthiness is no guarantee of authenticity. To quote the seventh of John Coles's fundamentals for experimental archaeologists: "Experimental results must not be taken as proof of ancient structural or technological detail. If a certain implement does function successfully in performing a certain act, it need not necessarily mean that the tool was actually used in this way in the past."[9]

Heyerdahl's reed boats proved eminently seaworthy and buoyant, and in that respect they may be called successful. In order to achieve the necessary buoyancy, however, Heyerdahl had to inflate the simple outline of an Egyptian rivercraft to such vast dimensions that the resulting behemoths literally could not be steered. Both the *Ra I* and the *Ra II* snapped their steering oars during attempts to alter or maintain course and reached the western side of the Atlantic for no better reason than that the winds and currents move in that direction. It is difficult to believe in the authenticity of any watercraft that cannot be used for practical workaday navigation.

Simple seaworthiness was also demonstrated in the case of the 1971 replica of a small boat or war canoe of the Scandinavian Bronze Age, a type known only from depictions in rock carvings and on small bronze artifacts. For the experimental model, the builders used the reconstruction of S. Marstrander, who had interpreted these forerunners of the Viking ships as skin boats, like those of the Arctic Inuit, with hides stretched over a wooden frame. Accordingly, the boatwrights constructed a self-sufficient *umiak,* or Inuit long boat, to which was added the high stem and stern posts and the upward-curving beak of the Bronze Age designs.[10] The resulting boat performed well in the waters of Oslo Fjord, but its credibility as an authentic skin boat was compromised by those very features which were added to make it conform to the Bronze Age depictions. The high stem and stern posts prevented it from being stored upside down when beached, as all skin boats should be, and the curved beak could be attached only by pegging right through the hides below the waterline, an expedient which the experimenters were the first to acknowledge as unlikely.

These various examples carry clear implications for the trireme replica. The possibility of omitting or misinterpreting structural details is particularly relevant to the trireme, which belonged to a boat-building tradition which has been defunct for over 1,500 years. The shipwrights now working on the replica at Piraeus are necessarily employing twentieth-century tools and techniques to recreate a fifth-century B.C. ship. Since the trireme is the largest and most complicated reconstruction ever attempted, there is, unfortunately, ample opportunity for small details to depart from ancient practice, even though the overall plan of the replica may be demonstrably correct. As small a matter as the shaping and securing of the tenons, using modern equipment and techniques, may alter the properties of the shell and thus affect the handling of the vessel as a whole.

The trireme replica, pieced together as it is from fragments of evidence, is particularly vulnerable to the risk of proceeding in ignorance of certain ancient boat-building techniques or tricks of the trade. Had a few chance references not proven the existence and nature of the hypozomata, or girding cables, what naval architect would have been willing to credit so long and slender a hull for an open vessel? Yet other specialized equipment or techniques may very well have left no trace behind in the dialogues of Plato or the dockyard lists—fittings which may have rendered clear and functional the structural details which now appear obscure and difficult.

The problem of illusory success in a trireme reconstruction has already been encountered in the oar system proposed by A.F. Tilley and tested in 1970. Tilley recreated the trireme as a glorified naval cutter with three men on each thwart, the middle man being required to scull, pulling oars on both sides at once.[11] The sea trial was a marked success, and the reconstruction fit enough of the ancient evidence to be taken seriously by more than one scholar.

The list of strictures is no more than an effort to throw into relief the many areas in which the new trireme may provide long-awaited answers to questions about this historic vessel. It is above all in the performance of the reconstructed hull design using Morrison's oar system that the unique value of the sea trial will lie.

True success, and the ability to duplicate the ancient feats of speed and maneuverability, must not be expected in the first few trials or even the first years. The Greek trireme was the most sophisticated oared vessel in history, and even the Athenian crews required several years of training to become proficient. The last word belongs to that greatest of Athenians, Pericles, who was himself a naval commander:

> As for seamanship, they will find that a difficult lesson to learn. You yourselves have been studying it ever since the end of the Persian Wars, and have still not entirely mastered the subject.... Seamanship, just like anything else, is an art. It is not something that can be picked up and studied in one's spare time; indeed, it allows one no spare time for anything else.[12]

NOTES

1. A. Brøgger and H. Shetelig, *The Viking Ships—Their Ancestry and Evolution* (Oslo, 1953; London, 1970).
2. J. M. Coles, *Experimental Archaeology* (London, 1979), 49–94.
3. J. S. Morrison, "The Greek Trireme," *Mariner's Mirror* 27 (January 1941): 14–44.
4. Thucydides 2.91.
5. Herodotus 4.42.
6. T. Heyerdahl, *The Ra Expeditions* (London, 1971), passim.
7. A. E. Christensen and I. Morrison, "Experimental Archaeology and Boats," *International Journal of Nautical Archaeology* 5 (1976): 275–84.

8. T. Heyerdahl, "Guara Navigation: Indigenous Sailing off the Andean Coast," *Southwestern Journal of Anthropology* 13 (1957): 134–43.

9. Coles, *Experimental Archaeology*, 47.

10. P. Johnstone, "Bronze Age Sea Trial," *Antiquity* 46 (1972): 269–74.

11. A. F. Tilley, "Rowing the Trireme," *Mariner's Mirror* 66 (November 1976): 357–69.

12. Thucydides 1.142, trans. Rex Warner (London, 1972).

Convoys and Squadrons: English Naval Strategy and Deterrence, 1674–88

SARI HORNSTEIN*

Following the claim by Samuel Pepys, many historians believed that the English navy was an inactive and ineffective force from the end of the Third Anglo-Dutch War in 1674 to the Glorious Revolution in 1688. Dr. Hornstein contends the opposite and shows that the navy was deployed successfully during these years in the Mediterranean in order to protect English merchantmen from the depredations of the Barbary corsairs.

****

During the latter part of the seventeenth century, particularly during the 1670s and 1680s, England enjoyed a period of marked economic buoyancy, as attested by the surge in its customs receipts. The role of the navy in that development has never been examined in any detail. Most historians have simply adopted the views of Samuel Pepys, the Restoration's foremost naval administrator, who argued that the English navy fell to its "lowest state of impotence" between 1674 and 1688.[1]

Contrary to what we have been led to believe by Pepys and by those who have followed him, however, the navy was indeed active during the period from 1674 to 1688, even though the commissioned fleet for the duration of the period was substantially smaller than that which had been commissioned during the Third Dutch War (1672–74) and the 1678 mobilization in anticipation of war with France.[2] The peacetime fleet, ranging in size from thirty to forty-five vessels,[3] was put to effective use by the combined deployment of convoys and squadrons. The efficient system of naval protection which had been evolved mitigated the need for an extensive deployment of naval vessels.

If one turns to the Admiralty list projections,[4] a succinct and clear picture emerges of the breakdown of the services which the navy was intended to, and indeed did, provide. Among the forty ships projected for service in 1680, for example, a small squadron of six vessels was designated for patrol in the Channel, furnishing when appropriate convoys for merchantmen sailing to the Canaries, Malaga, and the Iceland and Yarmouth fisheries.

*I would like to thank Bruce Collins for his helpful comments on an earlier version of this paper.

Six ships were to comprise the squadron in the Soundings, the approaches to the Channel several leagues west of the Lizard. Ten ships were designated for the Straits squadron, to cover the approaches to the Mediterranean, and one for Tangier duty. This last squadron was to operate independently of the eight ships earmarked for specific convoying services to the Mediterranean: two vessels each were appointed for convoy to Newfoundland, for the herring boats, the Turkey ships (those trading to the Levant), and vessels going to Spain and Italy. Finally, two ships were designed for Ireland, and one each for Jersey and Guernsey, Portsmouth and Sheerness (as guardships), the Leeward Islands, Barbados, and Jamaica.

What emerges very clearly from this projection and others like it, and indeed is confirmed in the Admiralty lists themselves,[5] is the relative importance of the Mediterranean as the navy's focus of attention. This contrasts sharply with the relative unimportance of the New World and is attested by the paucity of ships intended as convoy for vessels bound to the Caribbean or the Northern colonies. Ships sailing to Asia were another matter entirely. No naval vessels were assigned to the ships of the East India Company, since they were very heavily armed and could easily defend themselves from aggressors.

Not only was a special squadron designed to patrol the Mediterranean, but also regular convoys were arranged for merchant ships trading there. The ships bound for Spain, Italy, and the Levant could always rely on convoy protection. Likewise, the herring ships, which originated in Yarmouth or at the Iceland fishery, could depend on naval escort services to the Mediterranean. Moreover, the ships earmarked for specific convoy duty were not restricted to only those ships which they were designated to accompany abroad: vessels assigned to escort the Turkey ships to Constantinople, for example, were instructed to take into their convoy any other English ships which might be sailing their way but stopping at other points en route to their final destinations. Cadiz, Malaga, Alicante, Leghorn, Messina, and Zante typically were ports of call for the ships headed for the Levant.

The convoys to Newfoundland also must be included as an indication of the navy's Mediterranean orientation, for in spite of the fact that one normally supposes Newfoundland to be part of the New World, in the seventeenth century it functioned economically as a part of the Old. The Navigation Laws,[6] strengthened and reformulated in 1660, illustrate why this was so. Fish, the primary export of Newfoundland, were exempt from the list of commodities of colonial origin which were enumerated in 1660 and decreed must be processed via England before going on to other European destinations. The logic behind the exception was irrefutable: it was too much to expect Newfoundland fish to travel first to England and then on to their markets in southern Europe, where Catholic consumers were regularly demanding fish, and still be edible.[7] Since Newfoundland fish traveled directly to the Mediterranean from the New World (just as the herring ships did from their fishing grounds in the North Sea and Iceland), convoy protection for the Newfoundland ships also must be regarded as representing England's naval commitment to Mediterranean merchants.

The Channel squadron too can be counted among the Mediterranean-bound ships, even if it represented only a fluctuating component of them. Unlike the squadron in the Soundings, which usually was directed to maintain almost constant bearings, the Channel squadron was meant to respond to the intermittent demands of merchants who needed convoy protection to various southern ports. Often it would undertake relatively brief voyages escorting merchantmen headed for Bilbao, Lisbon, or the Canaries, and immediately after having seen its charges safely into their intended harbors, would return to home waters, usually in the company of some other English vessels which had been ready to sail with it on their homeward journeys. Or perhaps it would be directed to escort merchant vessels on longer voyages, penetrating the Straits and touching at several important ports along the northern shore of the Mediterranean before turning around and repeating in reverse what it had performed on its outward leg.

If one adds to the number of regular convoys servicing Mediterranean-directed trade the flexibility provided by the Channel squadron in responding to merchants' additional requests for escort, it is quite clear that Mediterranean-bound vessels were the major focus of the Admiralty's attention. The figures in the following table bear this out, even if one does not include the ships of the Channel squadron among those naval vessels which were Mediterranean bound. If one does include them, the Mediterranean emphasis of the English navy's activities is overwhelming.

Mediterranean-Bound Vessels as a Percentage of the Fleet in Present Sea Pay
(excluding guardships, ships coming in to be paid off, and yachts)[8]

	Squadron	Squadron
6 September 1675	31/36...86%	25/36...69%
3 September 1676	20/27...74%	16/27...59%
1 September 1677	34/37...92%	23/37...62%
1 September 1678	72/79...91%	34/79...43%
1 September 1679	28/40...70%	25/40...63%
September 1680	31/42...74%	18/42...43%
September 1681	32/44...73%	25/44...57%
2 September 1682	30/40...75%	26/40...65%
September 1683	31/41...75%	13/41...32%
30 August 1684	16/27...59%	13/27...48%
1 September 1685	12/27...44%	7/27...26%
September 1686	15/30...50%	11/30...37%
1 September 1687	20/33...61%	7/33...21%
24 September 1688	26/35...74%	5/35...14%

Since the principal threat to English shipping throughout the period came from the Barbary corsairs—privateers who operated from bases on the northern and northwestern coasts of Africa and whose raison d'être was to prey mercilessly on the commercial vessels of those nations with whom they were at war—it is no wonder that English naval vessels were concentrated in the Mediterranean region. For while it is true that England fought no wars against any European nation from 1674 to 1688, it did fight a series of wars against several of the Barbary Regencies: from 1674 to 1676, against the corsairs of Tripoli; from 1677 to 1683, against the corsairs of Algiers; and from 1684 to 1688, against the corsairs of Sally.[9] For one year only, during the fourteen-year interval from 1674 to 1688, was England spared the expense and the associated dangers of a declared war against any of the Barbary States.[10] For the remaining thirteen, English shipping was especially vulnerable to attack from the privateers of whichever of those states with whom England was then at war.

Moreover, the fact that England was neutral both during the Messinese War (1674-78), when France was fighting against Holland and Spain, and during the Franco-Spanish War (1683-84), meant that its need would be greater than ever for convoy protection. The growth of English shipping generally in the 1670s and 1680s and its proliferation in the Mediterranean, particularly during the Messinese War when England was the major neutral carrier of the goods of foreign nations, left more English vessels subject to the depredations of the Barbary corsairs than ever before.

Although English (and Dutch) commercial vessels are known to have been larger and better equipped to ward off potential adversaries than their Mediterranean counterparts—and therefore somewhat less attractive targets to the Barbary corsairs than the smaller and less well-armed trading vessels of other Mediterranean states,[11]—they were still susceptible to the devastating activities of those privateers. The crucial point, however, is that when English trading ships were not so well equipped as to defend themselves, they could rely on the presence of fourth-, fifth-, and sixth-rate frigates of the Royal Navy to defend them from piratical attacks.[12] And although these consisted of the lesser rates in the navy's arsenal, they were particularly well suited to the task of securing English vessels from the depredations of the corsairs at sea. The fourth-rate frigates, sporting anywhere from thirty to fifty-four guns and carrying a complement of 115 to 280 men each, were the backbone of the peacetime fleet: these were maneuverable but seaworthy vessels, sufficiently well armed to take on most corsair adversaries, which were renowned for their speed and agility.

It is important to note as well that from 1684 to 1688 the percentage of naval vessels earmarked to service Mediterranean-bound merchantmen falls. These figures tie in nicely with the view articulated by Sir Julian Corbett, and many others after him, that England's abandonment of Tangier in 1684 marked its abandonment of the Mediterranean and with it any claims to influence in that sea. But the figures actually support this view only superficially. In fact, very few naval vessels were stationed at Tangier at any point during the peacetime interval, and while many did indeed stop there en route to other ports within the Straits, or before heading north after having completed a tour within the Straits, Tangier rarely seems to have been anything more than a port of call.

The reduction of ships convoying merchantmen to the Mediterranean and patrolling that sea after 1684 had most to do with England's successful negotiation of peace with Algiers in 1683. From that point on, the Mediterranean fleet could be and was gradually reduced, and in its place a squadron designed to cruise along the coast of Sally and at the mouth of the Straits was gradually built up in response to the threats to English shipping posed by the corsairs of

Sally. By mid-1685 there was no longer a Straits squadron at all, while the Sally squadron had stabilized at six vessels, continuing at that level for the duration of the period. It was not until October 1688 that the recall of the Sally ships began, and within four months the Sally squadron ceased to exist altogether.

It was not the abandonment of Tangier which marked the end of England's Mediterranean presence, but the political difficulties of James II and particularly the military undertaking of his successors in 1689. The exigencies of naval war in home waters demanded the wholehearted application of the navy and came at the expense of the convoy system as it had evolved over the previous thirty-odd years. Testimony of the demise of that system is found in the parliamentary debates of the 1690s, which culminated in the Cruiser and Convoy Legislation of 1694.

In spite of the relative fall in the concentration of Mediterranean-bound naval vessels between 1684 and 1688, then, there was nevertheless a distinct Mediterranean emphasis in England's naval strategy for the duration of the peacetime interval from 1674 to 1688. If one bears in mind that the essence of successful piracy and privateering in the seventeenth century—as in the twentieth—was its dependence upon shipping traffic which sailed on predictable and fairly restricted routes, it is hardly surprising that this should have been so.

The danger to English shipping was not restricted to the Mediterranean basin. Since the privateers were fitted out with swift, maneuverable, and well-armed vessels, they could and did extend their field of operations along the Atlantic coast of Europe, as far north as the Channel and the North Sea. But the chances of a corsair intercepting and overcoming a vessel or group of vessels on the high seas were very remote indeed. For this reason the Admiralty could rest pretty well assured that the Soundings squadron would satisfy the safety requirements for those merchantmen which sailed to and from the New World, for the ships in the Soundings squadron would see those vessels bound thither safely out of European waters, well beyond the area where corsairs could cause them grief, and escort them safely into home waters on the last leg of their homeward journeys. Merchantmen sailing to and from the New World thus were not ignored when it came to their safe transatlantic crossings.

Indeed, in keeping home waters free of corsairs, the ships of the Soundings squadron actually provided a valuable service for all sailing ships. Moreover, they also escorted merchant vessels short distances both outward and homeward on their southern and Mediterranean voyages. But the ships of the Soundings squadron simply could not provide adequate protection for merchant ships sailing to the southward, for these ships did not enjoy the advantages of sailing in open seas as did their transatlantic counterparts. They sailed instead along the European Atlantic and Mediterranean coastlines, which, punctuated as they are with an infinite number of coves and inlets, provided perfect cover for corsairs, who could emerge swiftly from hiding and surprise and overwhelm unsuspecting merchant prey.

Given the nature of the coasts along which these merchantmen had to sail and the fact that their sea routes were fairly restricted, merchant vessels were in constant danger of corsair attack and therefore in need of protection for the duration of their voyages, and not merely some short portion of them. Under these circumstances it is hardly surprising that the Admiralty arranged for such a large concentration of naval vessels to be deployed to southern Europe and the Mediterranean.

To sum up, the Admiralty commissioners evolved what seems to have been a highly efficient naval strategy for protecting English ships sailing abroad: convoys operated in conjunction with regional squadrons, so that the overall number of ships in commission could be kept to a minimum and still remain effective.[13] Convoys, naval vessels which were assigned to groups of merchantmen, served in a defensive capacity and escorted the merchant ships under their care into their respective harbors. Patrols, groups of vessels which sailed in fixed stations, served in an offensive capacity in the overall naval strategy, intercepting and pursuing enemy corsairs.

How the Strategy Evolved: The Algerine Campaigns

The strategy of deploying naval convoys in conjunction with regional squadrons was applied more or less for the duration of the period from 1674 to 1688. It was only articulated and defined at the Admiralty, however, in the latter part of the Algerine War, largely as a result of the errors in the navy's application in the first part of that war and its failure to secure English merchant vessels which sailed to southern Europe and the Mediterranean. Between 1677 and 1679, Sir John Narbrough commanded the Mediterranean squadron with a view to negotiating a treaty with the Regency of Algiers. He returned to England in 1679 without having secured a peace, leaving behind a small squadron of ships under the command of Arthur Herbert. Herbert continued to press for a peace with that regency and succeeded in securing an agreement with the dey of Algiers in 1683 which proved to be durable: in its essentials, it was to be binding for nearly 150 years.[14]

The campaigns of Narbrough and Herbert were bent on achieving the same goals, namely, the subjugation of the corsairs of Algiers and the negotiation of a peace favorable to England. But the strategies employed in each campaign were quite distinct. The differences illustrate well the evolution and articulation of England's naval strategy during this interwar period.

From April 1677, when the Admiralty first reacted to the news of the escalation of Algerine privateering against English vessels, until May 1679, when Narbrough was preparing to return home with a substantial portion of his squadron, the number of ships stationed in the Straits and at Tangier grew from eight to thirty-five. A force which consisted of five 4th-rate vessels, two 5th-rates, and one sixth-rate in May 1677 grew to an immense one by May 1679 of five 3rd-rates, sixteen 4th-rates, four 5th-rates, nine 6th-rates, and one hulk. This formidable force was maintained until mid-May 1679, when Narbrough returned home with nineteen ships, leaving Herbert in the Straits with sixteen under his command. The expansion of the Mediterranean squadron in mid-1677 coincided with a corresponding buildup of the Channel squadron, which numbered only six vessels in May 1677 and eventually peaked at sixty-two in August 1678. That squadron only resumed its premobilization size, at nine vessels, in July 1679.[15]

The significance of the variation in the sizes of both the Channel and Mediterranean squadrons lies in the fact that as each was expanded, there emerged a certain specialization of naval functions. Apart from the assignment of several vessels to convoy duty for the Newfoundland fish ships and for the ships trading to the Canaries and to Bilbao, those ships comprising the Channel squadron were designed principally to patrol the Channel and adjacent waters.

The responsibility for providing convoy services for the merchants trading to the Mediterranean, hitherto arranged by the Board of Admiralty from London, now devolved entirely upon the commander in chief of the squadron in the Mediterranean. It was incumbent upon Narbrough to see to it that convoy was provided for merchants trading in that region. It was also his task to use the force under his command to subdue the corsairs of Algiers and to bring enough pressure to bear upon that regency to extract a peace honorable to England.

Narbrough had to divide up the squadron under his command to fulfill these twin duties of convoying to protect English Mediterranean trade and cruising to constrain the privateers, both daunting tasks, given that his Algerine adversaries had an impressive fleet at their disposal. In 1676 the Algerine fleet consisted of thirty men-of-war with 16 to 50 guns each, three smaller vessels armed with 8 guns each, seven brigantines, three galleys, and three more ships which had only recently been launched.[16]

In the course of the first six months of his Mediterranean tour of duty, Narbrough discovered two weaknesses in his strategy which would have to be modified. First, cruising about the Straits' mouth had proved sorely inadequate for protecting merchantmen, many of which were bringing supplies indispensable for the squadron's viability. Second, the naval convoys had to be strengthened because the Algerine corsairs sailed in groups: naval escorts meeting up with the corsairs were easily overwhelmed or diverted from the merchantmen in their care, which left them as easy pickings for the Algerines. If Narbrough required confirmation that his strategy was misguided, he received it in December 1677, when his peaceful overtures before Algiers came to nought. The Algerines simply had no reason to be interested in negotiating a treaty, given that they had taken as many as sixty-five English vessels during the second half of 1677.[17]

Narbrough's determination to overcome these weaknesses is reflected clearly in the naval strategy which he pursued over the next twelve months. Unfortunately, the exigencies of maintaining a fleet abroad considerably delayed his progress against the Algerines. Between January and June 1678, most of the vessels in Narbrough's fleet were fully occupied in refitting for service at Leghorn.[18] Only six vessels were convoying merchant ships, and no vessels were patrolling the Straits. The need for convoy preempted it.[19] During the latter part of the year, most of the vessels in Narbrough's squadron converged on Tangier, with a view to preparing for another visit to Algiers in an effort to persuade the Algerines to agree to a peace.[20]

Narbrough hoped that the English fleet might be able to pull off a repeat of Sir Edward Spragge's impressive performance of 1671, when eleven Algerine ships were destroyed in Bougie harbor,[21] or that the fleet's appearance off the coast of Algiers would at least intimidate the Algerines into agreeing to a peace. But the strategy would not work for two reasons. In the first place, the Algerines had fortified their mole to preempt a repeat of the 1671 fiasco.[22] And in the second place, the Algerines had been very successful in taking English merchantmen as prizes throughout 1678.[23] They had no more reason to want a peace with England now than they had the previous year.

Although Narbrough had arranged for the bulk of his fleet to accompany him on his second visit to Algiers, he directed a small division of seven ships to patrol the Straits' mouth from late November 1678, under Herbert's command.[24] It was, he claimed, "the only station to cruise in to annoy the Algerines, [for] both in the going out and returning [from the Straits], they are liable to be destroyed by our frigates."[25] And indeed, Herbert's squadron at the Straits' mouth remained intact throughout the next half year, while Narbrough and fourteen other ships refitted at Port Mahon in preparation for yet a third visit to Algiers.[26]

From mid-January to mid-March 1679, in addition to the small squadron of ships patrolling the Straits, patrols of two, three, and finally four vessels were directed to cruise between Capes Paul and Martin on the southern coast of Spain, "to annoy the Algerines lying on that coast,"[27] and "as the wind presents, to stretch to Cape Tres Forcas [Trois Fourches]" for twenty days, after which they were to cruise again between Capes Paul and Martin.[28] The captains of these vessels were directed to keep each other's company "both night and day"—presumably a function of the strength of their adversaries and their tendency to sail in small groups; to attempt to take or destroy any Algerines they might encounter; and to convoy any merchantmen they might meet with at sea.[29] Of a fleet of twenty-four vessels, excluding Herbert's force at Tangier, only two were assigned to convoy duty in the Mediterranean, although several vessels which were refitting would soon be in a position to escort merchantmen within the Mediterranean and did so.[30] So as not to lose any opportunity to do the Algerines any damage, Narbrough instructed the captains he assigned for convoy duty to endeavor to take any Algerines they might meet with, provided that they "be careful...not [to] lose [the] company of your convoys under your charge."[31]

This modified deployment of the vessels in the Mediterranean squadron did achieve some success in capturing or destroying some Algerine corsairs, but the returns to effort were not great.[32] Indeed, when Narbrough finally returned to Algiers at the end of March 1679 with twelve vessels—his third attempt to treat for peace with the Algerine government—he was rebuffed yet again. As Narbrough put it himself, "no peace can be thought of with the... [Algerines] until they be further chastised."[33] But Narbrough had failed to do that.

His strategy of presenting the Algerines with a formidable display of English naval strength at Algiers was misconceived: in spite of the fact that Narbrough had deployed ships to sail on the Algerine coast on a regular basis throughout his tenure as commander in chief in the Mediterranean, the corsairs did not fail to venture abroad. To demonstrate to the corsairs that they stood to gain little by being at war with England, Narbrough had to deprive them of those things for which they reckoned it was worth fighting, namely, prizes.[34] Since the Algerines did not fight in battle-fleet formation, the English fleet stood to gain virtually nothing by concentrating its force to impress them. This was especially true, given Narbrough's realization after his first appearance before Algiers in December 1677, that any attempt to burn the enemy fleet within the mole at Algiers would be fruitless. And indeed, the fact that he had decided to keep his ships "in a body" in response to the uncertainty of England's relations with France need not have entailed concentrating them on the coast of Algiers.[35] They could have been deployed more effectively in a body elsewhere.

A judicious application of Narbrough's force to convoy duty and to cruising along limited, well-defined stations might well have prevented the Algerines from taking so many English merchantmen as prizes. Instead, Narbrough assigned relatively few vessels to cruise in the Straits' mouth. Those which were deployed along the Spanish coast were expected to cover vast stretches over periods which were too short to be effective.[36] And Narbrough kept the bulk of the fleet which was free of convoying duty in his own company, cruising on the Algerine coast.

At its peak, the fleet under Narbrough's command numbered thirty-five, and yet he had little to show for nearly two years of effort. The squadron had captured five Algerines which were taken into the service of the navy, of which two were fourth-rates and three were fifth-rates. The total number driven ashore and burned or destroyed came to seven. Although Narbrough claimed to have put twelve corsair vessels out of action, the Algerine fleet still consisted of a further twenty-two well-armed ships.[37] Moreover, Narbrough's tenure in the Mediterranean coincided with the taking of upwards of 123 English merchantmen by the corsairs. And perhaps most important of all, Narbrough returned home with no peace in hand. He had been spurned by the Algerines.

It should be stressed, in fairness to Narbrough, that his mission to the Mediterranean was not facilitated by the conflicting demands on his squadron. In this respect, the judgment of Admiral Sir Herbert Richmond is compelling. In another context, he wrote: "On more occasions than one the commander was to be placed, like the ass between two bundles of hay, in doubt from which he should make his dinner; for the objects were given equal importance."[38] The split demands on Narbrough similarly undermined the effectiveness of the fleet's operations. Should he have concentrated his efforts on protecting English trade or on patrolling the seas with a view to hounding down the corsairs and taking or destroying them? Moreover, should he have imparted similarly schizoid instructions to the commanders of the ships in his fleet, burdening those who were deployed to cruise particular stations with the additional responsibility of accommodating merchantmen which they might meet at sea? Or, alternatively, burdening those who were deployed to convoy merchantmen with the additional instructions that they try and take any Algerines they might meet with at sea?

The Admiralty in London, fully occupied by the mobilization of the fleet for imminent war with France, provided Narbrough with no guidance regarding convoy provision. It merely provided him with a formidable fleet on which to draw in his campaign to subdue the corsairs. Narbrough was left in total command, answerable to no one, and ultimately responsible for the direction of Mediterranean affairs. It is perfectly likely that the Admiralty's faith in his ability to dispatch effectively the squadron was warranted: that the growth of English commercial activity, particularly between 1674 and 1678, when merchantmen profited by their neutrality, should not have warranted any extra particular consideration or advice. The fact of the matter is that, left to his own devices, the strategy Narbrough pursued was hardly optimal.

Throughout his Mediterranean stay, Narbrough was very much like Richmond's ass, "in doubt from which [bundle of hay] he should make his dinner." If the Admiralty still commended Narbrough's efforts to overcome the Algerines despite his failure, it was unwilling to leave to chance the outcome of Herbert's tenure as commander in chief in the Mediterranean. Herbert was to be liberated of all consideration of providing convoy to merchantmen. Unfortunately, in his view, he was to be burdened with a fresh obligation to distract him from his campaign against the Algerines.

When Narbrough left the Mediterranean in May 1679, leaving Herbert behind in command of the remaining sixteen ships, only nine of these ships, including his own, the *Rupert*, were designed to cruise under his command against the corsairs.[39] Rarely during his stint as commander in chief was Herbert instructed to dispatch any of his ships on convoying duty, and when so directed, it involved the temporary loss of only one or two vessels from his squadron. The provision of ships for convoy duty was practically the sole responsibility of the Admiralty in London. Convoy was provided separately, for the Turkey ships, the herring and Newfoundland ships, and those trading to Spain and Italy, Portugal, and the Canaries.

Also in marked contrast with Narbrough's Mediterranean experience, Herbert's was strictly controlled from the Admiralty Board in London. Although the rigidity of his orders abated somewhat as he proved himself an able commander and strategist, the limitations on his freedom to cruise, particularly in the first year and one half of his stay in the Mediterranean, had a profound impact on his successes against the corsairs. It was clear that the Admiralty was keen to direct the movements of Herbert's squadron and to see to it that the errors of Narbrough's venture in the Mediterranean be avoided.

The stations in which Herbert might cruise against the Algerines were restricted and well defined, extending no further than 100 leagues distant from the Straits of Gibraltar, westward or eastward; he was to take care not to allow all the vessels in his squadron to be cleaned at the same time and thus risk leaving the seas unguarded; but most important of all, Herbert was to attend on Tangier, England's garrison on the northwestern tip of Africa.[40] For in addition to the need to prosecute the war against Algiers, Tangier needed to be secured from the mounting pressure which the Moors of the Kingdom of Sally were bringing to bear on the garrison in an effort to claim it as their own. That assault, together with the rumored aid which the French were reported to be giving the Moors,[41] justified in the Admiralty's view the principal application of Herbert's naval squadron to providing whatever succor he might to the defense of the garrison.

Herbert protested that the limitations imposed upon him would undermine his campaign against the Algerines. But despite the constraints on his freedom to patrol the seas and his conviction that the squadron he commanded was too slight to achieve any lasting results, within a few months of his taking command of the Mediterranean squadron Herbert had succeeded in taking several vessels from the Algerines, in addition to having intimidated the Moors on the coast of Sally: the presence of four vessels of the squadron on that coast diverted the attention of the Moors from their designs on Tangier and cut into the supply lines which supported that effort.[42] Of the remaining vessels, two were stationed off Cape St. Vincent and two others were cruising between Cape Spartell and Cape Trafalgar,[43] with a view to intercepting Algerine corsairs.

From mid-1679 until April 1681, when a truce was finally agreed with the Moors, Herbert adjusted the distribution of the ships in his squadron to facilitate his assisting Tangier. The limitations of these stations, in view of the wider war against Algiers, proved to be choice.[44] In just under one year from the time Narbrough had returned home from the Mediterranean, Herbert had destroyed or taken five Algerine men-of-war and nine prizes. Bearing in mind that Herbert's war effort had been interrupted regularly by the demands from Tangier, "which hath not been inconsiderable and hath employed much of our time," this was no small achievement, as Herbert was only too happy to point out on his own behalf.[45]

From that point in time when Tangier required no special attention, Herbert and his squadron had some great successes in taking corsairs. Upon hearing of no Algerines cruising outside the Straits, Herbert was free to send his ships within the Straits in search of the enemy. Previous stations, lying close to Tangier, could now be reduced and were. Some of the ships which had been cruising in the Straits' mouth, between Cape Spartell and Cape Trafalgar, and just within the Straits' mouth, between Gibraltar and Ceuta Point, were now ordered on new stations within the Straits, to cruise between Cape de Gatt and Capes Paul and Martin on the coast of Spain.[46] Although this new flexibility now existed, the previous stations around the Straits' mouth were still maintained by some ships of the squadron.[47]

In May 1681, Herbert sent his first letter to the dey of Algiers in order to treat for peace, but nothing came of it.[48] For the next eleven months, the war against Algiers dragged on. The Mediterranean squadron, though limited in size, continued to harass the corsairs and Algerine shipping, taking men-of-war and smaller vessels, corn boats, and boats laden with supplies.

It is very likely that Algerine resistance to concluding a peace with England was influenced by proceedings between Algiers and France. The latter two had concluded a peace in September 1681, but by the following November, Herbert discovered that the Algerines were intending to break that peace. There were two issues at stake here for the Algerines. In the first place, Herbert appears to have had a good deal of success in subduing the corsairs and preventing them from taking English merchant vessels as prizes. In the second place, since the French were currently enjoying a peace with Algiers, merchantmen other than French ones were disguising their vessels with French colors and flags in order to deter the corsairs from attempting to prey on their vessels.

Baba Hassan, the dey's son-in-law and the de facto, if not the de jure, ruler of Algiers at this time,[49] could not maintain the political support of his subjects if the maritime policy he was supporting left them with little purchase at sea and a growing sense that the scope for plunder lay with the French, and not with the English, their avowed enemies. Hassan could buy off his political opposition by proclaiming a war against France and by giving his subjects an opportunity to take some prizes "before the French can do anything to hinder them."[50]

Herbert recognized that the Algerines were unlikely to maintain a peace which did not work to their advantage.[51] He was convinced that the pressure his squadron was bringing to bear on the Algerines, in conjunction with the success of the convoys in escorting English merchantmen and not leaving them unattended as prey for the corsairs, dictated that peace was really the only honorable alternative left to the Algerines.[52] He was right.

The Algerines simply could not support a war against two major adversaries at the same time. Together, England and France were too powerful to resist, particularly in light of the fact that Holland, with whom the regency had concluded a peace in 1679, was not proving to be the trading ally it was hoped for, nor supplying the Algerines with the ammunition they needed to prosecute their wars. Since Herbert had been successful in restraining their activities against English merchantmen at sea, the Algerines opted to declare war on France and conclude a peace with England.[53]

In the course of Herbert's three years as commander in chief, eight Algerines were taken into the navy's service—three fourth-rate ships, three fifth-rates, and two sixth-rates; one fifth-rate was sold and at least seven other corsair ships were driven ashore.[54] In all, some sixteen Algerines were put out of action. Taken together, Narbrough and Herbert took or destroyed twenty-eight Algerines, which left a force of some six corsair vessels, if the Algerine fleet did in fact consist of thirty-four vessels in 1676.[55] It was clearly Herbert who broke the back of Algerine intransigence, *pace* F. H. Dyer.[56] Moreover, very few English merchantmen appear to have been taken in the course of Herbert's tenure in the Mediterranean, in marked contrast to Narbrough's term there.[57]

The Lessons

In reviewing Herbert's tenure as commander in chief in the Mediterranean, it is clear that many of the strategic pitfalls which plagued the campaign of Narbrough were spared Herbert, in spite of the fact that, like Narbrough, Herbert was burdened with a double duty for a considerable part of his stay. Even when Herbert had to attend to the garrison at Tangier, he could still maintain some ships in stations which were key to the prosecution of the war against Algiers. This had the effect of achieving some limited goals by forcing the corsairs to beware as they sailed through the Straits' mouth, or when they cruised on the coasts of Portugal and Sally. It is quite ironic that, in spite of the tremendous drain which it placed on the nation, Tangier nevertheless served to intensify the effects of Herbert's squadron on the privateers of Algiers.

Narbrough's efforts to carry out his dual duties, in contrast with Herbert's, did not allow him strategically to kill two birds with one stone. Narbrough's force was usually either directed to convoy or to cruise against the Algerines, and when he attempted to divide his forces between the two sets of duties, this was not done as efficiently as it might have been. Narbrough simply had too much to attend to. This required a dispersion of his force, and that complicated his efforts to evolve a coherent and effective strategy.

These differences were not lost on the Admiralty Board in London. In June 1681, Herbert was beginning to despair of being able to sustain his offensive effort against Algiers because of a shortage of supplies, and he reckoned that all that could then be gained by his activities would be a peace dishonorable to England. Aware that "the charge of the fleet...[might be] uneasy to his Majesty," he recommended that the footing of the war effort be changed from an offensive strategy to a defensive one, in which the squadron would be disbanded and convoys would be supplied in its stead for the protection of English merchantmen.[58] The Admiralty commissioners, however, rejected this recommendation after careful consideration, for reasons which suggest they had a firm understanding of the weaknesses which plagued Narbrough's Mediterranean campaign.[59]

In the view of the commissioners, who responded to Herbert in November 1681, there were four reasons why such a strategy would be prejudicial to the interests of England. First, they argued that the current strategy had been highly effective in protecting merchantmen trading to the Mediterranean, few having been taken in the previous two years. Trade within the Mediterranean and outside the Straits had been secured. Second, such a strategy would take away "the advantage of building and trading in great ships." If extraordinary convoy protection were to be provided, the incentive to fit out larger ships would no longer obtain, and smaller vessels would be employed, which would in turn employ fewer people. Seamen turned out of work might seek employment elsewhere—possibly even in France, which might "prove a further mischief."

Third, and most importantly, a defensive strategy would not yield the desired results in prosecuting the war against Algiers. The absence of a regional squadron or patrol, it was argued, would weaken the effect of the convoying ships, which would not be free to chase opponents for fear of exposing their charges. Moreover, the corsairs' recognition of the convoy's inability to give chase would provide them the freedom to roam the seas with no need to worry about their own safety and to search out unsuspecting merchant prey with impunity. "So that we have a war and resolve not to hurt our enemies," wrote the commissioners. "But surely we ought not to tell them so if we desire a peace." This would be tantamount to declaring England's inability—"to her shame and reproach"—"to contend against seventeen little ships of pirates which to our great damage will quickly be increased by this method." Indeed, England could only expect, under such circumstances, for the Regencies of Tripoli and Tunis to follow suit and break their peace with it.

Finally, the commissioners argued that such a strategy, far from easing the financial strain, would be much costlier than the strategy presently being employed, and less effective at the same time. First, many more than nine additional vessels (the modest number in Herbert's squadron) would have to be deployed as convoys to secure English trade, and that would entail a vast increase in the navy's operating expenses. Second, the security afforded to English merchantmen by the combined deployment of convoys and squadrons could not be matched by convoys alone, "for 'tis impossible to contrive such orders for convoys as will answer all occasions and then too, the merchants will run from them, their losses will be frequent and great and their clamours greater. The enemy will be more at liberty to annoy us and incur no danger to themselves."

The commissioners had evolved a coherent and compelling naval strategy, whereby the combined use of naval convoys and patrols secured English merchantmen sailing to southern Europe. In its essence, the regional squadron acted as a deterrent force: Barbary corsairs studiously avoided English ships except where these were unprotected by convoy and English frigates were nowhere to be seen (or the odds favored their successful seizure of isolated vessels which were in convoy).

Moreover, the commissioners presided over a navy which was, comparatively, highly efficient. The total number of ships deployed to the Mediterranean during Narbrough's tenure there, at its peak, numbered thirty-five. This figure was far in excess of the number of vessels fitted out during the period from 1679 to 1683: the figure for those vessels deployed as convoys to the Mediterranean, in addition to those which formed Herbert's squadron, hovered around twenty. Fifteen fewer ships had been dispatched for Mediterranean service, and yet the results were so much better.

It must be stressed that, while this strategy was successful, it did not eliminate the Algerines altogether as a threat to Mediterranean shipping. Indeed, by 1686, after a brief war with France and just prior to its war with Holland, the Algerine fleet had been restored to a respectable force of twenty-four well-armed vessels.[60] The point is that England's naval strategy simply made it unattractive to the Algerines to continue to prey on English merchantmen. And the peace which Herbert concluded with the Regency of Algiers left no loose ends dangling which might become suitable pretexts for war in the future.[61]

The peacetime activities of the Royal Navy have been overlooked and underrated. England had evolved an efficient and effective naval strategy in this interwar period. The Royal Navy, *pace* Pepys, was a far cry from being at its "lowest state of impotence."

NOTES

1. Samuel Pepys, *Memoirs Relating to the State of the Royal Navy of England, 1679–88* (London, 1690), 130; also quoted in J. R. Tanner, *Samuel Pepys and the Royal Navy* (Cambridge, 1920), 77.
2. For a fuller treatment of the issues touched on in this paper, see my "The Deployment of the English Navy in Peacetime, 1674–1688" (Ph.D. dissertation, University of Leiden, 1985).
3. Great Britain, Public Record Office (hereafter PRO), ADM 8/1.
4. Ibid.

5. Ibid.

6. The Navigation Laws were designed to wrest the carrying trade from the Dutch.

7. Compare Benjamin W. Labaree, ed., *The Atlantic World of R. G. Albion* (Middletown, CT, 1975), 44, 50; Gillian Cell, *English Enterprise in Newfoundland* (Toronto, 1969), 4–5, 120–21, 127; C. L. Cutting, *Fish Saving: A History of Fish Processing from Ancient to Modern Times* (London, 1955), 36, 57, 67–68, 110, passim; H. Innes, *The Cod Fisheries* (New Haven and Toronto, 1940, 1954), 103–7.

8. Excluded are guardships, ships coming in to be paid off, and yachts from this calculation because of interest in determining where the focus of the Admiralty lay in deploying ships to protect merchantmen sailing abroad.

9. Salé, referred to by contemporaries as Sally, was situated on the northwest coast of Africa, just south of Tangier. It is part of present-day Morocco.

10. English shipping was subject to the depredations of the corsairs even during that year of peace from mid-1676 to mid-1677. Indeed, this led to the eventual outbreak of war with Algiers shortly after.

11. Peter Earle, *Corsairs of Malta and Barbary* (London, 1970), 16; Ralph Davis, "England in the Mediterranean," in *Essays in the Economic and Social History of Tudor and Stuart England*, ed., F. J. Fisher (London, 1961), 126–32; Ralph Davis, *The Rise of the English Shipping Industry in the 17th and 18th Centuries* (Newton Abbot, 1962), 250.

12. The appearance of English naval power in the Mediterranean from 1655 onward and the pass system protecting English ships from Barbary corsairs meant that English ships needed to rely less and less heavily on their own defenses, with the resulting drop in the ratio of men to tonnage and a corresponding drop in operating costs. Davis, "England in the Mediterranean," 131–32; compare also Davis, *Rise of the English Shipping Industry*, 250.

13. Although the Admiralty commissioners active between 1679 and 1684 articulated the reasoning behind the naval policy which was pursued, it is clear from the scattered evidence in the Admiralty orders and instructions between 1660 and 1674 that the essence of that naval strategy had been pursued prior to those commissioners' tenure at the Admiralty.

14. Sir G. Fisher, *Barbary Legend: War, Trade and Piracy in North Africa, 1415–1830* (Oxford, 1957), 265.

15. All the figures on the sizes of the squadrons are taken from PRO, ADM. 8/1.

16. "List of the Algerine Fleet Compiled by Samuel Martin," February 1676, PRO, S.P. 71/2/137; compare also "List of the Algerine Ships of War, 1676," London, British Library (hereafter BL), Sloane MSS 2755, fol. 53. The Algerine fleet totaled thirty-eight vessels in this latter list, in addition to seven brigantines and three galleys.

17. Narbrough to Admiralty, 8/18 December 1677/78, PRO, ADM. 106/326/357–58; PRO, S.P. 71/2/174, n.d.

18. Narbrough to Admiralty, 18/28 February 1677/78, PRO, ADM. 106/337/149; compare also Narbrough to Admiralty, 9/19 March 1677/78, PRO, ADM. 106/337/153.

19. Narbrough to Admiralty, 18/28 February 1677/78, PRO, ADM. 106/337/149.

20. Narbrough to Admiralty, 29 July 1678, PRO, ADM. 106/337/165.

21. W. B. Rowbotham, "The Algerine War in the Time of Charles II," *Journal of the Royal United Service Institution* 109 (1964): 165–66.

22. Narbrough's Testimony, 1 October 1676, Admiralty Minutes, PRO, ADM. 3/276; Narbrough to Admiralty, 8/18 December 1677, PRO, ADM. 106/326/357–58; Martin to Williamson, 3/13 March 1677/78, PRO, S.P. 71/2/227; Woolstone to John Ferreor, 4 March 1677/78, PRO, S.P. 71/2/231.

23. Martin to Williamson, 1/11 February 1677/78, PRO, S.P. 71/2/221; Woolstone to John Ferreor, 4 March 1677/78, PRO, S.P. 71/2/231. Also, Richard Fitzgerald to Sir Richard Bulstrode, 3/31 July 1678, BL, Addit. MSS 47899, fol. 175v; Thomas Hees, diary entry, 6 December 1678, The Hague, Rijksarchief (hereafter RA); Samuel Pepys to Narbrough, 24 January 1678/79, Narbrough's Letterbook (hereafter Ltrbk), Maidstone, Kent County Record Office (hereafter KCRO).

24. Narbrough to Admiralty, 5/15 November 1678, PRO, ADM. 106/337/176–78; Pepys to Narbrough, 23 September 1678, and List, 5/15 November 1678, Narbrough's Ltrbk, KCRO. Narbrough intended to return to Algiers with eighteen ships of his squadron.

25. Narbrough to Admiralty, 5/15 November 1678, PRO, ADM. 106/337/176–78.

26. Jeffries to [Secretary of State?], 27 February 1678/79, PRO, ADM. 106/343/310; Narbrough to Admiralty, 7/17 January 1678/79, PRO, ADM. 106/344/353.

27. Narbrough to Ernle, 23 December 1678, Narbrough's Ltrbk, KCRO; Roomcoyle to Admiralty, 18 March 1678/79, PRO, ADM. 106/345/393.

28. Narbrough to Strickland, 28 January 1678/79, Narbrough's Ltrbk, KCRO.

29. Narbrough to Strickland, 16 February 1678/79, ibid.

30. Narbrough to Admiralty, 7/17 January 1678/79, PRO, ADM. 106/344/353; Narbrough to Gardiner, 19 January 1678/79, Narbrough's Ltrbk, KCRO.

31. Narbrough to Killigrew, 12/22 February 1678/79, ibid.

32. Narbrough to Sheres, 12/22 February 1678/79, ibid.

33. Narbrough to Pepys, 13 April 1679, ibid.

34. Compare letter to Sir Richard Bulstrode, 7 April 1678 n.s., BL, Addit. MSS 47899, fol. 156.

35. Pepys to Narbrough, 23 September 1678, Narbrough's Ltrbk, KCRO; Narbrough to Admiralty, 16/26 June 1678, PRO, ADM. 106/337/157-58.

36. Narbrough to Roomcoyle, 11 February 1678/79, ibid.

37. Narbrough to Ball, 13 April 1679, ibid.

38. Sir Herbert Richmond, *The Navy as an Instrument of Policy, 1558-1727* (Cambridge, 1953), 151.

39. The *Rupert* was the only third-rate ship in his squadron, but in April 1680, Herbert transferred to the *Bristol*, a fourth-rate. The bulk of the vessels in his squadron were fourth-rates. PRO, ADM. 8/1.

40. Narbrough to Herbert, 10 May 1679, Narbrough's Ltrbk, KCRO; Admiralty Instructions to Herbert, 1 August 1679, PRO, ADM. 2/1726.

41. E. M. G. Routh, *Tangier, England's Lost Atlantic Outpost, 1661-1684* (London, 1912), 166.

42. Herbert to Pepys, 19 June 1679, Herbert's Letterbook, Yale University Library (hereafter Yale).

43. Herbert to Pepys, 17 July 1679, ibid.

44. Herbert to Brisbane, 9 April 1680, ibid.

45. Herbert to Brisbane, 24 April 1680, ibid.

46. Herbert to Goodrick, 15 April 1681, ibid.

47. Herbert to Jenkins, 15 May 1681, ibid.

48. Herbert to the bay [dey] of Algiers, 22 May 1681, ibid.

49. Samuel Martin, "The Present State of Algiers," PRO, S.P. 71/2/333.

50. Herbert to Jenkins, 19 November 1681, Herbert's Letterbook, Yale.

51. Herbert to Brisbane, 9 December 1681, ibid.

52. Herbert to Jenkins, 30 January 1680/81, ibid.

53. G. H. P. de Jonge, "Presenten en Protesten: De republiek en de Barbarijse Staten, 1675-1688" (Presents and protests: The Republic and the Barbary States, 1675-1688), (M.A. thesis, University of Leiden, 1984), 57-58. On the competition between these states to secure a peace with Algiers, see *Relation du voyage et de la négociation faite en Alger par l'ordre du Roy pendant le mois Février 1681*, Paris, Archives Nationales, AE B1, fols. 266-75; M. du Sault au [Bastion de France?], 20 November 1681, ibid., fols. 317-18; M. du Sault au Bastion de France, 10 March 1682, ibid., fols. 329-32.

54. Oxford, Bodleian Library, Carte MSS 40, fol. 208.

55. Autobiographical Fragment of Daniel Fitch, Earl of Nottingham, Leicester, Leicester Record Office, Finch MSS, Political Papers 148. Compare p. 27 above and note 60 below.

56. F. E. Dyer, *The Life of Admiral Sir John Narbrough* (London, 1931), 186-88; Florence E. Dyer, "The Journal of Grenville Collins," *Mariner's Mirror* 14 (July 1928): 214-15.

57. Narbrough to Admiralty, 8/18 December 1677, PRO, ADM. 106/326/357-58; Jeffries to Admiralty, 22 February 1678/79, PRO, ADM. 106/343/310, 312, 314; Pepys to Narbrough, 24 January 1678/79, Narbrough's Ltrbk, KCRO; Hees diary entries, 6 December 1678, 8 April 1679, The Hague, RA.

58. Herbert to Jenkins, 19 June 1681, Herbert's Letterbook, Yale; Herbert to Brisbane, 21 October 1681, ibid.

59. Admiralty commissioners to Herbert, August 1681, PRO, ADM. 2/1750. The following argument and quotations are taken from this document. The four arguments have not

been footnoted separately; compare Rowbotham, "Algerine War," 353, who paraphrases both Herbert's suggestions and the commissioners' response but failed to put them in context.

60. L. Sylvius, *Historien Onses Tijds, behelzende Saken van Staet en Oorlogh (The history of our time, regarding the affairs of state and war)*, Part 3, Book 24, August 1686, 95.

61. "Articles of Peace between England and Algiers, 29 November 1672," PRO, S.P. 108/9; "Articles of Peace between England and Algiers, 15 July 1683," PRO, S.P. 108/12; "Articles of Peace between England and Algiers, 10 April 1682," in C. Parry, *The Consolidated Treaty Papers* (New York, 1969), 205–11.

The French Raid upon the Newfoundland Fishery in 1762: A Study in the Nature and Limits of Eighteenth-Century Sea Power

OLAF UWE JANZEN

As part of a plan to damage British commerce in the North Atlantic and thus pressure the British to negotiate an end to the Seven Years' War, a French expedition attacked the Newfoundland fishery and captured St. John's. What began as a raid with a good chance at success in the overall strategy resulted in an attempt at permanent occupation. Dr. Janzen traces this expedition and shows how and why the change in plans spelled its certain doom.

****

On 8 May 1762 four French warships slipped out of Brest in thick weather and eluded blockading British cruisers. On board were 560 soldiers and officers under the command of Joseph-Louis-Bernard de Cléron, comte d'Haussonville.[1] Most of the men believed that their destination was St. Domingue, France's only remaining possession in the West Indies, the rest having been captured by British forces. Not until they had reached the open sea did the expedition's commander, *Chef d'escadre* Charles-Henri-Louis d'Arsac, chevalier de Ternay, reveal their true objective: the destruction of British trade and commerce in the North Atlantic, beginning with the British fishery at Newfoundland.

The choice of this objective said a great deal about France's situation by that point in the Seven Years' War. For over four years, it had suffered a nearly unremitting series of defeats which left much of its colonial empire in enemy hands, its navy in a shattered condition, and its financial and material ability to continue the war very much impaired. Yet attempts to negotiate an end to the war had ended in failure; when the government of William Pitt had refused to satisfy the minimum French demands concerning the fishery in the Gulf of St. Lawrence and at Newfoundland, the French broke off negotiations. That had been in September 1761. The duc de Choiseul, who was then minister of marine, of war, and of foreign affairs, had to find some way of pressuring the British into a more reasonable attitude. On the diplomatic side, this would mean bringing Spain (with whom France had concluded an alliance in August) into the war. On the strategic side, it would mean continuing operations against England's maritime empire. Since France's ability to conduct operations was by then quite limited, the campaign for 1762 would have to be planned with careful attention to the selection of the objectives, the organization of the expedition, and the appointment of the officers whose responsibility it would be to carry out the mission.

The *Plan de Campagne par Mer pour l'Anneê* 1762 which Choiseul read and endorsed during the winter of 1761–62 probably provided the inspiration for Ternay's mission.[2] It recommended raids against Brazil (a possession of England's ally, Portugal), the British fishery at Newfoundland, and British trade along the European and West African coasts. The plan was never fully adopted; France did not have the naval resources to undertake so ambitious an assault on the British maritime empire. Nevertheless, the object of the proposed campaign, "to make the most of these forces and keep the enemy as busy as possible...," was exactly what Choiseul had in mind. By combining some aspects of the plan and discarding others, he was able to prepare a campaign which was much more consistent with French resources and aims.

Choiseul's high regard for the migratory fishery was already a matter of fact; it had been his insistence that French access to the North American fisheries be a sine qua non to any peace settlement which had contributed to the breakdown of the peace negotiations in 1761. Both France and England regarded the migratory fishery as an economic resource of the first order.[3] Both countries also valued the fishery as a "nursery for seamen." According to the conventional wisdom of the day, the thousands of landsmen who found annual employment in the fishery became skilled seamen and mariners, thus providing their homelands with a strategic reserve of experienced manpower whenever the onset of war demanded the rapid expansion and deployment of the national navies.[4] In an age of rival mercantile empires, a country's response to a crisis could well be determined by the war-readiness of its fleets which, in turn, could depend upon the availability of trained seamen.[5] It was this dual role as an economic and strategic resource which made the fishery a particularly appropriate target. On the assumption that it represented one of France's better options to bring the war to an end, Choiseul prepared to attack the British fishery at Newfoundland.

The object of the mission, according to Ternay's instructions, was "to ravage and destroy, as much as he could, the commerce of the English fishery at the island and on the banks of Newfoundland." Ternay was to attempt the capture of St. John's, which served the fishery at Newfoundland as a rendezvous, refuge (by virtue of its defenses), and administrative center. He was to proceed with the destruction of that fishery, using St. John's as a base. These operations were to occupy Ternay for no more than a month ("Ces opérations ne pouvant pas retenir Le S'r. Ch'er. de Ternay plus d'un mois sur ces parages"). He was then to use his discretion in selecting further targets before returning to Brest in the fall ("Sa Majesté se remet à Son Zèle pour son service d'employer le reste de sa campagne, qui ne droit finir qu'au commencement de Novembre"). The fishery and commerce at Ile Royale were suggested as one possibility, provided the British forces there were weak. Otherwise he might return to Europe immediately in order to raid the seaports of Scotland and Ireland. In any case, Ternay was always to destroy enemy shipping,

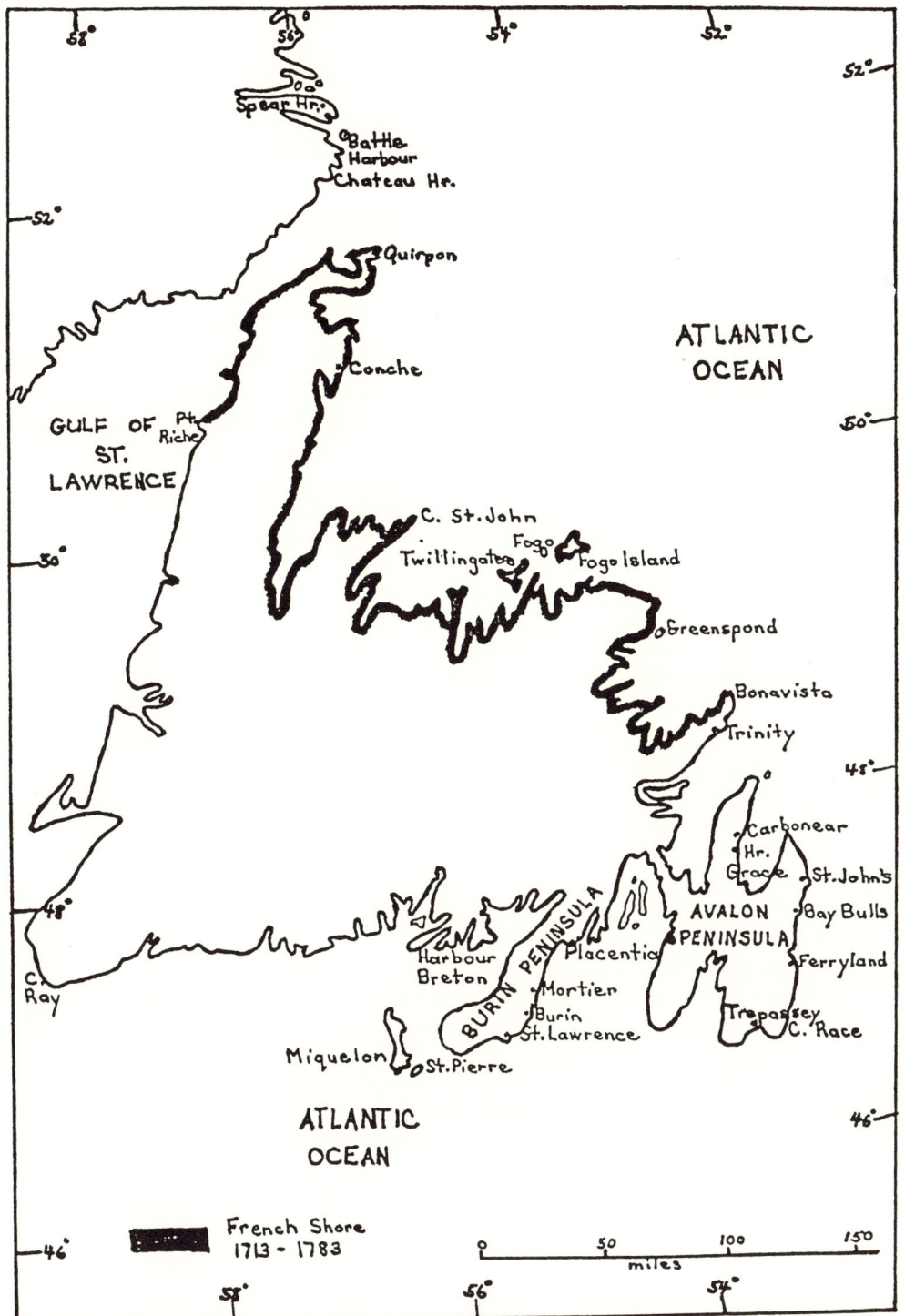

Map 1. Newfoundland in the late eighteenth century

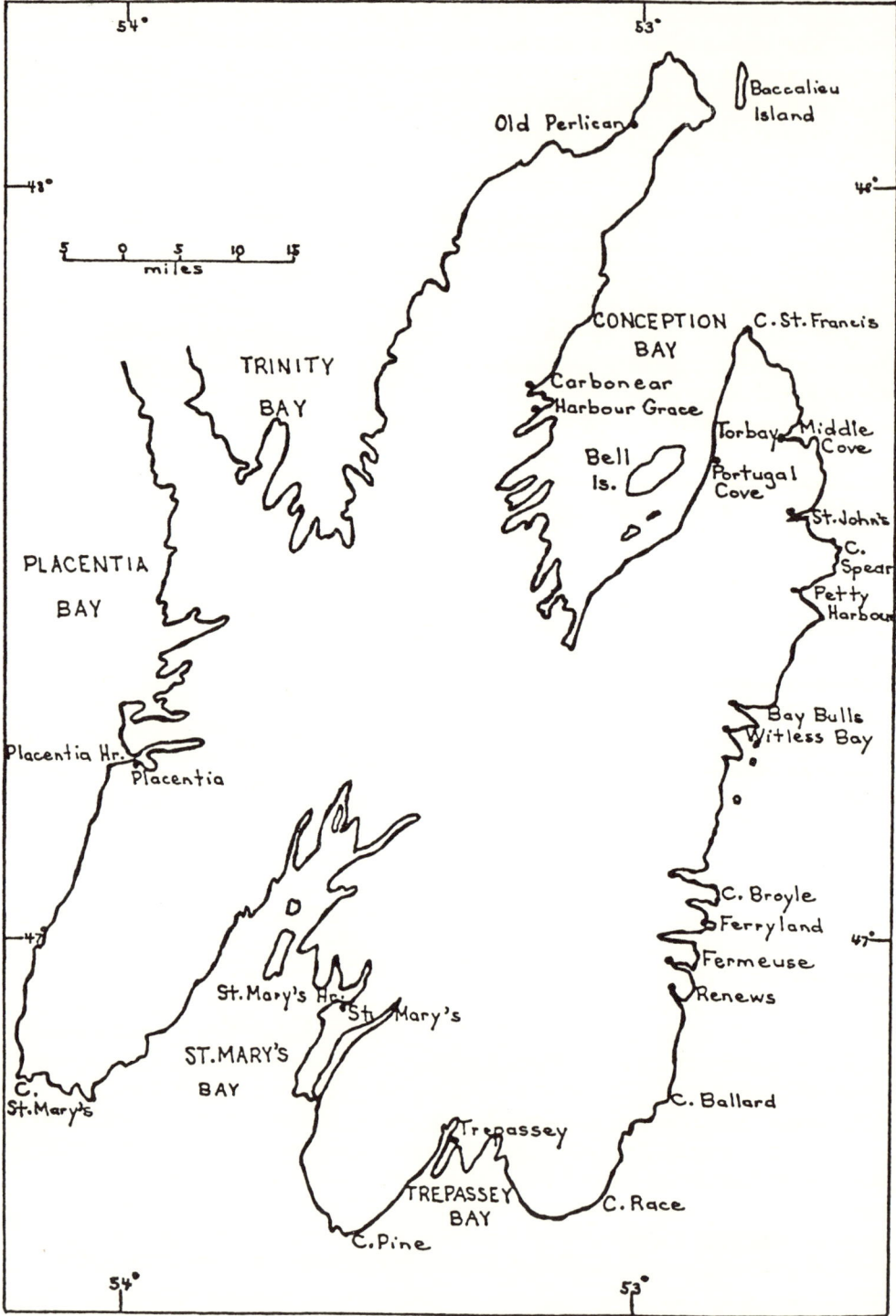

Map 2. Newfoundland's Avalon Peninsula

commercial buildings, and government structures, while exacting wealth from the towns and villages on pain of pillage should they refuse ("il brusquera toutes les descentes qu'il fera en brûlant tous les Bâtimens qu'il trouvera dans les Ports, Rades et anses, ainsy que les Magazins et autres Bâtimens civils appartenant à La Marine et au Commerce, et à L'égard des Villes, Bourgs et Villages, il tâchera d'en tirer les plus fortes contributions sous peine de pillage en cas de refus").

Finally, Ternay's instructions included a sentence which granted him virtually complete freedom to select other targets, should he think that they would better serve the object of his mission ("Sa Majesté... lui laisse une entière liberté sur le chois des objets auxquels il croira devoir s'attacher de préférence pour achever sa campagne"). Such a concession was not uncommon in the eighteenth century. It left a good commander free to respond to an unexpected contingency or opportunity. There was always the danger, however, that a weak or inexperienced commander would abuse that freedom to limit or even to abandon the mission altogether. In Ternay's case, this is precisely what would happen.[6]

While there are some who view Ternay's expedition as an attempt to capture and secure a bargaining counter with which France could negotiate a more equitable peace, it is clear that the attack on the fishery was planned as a raid.[7] Indeed, the successful outcome of the mission was assured only if Ternay avoided conquest. So long as his force continued to move from objective to objective, the British response would have to be a limited one, despite overwhelming superiority in sea power. It was precisely for this reason that Ternay was nervous about seizing and occupying St. John's, even for only a month; as he later explained to Choiseul, "I do not see how it would be possible to hold a post which is surrounded by the enemy and far from all help."[8] But given the slow rate of speed with which news of his presence at St. John's could be transmitted in an age of sail, a stay of one month ought not to have jeopardized the success of the mission. Apparently Choiseul had recognized what Julian Corbett would later articulate, namely, that "command of the sea means nothing but control of sea communications."[9] So long as Ternay did not remain too long, his precise location would remain unknown, and any British response to his presence in the North Atlantic would be unlikely to intercept him.

Certainly, by the spring of 1762, the benefits to be won outweighed the risks; by then it was apparent that Choiseul's diplomatic initiative had failed. The alliance with Spain brought that country into the war in January 1762. Choiseul had been encouraged by the prospect of adding Spain's naval resources to those of France, even as England's Royal Navy would be taxed by the need to contain this new threat. Moreover, Spain's entry into the war would terminate England's lucrative commercial relations with that country, thereby increasing the strain on England's ability to finance the war. Finally, Spain's participation would threaten England's ally, Portugal, and force the British government to disperse its military resources even further.

But Spain's entry into the war proved to be a disappointment. Hostilities against Portugal did not begin until May 1762, by which time British forces had seized Martinique, leaving St. Domingue the last remaining French possession of significance in the Caribbean. The capture of Martinique in February was immediately followed in March by the commencement of operations in Cuba. Choiseul was quite willing to resume negotiations at this point, particularly since the hated Pitt had resigned in October 1761 and had been replaced by the earl of Egremont. Nevertheless, Choiseul "was too able a statesman to abandon his plans for war simply because of the apparently favourable attitude of the British Cabinet toward peace."[10] The attack upon the British fishery proceeded even as negotiations between France and England resumed.

Ternay's expedition therefore must have served Choiseul's purposes well. Not only did it make use of what few ships were still at his disposal, but it also might even lead to dividends at the peace table—and at relatively modest cost and risk. Nevertheless, any success which might ensue would depend not so much on the logic of the expedition as upon the men responsible for its execution. The military contingent which embarked at Brest was as powerful as space on the warships would allow; according to later British reports, the soldiers were all "Choice men."[11] However, the crews of the four warships in Ternay's squadron—the 74-gun *Robuste,* the 64-gun *Eveillé,* the 30-gun frigate *Garonne,* and the 26-gun storeship *Licorne*—were sickly and understrength.[12] Aggressive action would be avoided as a result, and Ternay's leadership would be uncertain. Moreover, he had only recently been promoted to the rank of ship's captain, and he had never commanded a ship in action, let alone a squadron entrusted with the complex task of carrying out a combined operation. On the other hand, he had recently distinguished himself for his role in bringing the warships *Robuste* and *Eveillé* out of the Vilaine River to Brest. They had been driven over the bar at the river's mouth by pursuing British warships during the Battle of Quiberon Bay in 1759 and had idled there ever since, secure but useless.[13] For this action, Ternay received his captaincy and the command of the Newfoundland expedition. Evidently, for such a mission, Choiseul valued audacity and initiative more than he did experience.

While success therefore seemed possible, Ternay cautioned that "only secrecy and extreme diligence can assure a project's success."[14] Toward this end, various precautions were taken to disguise the purpose behind the activity at Brest. Mail intended for St. Domingue was sent on board Ternay's ships, as were two or three officers attached to regiments serving there. Ternay also was to send dispatches from Newfoundland, which implied that St. Domingue was still his ultimate destination. Finally, he was instructed to chart a course for Newfoundland which would minimize the risk of being seen or of revealing his true objective; should he encounter any enemy merchantmen, he was to take or destroy them.[15]

Most of these measures had the desired effect. The London newspapers were aware that something was up, but they could only speculate about Ternay's destination. And the British did not immediately detect his departure.[16] But in one of those examples of bad luck for which no amount of careful planning can allow, Ternay's squadron was barely three days out of Brest when it crossed the path of a British convoy. The convoy escort formed a disposition for battle, but the French, who were undermanned and had one ship *en flûte,* were in no mood to risk their mission for a battle whose outcome was uncertain. Consequently, the French squadron tacked to the northward and escaped.[17] Although the object of the French expedition was still unclear, the British were now alerted as to its presence in the North Atlantic.[18]

The encounter left Ternay worried that British warships assigned to the Newfoundland station would soon be responding to his presence there. As the French squadron approached the Grand Banks, another incident intensified his concern. The *Garonne* became separated from the squadron and, contrary to instructions, attempted unsuccessfully to capture an English vessel. The merchantman was last seen making for St. John's, and Ternay was certain that not only the fishery but also the naval establishment at Halifax, Nova Scotia, would know that he was loose in Newfoundland waters. It was therefore with a sense of extreme urgency that Ternay brought his ships into Bay Bulls, a few miles south of St. John's, on 24 June. D'Haussonville and the troops were quickly landed with instructions to march upon St. John's—an arduous task since there were no roads, only primitive wilderness paths; they were expected to complete the trek in three days. Ternay would remain at Bay Bulls, destroying the shipping and fishing facilities found there. By descending upon St. John's from the rear instead of from the sea as expected, he hoped to salvage some of the element of surprise which he believed had been compromised.[19]

Ternay did not yet realize just how vulnerable the Newfoundland fishery was to a raid at that time. Despite the high regard in which the fishery was held, it had been traditional British practice to defend it through the exercise of sea power in metropolitan waters.[20] Little had been done in Newfoundland itself to provide the fishery with an effective local defense. The only significant fortifications on the island were at Placentia and St. John's. These were so poorly situated and in such a decrepit state by 1762 that their ability to repulse an attack was in doubt. Ternay would be shocked by the condition of the defenses at St. John's, observing that "they say that this place, which has been in England's possession for a long time, has cost that country £190,000. To see its actual state, you would not think so."[21]

The fortifications were garrisoned by two companies of the 40th Regiment of Foot which had been serving in Newfoundland since 1717, the year in which their parent regiment had been formed; by 1762 the company at Placentia was described as being "very defective," and there is nothing to suggest that the condition of the company at St. John's was any different.[22] A company of the Second Battalion, Royal Regiment of Artillery, also was serving in Newfoundland, but the largest detachment was at Placentia, not St. John's.[23] Finally, the British warships stationed at Newfoundland every year from late spring to early fall for the regulation and defense of the fishery must be considered. In 1762 these were the 50-gun *Antelope* and two 20-gun frigates, the *Syren* and the *Gramont*. At the time of Ternay's appearance off St. John's, only the frigates had arrived from England; the *Antelope*, with Captain Thomas Graves, the commander in chief of the Newfoundland station and governor of the island, was still at sea. To all intents and purposes, there was no effective local defense.

This is not to say that some sort of resistance was not possible. The *Gramont* had arrived at St. John's a few days earlier with some of the trade and was moored in the harbor. Its commander, Captain Patrick Mouat, was able to send about 100 of its sailors and marines up to Fort William to help serve the guns. At the same time, Captain Lieutenant Rogers was keen to have his artillery detachment open fire upon the French. A large number of fishermen and inhabitants—about 370 men by one report—had volunteered to assist the garrison in the defense of the town, and many were subsequently issued arms and ammunition. But the garrison commander, Captain Walter Ross, would give them no further encouragement or direction, nor would he permit Rogers to begin bombarding the French, except for two ineffectual shots fired while the enemy was still half a mile away. As a result, d'Haussonville advanced his men to within 300 yards of the fort, where they found shelter behind a hill. He then summoned the garrison to surrender. Even then, defeat was not inevitable, for it had been impossible for the French to bring their artillery with them on the difficult march from Bay Bulls; they would have had to take the fort by storm. But Ross believed that the French numbered more than 1,500 and that, in the face of such numbers, resistance was futile. Incapable of providing decisive leadership even in surrender, and much to the disgust of the other officers, he called a council of war before agreeing to the French terms. Captain Mouat was particularly bitter because Ross's sudden surrender had left the *Gramont* trapped in the harbor. Mouat had to order its guns spiked and the ship scuttled in an attempt to keep it out of enemy hands.[24]

Immediately after the capitulation of Fort William on 29 June, the French began vigorous efforts to improve the state of defense at St. John's. Michael Gill, a local magistrate, was compelled to provide workmen to improve the fortifications.[25] The captured crew of the *Gramont* was put to work to raise the sunken frigate. Its guns were then drilled out, and the ship was prepared as swiftly as possible to be added to the French squadron.[26] Meanwhile, on 3 July, Ternay had brought his ships into the harbor and then secured its entrance with a boom and a new battery.[27] Four sloops and a schooner, armed with cannon and mortars and loaded with 150 soldiers, were sent north to destroy the defenses and fisheries of Conception, Trinity, and Bonavista bays. Two other vessels were sent to the Southern Shore on a similar mission.[28] M. de Clonard, who was directed to raise recruits for a marine regiment, had found numerous Irishmen willing to enter into the French service.[29] So far, the mission was proceeding much more smoothly than Ternay had anticipated.

Yet as success followed success, Ternay became increasingly reluctant to proceed with his mission by attacking the North American fishery. His instructions had directed him to stay in Newfoundland no longer than one month after the capture of St. John's, but within a week of his arrival at that port he had already postponed his departure to the beginning of September.[30] Ternay offered several explanations for the delay, he needed time to complete the improvements to the harbor defenses, he needed time to careen and repair the *Gramont*, and he was concerned that the British warships stationed at Halifax had been alerted about his presence and were expecting him.[31] Possibly the best explanation came from the British commander at Louisbourg, Lieutenant Colonel Tulleken. He was confident that the French would make no further attempts upon British possessions in the region. "It seems to me," he wrote to Sir Jeffrey Amherst, his commander in chief, "that what they have got has been more fortunate than from any Expectations they would have had of success; and finding themselves so lucky, they endeavour to fix where they are in hopes of being speedily reinforced from Home." In effect, the French were stunned into immobility by their own success.[32]

It was a perceptive observation. Before sailing from Brest, Ternay had questioned whether St. John's should or even could be taken.[33] When, contrary to his expectations, St. John's fell with scarcely a shot being fired, he tried lamely to cover his surprise by declaring that "in war it is usually the most difficult tasks which succeed most easily."[34] Nevertheless, he was unwilling to test this observation any further. Rather than proceed with his attack upon British commerce in the North Atlantic, Ternay decided to remain where he was and prepare St. John's for permanent occupation. It was a decision which ignored a fact which he had recognized before leaving Brest, namely, that by 1762 France no longer had the means to support a prolonged occupation of Newfoundland.

It was also a decision which ignored the facts of Ternay's own experience. Despite having landed over 500 troops with ease at Bay Bulls, he now maintained that the entire coast was too sheer to be accessible even by shallops. Despite d'Haussonville's success at marching his men twenty-five miles in three days, Ternay now claimed that overland travel was almost impossible, owing to the bad terrain and lack of roads. Despite capturing St. John's from the landward side, Ternay assumed that any British countermeasures would come from the sea. With the dust still settling from the French seizure of the town, Ternay now assured Choiseul that St. John's could be made invincible with very little extra work.[35] To Ternay, the security of having a bird in the hand was incalculably more attractive than the risks of seeking more in the bushes.

Having made his decision, Ternay then had to solve the pressing problem of securing the provisions necessary for a prolonged occupation. Troops were sent through the town to survey the supplies in the storehouses of the local merchants and to post sentinels over them. Livestock and poultry were confiscated for garrison use. The detached force which had been sent to destroy the fishery north of St. John's also was ordered to collect provisions for the French garrison; indeed, Ternay regarded that as being "one of the principal objects of his mission."[36] He had arrived shortly after the winter's consumption of food reserves and before the spring trade had arrived with fresh provisions and supplies.[37] A few vessels did arrive after the French had taken St. John's; these were seized as they entered the harbor, before they realized the true situation.[38] However, most of the trade was warned in time and either turned back or headed elsewhere.

Unless measures were taken to reduce the numbers of mouths to be fed, Ternay simply could not expect his force to hold St. John's until relief could be sent from France. Consequently, most of the inhabitants, except for a few people who had value as hostages, were loaded onto captured merchantmen and allowed to make their way as best they could to England or the American colonies.[39] Only the Irish Catholics who were sympathetic to the French were allowed to stay.[40] The French garrison also would be reduced to 350 men under the command of Lieutenant Colonel de Bellecombe, while the rest of the soldiers would return to France with d'Haussonville and Ternay's squadron, together with as many Irishmen as would enter into French service. In this way the total population of St. John's would be reduced to a maximum of 500 people by the time winter arrived. With a little belt-tightening and the help of supplies and stores which Ternay hoped could be sent from France before the year was out, the provisions would last until early 1763. Provided another squadron were then to bring reinforcements and supplies to Newfoundland, France would be guaranteed possession of St. John's through 1763.[41]

If Choiseul was disturbed by the way in which Ternay had transformed what was to have been a raid into a conquest, he gave no sign of it when the news reached him early in August 1762. Instead, he expressed both his and the king's pleasure and satisfaction with Ternay's achievement.[42] It is possible that Choiseul was reluctant to admit in any way that Ternay had proved to be an unwise choice as commander of the expedition. A more likely explanation for Choiseul's acceptance of Ternay's fait accompli is suggested by the peace negotiations between France and England. These had resumed during the winter of 1761–62 and were being conducted through the intermediation of the Sardinian envoys to Paris and London, the bailli de Solar and Count Viry.

By the summer of 1762, these negotiations had reached a critical stage; Choiseul was anxious to make peace, but France's ally, Spain, was being obtuse and the British cabinet was divided over the terms.[43] Although de Solar believed that further delay in the progress of the peace talks would encourage the French to think seriously about keeping Newfoundland, there is no evidence to suggest that Choiseul tried to use the island as a "bargaining counter," nor does it seem likely, at so critical a juncture in the negotiations, that Choiseul would have jeopardized a settlement by assuming a position which seemed certain to prolong the war.[44] Nevertheless, he did agree to send two supply ships to St. John's before winter set in.[45] Ternay may not have adhered to his instructions, but his success at St. John's had given France a momentary moral advantage which Choiseul would be anxious to preserve, at least until the terms of the peace were worked out.

The questions which now had to be faced were how quickly and how effectively the British would respond to the capture of St. John's. Ternay and d'Haussonville were confident that the British would be able to do no more than send some warships to Newfoundland which might menace the French but not dislodge them. This was why Ternay saw no contradiction in improving only the seaward defenses of St. John's, despite having taken the town from the landward side. Similarly, when de Cirq, the French engineer, encouraged d'Haussonville to entrench upon the hills which commanded Fort William, his advice was ignored.[46] Even Choiseul agreed that a British counterattack with soldiers and artillery seemed out of the question before 1763.[47] And, so long as the British were uncertain about Ternay's intentions, this remained a valid conclusion.

When the news of the capture of St. John's reached London around 21 July, the government sent a squadron of warships under Captain Hugh Palliser to Newfoundland. There, he was to reinforce Captain Graves who, it was expected, would already have been joined by Lord Colvill and the North America-stationed ships.[48] No troops were sent with Palliser, nor was there any reason to suggest that troops were thought necessary. Meanwhile, the HMS *Syren* came into Halifax on 30 June with the news that enemy ships were in the vicinity. The frigate was part of Graves's command and had been patrolling the fishery out of Placentia when it spoke to a schooner which claimed to have encountered five enemy ships: "Suppose to be Spanish Men of War."[49]

Lord Colvill received the report with skepticism and suggested that the schooner had probably seen some enemy frigates or privateers, but he was prepared to cruise with his ships toward Newfoundland "to take, or Drive them off the Coast."[50] However, the civil authorities at Halifax were convinced not only that the report was accurate but also that their colony, Nova Scotia, was the enemy's real objective, and they refused to let Colvill sail.[51] Martial law was declared, an embargo was imposed on all shipping, and a militia company was hurriedly placed on daily guard duty.[52] No one suggested that a military force be assembled for any purpose other than defending Nova Scotia from the expected attack.

Throughout the month of July British military and naval authorities in North America remained alert to the possible presence of an enemy force in their vicinity but, without more precise information, they could not act. At Halifax, Lord Colvill was prepared to lead an expedition to Newfoundland once it became apparent, late in the month, that the fishery there was the enemy's main objective. But without orders from General Amherst in New York, the military commanders at Halifax and Louisbourg refused to provide Colvill with troops.[53] Amherst had been puzzled by the reports he was receiving and had adopted a wait-and-see attitude. Some of the reports continued to describe the enemy as Spanish; this made little sense since, at that moment, British forces were attacking Cuba, and one would therefore expect all available Spanish warships to be sent to the Caribbean.[54] One report implied that there was in fact no enemy force, only "some Victuallers bound for Quebec" which may inexplicably have fired upon some fishing vessels.[55] Consequently, Amherst would only caution the garrisons in Nova Scotia, Louisbourg, and Quebec to be on their guard.[56]

Even after 20 July, when he received confirmation about Ternay's attack upon the fishery and the capture of St. John's, Amherst would not initiate a counterattack. He still believed that the assault on Newfoundland was only a raid, which would be followed by another upon one or more of the North American colonies. Amherst was all too conscious of his weakness in such an event. Most of the soldiers stationed in North America were serving in the campaign against Cuba; according to one New York merchant, "the Troops are so drained that General Amherst has not so much as a sentinel."[57] Of even greater concern to the general was the fact that the same campaign had taken nearly every ship belonging to the North American station; in a letter to Rear Admiral George Rodney, Amherst revealed that "this coast... is Entirely bare from Newfoundland to Florida."[58] Consequently, when he began to seek reinforcements, it was warships that he requested rather than troops.[59] Although Amherst did order all the transport vessels then in New York into a state of readiness, this must be seen as a general measure, taken for "the protection of every part of this Continent," and not as evidence that he was already organizing an expedition for the relief of St. John's.[60] Until he knew for certain where the French would be, Amherst could only wait and prepare.

Ternay thus had been proven correct, for he had predicted that the British would do nothing until they knew with certainty where the French were.[61] But he was quite mistaken in assuming that, once the location of the French had been determined, the British would not organize a counterattack before 1763. On the contrary, when General Amherst learned on 8 August that "it appears the Enemy intend to Keep possession of that place [St. John's]," he acted with impressive speed and force.[62] Amherst correctly assumed that the British government would probably send warships, but not troops, to assist in the recapture of St. John's. He also recognized, now that the danger of further attacks by Ternay upon North America had been dispelled, that the colonies could be safely stripped of their defenses in order to assemble a counterstroke.

Amherst had no troops of his own, but he was able to scrape together about 200 regulars out of the hundreds convalescing at New York from wounds and sickness contracted during the campaign against Martinique.[63] These men would form the nucleus of the expedition, and Amherst's brother, Lieutenant Colonel William Amherst, would be its commander. The transports were quickly loaded and sailed on 14 August for Halifax and Louisbourg where they received another 1,300 regulars, provincials, and artillerymen before continuing on to Newfoundland. On 10 September the transports made Cape Race. Barely a month had elapsed since General Amherst had begun to organize the expedition.[64]

It was a remarkable accomplishment, not only for the speed with which the expedition had been organized but also for the way in which it demonstrated how well General Amherst, like Choiseul, had grasped that "command of the sea means nothing but control of sea communications."[65] Amherst had recognized that the French decision to remain at St. John's had changed the complexion of the situation completely. By abandoning any hope or pretense of threatening their sea communications, Ternay had surrendered the initiative to the British. Had he continued to attack the British trade in North American waters, Amherst would have been forced to proceed much more cautiously with his preparations for the recovery of St. John's; Captain Graves and Lord Colvill barely had sufficient ships between them to face Ternay in battle, let alone be able to spare any to escort Colonel Amherst's transports. But by remaining at St. John's, Ternay allowed the transports to proceed from New York to Halifax, then to Louisbourg, and finally on to Newfoundland without any escort whatsoever. Although the task of dislodging the French from their improved defenses at St. John's still lay ahead, to all intents and purposes the defeat of Choiseul's campaign against the British fishery at Newfoundland was virtually assured.

Lord Colvill's warships were already in Newfoundland waters when Amherst arrived. Frustrated by his failure to organize a relief expedition in Nova Scotia, Colvill had finally sailed from Halifax on 10 August with the *Northumberland* (74), the *Gosport* (44), and the Massachusetts provincial armed ship *King George* (20) to join Captain Graves at Placentia. Graves had been waiting there since his arrival in Newfoundland one month earlier. He had been convinced that the French would descend upon Placentia once their conquests elsewhere on the island had been consolidated. With only the *Antelope* (50) and the *Syren* (20), both of which were old ships, at his disposal,

Graves had set the small garrison and his marines feverishly to work improving the harbor defenses. Lord Colvill's appearance on 14 August therefore came as a great relief, and Graves looked forward with enthusiasm to abandoning "the defensive to go to seek the Enemy." On 22 August the warships left Placentia and made for St. John's, where they would cruise in an attempt to sever Ternay's communications with France.[66]

Ternay was not overly disturbed by the appearance of Lord Colvill's little squadron on 24 August. He had been expecting British warships since July and was confident that without troops they could do him no harm. For the next two weeks the British ships were a familiar sight as they cruised before St. John's.[67] His complacency gave way to alarm as Ternay began to receive information that Colvill's warships were about to be joined by an expedition numbering 4,500 men. He was certain that St. John's, which he had described as "impenetrable" two months earlier, could not be held against such a force. He therefore convinced d'Haussonville on 8 September to evacuate most of the garrison and prepare to debark immediately for France; 300 men under the command of de Bellecombe would remain to surrender the fort honorably or else hold it through the winter, should the British expedition be delayed or prove to be imaginary. The embarkation was completed by 11 September, but contrary winds prevented Ternay's departure. By the time the wind shifted to a favorable direction on the following day, Colonel Amherst's transports had made their appearance, and Ternay realized that the English expedition sent against him was smaller than he had been given to believe. Consequently, he decided to stay at St. John's, after all; the lengthy embarkation was reversed and the grenadiers, together with the marines of the squadron, returned to shore.[68]

Ternay was confident that the British could be repulsed. The narrow entrance to Quidi Vidi Harbor, which was about a mile from St. John's and which was the only place where the British could land artillery and stores, had been blocked useless by sinking several shallops; without artillery, the British could not hope to take Fort William. Ternay also knew that d'Haussonville had stationed detachments of troops at the more distant landing places, so that the British would be unable to achieve the degree of surprise which had made the French capture of St. John's possible. However, events were to show that Ternay's confidence was misplaced.[69]

Under the watchful protection of the *Syren*, Amherst's transports had made for Torbay, a few miles to the north of St. John's, and anchored there in the evening of 12 September. The French detachments there were too small to impede either the landing of the troops in the morning or the march south later that day. An attempt to stop the British advance at the river which empties into Quidi Vidi Harbor was equally unsuccessful. By 14 September the British were clearing that harbor of its obstacles and had even begun to unload light artillery and stores by shallop, despite a bombardment from a small French battery which had been hastily thrown up on Signal Hill.

When the French were forced from their positions by a daring assault under cover of fog the next morning, Ternay's situation became truly desperate. Not only Fort William but also his entire squadron would be at the mercy of the British once they hauled heavy artillery onto the heights they now controlled. As a result, Ternay abandoned all thoughts of resistance and concentrated instead upon escape. In the fog which continued to enshroud St. John's, he prepared to evacuate the troops from Fort William and take his ships through the harbor narrows. When the wind shifted favorably for an immediate departure, Ternay decided that the additional delay needed to embark the troops might only bring another shift of wind, a shift which would leave him trapped in the harbor. Ternay therefore sailed from St. John's, leaving behind almost all of the French land forces together with most of the marines of the squadron.

Lord Colvill, who did not detect Ternay's escape, peevishly regarded it as a "shamefull Flight," adding that, "had the French any naval Honour to loose, this Flight of Monsieur Ternay's woud finish it."[70] Captain Hugh Debbieg, the military engineer attached to Amherst's expedition, offering a more realistic assessment of Ternay's predicament, suggested that:

> Monsieur De Ternai... shewed his wisdom in retreating from St. John's Harbour the moment we got Possession of the Hills he knew well enough, there was much less risque in meeting with Lord Colvill's Fleet, than to remain in the Harbour, where the Fate of his Squadron was so certain.[71]

Ternay's departure from St. John's sealed the fate of the French troops who, under the command of Colonel d'Haussonville, continued to hold Fort William in defiance of British demands to surrender. Only when the British managed to set up a mortar battery and began to shell the fort did d'Haussonville agree to capitulate. By the end of 18 September, St. John's was once more in British hands.[72] As for Ternay, his squadron was too undermanned and wracked with disease to attempt any further attack upon British trade or territories. It headed instead for Brest and, when that refuge proved to be too well guarded by British cruisers, for Corunna.[73]

Ternay would remain there for several months until the war dragged to an end, trying to convince Choiseul, and perhaps himself, that his mission had been a success. The cost to the British economy of the interrupted cod fishery alone, he estimated at £1 million. Some 460 vessels of all kinds, together with the shore facilities of the fishery, had been destroyed. Over 100 hostages had been taken, 350 Irishmen had been recruited into French service, and most of the residents of St. John's had been expelled. An English frigate had been captured and added to Ternay's squadron, and another ship, an English privateer, had been taken just before entering Corunna. "All these losses," he concluded, "cause me to view this campaign as being completely advantageous to the State."[74]

To a limited extent, Ternay was correct in insisting that his attack on Newfoundland had been a blow to the fishery. The physical damage to the boats and facilities there would take time and money to repair. The effect on the trade, which had already suffered a setback when Spain entered the war and closed that country as a market for British fish, was equally serious. Although the news that St. John's had been recaptured created "universal joy" among the English merchants of the Italian markets, it was highly unlikely that very much of the trade for 1762 could be salvaged.[75] The French occupation had completely disrupted the fishing industry in Newfoundland and frightened off many of the employers and merchants "till it was too late for the fishery."[76] Nevertheless, the damage was much less severe than it could have been. The French detachment which had been instructed to destroy the fishery to the south of St. John's evidently stopped short of Ferryland, where British marines belonging to the *Syren* had been stationed in June and later reinforced.[77] A significant portion of the British fishery at Newfoundland was therefore spared. Even in those parts of the island where the French did appear, many of the merchants had been able to send away their best goods and effects before they could be confiscated. Moreover, many of the warehouses were left intact, together with their contents, after Ternay decided to hold St. John's. Had they been destroyed according to Ternay's instructions, the injury to the British fishery would have been very severe.

In earlier wars the fishery had survived repeated destruction of its shore facilities because it was then still a migratory fishery, with relatively few permanent structures or investments on the island. This was no longer the case by 1762. Extensive storage, service, and trading facilities in many of the harbors gave proof that the age of the so-called great merchant had arrived. Some of the establishments were worth tens of thousands of pounds. More importantly, the fishery was developing a considerable dependence upon the presence of permanent facilities in Newfoundland. Their destruction would therefore have been a considerable blow to the fishery.[78] Finally, a considerable number of captured ships and vessels were found in the harbor and retaken after the French were defeated.[79] In purely quantitative terms, then, Ternay had failed to damage the fishery as severely as he had claimed.

Responsibility for this failure must rest squarely with Ternay himself. While Choiseul condoned Ternay's decisions even when they went against his instructions, the minister of marine was hardly in a position to influence them as they were made. When Ternay presented him with a fait accompli, Choiseul presumably decided to make the best of what limited success Ternay had achieved. If any blame can be placed on the minister, it was for appointing Ternay in the first place. The initiative and courage which Ternay had demonstrated in rescuing the *Robuste* and the *Eveillé* from the Vilaine were desirable qualities, but so too were experience, a sound grasp of strategical principles, and steadiness in the face of an unpredictable situation which, in Ternay, were not proven qualities. His determination to keep his warships out of English hands was admirable; at one point he had told Choiseul that "they didn't leave the Vilaine River just to be captured at St. John's."[80] But such sentiments resulted in cautious tactics and may even have influenced his decision to hold St. John's. Ternay's uncertainty was most evident as he vacillated between resistance and flight in the face of English measures to recover St. John's. Time and again, he behaved more as the junior captain he actually was, accustomed to the relatively limited responsibility of commanding a single warship, than as the *chef d'escadre* Choiseul had made him, responsible for the leadership of a combined expedition.

Ternay's weak grasp of strategical principles was, however, his greatest flaw. His mission had been to conduct a series of raids against British trade and possessions in the North Atlantic. The descent on Newfoundland was conceived as an indirect assault on Great Britain's ability to finance the war. As such, Choiseul's plan was indicative of the way in which the French were capable of glorious gambles which hinted at an intuitive understanding of the limitations of British sea power. Yet Ternay's decision to transform his mission into one of conquest shows that he, at least, did not grasp the full implications of those principles of maritime strategy which the Royal Navy was on the way to mastering. Thus, so long as he adhered to Choiseul's plan, Ternay had demonstrated brilliantly that local command of the sea, which the British were exercising so thoroughly by 1762, did not preclude the continuation of French maritime operations. Ternay did not need a squadron capable of disputing command of Newfoundland waters with local British forces because "command," as Corbett would later argue, did not mean the occupation or control of the sea itself but rather of sea communications.

So long as his objectives remained unclear, the British response to Ternay's activities remained a limited one. Only when Ternay departed from his instructions by attempting to establish a French base at St. John's was General Amherst given both a fixed target and the time in which to prepare a counterstroke. Moreover, by remaining in one place, Ternay had to abandon the rest of his mission; Ile Royale and its fishery, and the coasts of Scotland and Ireland, were left untouched. Although the negotiations which brought the war to an end followed close on the heels of the French capture of St. John's, no one, including Ternay (who had the most to gain by advancing such a claim), ever suggested that the one contributed to the other. The moment St. John's became the object rather than an objective of Ternay's expedition, his mission lost any hope for success.

Notes

1. Addendum to Ternay to Choiseul, 5 May 1762, Public Archives of Canada (hereafter PAC), MG 2, transcripts, 27–28, Ottawa for Archives de la Marine (hereafter AM) B4, vol. 104, Paris. The force which would eventually occupy St. John's was substantially larger, having been augmented by about 300 marines from the ships, Colvill to Sir Jeffrey Amherst, 16 August 1762, PAC, MG 13, microfilm for Public Record Office (hereafter PRO), War Office (hereafter WO), WO 34/42, fols. 98–99, London.

2. PAC, transcripts, 3–9 for AM B4, vol. 104.

3. Ralph G. Lounsbury, *The British Fishery at Newfoundland, 1634–1763* (New Haven, 1934), 311–13; "Mémoire sur la pesche de L'amérique septentrionale," no date [1760–62], PAC, MG 5, transcripts, 143–46 for Archives des Affaires Etrangères, B1, vol. 22, Paris. In fact, both the French and English governments made virtually identical and simultaneous assessments of the value of the migratory fishery. Comparing the resources of Louisiana, Canada, and Newfoundland, the British Board of Trade in 1761 concluded that "the Newfoundland Fishery as a means of wealth and power is of more worth than both of the aforementioned provinces," while during the negotiations which brought the war finally to an end, Choiseul maintained that "the codfishery in the Gulf of St. Lawrence is worth infinitely more for the realm of France than Canada and Louisiana." Board of Trade cited in Gerald Graham, "Fisheries and Sea Power," Canadian Historical Association, *Annual Report 1941*, reprinted in *Historical Essays on the Atlantic Provinces*, ed. George Rawlyk (Toronto, 1967), 8; Choiseul cited in Max Savelle, *The Origins of American Diplomacy; The International History of Anglo-America, 1492–1783* (New York, 1967), 475n.

4. Keith Matthews, "A History of the West of England-Newfoundland Fisheries" (D.Phil. dissertation, Oxford University, 1968), 396; Olaf Janzen, "Newfoundland and British Maritime Strategy during the American Revolution" (Ph.D. dissertation, Queen's University, 1983),

chap. 1; J.-F. Brière, "Pêche et politique à Terre-Neuve au XVIIIe siècle: La France véritable gagnante du traité d'Utrecht?" *Canadian Historical Review* 64 (June 1983): 168-69.

5. In June 1770 the North administration was slow to respond to a dispute with Spain over the Falkland Islands, in part because the start of the fishing season had effectively removed thousands of men needed to put the Royal Navy on a war footing. See Nicholas Tracy, "The Falkland Islands Crisis of 1770; Use of Naval Force," *English Historical Review* 90 (January 1975): 49.

6. "Mémoire du Roy pour Servir d'Instruction au S'er. Ch'er. de Ternay," PAC, MG 2, transcripts, AM B4, vol. 104.

7. The French attack upon the fishery in 1762 is identified as a raid in Julian Corbett, *England in the Seven Years' War: A Study in Combined Strategy*, 2 vols. (London, 1907), 2:323; and in Maurice Linÿer de la Barbée, *Le Chevalier de Ternay* (Grenoble, 1972), chap. 8. It is identified as a conquest by Daniel Prowse, *A History of Newfoundland from the English Colonial and Foreign Records*, 2d ed. (London, 1896), 305; Gordon O. Rothney, "The History of Newfoundland and Labrador, 1754-1783" (M.A. thesis, University of London, 1934), 49; David Webber, "The Recapture of St. John's, 1762," *Newfoundland Quarterly* 61 (Fall 1962): 1-10; Glanville Davies, "England and Newfoundland: Policy and Trade, 1660-1783" (Ph.D. dissertation, University of Southampton, 1980), 122; Bernard Ransom, "A Century of Armed Conflict in Newfoundland," *Newfoundland Museum Notes* 10 (St. John's, 1982). Gerald Graham refers to the attack as both a raid and an attempt "to win one substantial bargaining counter," which implicitly would mean a conquest. Gerald Graham, *Empire of the North Atlantic; the Maritime Struggle for North America* (Toronto, 1950), 191. This is a contradiction since, by definition, "over-sea invasion is a continuous process which...requires the maintenance of unbroken communications during the period necessary to ensure complete military success. A raid, on the other hand, is an attempt to seize by surprise some strong point on or close to a coast-line, with a view to inflict an injury—moral or material—which might cripple, or at least diminish, the fighting resources of an enemy." Sir George Sydenham Clarke, *Fortifications: Its Past Achievements, Recent Development, and Future Progress*, 2d ed. (London, 1907), 170-71.

8. Ternay to Choiseul, 9 July 1762, PAC, MG 2, transcripts, 37 for AM B4, vol. 104.

9. Corbett, *England in the Seven Years' War*, 1:308.

10. Savelle, *Origins of American Diplomacy*, 497.

11. Colvill to Amherst, 16 August 1762, PAC, MG 13, microfilm for PRO, WO 34/42, fols. 98-99.

12. Ternay had difficulty bringing his crews up to strength, despite stripping men from the ships still trapped in the Vilaine River. Ternay to Choiseul, 7 April, 5 May 1762, PAC, MG 2, transcripts, 29-30 for AM B4, vol. 104. Few of the men had been to sea, and most were dressed in rags, according to Linÿer de la Barbée, who describes them as "a wretched herd which was therefore assured a frightening mortality rate." Linÿer de la Barbée, *Chevalier de Ternay*, 155. The *Biche*, which some sources add as a fifth vessel to Ternay's squadron, was in fact an English privateer taken as Ternay returned to European waters following the failure of his expedition. Ibid., 169-70.

13. La Perouse to Ternay, 1 February 1762, "Journal et Lettres du Chevalier de Ternay," 273-73v, Bibliothèque Nationale, Département des Manuscrits, Nouvelles acquisitions françaises 9410, Paris. The entire operation is described in Linÿer de la Barbée, *Chevalier de Ternay*, chap. 7.

14. Ternay to Choiseul, 7 April 1762, PAC, MG 2, transcripts, 29 for AM B4, vol. 104.

15. Ternay's instructions, enclosed in Choiseul to Ternay, 30 April 1762, ibid., transcripts, 18-21; Choiseul to Ternay, 9 April 1762, ibid., transcripts, 22-23.

16. "[They] are the very armament the Papers mention'd before we left England," Graves to Clevland, 21 September 1762, PAC, MG 12, microfilm for PRO, Admiralty Papers (hereafter ADM) 1/1835, pt. 3.

17. John Campbell, *Lives of the British Admirals*, 8 vols., rev. ed. (London, 1812-17), 5:192-93; William L. Clowes, *The Royal Navy: A History from the Earliest Times to the Present*, 7 vols. (London, 1897-1903), 3:250-51.

18. On 27 June 1762 orders were sent to Captain Graves, the senior officer on the Newfoundland station, "acquainting [him] with Mons'r Ternays force, and directing [him] how to act if he came to Newfoundland." Graves to Clevland, 21 September 1762, PAC, MG 12, microfilm for PRO, ADM 1/1835, pt. 3.

19. Ternay to Choiseul, 9 July 1762, PAC, MG 2, transcripts, 33-36 for AM B4, vol. 104.

20. Gerald S. Graham, "Britain's Defence of Newfoundland; A Survey from the Discovery to the Present Day," *Canadian Historical Review* 23 (September 1942): 260-79.

21. Ternay to Choiseul, 9 July 1762, PAC, MG 2, transcripts, 33-36 for AM B4, vol. 104. The defects of the works at Placentia are described in Report of Leonard Smelt, Engineer in Ordinary, to the Board of Ordnance, 22 November 1751, PAC, MG 11, transcripts, 45-49 for PRO, Colonial Office (hereafter CO), 5/161; see also Jean-Pierre Proulx, *Placentia, Newfoundland*, two volumes bound in one: *The Military History of Placentia: A Study of the French Fortifications* and *Placentia: 1713-1811* (Ottawa, 1979), 143-45. The works of St. John's are described in Captain Richard Edwards to Admiral Francis Holbourne, 17 July, 6 September 1757, PAC, MG 12, microfilm for PRO, ADM 1/481, fols. 384-86, 423-24.

22. J. A. Houlding, *Fit for Service: The Training of the British Army, 1715-1795* (Oxford, 1981), 18-19; R. H. Raymond Smythies, *Historical Records of the 40th Regiment (2nd Somerset) Regiment, Now 1st Battalion The Prince of Wales Volunteers (South Lancashire Regiment) from Its Formation in 1717, to 1893* (Devonport, 1894), 34; Graves to Board of Trade with enclosure, 18 August 1762, PAC, MG 11, microfilm for PRO, CO 194/15, fols. 31-34; Graves to Clevland, 18 August 1762, PAC, MG 12, microfilm for PRO, ADM 1/1835, pt. 3; Edwards to Holburne, 6 September 1757, PAC, MG 12, microfilm for PRO, ADM 1/481, fols. 423-24.

23. M. E. S. Laws, *Battery Records of the Royal Artillery, 1716-1859* (Woolwich, 1952), 30.

24. Account compiled from information provided by soldiers on board the brig *Dorothy*, a cartel carrying prisoners from Newfoundland to England, enclosed in Governor Francis Bernard to General Jeffrey Amherst, 29 August 1762, PAC, MG 13, microfilm for PRO, WO 34/26, fols. 202-3; "An Account of the Enemy Fleet & Army at Newfoundland as Given by Lt. Fade to Col. Tulleken," 29 July 1762, ibid., WO 34/18, fols. 53-53v; statement of Captain Lamb, 1 August 1762, PAC, MG 11, transcripts, 477-80 for PRO, CO 5/62; Colvill to Clevland, 24 July 1762, PAC, MG 12, microfilm for PRO, ADM 1/482, fols. 210; Captain Mouat to Clevland, 28 February 1763, ibid., for ADM 1/2115.

25. Statement of Captain Lamb, 1 August 1762, PAC, MG 11, transcripts, 477-78 for PRO, CO 5/62.

26. Ternay to Choiseul, 9 July 1762, PAC, MG 2, transcripts, 34-35 for AM B4, vol. 104.

27. Ibid., transcript, 34.

28. Ibid., transcript, 40; "Relation d'une Action de Guerre qu'a fait Le Ch'r. De La Motte Vauvert... en 1762," 25 February 1775, ibid., transcripts, 42-49.

29. Choiseul to Ternay, 12 April 1762, ibid., transcripts, 24-25; Ternay to Choiseul, 9 July 1762, ibid., transcript, 41; de Clonard to Choiseul, 16 October 1762, PAC, MG 4, transcript, 147 for Archives de la Guerre, B1, A1, vol. 3628, Paris.

30. "Mémoire du Roy pour Servir d'Instruction au S'r. Ch'er. de Ternay," enclosed in Choiseul to Ternay, 30 April 1762, PAC, MG 2, transcripts, 18-24 for AM B4, vol. 104; Ternay to Choiseul, 9 July 1762, ibid., transcript, 39.

31. Ibid., transcripts, 39-41; Ternay to Choiseul, 20 July 1762, ibid., transcript, 50.

32. Tulleken to Amherst, 20 July 1762, PAC, MG 13, microfilm for PRO, WO 34/18, fol. 49v.

33. Ternay to Choiseul, 9 July 1762, PAC, MG 2, transcripts, 37-38 for AM B1, vol. 104.

34. Ibid., transcript, 34.

35. Ibid., transcripts, 37-39.

36. Ibid., transcript, 40; "Relation d'une Action de Guerre qu'a fait Le Ch'r. De La Motte Vauvert... en 1762," ibid., transcript, 42; statement of Captain Thomas Lamb, 1 August 1762, PAC, MG 11, transcripts, 477-78 for PRO, CO 5/62; Rev. Edward Langman (St. John's) to Rev. Secretary Daniel Burton, 14 July 1762, PAC, MG 17, B1, transcripts, 44-45 for Society for the Propagation of the Gospel in Foreign Parts, Letters, ser. B, 1700-86, vol. 6, London (hereafter SPG, B/6).

37. Langman to Burton, 2 November 1762, ibid., transcripts, 46-47.

38. Ibid.

39. Ibid.; Ternay to Choiseul, 9 July 1762, PAC, MG 2, transcript, 39 for PRO, AM B4, vol. 104; Colvill to Clevland, 16 August, 20 September 1762, PAC, MG 12, microfilm for PRO, ADM 1/482, fols. 223, 215.

40. How many Irish Catholics actually were in St. John's in 1762 is not certain. During the winter of 1760-61, the Irish population was described as being 400 men, 100 women, 60 boys,

and 60 girls, figures which clearly were meant to be estimates; see Langman to Bearcroft, 4 November 1762, PAC, MG 17, transcript, 39 for SPG, B/6.

41. Ternay to Choiseul, 9 July 1762, PAC, MG 2, transcripts, 39-40 for AM, B4, vol. 104.

42. Choiseul to Ternay, 14 August 1762, PAC, MG 1, transcripts, 59-63 for Archives des Colonies (hereafter AC), B, vol. 104, Paris.

43. Savelle, *Origins of American Diplomacy*, 489-510; Ronald Hyam, "Imperial Interests and the Peace of Paris (1763)," in *Reappraisals in British Imperial History*, eds., R. Hyam and G. Martin (Toronto, 1975), 21-43; Zenab Esmat Rashed, *The Peace of Paris*, 1763 (Liverpool, 1951), chaps. 4-5.

44. De Solar to Viry, 26 August 1762, PAC, MG 23, transcripts, 2: 125-26 for Earl of Shelburne Papers, vol. 10, William L. Clements Library, Ann Arbor, Michigan (hereafter Shelburne Papers).

45. Choiseul to Ternay, 14 August 1762, PAC, MG 1, transcripts, 59-60 for AC, B, vol. 104.

46. Ternay to Choiseul, 9 July 1762, PAC, MG 2, transcripts, 38-39 for AM B4, vol. 104; Captain Hugh Debbieg to Lord Shelburne, 19 February 1767, PAC, MG 23, transcripts, 28:58 for Shelburne Papers, 86.

47. Choiseul to de Bellecombe, 14 August 1762, PAC, MG 1, transcripts, 64-67 for AC, B, vol. 114.

48. *London Daily Advertiser*, 26 July 1762, in *Horace Walpole's Correspondence*, vol. 22, *Correspondence with Mann*, ed. W. S. Lewis (New Haven, 1960), 52n-53n. Palliser sailed on 7 August 1762 with three 74s and a 32-gun frigate. He arrived at St. John's on 19 September, too late to participate in the recapture of the town. Palliser to Clevland, 22 August [*sic*] 1762, PAC, MG 12, microfilm for PRO, ADM 1/2299, pt. 8.

49. Major General Sir Jeffrey Amherst to Rear Admiral Rodney, 20 July 1762, PAC, MG 11, transcripts, 412-13 for PRO, CO 5/62; Captain Thomas Graves to Clevland, 18 August 1762, PAC, MG 12, microfilm for PRO, ADM 1/1835, pt. 3; Graves to Board of Trade, 18 August 1762, PAC, MG 11, microfilm for PRO, CO 194/15, fols. 31-34.

50. Amherst to Rodney, 20 July 1762, PAC, MG 11, transcripts, 412-13 for PRO, CO 5/62.

51. J. B. Brebner, *The Neutral Yankees of Nova Scotia* (1937; reprint, Toronto, 1969), 37-39; Colvill to Clevland, 2 July 1762, PAC, MG 12, microfilm for PRO, ADM 1/482, fol. 208.

52. Philip Chadwick Foster Smith, ed., *The Journals of Ashley Bowen (1728-1813) of Marblehead, vol. 1*, Publications of the Colonial Society of Massachusetts (Boston, 1973), vol. 44, 133; letter of 15 July 1762 from Halifax and printed 29 July 1762 in the *Boston News-Letter and New England Chronicle*, ibid., 133n.

53. Colvill to Clevland, 30 July, 6 August 1762, PAC, MG 12, microfilm for PRO, ADM 1/482, fols. 211-13.

54. Statement of Ganeston Meers, 11 July 1762, enclosed with Amherst to Rear Admiral Rodney, 20 July 1762, PAC, MG 11, transcripts, 420-21 for PRO, CO 5/62.

55. Statement of Samuel Dogget, 11 July 1762, ibid., transcripts, 422-23; Amherst to Admiral Sir George Pocock, 20 July 1762, ibid., transcript, 416.

56. Amherst to Secretary of State Egremont, 20 July 1762, ibid., transcripts, 306-7; J. Clarence Webster, ed., *The Journal of Jeffrey Amherst, Recording the Military Career of General Amherst in America from 1758-1763* (Toronto, 1931), 287.

57. Cited in John Shy, *Toward Lexington: The Role of the British Army in the Coming of the American Revolution* (Princeton, 1965), 106.

58. Amherst to Rodney, 20 July 1762, PAC, MG 11, transcript, 412 for PRO, CO 5/62.

59. See Amherst's letters of 20 July 1762 to Secretary of State Egremont, General Lord Albemarle, Admiral Pocock, and Rear Admiral Rodney in ibid., transcripts, 304-5, 409-19. Pocock's response can be found in his letter of 9 October 1762 to Clevland in David Syrett, ed., *The Siege and Capture of Havana, 1762* (London, 1970), 299-300.

60. Amherst to Colvill, 9 August 1762, PAC, MG 11, transcript, 453 for PRO, CO 5/62; Amherst to Egremont, 20 July 1762, ibid., transcripts, 306-7.

61. Ternay to Choiseul, 9 July 1762, PAC, MG 2, transcript, 37 for AM B4, vol. 104.

62. Amherst to Egremont, 15 August 1762, PAC, MG 11, transcript, 427 for PRO, CO 5/62.

63. Ibid., transcripts, 427-28; Amherst to William Amherst, 13 August 1762, ibid., transcripts, 436-40; "List of the Troops Ordered to Form the Corps under the Command of Lt. Colonel Amherst," 13 August 1762, ibid., transcript, 445.

64. William Amherst to General Amherst, 27 August 1762, ibid., transcripts, 527–29; J. C. Webster, ed., *The Recapture of St. John's, Newfoundland in 1762 as Described in the Journal of Lieut.-Colonel William Amherst, Commander of the British Expeditionary Force* (Shediac, New Brunswick, 1928), 5–6.

65. Webster, *Recapture of St. John's*, 5.

66. Colville to Clevland, 9 August, 20 September 1762, PAC, MG 12, microfilm for PRO, ADM 1/482, fols. 214–18; Colvill to General Amherst, 19 August 1762, PAC, MG 13, microfilm for PRO, WO 34/42, fols. 97–97v; Graves to Board of Trade, 18 August 1762, PAC, MG 11, microfilm for PRO, CO 194/15, fol. 34v.

67. Ternay, "Journal de ce qui s'est passé à St. Jean depuis le 8. Septembre jusqu'au 15 du même mois, Jour de mon départ" (hereafter "Journal"), PAC, MG 2, transcript, 57 for AM B4, vol. 104; Colvill to Clevland, 9 August, 20 September 1762, PAC, MG 12, microfilm for PRO, ADM 1/482, fols. 214–18.

68. Ternay to Choiseul, 9 July 1762, PAC, MG 2, transcript, 39–40 for AM B4, vol. 104; Ternay, "Journal," transcript, 57–58.

69. Ibid., transcript, 57–59. Other primary accounts of the recapture of St. John's are provided in Webster, *Recapture of St. John's*; "Col. Amherst's Account," *Gentleman's Magazine* 32 (1762): 487–88; C. H. Little, ed., *The Recapture of Saint John's, Newfoundland. Dispatches of Rear-Admiral Lord Colvill 1761–1762* (Halifax, 1959). The best secondary accounts of the events of 1762 include Major Evan W. H. Fyers, "The Loss and Recapture of St. John's, Newfoundland in 1762," *Journal of the Society for Army Historical Research* 11 (1932): 179–215; Georges Cerbelaud Salagnac, "La reprise de Terre-Neuve par les Français en 1762," *Revue française d'histoire d'outre-mer* 63 (1976): 211–12; Linÿer de la Barbée, *Chevalier de Ternay*, chap. 8.

70. Ternay, "Journal," transcript, 62–64; Colvill to Clevland, 20 September 1762, PAC, MG 12, microfilm for PRO, ADM 1/482, fol. 217; Colvill to William Amherst, 16 September 1762, PAC, MG 11, microfilm for PRO, CO 194/26, fol. 13.

71. Debbieg to the Board of Ordnance, 8 January 1766, Shelburne Papers, vol. 86, fol. 31.

72. Webster, *Recapture of St. John's*, 11; "Col. Amherst's Account," 485.

73. Ternay to Choiseul, 5, 23 October 1762, PAC, MG 2, transcripts, 51–52, 65–66 for AM B4, vol. 104; Linÿer de la Barbée, *Chevalier de Ternay*, 169–71.

74. Ternay to Choiseul, 5, 15 October 1762, PAC, MG 2, transcripts, 51–56 for AM B4, vol. 104.

75. Mann to Walpole, 6 February 1762, *Walpole's Correspondence*, 22:5; Dick (Leghorn) to Egremont, 5 November 1762, ibid., 100n; Mann (Florence) to Walpole, 13 November 1762, ibid., 99–100.

76. Rev. Langman to Burton, 2 November 1762, PAC, MG 17, transcripts, 46–50 for SPG B6; Graves to Board of Trade, 4 October 1762, PAC, MG 11, microfilm for PRO, CO 194/15, fols. 42–43v.

77. Graves to Clevland, 18 August 1762, PAC, MG 12, microfilm for PRO, ADM 1/1835, pt. 3.

78. When Joseph White, the Poole merchant with extensive holdings at Trinity, died in 1771, the estate was valued at £150,000; W. Gordon Hancock, "The Poole Mercantile Community and the Growth of Trinity, 1700–1839," *Newfoundland Quarterly* 80 (Winter 1985): 22. The presence of a resident fishery helps explain why the British fish trade overshadowed that of France during the eighteenth century; see Christopher Moore, "The Markets for Canadian Cod in the Eighteenth Century: France's Cod Trade and the Problem of Demand," paper presented at the Annual Meeting of the Canadian Historical Association, Guelph, Ontario, 1984, 18–19. The rise of the resident fishery is described in Matthews, "History of the West of England-Newfoundland Fisheries," 365–68, 378–81.

79. Graves to Board of Trade, 4 October 1762, PAC, MG 11, microfilm for PRO, CO 194/15, fols. 42–43v. For an example of how one British merchant responded to the French attack, see the survey of Benjamin Lester's career at Trinity in W. Gordon Hancock, "A Biographical Profile of 18th and Early 19th Century Merchant Families and Entrepreneurs in Trinity, Trinity Bay," unpublished manuscript at Centre for Newfoundland Studies, Memorial University of Newfoundland, Corner Brook, Newfoundland (1980), especially 91–92.

80. Ternay to Choiseul, 9 July 1762, PAC, MG 2, transcripts, 40–41 for AM B4, vol. 104.

The Battle of Grenada and Caribbean Strategy, 1779*

ALAN G. JAMIESON

Following the Franco-American Alliance in 1778, Britain concentrated its attack against the French in the Caribbean. Dr. Jamieson's essay examines how British naval supremacy there was undermined in early 1779, leading to the loss of St. Vincent and Grenada and the defeat of a British fleet; how command of the sea in this war would not be the British monopoly it had earlier been; and how hopes of conquering enemy islands gave way to a realization that safeguarding Britain's colonies in the Caribbean would stretch the Royal Navy to its limits.

****

On 20 July 1779 a battered 64-gun ship of the line, the HMS *Lion*, arrived at Port Royal, Jamaica. It had come down from the Lesser Antilles, a thousand miles to the east, and brought news of a naval action off the island of Grenada. The British fleet had been beaten, the island lost, and the *Lion* had been forced to run westward before the prevailing winds to avoid being captured by the French fleet. The captain of the *Lion* was William Cornwallis, younger brother of Charles, second Earl Cornwallis, who was to surrender his army at Yorktown in 1781. Although not as decisive as Yorktown, the British defeat at Grenada in 1779 had an important influence on the course of the American War of Independence.

Some idea of the impact the Grenada disaster had upon British public opinion can be gained from a letter written by another of William's brothers, James, shortly after news of it reached England in early September. James Cornwallis told William that:

> Admiral Barrington is come home in very ill-humour, and represents our situation in the West Indies as truly lamentable, where we thought ourselves strongest. Upon the whole, nothing can look worse than our affairs, although we have not yet had any great loss excepting Grenada, we are every day in apprehension of some bad news. How different from the last war, when we were only accustomed to hear of victory.[1]

---

*This paper is adapted from Alan G. Jamieson, "War in the Leeward Islands, 1775–1783" (D. Phil. thesis, University of Oxford, 1981), chap. 6, passim. Full references are given in the thesis, and only essential references are given here.

In January 1779, Admiral Samuel Barrington's Leeward Islands squadron, fresh from the conquest of the French island of St. Lucia, had been joined by Admiral Sir John Byron's fleet from North America, giving the British superiority over the French naval forces in the Lesser Antilles. Yet, by mid-July, the French fleet, under the comte d'Estaing, was superior to that commanded by Byron, had defeated him in battle and, in conjunction with French land forces, had captured St. Vincent and Grenada, the latter island being considered by the British as their most valuable West Indian colony after Jamaica. How had this dramatic reversal of fortunes come about? And what were the consequences of the loss of Grenada, the most serious blow to Britain since the American rebellion had been transformed into a global war?

When, in mid-1778, France joined the Americans in their war against Britain, the London government chose to strike at the new enemy in the Caribbean. A force of troops under General James Grant was sent from North America and, with the assistance of Admiral Barrington's squadron, captured the island of St. Lucia, near the major French base of Martinique, in December 1778. This operation was almost defeated by the arrival of a superior French fleet under the comte d'Estaing which had been in North America attempting to assist the Americans. However, d'Estaing's fleet was being pursued by a British squadron under Admiral Byron which arrived at St. Lucia early in January 1779 and restored naval superiority to the British.

It soon became clear that Admiral Byron could not decide how to exploit this British superiority. He made no attempt to recapture Dominica, the British island taken by the French in September 1778. Instead, he kept all his forces at St. Lucia, supposedly blockading the French fleet at Martinique. In fact, he seems to have had little idea how to blockade the island effectively. There was no close blockade of d'Estaing's fleet in Fort Royal Bay, Martinique, merely a few watching cruisers, and St. Pierre, the northern port of the island, did not receive even that inadequate attention. The mass of Byron's fleet remained inert in Gros Islet Bay.

The result of the ineffective blockade of Martinique was that naval reinforcements were able to reach the island from France and steadily undermine British naval superiority. By the end of April 1779, d'Estaing had seventeen ships of the line and two 50-gun ships with which to oppose Byron's fleet. The British had twenty-two ships of the line and three 50-gun ships, but more French reinforcements set off across the Atlantic in May. This force of four ships of the line and one 50-gun ship, under the command of La Motte-Picquet, made slow progress and did not reach Martinique until 27 June. However, its arrival was to have a decisive influence on a situation already much changed since the days of undisputed British naval superiority back in January.

Byron cannot take all the blame for failing to intercept the French reinforcements, for the easiest way to stop them would have been to blockade the naval bases in France from which they were dispatched. But the British navy in home waters was unable to do that. One responsibility which rested solely on Byron's shoulders was the security of the British islands in the Lesser Antilles, and some of their governors were highly critical of his conduct. Although Byron's blockade kept d'Estaing's fleet at Martinique, it failed to stop enemy frigates and privateers from sallying forth to harass the British islands and their trade. Lord Macartney, the governor of Grenada, was particularly angry at the lack of naval protection for his island which, he wrote, "is in point of consequence the second of our West India islands, being in produce next to Jamaica."[2] Governor Burt of Antigua was equally dissatisfied, and for him the final straw came in late April when a small French squadron, under de Grasse, slipped away from Martinique, cruised unopposed near Antigua, and seemed to threaten an attack on the island.

Burt's cries for help finally provoked Byron into taking action. After General Grant assured him that the army could hold St. Lucia during his absence, the admiral sailed northward with the fleet on 30 April and was off Nevis on 3 May, only to discover that de Grasse's squadron had already returned to Martinique without attacking any British island. If de Grasse's cruise to leeward was a feint to draw Byron away from St. Lucia, it worked brilliantly. However, when a French squadron of eight ships of the line appeared off St. Lucia on 5 May, it found Grant ready to defend the island. The French decided against making a landing and returned to Martinique. Byron's fleet returned to St. Lucia on 10 May, and the crisis was over.

It might be thought that after this experience Byron would be wary of removing his fleet from St. Lucia while the main French fleet stayed at Martinique. However, less than a month later, Byron took his fleet to leeward once again, this time sailing to St. Kitts. On this occasion the French were more successful in exploiting their opportunity and captured both St. Vincent and Grenada. Byron's excuse for not sending aid to Burt and Macartney earlier in the year had been that his fleet must remain concentrated at St. Lucia to bottle up d'Estaing's ships at Martinique. Only when a definite threat seemed to be posed to Antigua by de Grasse in late April did Byron reluctantly leave his post and take the fleet to leeward. No such threat existed at the start of June, so why did Byron remove his fleet a second time?

Previous accounts of these events have always accepted the explanation that Byron sailed to leeward once more because he wished to cover the departure from St. Kitts of the first homeward-bound trade convoy of the year. At one level, this seems a reasonable explanation. The security of the trade was a vital, even a paramount, consideration for all British admirals, and when General Grant asked Byron if he might send some troop transports with the convoy, he was told this would delay its sailing; "a further delay might be attended with very bad consequences to public credit and occasion great complaints from the merchants."[3] Lord Macartney at Grenada, in no doubt about the importance of the June convoy, supposed that when all the ships were collected at St. Kitts:

> The whole merchant fleet for Great Britain and Ireland will then consist of about two hundred sail, not less in value than two millions sterling, to which if we add 4,000 seamen, the number I calculate on board to navigate them, the safe arrival of this convoy will be an event of immense importance as a political and a commercial object.[4]

However important the convoy might be, can one really accept the view that the sailing of two hundred merchant ships demanded the presence of more than twenty ships of the line before it could be accomplished safely?

It is clear from the entries in Byron's journal, made during April and May, that the admiral had already collected an adequate escort for the June convoy. The convoy itself was to be escorted all the way to the British Isles by a 64-gun ship of the line, a 50-gun ship, a 26-gun supply ship, and a 14-gun sloop, while a number of frigates and sloops had been ordered to see it clear of the Caribbean islands and then return. Such an escort as this could deal with any danger up to and including an attack by some of d'Estaing's frigates. Only if the main French fleet from Martinique, or a large detachment from it, made an attack would the escort be overwhelmed, and this danger could best be prevented by Byron's fleet remaining at St. Lucia to watch Fort Royal, and not by its going to St. Kitts.

Thus, it seems unlikely that Byron went to leeward merely to protect the convoy. His decision to leave d'Estaing unopposed was later much criticized, and Sir Charles Middleton, comptroller of the navy, outlined what the admiral should have done when he wrote:

> It should be recommended to the commanding officer at the Leeward Islands never to quit the neighbourhood of a French squadron of force while they continue at Martinique, but to leave the protection of the homeward bound trade to its own convoy [that is, escorts] and a proper escort of frigates till clear of the islands. By pursuing this conduct he will secure the islands, as well as the trade, but if he acts otherwise, he will protect one at the expense of the other.[5]

This is not only what Byron should have done, but also it is clear from his journal that it is what he intended to do up until late May. Then he decided to take his whole fleet to leeward. If, as had been argued, the fleet was not needed to safeguard the convoy, then why did Byron decide on this course of action?

A clue to one possible reason for Byron's decision is provided in a letter sent to Lord North, George III's chief minister, by a correspondent in Bristol toward the end of July. The letter records the safe arrival of the Bristol ships that sailed from St. Kitts with the June convoy. It goes on to note:

> Admiral Byron with his whole fleet were at St. Kitts, and sailed with them [the convoy] having given out that he intended to see them as far as the island of Bermudas; d'Estaingn [sic] gave out that as soon as they were sail'd, he would attack the island of Barbadoes; Admiral Byron with his fleet left them the second day after they sail'd, and from the course they [Byron's fleet] steered, they imagined his sailing with them was only a feint to draw the French fleet out.[6]

The idea that Byron was attempting a daring feint to draw out d'Estaing and at last bring him to battle is a possibility, but if that was Byron's intention, he was being extremely rash. Returning from leeward, the British fleet would face contrary winds and currents for much of the way. Such winds and currents also might delay the French fleet if it sought to execute a similar movement from leeward by sailing from Martinique to Barbados, but it was most unlikely that the French would be so long delayed that the British fleet returning from St. Kitts could intercept them. Also, such an interception would only be possible if Byron had excellent intelligence of the location of the French fleet, but since he neglected to leave any cruisers to watch d'Estaing, such enlightenment was denied him. If Byron's second movement to leeward was intended as a feint, it was an extremely ill-considered maneuver. Its consequences were to be disastrous for the British.[7]

After leaving St. Lucia on 26 May, Byron took his fleet to windward of Martinique in the hope of intercepting the expected French reinforcements under La Motte-Picquet, but on 5 June the British squadron left its cruising station and headed to leeward. The fleet anchored in Basseterre Roads, St. Kitts, on 10 June and found the homeward-bound trade already assembled. The day before, d'Estaing, noting Byron's absence and hoping he had gone to leeward, ordered a small French force to attack St. Vincent. The convoy sailed from St. Kitts on 16 June, and Byron accompanied it with the fleet. On that same day, as the British fleet and convoy headed into the Anegada Passage, the French landed on St. Vincent. The stalemate in the Leeward Islands was over, and the British were now to pay dearly for wasting their six months of naval supremacy.

St. Vincent was captured with little difficulty, and a further boost to French morale came a short time later with the arrival of La Motte-Picquet's reinforcements. Emboldened by one success and the continued absence of Byron's fleet, and with his forces strengthened by the reinforcements, d'Estaing now set out to attack Barbados. His fleet of twenty-one ships of the line, four 50-gun ships, and twelve frigates carrying 6,500 troops left Martinique on 30 June. Contrary winds prevented the French from approaching Barbados, so d'Estaing moved against Grenada instead. Despite a spirited resistance by a small force led by Lord Macartney, the island was in French hands by 4 July.

While the French had been going from success to success, Byron had been laboring to bring his fleet back from leeward. He had left the trade convoy on 17 June and headed southward down the windward side of the island chain, apparently heading for Barbados. However, contrary winds and currents made progress slow, so Byron took his ships to St. Lucia on 1 July. There he was told of the loss of St. Vincent, so he returned to sea with twenty-one ships of the line, a frigate, and a convoy of transports carrying troops commanded by General Grant. Byron's intention was to recapture St. Vincent, but at sea he learned of the attack on Grenada and took his forces to that island instead.

From what little intelligence he could gather, Byron had gained the impression that a French fleet of between fifteen and twenty ships of the line had attacked Grenada, so he hoped to enjoy a superiority of forces in any encounter with the enemy. On the morning of 6 July, the British fleet was heading southward in line of battle off the west coast of Grenada and nearing the island's capital, St. George's. Byron saw d'Estaing's fleet emerging from St. George's Bay, its numbers as yet uncertain, and it appeared to be in some confusion. Both in the hope of taking advantage of this confusion and of preventing d'Estaing from avoiding battle (as he had done so often before by a timely withdrawal), Byron abandoned the line of battle and ordered a general chase in the southeast quarter.

Once the signal for general chase had been made, "the British squadron bore down upon [the French] with all the sail they could crowd and were apprehensive, I believe, of [the French] making their escape."[8] To General Grant and his officers, it was a stirring sight, and "we lookers on not knowing the strength of the enemy were sanguine in our hopes of taking the [French] ships."[9] As the first British vessels approached them, the French ships began to form a rough line of battle, heading northwestward. It was soon clear that d'Estaing's fleet was much larger than Byron had expected. This advantage was further increased by the fact that, due to the general chase, the British ships came up to the French line one or two at a time and so each received the concentrated fire of a number of French ships.

The leading British ships, heading southeastward, came up with the rear of the French line and then began to work their way northwestward up that line toward the van. This promised to be a slow and damaging process, so Byron ordered all those ships still chasing toward the southeast to wear and chase to the northwest, with the intention of getting them into line against the French as soon as possible. This order has been overlooked by previous historians, and this left them with the problem of explaining how the *Monmouth*, which was in the rear of the formation chasing to the southeast, suddenly appeared at the head of the British line sailing toward the northwest. Mahan sought to explain this oddity by crediting Captain Fanshawe of the *Monmouth* with having, on his own initiative, cut across in a movement similar to that so daringly undertaken later by Nelson at the battle of Cape St. Vincent in 1797. Now it is clear that Fanshawe was simply obeying orders.[10]

Three British ships—the *Grafton*, the *Cornwall*, and the *Lion*—had been too badly damaged to follow the British fleet as it headed northwestward in line of battle, and they were left behind. This gave the French a considerable numerical superiority, but they were content to keep their distance from the British line and engage in a desultory exchange of fire which eventually ceased. Both lines were heading toward the northwest. Since the French line was longer than that of the British, Byron feared that d'Estaing might bring the French round until they stood between him and Grant's troop transports. Given the French superiority in frigates, this was a real danger, for the frigates could snap up the convoy while d'Estaing kept Byron at bay. Fortunately, the French did not attempt such a maneuver.

In the middle of the afternoon, the French fleet tacked, and Byron did the same. Both fleets were now heading southeastward back toward St. George's Bay and the three crippled British ships. The French steered straight toward the vessels, and it seemed certain that they would be captured unless Byron was willing to renew the battle in order to save them. Conscious that his now inferior fleet contained many ships almost as badly damaged as the cripples, Byron refrained from action. Nevertheless, although fired on by the French, the *Grafton* and the *Cornwall* escaped northward. Captain Cornwallis's *Lion*, far to leeward and a target for all the French ships, made off westward.

At nightfall Byron tacked his fleet and led them away northwestward. D'Estaing did not pursue the beaten British and was content to return to Grenada. His unenterprising conduct of the battle has been criticized by many later historians, but his conduct merely reflected the outlook of contemporary French naval officers. As one of them observed later in the century, "the French navy has always preferred the glory of assuring or preserving a conquest to that, more brilliant perhaps, but actually less real, of taking a few ships."[11] D'Estaing had preserved his conquest, Grenada, but if he had destroyed Byron's fleet, all British West Indian islands might have been at his mercy.

News of the Grenada disaster "produced a considerable sensation in Barbados," and at the eleventh hour, the planters made desperate attempts to put their defenses in order. While the British fleet and troop convoy fled to St. Kitts, the French fleet slowly followed them, calling at Guadeloupe on the way. On 22 July, d'Estaing led his fleet into Basseterre Roads, St. Kitts, apparently intent upon delivering the final blow to the British squadron anchored there. However, when almost within gunshot, the French fleet tacked and withdrew. Instead of further battle, d'Estaing led his fleet to leeward, heading for St. Domingue from where he could attack the British in either Jamaica or North America.

When the topsails of d'Estaing's fleet dipped below the western horizon, the naval superiority of the Lesser Antilles which the French had won at Grenada disappeared. D'Estaing had stripped the French islands of almost all their naval forces and a large number of troops before he left the area, and the marquis de Bouillé, governor of Martinique, was alarmed that not only would the British be able to recapture the islands they had so recently lost, but they also might then attack Martinique and Guadeloupe. However, the French governor underestimated the impact of the Grenada disaster on the British. Admirals Byron and Barrington were in no mood for offensive operations. Once d'Estaing had quit the Lesser Antilles, they both left the British fleet and returned home, anxious to defend their conduct and explain how Grenada was lost.

When news of the Grenada disaster reached Britain, public dismay was considerable. Their second most important possession in the West Indies had been lost, and the navy had suffered its worst defeat at the hands of the French since the battle of Beachy Head in 1690, or at least since Byng's battle off Minorca in 1756. Public outrage was all the greater because the Caribbean was the area in which Britain was seen to have a clear superiority over the French, the area "where we thought ourselves strongest." Unlike the public, the government knew that British superiority in the Lesser Antilles had been slowly ebbing away since the start of 1779, and the loss of Grenada forced ministers to consider urgent measures to halt further collapse in the West Indies, lest Jamaica itself be lost. Middleton thought that, to reestablish British naval supremacy, every ship of the line that could be spared from home waters should be sent out to the Caribbean, for "this war can never end without success, but in that country."[12] Lord George Germain, secretary of state for the colonies, had thoughts similar to Middleton's. The war in North America was to be run down and invasion was to be risked at home so that all efforts could be concentrated in the Caribbean, for Germain believed "that the West Indies will become the principal theatre of the war."[13]

At the beginning of 1779 the British had possessed naval superiority in the Lesser Antilles, but during the first six months of that year this superiority was whittled away by the arrival of reinforcements from France. That these reinforcements got through to Martinique unopposed was due both to the inactivity of Admiral Byron and the inability of the government in London to arrange a close blockade of naval bases in France. By June the French had superior forces and, thanks to rash decisions by Byron, had the opportunity to capture St. Vincent and Grenada and inflict a humiliating defeat on the Royal Navy.

The immediate consequences of the Grenada disaster might have been worse than they were but for the shortsighted strategic outlook of the French commander, d'Estaing. If he had completed the destruction of Byron's fleet, all the remaining British islands in the Caribbean, including Jamaica, might have fallen to him. Instead, however, he was content to have taken St. Vincent and Grenada, leaving the battered British fleet to fight again another day.

In the wider strategic context, the circumstances of the loss of Grenada clearly demonstrated to the British that they could no longer sustain the naval superiority which had been such a feature of wars earlier in the eighteenth century. Opposed by the naval strength of the Americans and the French, joined during 1779 by the Spanish, the Royal Navy was severely stretched to meet its worldwide commitments. The conquest of St. Lucia in December 1778 had given hope that it would be as easy to snap up French Caribbean islands in this war as it had been during the Seven Years' War, but the Grenada disaster exposed the true situation. Just to defend the colonies in the West Indies would demand a concentration of British naval power at the expense of most other theaters of the war. This was what the London government, sobered by the loss of Grenada, hoped to do in 1780, only to be distracted by renewed hopes of victory in North America. These hopes were finally dashed at Yorktown in 1781, and the concentration on the West Indies proposed in late 1779 soon became a reality. In 1782, Admiral George Rodney's victory at the battle of the Saints expunged the stain of the Grenada defeat and allowed Britain to salvage some glory from a lost war.

NOTES

1. G. Cornwallis-West, *The Life and Letters of Admiral Cornwallis* (London, 1927), 90–91.
2. London, Public Record Office (hereafter PRO), Lord Macartney to Lord George Germain, 2 April 1777, Colonial Office (hereafter CO) 101/20.
3. PRO, Admiral Byron to General Grant, 3 June 1779, (Admiralty) ADM 1/312.
4. PRO, Macartney to Germain, 6 June 1779, CO 101/23.
5. Middleton's memorandum (n.d.; probably September 1779) in *Private Papers of John, Earl of Sandwich, 1771-82*, vol. 3, ed. G. R. Barnes and J. H. Owens (London, 1933), 172–77.
6. [?] to Lord North, 30 July 1779, in *The Correspondence of George III, 1760–1783*, vol. 4, ed. J. W. Fortescue (London, 1927–28), 402–3.
7. This paragraph has been rewritten to take account of criticism from Professor Daniel Baugh of Cornell University, to whom gratitude is extended.
8. PRO, Grant to Germain, 8 July 1779, CO 318/5.
9. Banffshire, Scotland, Ballindalloch Castle, Macpherson-Grant Papers, Grant to General Clinton, 28 July 1779.
10. A. T. Mahan, *Major Operations of the Navies in the War of American Independence* (London, 1913), 109. For the order to chase northwest, see Oxford, Bodleian Library, Admiral Byron's Journal, 1778–79, MS. ADD.c.70.
11. Ramatuelle, quoted in A. T. Mahan, *The Influence of Sea Power upon History, 1660–1783* (Boston, 1890), 371–72.
12. Middleton's memorandum, *Sandwich Papers* 3:172–77.
13. PRO, Germain to General Vaughan, 8 February 1780, CO 318/6.

Naval Medicine in an Emerging Crisis, 1845-63

ALLEN RICHMAN

Physicians on board U.S. warships were able to deal with medical problems in the Mexican War rather effectively, due to the limited nature of the war. When the Civil War broke out, however, they were soon overwhelmed by the vast number of wounded and diseased. In this essay, Dr. Richman examines these difficulties and emphasizes how the campaigns on the Virginia Peninsula and in the Mississippi Valley overpowered the physicians' resources.

****

> Of all classes of our fellow-citizens there is perhaps no one which requires more sympathy, more individual attention from the government, than the class of sailors. They live hard, and die early; they receive less for their labor, and are more heavily taxed, than any other men in society.[1]

The words are those of William Ruschenberger, a senior surgeon in the U.S. Navy, writing to a friend during the Mexican War. It was the first major American conflict fought primarily beyond its own frontiers. Within a few months the navy would convoy a force of nearly 10,000 fighting men to the central Gulf coast of Mexico. Winfield Scott, the army's brilliant commander, was preparing to strike at Vera Cruz. If successful there, he intended to push on to Mexico City itself and bring this already spectacular war to a triumphant conclusion.

At the height of the conflict, the navy had more than 200 vessels of all types operating in the Gulf of Mexico. Some were civilian craft pressed into service; others were the spoils of war, seized when American naval units raided ports like Tampico and Alvarado. The most useful prizes were two small paddle-wheel steamers and several shallow-draft schooners being built in the United States for the Mexican government.[2] Since the enemy had no naval force capable of serious resistance, the greatest hazards faced by the navy were those involving routine blockade duty far from home in a semitropical climate. Although almost one hundred years had passed since Dr. James Lind had published *A Treatise of the Scurvy,* medical science had not fully impressed on the navy the vital importance of supplying the men with an adequate amount of citrus fruit or other foods which contain vitamin C.[3] The scurvy rate rose out of control on two of the larger vessels which had just returned from extended sea duty in South America; they could not be spared to return to Pensacola, Florida, for fresh supplies.

Unsafe drinking water proved even more damaging than scurvy to the health of the blockading squadron. Fresh fruits and vegetables could alleviate the one problem, but there was virtually no way to deal with the other. Surgeons' letters dating back many years indicate that the standard procedure for drinking water was to draw fresh water from the mouth of coastal rivers—a practice for which there was no alternative for vessels trying to maintain their wartime stations. Commodore David Connor ordered a flying hospital established at Salmadina Island near Vera Cruz in December 1846. Fleet Surgeon Waters Smith, who opposed the idea, urged that seriously ill men be transferred to Pensacola. He did not believe that a swampy coastal island was a proper place to treat men debilitated by dysentery and other diseases.[4]

It was tropical fevers, however, rather than scurvy or water-borne infection, which so harmed navy personnel. Any vessel which touched the coast or sent expeditions up river was soon threatened by the rapid spread of "remittent" or "intermittent fever," or malaria. Even more terrifying was the *vomito negro*, or "black vomit," as yellow fever was called in the tropics. It was the fear of these dreaded diseases which caused Scott to land his men so early in the spring near Vera Cruz. It also convinced him to leave the city as soon as he had secured it[5] and to fight his way up the Central Mexican Plateau without an adequate supply line behind him.

However, if the army escaped most of the problems of coastal fever, the navy did not. The ports of Tampico in the north to Alvarado in the south were quickly neutralized, but the fever lists rose alarmingly. Even before the seizure of Vera Cruz, four assistant surgeons had been sent home due to broken health. This left some of the blockading vessels without medical officers.[6] As early as the autumn of 1846, the Home Squadron was facing a health crisis. With almost 1,800 men on duty, 126 were sent by steamer back to Pensacola and another 82 were under treatment with fevers of one sort or another. There were an additional 163 cases of scurvy to worry about, most of the latter aboard the frigate *Raritan*.[7] The crew was so decimated by disease that only a return to Pensacola enabled those still alive to receive proper treatment.

By midsummer 1847 the hospital at Pensacola was filled to overflowing, its 175 beds nowhere near enough.[8] Surgeons used phrases like "malignant" and "violent intertropical fever" to describe the terrible ordeal, and yet they were surprisingly successful in arresting the spread of most of the afflictions other than yellow fever. Physicians had begun experimenting with large doses of quinine for the treatment of malaria, and the reports found their way into medical journals as well as military correspondence. Dr. Austin Flint of Buffalo, New York, raised the traditional three-to-five-grain doses to as high as forty grains every hour and discovered that he could break almost any case of malaria.[9] Such efforts had inspired the American military to conduct their own investigations at Tampa Bay, Florida, between 1839 and 1841. Assistant Surgeon John B. Porter treated over 1,800 cases of "climatic disease" in a two-year period. Traditional alternatives like bleeding and purging the patients proved to be useless, but when a controlled experiment was attempted with large doses of quinine, the results were astonishing.[10] While some patients were given the traditional three-to-five-grain doses, the great majority

Courtesy of National Archives

received quantities up to twenty-five grains several times per day, and most fevers were quickly broken. Equally important, the chance of future attacks was greatly reduced. This knowledge, gained on the eve of the Mexican War, reduced fatalities dramatically.

Perhaps two hundred sailors died from all causes during the hostilities with Mexico. Estimates are that no more than twenty died from enemy action. Of the remaining fatalities, more than thirty drowned when the brig *Somers* went down in a Gulf storm. Several dozen died of problems related to scurvy. The remaining deaths can be divided between water-borne infectious diseases and, more commonly, tropical fevers. A dozen surgeons, supported by no more than fifty assistant and passed assistant surgeons, had done a surprisingly good job at reducing fatalities within the limits of their equipment, facilities, and knowledge. The brevity of a one-sided war helped them manage with inadequate resources.

The years that followed produced dramatic changes. Most important was the widespread application of steam power to naval vessels, so that by 1861 the sailing navy was largely a part of the past. Steam gave the navy the capability to take out casualties and bring in medical supplies quickly. The universal application of ether and chloroform made surgery painless if adequate supplies were on hand. Furthermore, storage of water in tin and other noncorroding containers preserved it "sweet," as the sailors said, for many weeks. Reliable delivery of fresh fruit, fruit juices, and vegetables virtually caused the disappearance of scurvy. The widespread use of disinfectants like chloride of lime prevented bilge water from becoming a breeding ground for infectious disease. And general improvements in ship cleanliness gave doctors hope that most of the health problems of the past were controllable, if not solvable. This was the prevailing attitude in the spring of 1861 as the United States approached the precipice of civil war. The military was totally unprepared for the scope or the magnitude of the impending crisis. Therefore, when the Union broke apart, the U.S. Navy found itself with a job of incredible complexity and enormous hidden dangers.

Blockade duty along some 2,000 miles of coastline led to all the traditional problems of weather, supplies, and distance, but these were mitigated by rapid communication and transportation. However, if the navy's casualties were nowhere as high as the army's, naval personnel and appropriations were much lower, and resources were stretched beyond imagined limits. The problems which appeared threatened to overwhelm the small professional cadre of officers and physicians. Moreover, multiple responsibilities were not always mutually supportive. For example, closing the rebel harbors and eliminating coastal strong points required a total commitment, but this was impossible because of critical secondary responsibilities—aggressive combat on the western rivers, especially the Mississippi. General Ulysses S. Grant's efforts at Forts Henry and Donelson would have been unimaginable without Andrew Foote's gunboats. The same is true of Vicksburg; New Orleans, the Queen City of the South, fell by a naval operation. But the fever and dysentery rate on the rivers crippled a significant portion of the navy's freshwater western force. Serious as these problems were, however, they were dwarfed by the news coming from Hampton Roads, Virginia, and the estuary of the James River.

Union General George B. McClellan saw his theater of the war as one where the prize would be achieved by seizing the Confederate capital of Richmond. If the door had been slammed shut at Manassas Junction, then a seaborne invasion of the lower peninsula was a clever alternative, a fact which even Robert E. Lee admitted. As Union troops came ashore near Fortress Monroe, where the York and James rivers come together, the navy saw its responsibilities primarily in terms of support, not combat. It also did not consider the implications of a long campaign. It soon would have to reevaluate its role.

The 50-gun steam frigate *Merrimack* had been burned at Norfolk by retreating Union naval personnel on 20 April 1861. On 8 March of the following year, it reappeared in Hampton Roads as a refloated ironclad—the terrifyingly powerful gunboat *Virginia*. A strong blockading force of Union warships controlled the northern shore of the James River. The great 50-gun frigate *Congress* was supported by the 24-gun sloop *Cumberland*. Several miles to the east rode the steam-powered 50-gun *Minnesota*, the equally powerful *Roanoke*, and the 12-gun *St. Lawrence*.

In addition to being hit by a number of shells, the *Cumberland* was rammed so hard that the iron prow of the *Virginia* twisted off. The *Congress* was devastated by shells, many fired from no more than one hundred yards away.[11] On both vessels the lower decks were covered with the dead and wounded. When the *Cumberland* went down in fifty-four feet of water, it took many of its wounded with it. Others drowned, being too weak to reach shore. Perhaps 150 of the *Cumberland*'s 376 men were never accounted for. The *Congress* with 434 men did not sink until evening, but it went down in a mass of flames, having lost almost as many men. Both the *Minnesota* and the *Roanoke* went aground while moving over to help their stricken and dying comrades. The *Roanoke*'s propeller shaft was giving so much trouble that steam tugs attempted to tow the ship into battle. Although shallow waters prevented the *Virginia* from destroying them, it did fire at the helpless vessels for a while. Several shells hit the *Minnesota* and did considerable damage.

By nightfall there was chaos at Hampton Roads. Surgeon Edward Shippen of the *Congress* was himself a casualty, with a serious concussion. Dr. Charles Martin told of harrowing events on board the *Cumberland*. More than thirty of the men were "so mangled and burned by explosion of shell, that but a very small percent would have survived the necessary operations." As the wounded were laid out in the sick bay, a shell burst over the skylight and killed four of the men below. When the ship sank, sailors threw mess chests and wooden casks into the river for the wounded to hold on to in the swirling waters.[12] That night physicians worked among men battered in hours of combat, unable to strike back at the enemy. Many had been injured by metal fragments from exploding shells or by the force of objects hurled by the explosions. Arms, legs, and bodies were torn by wooden splinters. Everywhere, there were men with fractures of limbs. (If it were a compound fracture, the arm or leg was amputated.) Men were covered with lacerations, contusions, and abrasions. Some, relatively uninjured by the day's combat, were exhausted from hours in the water.[13]

The log of the *Monitor* records that at 10:00 P.M. on 8 March 1862, it came to anchor alongside the grounded *Minnesota*.[14] Within the next half day it would change the history of naval warfare. But during a pause in the famous fight between the ironclads—due to the wounding of the *Monitor's* commander, Lieutenant John Worden—the *Virginia* again began to hammer the *Minnesota*. Six men were killed and twenty wounded. One shot fired at the *Minnesota* hit the little tugboat *Dragon*, wounding three men and sending it to the bottom. Several sailors had to be treated for ghastly wounds, since they had inhaled live steam and were burned internally as well as externally. Once the balanced contest between the iron ships resumed, physicians had time to begin the orderly treatment of the wounded. Many were dispersed to shore hospitals, where possible, but others remained on board the surviving ships until they too could be moved. The vast majority were transferred to the naval hospital at New York, a process not completed until the latter part of April. By that time General McClellan was beginning to land large numbers of men for his ill-fated Peninsula campaign.

Naval physicians were almost overwhelmed by their problems. Burns, open wounds, and imperfect amputations led to rampant infection in the hospital wards and sick bays of the warships. The blockade of Hampton Roads was now more critical than ever, especially as Union ships watched for another sally of the *Virginia*. Most of the vessels took their drinking water from the James River, a practice which appalled Fleet Surgeon William Wood. He reminded the medical bureau that it was an open sewer for the army of 100,000 encamped along its banks, as well as for countless vessels anchored there.[15] Dysentery, typhoid fever, and other intestinal disorders were so common that doctors were running short of ipecac and opium, the drugs of choice in the treatment of such diseases. Malaria made its usual appearance ashore and afloat all along the James, and there never seemed to be enough quinine. Reports from flotillas on the upper and lower Mississippi indicate that the Bureau of Medicine and Surgery could not ship the drug fast enough to satisfy the frantic doctors in the combat zones.

While the casualty lists expanded beyond any rates the military was prepared for, physicians began employing new techniques which improved conditions immeasurably for the injured and diseased. One of their most startling successes came from the very technology which was changing the nature of combat. Steam-powered ironclads might revolutionize warfare, but steam engines also could banish dysentery and other water-borne infectious diseases patrolling Union warships. The chief engineer of the *Minnesota* convinced Fleet Surgeon Wood that any of the larger steam vessels could condense a thousand gallons of pure water per day via a drip pipe from the boiler safety valves.[16] A few days later an excited bureau chief not only congratulated Wood but also ordered him to prohibit the use of James River water by any vessels of the flotilla.[17] Navy Secretary Gideon Welles was informed of the decision that same day and added one more proviso to it. Steam condensers in recently captured Norfolk were to be put to use distilling additional quantities of fresh water which then would be carried to the remaining vessels on station in the estuary.[18]

As time passed, doctors were so busy disinfecting ships and hospitals ashore that some of the senior engineers became alarmed by their overzealousness. The result was a general order to reduce the problems incurred. Chloride of lime was no longer to be used as a disinfectant in the bilges of vessels. "It destroys the copper and iron pipes with which it comes in contact, about the engines, boilers and their attachments."[19] This penchant for dumping chemicals into the holds of ships was characteristic of an era when amateur chemists in the medical branch tried countless combinations and occasionally stumbled upon surprising successes. Hospital floors were painted and mopped with a variety of compounds, and some of the less lethal were applied to wounds and injuries.

Although cold water irrigation remained a standard treatment for cleansing wounds, the literature of the era is full of some fairly sophisticated experiments. Military surgeons were quite successful with diluted nitric acid and even more successful with diluted bromine. Both were applied to particularly nasty wounds and especially to amputations which, in overcrowded hospitals, often led to gangrene. The results were nothing less than astonishing and certainly more successful than buttermilk, which one surgeon continued to swear by. Like iodine and chlorine, bromine is a toxic halogen which fumes with a reddish brown vapor. It disinfected with such reliability that in some hospital wards gangrene was almost banished.[20] Once the patient was removed from the battlefield area, doctors had an opportunity to work leisurely and in a cleaner environment to treat him effectively.

It should be noted that this led to the designation of the navy's first hospital ships. Within six months of the First Battle of Bull Run, Commodore David Farragut asked for such a vessel. The first ship proposed was the frigate *Congress*, but the *Merrimack* ended that possibility. What the navy got instead was the 400-ton storeship *Ben Morgan*, on duty off the coast of North Carolina. Fleet Surgeon Wood accepted it for the duration of the fight for the Virginia Peninsula, but even as a temporary floating hospital it was unacceptable. The *Ben Morgan* was a coal ship which served the North Atlantic Squadron. As soon as the army secured the old Norfolk Naval Hospital from the Confederates, the collier was returned to its former duties.[21]

On western waters the navy found a more satisfying situation when it obtained the 187-ton side-wheel riverboat *Red Rover*. The gift of the privately financed Western Sanitary Commission, it was properly outfitted. For the duration of the war it provided invaluable medical service for the western rivers flotilla.

The use of such vessels is one of the clearest reminders of the scope of the conflict and the magnitude of the dangers for the fighting navy. Their trials were just beginning, as Americans learned the price for total war within their own borders.

NOTES

1. In a letter to Congressman Henry J. Seaman, 4 January 1847, quoted in House of Representatives Doc. No. 68, 5-6, 29th Cong., 2d sess. Ruschenberger was an articulate, reform-minded physician, who was at the time running the New York Naval Hospital.

2. K. Jack Bauer, *Surfboats and Horse Marines: U.S. Naval Operations in the Mexican War, 1846-48* (Annapolis, 1969), 15-22 passim.

3. Christopher Lloyd, ed., *The Health of Seamen: Selections from the Works of Dr. James Lind, Sir Gilbert Blane and Dr. Thomas Trotter* (London, 1965).

4. Fleet Surgeon Waters Smith to Thomas Harris, chief of the Bureau of Medicine and Surgery, 30 January 1847, No. 88, National Archives and Records Service, *Naval Records Collection of the Office of Naval Records and Library* (hereafter *NRC*), Group 52. Record Group 52 is officially entitled "Surgeons and Assistant Surgeons: Bureau of Medicine and Surgery: Letters Received."

5. The city fell on 29 March 1847 after a siege of less than three weeks. By 8 April advanced units under General Twiggs were already on the move west toward Mexico City, 260 miles away.

6. Smith to Harris, chief of the Bureau, 31 August 1846, No. 88, *NRC*, Group 52, "Letters Received."

7. Smith to Harris, 10 October 1846, No. 39, ibid.

8. Isaac Hulse to Harris, 14 August 1847, No. 188, ibid.

9. "On the Treatment of Intermitting Fever," *American Journal of the Medical Sciences* (hereafter *AJMS*) 4, New Series, 2 (October 1841): 278.

10. "Analysis of an Official Report to the Surgeon-General, U.S. Army, on the Use of Large Doses of Sulphate of Quinine in Diseases of the South, with Notices of Climate and Diseases of Florida, &c., &c.," *AJMS* 19, New Series, 10 (July 1845): 296-310.

11. One of the best contemporary accounts is found in William J. Tenny, *The Military and Naval History of the Rebellion in the United States with Biographical Sketches of Deceased Officers* (New York, 1865), 223-26.

12. Martin to William Whelen, chief of the Bureau, 21 March 1862, No. 580, *NRC*, Group 52, "Letters Received."

13. Because several vessels were lost with all records and logbooks, the story of medical casualties must be pieced together from such sources as *NRC*, Group 52, Entry 36, "Casualties in the U.S. Navy, April 1861-July, 1865," 4 vols., 1:24-26. In the same record group see "Medical Journal: U.S.S. *Ben Morgan*, Oct. 24, 1861 to July 25, 1862," 66-72. Fleet Surgeon William Maxwell Wood, on board the USS *Minnesota*, was able to summarize much information in his letters of 12 and 14 March 1862 to Flag Officer Louis M. Goldsborough, commanding the North Atlantic Blockading Squadron, *NRC*, Group 45, Subject File MK. Record Group 45 is made up of seventeen files containing unorganized materials pertaining to all aspects of naval service in the nineteenth century. Finally, see Wood to William Whelen, chief of the Bureau, 19 March 1862, No. 561, *NRC*, Group 52, "Letters Received."

14. Log of the USS *Monitor*, *NRC*, Group 45, Appendix D (List of Logs and Journals), No. 110.

15. William Whelen, chief of the Bureau, to Gideon Welles, secretary of the navy, 5 August 1862, *NRC*, Group 52, "Letters Sent" 1:125.

16. Wood to Whelen, 2 August 1862, No. 32, *NRC*, Group 52, "Letters Received."

17. Whelen to Wood, 5 August 1862, *NRC*, Group 52, "Letters Sent" 1:120-21.

18. Whelen to Welles, 5 August 1862, ibid., 125-26.

19. Rear Admiral David Porter, North Atlantic Squadron, "General Order No. 32," 4 November 1864, *NRC*, Group 45, Subject File MH. Sulphate of iron was to be used as a substitute.

20. Dr. M. Goldsmith, "Bromine in Hospital Gangrene," *AJMS* 92, New Series, 46 (October 1863): 564–67. Dr. I. Moses, "Surgical Notes of Cases of Gunshot Injuries Occurring during the Advance of the Army of the Cumberland in the Summer of 1863," *AJMS* 94, New Series, 47 (April 1864): 324–43.

21. Wood to Whelen, 13 June 1862, No. 558, *NRC*, Group 52, "Letters Received," Also see Whelen to Wood, 17 June 1862, *NRC*, Group 52, "Letters Sent" 1:493–94.

THE *MONITOR* PROJECT

In 1975 the site of the shipwrecked USS *Monitor,* off Cape Hatteras, North Carolina, was designated a national marine sanctuary. The USS *Monitor* Project, under the auspices of the National Oceanic and Atmospheric Administration, is to develop a master plan for that sanctuary. In these essays, Edward Miller, William Still, Ernest Peterkin, and Richard Gould discuss the major questions and problems in creating a master plan for the *Monitor* and thus contribute to developing a national cultural policy for historic shipwrecks.

The USS *Monitor* as a National Marine Sanctuary

EDWARD M. MILLER

The Civil War ironclad, USS *Monitor*, was discovered in August 1973 by a Duke University research team and designated as the first National Marine Sanctuary on 30 January 1975 by the National Oceanic and Atmospheric Administration (NOAA), under provisions of Title III of the Marine Protection, Research, and Sanctuaries Act of 1972. Managed by the Sanctuary Programs Division of NOAA, the *Monitor* is part of a growing network of eight national marine sanctuaries designed to enhance specific resource protection through a structured program of management, research, and public education.

NOAA's fundamental approach to the management of the *Monitor* sanctuary recognizes the importance of the shipwreck as an irreplaceable and nonrenewable cultural resource of national significance. Due to the ship's perceived historical importance and the high public interest in it, there is widespread consensus that the project warrants careful and deliberate planning so that maximum return and benefit can be derived for the American public. Additionally, there is consensus that the manner in which the *Monitor* is treated will establish a major precedent for other historic shipwrecks in the United States. Thus, the promise of the *Monitor* sanctuary is to have a major influence in the development of a national cultural policy for historic shipwrecks.

At the 1978 national conference on the *Monitor* held in Raleigh, North Carolina, the focus of research was set on the fundamental question of what should be done with the vessel in contrast to what we can or want to do. Thus, a significant emphasis was placed on the process of decision making in order to ensure the maximum benefit for the American people, without degrading the historical or archaeological value of the site.

The true value of the *Monitor* must somehow be determined. Is it archaeological? Is it historical? Is it symbolic? Or, more likely, is it some combination of all three? Then, once this is done, decisions must be made on how best to preserve whatever is determined to be the value of the *Monitor*. Principal goals for the sanctuary include the protection and preservation of the ironclad and all its associated historical records, documents, and archaeological collections.

Since the designation of the sanctuary, NOAA has sponsored three major expeditions to the site. In 1977 a photo survey was conducted; a piece of hull plate and the lantern, now on display in the U.S. Naval Academy Museum, were recovered. In 1979 a team of archaeologists conducted forty-nine dives in twenty-six days from a lock-out submersible, to complete a test excavation, and they recovered 106 artifacts which have been conserved and have been part of the *Monitor* displays at numerous museums around the country.

In 1983 the *Monitor*'s anchor was located and recovered and is now undergoing conservation at East Carolina University in Greenville. Two years later, a remote sensing survey and mapping effect were made which laid the groundwork for future archaeological work. But the on-site activities, perhaps the most visible, represent only a small portion of NOAA's efforts. Extensive investigations have been made into the historical records of the ship, including biographical studies of the commanding officers and a catalogue of drawings of the *Monitor*. The research program has placed equal emphasis on the archaeological record at the site, as well as existing historical records of the ship, recognizing the linkage and tremendous value the historical records will have for future investigation of the ship.

Results of the research to date have revealed the tremendous amount of material available for study, leaving the impression that the serious investigation of the *Monitor* has barely begun. The on-site research has been exploratory and has identified a serious threat of collapse to the remaining ship structure, due to its continued exposure to a highly corrosive submarine environment and to the unequal and highly stressed support provided by the displaced turret. What this means is that the decision of what should be done cannot be deferred to future generations, who most likely will have more advanced archaeological and conservation techniques available to them.

This does not imply, however, that there should be immediate archaeological excavation and recovery of material. There may be alternative ways to preserve the yet undetermined value of the *Monitor* without committing to the difficult, lengthy, and costly processes of recovery and conservation of structural material. These other options may include preservation through professionally filming the *Monitor* as a shipwreck so that everyone may see it resting on the seafloor, or preservation through documentation.

Preservation of the actual artifact, however, is considered by many to be the ultimate documentation, so this needs to be considered also. All possible options to preservation must be evaluated in order to estimate the full cost in terms of the archaeology involved, engineering required, and the conservation obligation. Then, an option must be selected that meets the following criteria: feasibility, suitability, and acceptability. Feasibility is a measure of the availability of the technical and fiscal resources required. Suitability is a measure of how well the option achieves the goals set for the sanctuary. Acceptability is a measure of the cost involved and asks the hard question, are the expected end results worth it?

This is the major task confronting researchers today. Only by measuring these factors will there be results. Anything else is merely speculation. Until the effort to do this is expended, the *Monitor* is not being treated in a scientific and responsible manner, and thus its potential as a submerged cultural resource will not be realized. Perhaps even more importantly, the promise of the *Monitor* stated in other meetings over ten years ago will not be fulfilled.

To address these questions systematically requires the development of a master plan for the *Monitor* National Marine Sanctuary. It is the responsibility of the Marine and Estuarine Management Division of NOAA to develop this plan. The National Trust for Historic Preservation recently has been asked to join in this effort for several reasons. First, as the only national, nonprofit, private membership organization, chartered by Congress to encourage public participation in preservation of sites, buildings, and objects significant in American history and culture, the National Trust will facilitate the organization of the national and international talents required to develop the master plan, to be called the "USS *Monitor* Project."

Second, the National Trust will facilitate the raising of private funds to support the objectives of the project. Whatever is decided, one thing is sure: it will be expensive, and the government today can ill afford to add to the public debt. A more appropriate solution is to require that the project stand on its own merit and, similar to the Statue of Liberty restoration, that it be supported individually and voluntarily by the American people. If the *Monitor* is of any value whatsoever, then we must decide in our time what its ultimate disposition will be. NOAA thus is soliciting the assistance of this nation's best historical expertise to help in the decision.

The downside of any archaeological excavation and recovery, besides the cost, is that they can never be repeated. They can be done only once. Decisions and preparations must be made before anyone begins to "dig." Previous projects, both here and abroad, have taught that to proceed with any recovery plans before questions concerning conservation, display, and required funding are fully answered surely will jeopardize the resource and the success of the project.

The Historical Importance of the USS *Monitor*

WILLIAM N. STILL

In 1851, John Ruskin wrote: "Take it all in all a Ship of the Line is the most honorable thing that man, as a gregarious animal, has ever produced." In that same year, however, Sir Henry Bessemer gave his first demonstration that molten iron could be converted to steel. Ten years later, a ship would be laid down, constructed partially of iron, that would symbolize the end of Ruskin's "most honorable thing."[1] That ship was the ironclad warship, USS *Monitor*.

A recent authority has written: "Of all the warlike technology of the zenith of the Industrial Revolution and of the Age of Progress, none has loomed more impressively, generated more public controversy, or captured the general imagination of powers with naval pretentions than the ironclad warship."[2] Today, only one ironclad, the HMS *Warrior*, is still afloat, presently being restored in England. Although it is one of the first of the armored warships, it is by no means the most famous. That distinction probably belongs to the *Monitor*, presently lying some sixteen miles off Cape Hatteras, North Carolina, at a depth of approximately 230 feet.

Virtually from the time it was under construction during the first year of the Civil War, its fame was assured. Its unique raft-like structure supporting a turret generated thousands of words in the newspapers. The controversy surrounding the *Monitor*'s inventor-builder, the Swedish-American, John Ericsson, contributed to its fame. Then came its celebrated battle with the CSS *Virginia* (formerly the USS *Merrimack*), perhaps the only naval combat which achieved its place in history mainly because it was indecisive. As Bernard Brodie wrote:

> The engagement in Hampton Roads on March 9, 1862 would never have gained so much renown had either the *Merrimac[k]* or the *Monitor* sunk the other. It was the uselessness of their long and furious cannonade, contrasted with the signal victories of the *Merrimac[k]* over unarmored ships on the previous day, that made the affair a landmark on the story of the warship.[3]

Writing of this battle, Oliver Wendell Holmes asked: "Is it not the age of fable, and of heroes, and demi-gods over again?"[4] The combat captured the imagination of the American public then and later. Various naval officers, members of Congress, as well as newspapers and periodicals, including the influential *Army and Navy Journal*, discoursed on the epochal importance of the encounter.[5]

The *Monitor* action in Hampton Roads produced such an intense enthusiasm in the North that a "monitor craze" swept the Union. Three weeks after the battle, ten improved Ericsson monitors were contracted—the *Passaic* class—which would see more service than any other class of monitors. Until the end of the war the navy would concentrate on monitor construction.[6]

The monitor craze crossed the Atlantic. Shortly after the battle, Charles Francis Adams, U.S. minister to Great Britain, wrote to his son that the *Monitor* had become the "main talk of the town."[7] The London *Times* wrote: "Whereas we had available for immediate purpose 149 first-class warships, we now have two, both armored vessels.... There is not now a ship in the English Navy, apart from these two, that it would not be madness to trust to an engagement with the little *Monitor*." In a similar tone, Ephraim Douglas Adams wrote: "More than any other battle of the Civil War the duel between the *Merrimac* and the *Monitor* struck the imagination of the British people."[8]

The Hampton Roads engagement was not only a sensation in England but also throughout Europe.[9] John Bigelow, U.S. consul general and minister in Paris, wrote in his memoir:

> That event had done more to re-establish [the U.S.] as a national power in Europe and inspire respect for our military resources than anything that has occurred since the rebellion. The Nations who were rejoicing in our weakness...two months ago...have suddenly discovered that the race is not always to the strong, and that it was the mercy of Providence rather than their own wisdom or sense of justice which prevented their being plunged into a war which in the natural course of things might have resulted in sinking half their navy before they would have heard of its arrival in our country.[10]

Although Bigelow exaggerated the *Monitor*'s power as well as the effect the battle had on European governments, he nevertheless was correct on the ironclad's impact on public opinion.

The Hampton Roads engagement did, however, impress the French government. A French frigate observed the combat from the southern entrance to Hampton Roads. Its commanding officer wrote a long, detailed account of it, concluding that "I can right now foresee how useless it will be for ordinary ships to try to fight against these floating fortresses armed with rifled guns of nine and eleven inches in diameter." Referring to the *Monitor* as a "work of genius, his report influenced Napoleon III to hasten the modernization of his fleet.[11]

Historians would continue to perpetuate the fame and importance of the *Monitor* after the war. A majority of historians writing in the latter decades of the nineteenth century agreed with James Ford Rhodes in that "the *Monitor-Merrimac[k]* struggle was undoubtedly a great turning point in naval warfare." Bruce Catton wrote in 1956, "March [1862 was] memorable for the most momentous drawn battle in history—a battle that nobody won but that made the navies of the world obsolete." Winston Churchill also commented that "the combat of the *Merrimac[k]* and the *Monitor* made the greatest change in seafighting since cannon fired by gunpowder had been mounted on ships about four hundred years before." And finally, William C. Davis described the *Monitor* as a "model for the warship of the future."[12]

James P. Baxter demonstrated some thirty years ago in his brilliant study on the ironclad, however, that the influence and importance of the *Monitor* both on the naval construction policies of the European governments as well as on the development of the modern capital ship have been greatly exaggerated. At the time of the Hampton Roads contest, more than one hundred ironclads were under construction in various countries. Baxter went on to say:

Though the influence of the battles of Hampton Roads on the policy of European governments has been greatly exaggerated, few naval actions in history have made so profound an impression on the popular imagination. The combats of March 8 and 9 symbolized the passing of the old fleets and the coming of the new. Symbols they were, and not the cause, for they did not initiate the great revolution in naval architecture, they crowned it. They taught the man in the street what the naval constructors already knew: that shell guns had sounded the doom of the wooden navies of the world. On the chief problem confronting the naval constructors of Europe—the best design for *seagoing* ironclads—these battles threw little light. Nevertheless fate had provided for the first fight of ironclads so incomparable a setting that the *Merrimack* and *Monitor* have monopolized public attention in the United States, to the exclusion of the scores of ironclads then already built or building in Europe.[13]

In an article published in 1981, Larry E. Tise, then director of the North Carolina Division of Archives and History, emphasized the historic and symbolic value of the *Monitor* to the American people.[14] Dr. Tise is correct. To the majority, however, the value of the *Monitor* is related to the Battle of Hampton Roads—a military or naval value. The vessel has another symbolic value, perhaps equally important: its place as an example of American technology and industry.

The Civil War was fought at a time when the United States was beginning to accelerate toward industrial importance. The nation was already one of the industrial leaders in the world in 1860, with manufacturing employing almost one-seventh of the labor force.[15] Before the war American contributions in technology were gaining recognition. The U.S. exhibits at the Crystal Palace Exposition in London in the mid-1850s impressed Europeans.[16] New inventions illustrated American ingenuity. Cyrus McCormick's reaper and especially the sewing machines of Elias Howe and Isaac Singer were sold abroad. By the war's outbreak Singer's European outlets were selling more sewing machines than some 3,000 salesmen were able to market in the United States.[17]

Recent writings in the economic history of the United States in the mid-nineteenth century have suggested that the Civil War actually retarded the nation's growth.[18] This may well be true, but the war clearly stimulated developments in technology. "It was the first struggle," John W. Oliver wrote, "in which science and machinery played a dominant part, and it was the first time that technological innovations and improvements were applied on a large scale in a major war."[19] Bernard and Fawn Brodie wrote: "The American Civil War was a colossal proving ground for improved weapons of all kinds. For the first time the achievements of the industrial and scientific revolution were used on a large scale in war."[20] Ericsson himself wrote that "the time has come, Mr. President [Lincoln], when our cause will have to be sustained not by numbers, but by superior weapons. By a proper application of mechanical devices alone will you be able with absolute certainty to destroy the enemies of the Union."[21] The most famous of the "mechanical devices" was designed by Ericsson, the ironclad *Monitor*.

"A . . . feature of the *Monitor* story, perhaps the most important one for her place in the international history of technology," wrote Theodore Ropp, is that she was one of the most successful ship prototypes in history. *Monitor*, like the later *Dreadnought*, became a generic term, in the *Monitor*'s case for light-draft, coast defense ironclads and for vaguely similar light-draft ships which were used in both world wars and Vietnam.[22]

Monitor-type warships were used by various navies. The last American naval vessel designated a monitor, the *Cheyenne*, was decommissioned and scrapped in 1925.[23] The *Passaic*-class monitor, *Comanche*, remained afloat as a coal barge in San Francisco at least until World War II.

Baxter in his study on ironclads stressed the revolutionary importance of these early armored vessels. The ironclads were the transitional warships from wood to iron. However, armor was only one of the technological innovations in the nineteenth century that revolutionized the navies of the world. During the century occurred the shift from sail to steam. The screw propeller, rifled and breech-loading ordnance, shells, and the revolving turret were other innovations.[24]

The *Monitor* incorporated many of these technological improvements. It carried two 11-inch Dahlgren smoothbore cannon that could fire shells, it was driven by screw propellers of Ericsson's design, and it was steam-powered by two single-cylindered steam engines also designed by Ericsson. Of the naval technological developments of the century, the introduction of the steam-powered warship was, in its tactical, strategic, and ultimate political consequences, by far the most important. Although historians have emphasized the engagement between the *Monitor* and the *Virginia* as the first combat between two ironclads, they rarely point out that this was also one of the earliest engagements between two warships maneuvering entirely under steam propulsion.[25]

In addition to steam machinery and propellers, there were more than 250 patentable inventions by Ericsson on the *Monitor*. Isaac Newton, the ship's first engineer, estimated "that she contained at least forty patentable contrivances" in the turret.[26] And the turret itself was the most important of these technological innovations.

Although the *Monitor* was not the first ironclad in action, it was the first turreted armored vessel to engage an enemy. The success of Ericsson's vessel gave a great impetus to the adoption of the armored turret. The concept of a turret was not new, however. Ericsson himself recognized this when he wrote: "A house, or turret, turning on a pivot for protecting apparatus intended to throw warlike projectiles, is an ancient device.... Thinking back, I cannot fix any period of my life at which I did *not* know of its existence."[27]

Along with Ericsson's gun tower, several turrets were either under construction or had been proposed. Theodore R. Timby of New York later would claim that the idea was his; James B. Eads, a western river builder, designed a turret that was installed on the *Milwaukee*-class monitor; and Captain Cowper P. Coles of the Royal Navy developed a cupola that the British government adopted even before they learned what had happened at Hampton Roads.[28] Nonetheless, the *Monitor*'s success provided the turret concept with credibility, and it was a major factor in the emphasis on turreted warships both in the United States and abroad. Until the end of the war the U.S. Navy would concentrate on monitor construction. Of the forty ironclads laid down by the Union during the war, thirty-five were of the monitor type.[29]

As Davis said, the "turret alone would have made Ericsson immortal; it was the most successful innovation in nautical warfare of the century."[30] Although Davis's statement is probably exaggerated as to the turret's significance, there can be no question about its importance.[31] The centerline turret would be a major characteristic of the modern capital ship.

It is almost certainly questionable that the *Monitor* was the forerunner of the modern warship, as has frequently been said. Both Baxter in his work on the ironclad and Stanley Sandler's on the modern capital ship convincingly disallow that theory. It was not the raft-like monitor but the large, high-freeboard, centerline, multiple-turret armored ship that was the forerunner of the modern capital ship. Modern ship design was primarily a result of developments in Europe. Yet, with its turret, forced-air ventilation in living spaces, and other unique features, the *Monitor* was, within the context of the mid-nineteenth century, a most advanced warship and unquestionably had a great impact on design in the United States for many years.

Today, the *Monitor* is undoubtedly the best known warship in American history, recognized by most children. Even compared to famous vessels still afloat, such as the *Constitution, Constellation, Missouri,* and *Olympia,* it stands alone. The *Monitor* is both a historic artifact and a symbolic monument of enormous importance to the American people. As such, it is worthy of the public and private resources necessary for its full documentation.

NOTES

1. Quoted in Elting E. Morison, *From Know-How to Nowhere: The Development of American Technology* (New York, 1974), 147–48.
2. Stanley Sandler, *The Emergence of the Modern Capital Ship, 1860–1870* (Newark, DE, 1979), 15–16.
3. Bernard Brodie, *Sea Power in the Machine Age* (Princeton, 1941), 171.
4. Quoted in Rear Admiral Albert Gleaves, *Life and Letters of Rear Admiral Stephen B. Luce* (New York, 1925), 3.
5. George T. Davis, *A Navy Second to None: The Development of Modern American Naval Policy* (New York, 1940), 9, 9n.
6. William N. Still, Jr., "Technology Afloat," *Civil War Times Illustrated* 14 (November 1975): 42.
7. Worthington C. Ford, ed., *A Cycle of Adams Letters, 1861–1865,* 2 vols. (Boston, 1920), 1:123.
8. Ephraim D. Adams, *Great Britain and the American Civil War,* 2 vols. (New York, 1925), 1:276.
9. Lynn M. Case and Warren F. Spencer, *The United States and France: Civil War Diplomacy* (Philadelphia, 1970), 266.
10. Ibid., 267.
11. Ibid., 265–67.
12. Bruce Catton, *This Hallowed Ground* (New York, 1960), 160–61; Sir Winston Churchill, *History of the English-Speaking Peoples,* 4 vols. (New York, 1956), 4:202; William C. Davis, *Duel between the First Ironclads* (Garden City, 1975), 165; Gleaves, *Stephen B. Luce,* 289.
13. James P. Baxter, *The Introduction of the Ironclad Warship* (Cambridge, MA, 1933), 285; Kenneth Bourne, *Britain and the Balance of Power in North America, 1815–1908* (Berkeley, 1967), 239–40. See also Regis A. Courtemanche, *No Need for Glory: The British Navy in American Waters, 1860–1864* (Annapolis, 1977), 157; Sandler, *Emergence of the Modern Capital Ship,* 65.

For an example of an exaggerated effect see Stephen B. Luce, "The Story of the *Monitor*," *Naval Actions and History, 1799-1899*, published in the Papers of the Military Historical Society of Massachusetts (Boston, 1902), 12:127-54.

14. Larry E. Tise, "Off Carolina Searching for the *Monitor*," *Civil War Times Illustrated* 20 (July 1981): 38-41, 44-45. This was a special issue devoted to the *Monitor*, the only issue of that magazine devoted to a particular ship.

15. Sidney Rather, James H. Soltow, and Richard Sylla, *The Evolution of the American Economy* (New York, 1979), 241.

16. Charles Singer et. al., eds., *A History of Technology*, 7 vols. (Oxford, 1985), 5:818.

17. Ibid., 819.

18. Susan P. Lee and Peter Passell, *A New Economic View of American History* (New York, 1979), 227-29. Thomas Cochran was the first historian to challenge the idea that the Civil War stimulated economic growth. See Thomas Cochran, "Did the Civil War Retard Industrialization?" *Mississippi Valley Historical Review* 48 (1961): 197-210.

19. John W. Oliver, *History of American Technology* (New York, 1956), 276. See also Singer, *History of Technology* 5:809.

20. Bernard Brodie and Fawn Brodie, *From Crossbow to H-Bomb* (New York, 1962), 133-34.

21. William C. Church, *The Life of John Ericsson*, 2 vols. (New York, 1890), 2:34.

22. Theodore Ropp, "The *Monitor*'s Changing Appeal," in *The Monitor: Its Meaning and Future* (Washington, 1978), 72-73.

23. *New York Times*, 4 October 1925.

24. Still, "Technology Afloat," 5.

25. Brodie, *Sea Power in the Machine Age*, 177.

26. Church, *Life of John Ericsson*, 1:261.

27. Ibid., 2:114.

28. Baxter, *Introduction of the Ironclad Warship*, 324; Still, "Technology Afloat," 42; Phillip K. Lundeberg, "The *Monitor*: Fragile Survivor," *The Monitor: Its Meaning and Future*, 67.

29. Still, "Technology Afloat," 43.

30. Davis, *Duel between the First Ironclads*, 18.

31. As mentioned earlier, most authorities place more emphasis on steam propulsion.

The Importance of Understanding the Construction of the USS *Monitor*

ERNEST W. PETERKIN

The conceptual phases of the master plan for the USS *Monitor* Project are: 1) pre-disturbance survey and documentation, 2) archaeological documentation and excavation, and 3) recovery of selected structure. The decision to progress from one phase to the next will depend upon the successful accomplishment of the preceding phase. The project now is in the first phase and is concerned with site surveys and the collection of historical data on the construction and contents of the vessel.

The expeditions to the wreck site over the past decade have collected photographic and video data providing a preliminary qualitative impression of the condition of the hull. The sonar and magnetic surveys, taken in the fall of 1985, have yielded for the first time bottom contours of the entire one-mile diameter sanctuary and debris pattern resulting from capsizing during sinking, environmental effects, and probable depth charges during World War II.

The planned photographic expedition for summer 1987 is expected to provide identification and quantitative information on much of the ship's exposed structure and debris. Despite this potential increase in information on the ship's configuration and damage obtainable by photographic techniques, photographic measurements are limited to visible surfaces. What lies below the collapsed hull, debris, and overburden will remain unknown until excavation, and, as excavation is part of Phase 2, a major decision will be required before that step is reached. The following research objectives should be addressed prior to moving from one phase to the next.

Archaeological Estimate. The number, type, size, weight, and location of thousands of artifacts thought to remain in the *Monitor* will influence their desirability and the estimate of resources necessary for their recovery. As there are no known records of the contents of the ship at the time of the sinking, these details must be derived from the historical record. Study of contemporary drawings, contracts, specifications, and allowance listings makes it possible to define the compartments of the hull and their probable contents.

Recovery Operations. Decisions concerning recovery techniques, costs, and resources will be determined by the condition, size, and weight of wreck compartments. Sinking, environmental, and depth-charging effects have had serious impacts on the vessel's structural integrity. The condition of the wreck can be estimated more precisely by comparing on-site data with the historical record.

Conservation Requirements. Preservation of the vessel and its contents requires an understanding of construction materials and their connections and the number and composition of artifacts. The magnitude of conservation could range from the entire wrought-iron hull to a sewing needle in a sailor's kit. The spectrum of materials and the number of items to be conserved can be estimated from the historical record and some wreck observation. The magnitude of the conservation effort would determine requirements for facilities, staff, and production rates.

Exhibit Planning. Since the exhibit for the USS *Monitor* Project could range from the current recovered artifacts through the possibility of displaying the entire vessel and its contents, planning for exhibition facilities can be estimated from the vessel's construction and contents studies.

Interpretation. As the *Monitor* class may have represented only 3 percent of the active number of ships in the Union navy during the Civil War, there seems to be a corresponding lack of documentation about life aboard this new type of vessel. Its construction and layout reflect the technology of the times for the most advanced form of naval warfare. Comparison of construction, arrangement of weapons, and employment of the crew with conventional men-of-war will lead to a better understanding of this experiment by the modern public.

It is apparent that all of the research goals for the project depend upon a detailed understanding of the construction of the *Monitor* and its contents. These two factors are the starting points for planning and decision making related to archaeological assessment, recovery planning, conservation requirements, and interpretation. As on-site documentation is limited to the amount of information that can be derived from the visible surface of the vessel, major reliance must be placed on examination and analysis of the historical record.

In support of this approach, three studies have been undertaken. First, the collection of mechanical drawings—a study, *Drawings of the USS MONITOR,* has been published which includes 154 drawings by Ericsson and his staff, plus some fifty related drawings, covering the general and detailed construction of the vessel. Second, the study of contents—*Contents of the USS MONITOR* is nearing completion. It provides the items likely to be found in some 112 compartments of the ship, based on navy allowance lists for Civil War vessels, contracts, specifications, official correspondence, drawings, and writings of the crew. Third, the development of new drawings—a reconstruction of contemporary information and detailed study of compartments not included in the original plans, now in progress, will provide comprehensive line drawings, general arrangements, deck arrangements, shell expansion, and selected transverse sections not previously illustrated.

With the above information, archaeologists, ocean engineers, conservators, exhibit interpreters, and management personnel will be provided with a comprehensive basis for planning and making recommendations for future courses of action during Phase 1 of the project.

The USS *Monitor* Project Research Design

RICHARD A. GOULD

Any use of the term "research design" in archaeology denotes a controlled approach to data recovery and a hypothesis-testing approach to data analysis. The present survey of the wreck site of the USS *Monitor* affords a unique opportunity to see how much a nondestructive, designed research project can say about the society that produced this ship and its relationship to the mid-nineteenth century origins of the modern arms race.

Much has been written about the "ironcladization" of world navies during the mid-nineteenth century, along with related technological changes involving the introduction of steam propulsion and advances in weaponry such as rifled cannons, turrets, and shell guns. Unique as the *Monitor* may appear, its development was embedded in the conditions of both the Industrial Revolution and the Anglo-French military rivalry. France, in particular, bought in to the ironcladization process early, and French observers watched the Battle of Hampton Roads with keen interest.

To what extent was the use of metal armor on ships determined by the advent of the shell gun? This is a familiar thesis to anyone who has read James P. Baxter.[1] Or was the advent of ironclads due more to the enormous consumption and depletion of suitable timber demanded by the wooden-walled navies of that era? This is an argument recently advanced by Andrew Lambert.[2] If we accept the idea that armor and the other innovations represented spurts or escalations in military technology, then to what extent were these responses to some action taken by the other side? Alternatively, we should consider the possibility that many of these developments may have been generated internally by the society that produced them, perhaps to solve problems of unemployment or to maintain the capacity for war production during times of peace.

Questions of this kind that seek to measure and explain the essential characteristics of the modern arms race represent what could be called a macro-level of the *Monitor* research design. But in order to begin to deal effectively with these kinds of questions, we must first consider a micro-level of specific operations and measurements required and the middle level of analysis needed to connect such micro- and macro-levels. Long before we can deal effectively with high-level questions about the relationship of the *Monitor* to the history of the world arms race, we must decide what kinds of low-level data are needed and what kinds of measurements are relevant to answering these almost cosmic questions about our present condition. All archaeological research designs involve this complementary relationship between general hypotheses about human behavior on the one hand and specific observations and measurements on the other.

Archaeological studies of the *Monitor* so far have tended to be descriptive and to view the wreck and related materials as historic relics. With all due respect to Civil War historians and buffs, another issue now is whether a scientifically controlled study of the wreck site can produce inferences that both are credible and extend our knowledge beyond the level of the ship's individual history and particular characteristics. Although detailed scholarly information about the *Monitor*'s history is essential in this effort, in the context of an archaeological research design, this historical information becomes a means to an end rather than an end in itself. In short, one goal of the USS *Monitor* Project is to posit general principles about how modern, industrial societies prepare for war, based not only on the written record but also on an archaeological study of the material residues and by-products of those preparations. Seen in this light, the wreck of the *Monitor* has wide significance and involves European nations as much as the United States, with possible lessons extending to the present world situation.

Assumptions about Underwater Archaeology

Perhaps the most commonly held assumption about archaeology is the idea that, above all, it involves excavation. The "underwater dig" is a corollary to this assumption. However, the first phase of the USS *Monitor* Project involves no digging at all. Instead, it will attempt to find out as much as possible about the wreck site through nondestructive methods. Systematic archaeological surveys of this kind are becoming common on land and are producing excellent results, leading to a greater appreciation for rigorous methods and the application of new technologies, including a variety of remote-sensing techniques.

Another frequent assumption equates the shipwreck with the site. Such congruence cannot be assumed for the *Monitor* wreck, where several items, including the ship's anchor, became detached from the vessel and were found at varying distances out on the sea bottom. Consequently, one of the first tasks on our research agenda was to determine the extent of the site.

It also is assumed in most cases that shipwrecks have a Pompeii-like quality in which all the observed attributes of the shipwreck co-occur in an association produced at the instant when the ship sank. While logical, this assumption must be examined in the case of the *Monitor*, since there may have been various factors affecting the integrity of the ship after it came to rest on the sea bottom. Clichés about the *Monitor* as a kind of time capsule can produce misleading and ambiguous results if no effort is made to control for postdepositional factors. Examples of these include sea bottom sedimentation and erosion, effects of marine vegetation and other natural processes at the site, and possible disturbances caused by human activities such as fishing and war (specifically, the possible damage due to depth charges during World War II).

Survey Methods and Procedures

Whatever the ultimate fate of the *Monitor*, any decisions about its future will depend on controlled studies that will provide a framework for convincing inferences about the behavior that structured both the ship and the wreck site. Phase 1 of the project represents a systematic effort to provide these controls and put them in place, before work of any kind begins on the *Monitor* that might affect the physical integrity of the wreck as it now lies. At this point, some discussion of these controls is appropriate.

Electronic Grid

All archaeology, whether on land or under water, requires that everything found be referrable to a horizontal grid system over the site. This applies equally to survey as well as to excavation. Underwater archaeologists have long made use of mechanical grid systems using string and pegged corners or PCV pipes, but such methods work well only in relatively shallow water, usually in conditions of good visibility and in areas where conventional scuba diving can be done. At a depth of 230 feet, the *Monitor* site is simply too deep for these conventional approaches, and a new method had to be devised.

Ocean Search, a division of Eastport International, a Maryland-based firm with experience in locating and recovering materials from deeply submerged aircraft wrecks and other similar sites, provided the solution in the form of an electronically operated grid system with the potential for accuracy up to present-day archaeological standards. In particular, the entire survey depends upon an electronic grid located on the seabed over a 2,500-square meter area with the *Monitor* near the center. This system, called the "ALLNAV," consists of two parts: the surface navigation component, Motorola Mini-Ranger; and the subsurface seabed component, EG & G SeaLink.

Mini-Ranger is based on two transmitters—in this case, one at Cape Hatteras Lighthouse and the other at Diamond Shoals Light—and an on-board receiver/computer system that continuously processes signals from the transmitters to produce real-time position fixes on the surface. These are accurate to within a few meters.

After establishing a position over the *Monitor* by means of an earlier Loran-C fix (not very accurate, as it turned out) and a systematic grid search using Mini-Ranger with side-scan sonar, the SeaLink underwater navigation system was deployed. This consisted of four underwater transponders placed in specially constructed stands out beyond the corners of the grid. At the end of the survey, these transponders were released from their stands and floated to the surface for recovery. These stands remain as archaeological datum points on the seabed. During the summer of 1987, plans are to return to the site with the DEEP DRONE remotely operated vehicle (ROV) and place the transponders back in their stands, thus reestablishing the electronic grid over the site.

SeaLink works acoustically by means of a transducer that interrogates each of the transponders to obtain the exact distance fixes, which are integrated and displayed on board the ship every thirty seconds. Unlike Mini-Ranger, this is not a real-time system, due to the length of time it takes for sound to travel through water and the complex geometry involved (requiring complex calculations by the computer). Thus, SeaLink's usefulness for surface navigation is limited to relatively smooth water conditions with minimal winds and currents, and even then it puts heavy demands on the ship's course-keeping abilities.

The first survey of the underwater grid was accomplished by using navigational inputs from SeaLink alone. It was done under ideal sea conditions and with the advantages of a long, narrow-hulled ship with bow thrusters and very competent course-keeping. As sea conditions deteriorated, so did the ability to maintain accurate courses using SeaLink navigation. Mini-Ranger, with its real-time capability (translated into continuous track indications for the helmsman to follow) worked much better on the surface, and it was used primarily for positioning the underwater transponders array and giving location data for the wreck. Despite the inaccurate Loran position fix for the *Monitor*, the wreck was relocated and the process begun of establishing the underwater grid only three hours after arriving on the scene. There were problems, however, with Mini-Ranger, involving gaps in the navigational coverage and excessive downtime, which was why the SeaLink system was used for surface navigation.

The electronic grid system represents the most important framework for controlling any kind of archaeological surveys or foreseeable excavations on the *Monitor*. Its use on this site is an important technological advance in underwater archaeology, especially when dealing with deeply submerged sites. When the next field season takes place in summer 1987, plans are to position another array of transponders around the *Monitor* but closer to the wreck site, permitting accurate locational fixes within centimeters instead of the meters obtained from the system presently in place. But we must always be prepared for technical problems when using an electronic grid system like this; it is especially important to have adequate technical expertise on board, redundancy of components, and liaison with shore-based backup. Without these kinds of preparations, valuable ship time and opportunities to work when the weather is most favorable may be lost.

The Remote Sensing Survey

A controlled survey was run along the underwater grid over the *Monitor* site, using 50-meter track spacing from north to south and 100-meter track spacing from east to west. Our first runs through the grid were done at fairly high speed (approximately three to five knots across the seabed, depending on the set of the surface currents, which are strong in the Cape Hatteras area). This speed was essential for good tracking. A side-scan sonar, operating at 100 kHz with ranges varying from 75 to 300 meters, was towed. At the same time, continuous bottom-depth readings were obtained from the ship's fathometer, and a digital fathometer was attached to the ship's side. The side-scan sonar revealed that the *Monitor* lies in essentially a featureless silty plain which extends throughout the 2,500-square meter gridded area. Beyond that area, however, there are indications of more complex geological formations with areas of exposed rock and with terrain features such as depressions and gullies. Within the gridded area, the *Monitor* itself appears to have become the principal feature to alter the local landforms, and one of the images noticed in the side-scan survey was a prominent northeast-southwest scour mark on the seabed extending from the wreck. Further data from two current meters and a transmissometer deployed approximately 300 meters east and west of the *Monitor* should help in understanding the dynamics of the currents and seabed deposition and erosion in the immediate area of the wreck before next season's work begins.

A further north-south survey of the gridded area using 50-meter track spacing was run using side-scan sonar, but with emphasis on use of the sub-bottom profiler and magnetometer. Good subbottom profiler and sonar data were obtained on this series of runs, but sea conditions by then required a ship speed that was too fast for highly detailed magnetometry. Further bathymetric data also were collected from the ship's fathometer during this second survey.

The second survey was performed using Mini-Ranger surface navigation, which permitted very accurate steering along each track but also required precise correlation and alignment between the surface and subsurface grids provided respectively by Mini-Ranger and SeaLink. This correlation was one of the final tasks performed during the voyage, and it ensured that exact positioning for the DEEP DRONE phase of the survey will be available within the 2,500-square meter grid when the survey resumes in the site in summer 1987.

Preliminary Evaluation of Results

Despite a combination of technical difficulties and some problems with weather, this initial ten-day season accomplished the following:

1. Establishment of an electronic grid system that will enable archaeologists to do controlled studies of deeply submerged sites with accuracy and repeatability comparable to current practices in good land archaeology. The methodological importance of this accomplishment extends far beyond the *Monitor*, because it opens the way for archaeology at many types of deeply submerged sites, including submerged terrestrial locations as well as shipwrecks, up to currently acceptable standards. This grid will be used for all subsequent studies of the *Monitor*.

2. Data collection using a variety of remote-sensing techniques to measure such variables as currents, salinity, and seabed geology in order to provide controls for all further research on the *Monitor* wreck site.

3. Data collection to help establish the parameters of the wreck site, which now extend out beyond the wreck itself. Metallic debris was "visible" on the side-scan sonar extending at least 100 meters to the north and northeast of the wreck.

All of these accomplishments represent essential first steps toward the larger archaeological questions raised earlier. Specifically, they provide a framework for evaluating the results of the rest of the nondestructive survey as well as for any further archaeology that may take place during subsequent field research on the *Monitor*. For example, the electronic grid now in place will make it possible to measure the ironclad's structure, along with objects that have become detached from the ship, with sufficient accuracy to begin systematic comparisons with the historical evidence already collected.

Finally, the 1985 field season afforded participants an opportunity to evaluate the technological systems available for this kind of research. These systems are extremely complex, with a high probability rate of failure while on the scene. No research design that employs such systems can afford to ignore this fact. In essence, much appreciation was gained on how well all of this high technology works, when it works.

It will be a practical requirement for all further remote-sensing studies of the *Monitor* to estimate the probability and severity of downtime resulting from technical failures and to make sure that there is adequate redundancy and shore-based support to avoid costly and wasteful delays. This should not be interpreted as negative criticism of these systems. Rather, it is part of a realistic appreciation of their value in opening up the possibilities for scientific research on the *Monitor* site, with the direct implications that such research will have on larger questions about the *Monitor*'s role in relation to the early history of an expanding, and ultimately worldwide, arms race.

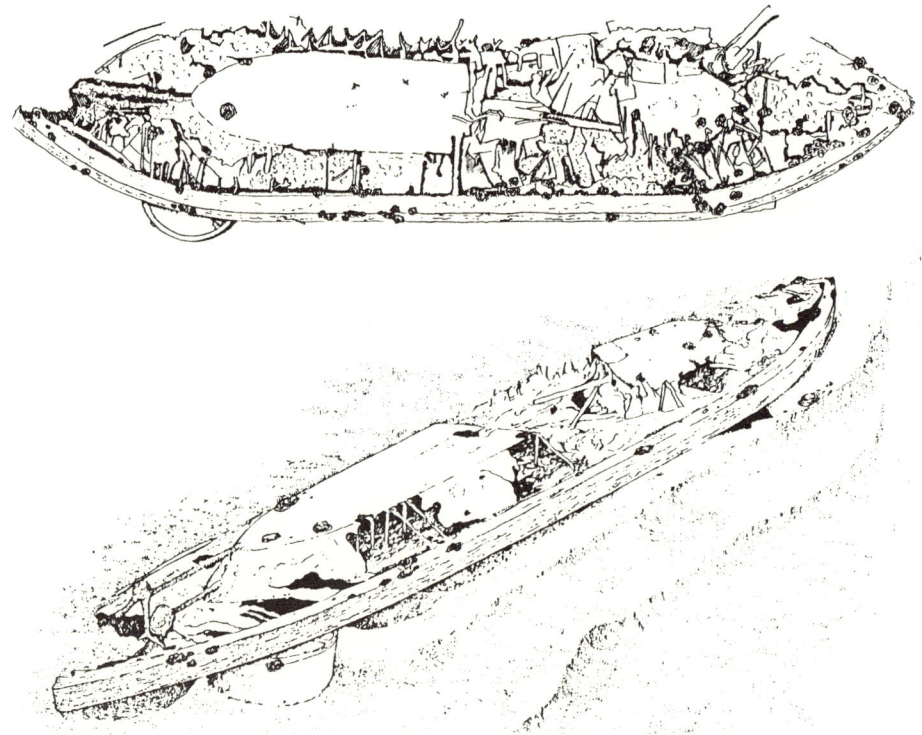

USS *Monitor* (Courtesy of Monitor National Marine Sanctuary)

NOTES

1. James P. Baxter, *The Introduction of the Ironclad Warship* (Cambridge, MA, 1933).
2. Andrew Lambert, *Battleships in Transition: The Creation of the Steam Battleships, 1815–1860* (Annapolis, 1984).

The Royal Navy and the Projection of British Power, 1863-1900

BRUCE COLLINS

Most general histories of empire and imperial wars ignore the Royal Navy's role in projecting British power in nineteenth-century expansion. By examining this role in the Maori War of 1863-66, the Ashanti War of 1873-74, and the first year of the Boer War, Dr. Collins shows the variety of ways in which naval squadrons helped launch, support, and sustain land campaigns. He argues for the more detailed study of the naval role of expansion.

****

In introducing *Victorian Military Campaigns,* Brian Bond asserted: "In summing up Britain's advantages in these colonial campaigns pride of place must be given to the Royal Navy." It conveyed troops and protected bridgeheads. It participated in the campaigns themselves by shelling coasts, sending boats up rivers to support the army, and lending guns and rockets for land use.[1] No historian asked to comment on Britain's ability to maintain and expand its interests in the late nineteenth century would disagree with Bond's general assertion, or with Anthony Preston and John Major's conclusion that the numerous bases and ubiquitous small gunboats constantly patrolling worldwide made the Royal Navy so distinctive and distinctively powerful.[2] No other nation deployed so many warships so widely in the nineteenth century. Yet having said that, it is remarkable that so little is written more precisely about the role played by these warships in projecting British power. Interestingly enough, in the essays on individual wars that Bond commissioned, there is scarcely any mention of the naval contribution, despite the large and just claim for the navy advanced in Bond's introduction. And important recent books on the empire by Ronald Hyam, Bernard Porter, and T. O. Lloyd, together with a survey by James L. Stokesbury on *Navy and Empire,* give little attention to the naval role in British expansion, other than to repeat that it was a vital one.[3]

One reason for this was the metropolitan bias of late nineteenth-century navalism. Technological revolution, the European naval race from the 1880s, Alfred Thayer Mahan's reemphasis upon decisive battles at sea, global strategic reappraisals in the 1900s, and, above all, menaces of mainly German but sometimes French or Russian navies dwarfed into Lilliputian insignificance the mere happenings of gunboat diplomacy. They naturally dominate late nineteenth-century naval historiography.[4] Indeed, this later historical orientation reflects the anxieties and preoccupations of the earlier period. For example, in 1891, Rear Admiral P. H. Colomb, regarded by Professor G. S. Graham as one of the nineteenth century's most astute naval writers, published a volume on naval warfare. Colomb noted and welcomed Mahan's *The Influence of Sea Power upon History, 1660–1789*, which had appeared the previous year and which indeed owed much to Colomb's earlier work. Unsurprisingly, Colomb, like Mahan, focused upon major fleet actions and the impact commanding the seas had upon competing Great Powers' fortunes. This preoccupation led to a concentration on the period before 1815; only a few references to the Crimean War and a brief discussion of the bombardment of Alexandria in 1882 acknowledged the naval role in projecting British power after Waterloo.[5] Again, a leading naval publicist of the 1890s, Sir George Sydenham Clarke, persistently pressed for a bigger, better navy by referring to grand strategy, the navy's past importance, and the empire's dependence on sea lanes and maritime trade. His journalism failed to recognize the navy as an instrument of colonial conquest or policing.[6] This omission is understandable enough among navalists concerned with the European theater, European rivalries, and European battlefleets, but it marred even the writings of those interested in colonial warfare.

C. E. Calwell was probably the foremost Victorian authority on small wars. Published in 1896 while he was only a junior army officer, *Small Wars: Their Principles and Practice* is still regarded as the best theoretical work on the subject.[7] As so often happened, it acknowledged the fundamental importance of sea power and naval support but did so cursorily in a chapter three pages long. In 1897, as if to rectify that anomaly, Calwell published a survey of the impact of sea power upon land campaigns after 1815; this also may have been a timely effort to apply Mahan's ideas to a later period, the master having only reached 1815 in a two-volume treatise that appeared in 1892. But Calwell's attention centered on major wars, especially those in the eastern Mediterranean and mostly not involving the British closely or directly. Fleeting mention was made of the Egyptian campaign of 1882, which showed better than any event since 1855, according to Calwell, "the potentialities of the British Empire's great amphibious strength," since "the suddenness with which such blows can be delivered goes far . . . to compensate for deficiency of numbers." In 1905, however, as controversy raged over the concentration of the Home Fleet, Calwell wrote at length that a worldwide empire needed to maintain squadrons and a capacity for both rapid development and amphibious warfare "in every ocean and in every sea." Sea power was required to protect maritime trade and mercantile marine, to transport soldiers between dependencies and colonies, and, in "almost innumerable examples," to provide sailors for land operations. While taking full cognizance of small squadrons' historical and continuing importance, Calwell in fact devoted scant attention to precise cases of Victorian Britain's projection of power.[8]

Even more curiously, when Brigadier General G. G. Aston of the Royal Marine Artillery wrote up his staff college lectures on amphibious warfare for publication in 1911, he scrutinized no British examples, considering instead the Chilean War of 1891, the Spanish-American War of 1898, the Sino-

Japanese War of 1894-95, and the Russo-Japanese War of 1904-05.[9] Given such oversights at the turn of the century, no one would be puzzled to find that Geoffrey Callender's *The Naval Side of British History* (1924) devoted only 22 of its 280 pages to the period from 1815 to 1914, that it said nothing of gunboat diplomacy or the naval side of actual imperial history, that it insisted on naval power having been used to succor free trade generally rather than for British advantage, and that it portrayed naval activity in such vacuous terms as "the British sailor came to be regarded by races of every colour and every creed as a warrior, capable of delivering trenchant blows, but preferring always in any one of a thousand ways to lend a helping hand." Such an approach was the more peculiar, if not perturbing, because Callender was professor of history at the Royal Naval College, Greenwich.[10]

If writings on naval warfare, when they burgeoned in the 1890s and 1900s, failed to offer any thorough analysis of the role actually played by naval power in advancing British interests after Waterloo, one outstanding exception emerged to fill that gap. From 1897 to 1903, Sir William Laird Clowes published a seven-volume history of the Royal Navy, with his last volume covering the years from 1857 to 1900.[11] Here indeed was an exhaustive account of the navy's far-flung doings. Yet Clowes's narrative was tedious and unreflective, wedded to the relentless agenda laid down by the dispatch writer and very largely devoid of political concerns or interservice relations. Clowes tells when and where naval forces intervened and how the fighting went, but he offers no rounded assessment of either individual squadrons' work or of the nature of the naval contribution to the projection of British power. Incident and information predominate without yielding insight and without even being encyclopedic. No wonder his work is very largely overlooked beyond the circle of strictly naval historians.

Given such typical neglect, this paper reexamines the naval role in defending and extending British interests. It does so in order to offer some working generalizations concerning the naval contribution to the projection of power. It focuses on that projection of power rather than on policies or principles discussed in the Cabinet or the clubs of London. The vast subject of comparing the Royal Navy with the navies of other European powers or of the United States is necessarily ignored in so brief a survey. To consider what the navy did and how it met the tasks assigned to it, three case studies of the period from 1863 to 1900 have been chosen. These examples are not cases of gunboat diplomacy classically defined. Indeed, only one of the three is mentioned—and that very briefly and unsatisfactorily—in Preston and Major's *Send a Gunboat!*, although two of these examples did involve gunboats.[12] The three cases—the Maori War of 1863-66, the Ashanti campaign of 1873-74, and the first, most precarious year of the Anglo-Boer War of 1899-1902[13]—all relate to the projection of British power on land. These conflicts were different in kind. The first was, in essence, a white settler war of conquest; the second was a war of prestige to roll back the Ashanti from their encroachments upon the coastal settlements of the British and their allies; and the third was an interior war between the white settler groups in South Africa. Naval involvement in all three was described by Clowes but typically has been forgotten since. And, as will be shown, Clowes's accounts were inadequate as well as unsystematic.

The Maori War of 1863–66 was the most significant of a series of conflicts with the Maoris of North Island, New Zealand; it was also the last major war against the dwindling Maori population, although fighting continued sporadically into the 1870s.[14] The fact that 12,000 imperial troops (exclusive of colonial volunteers) had been deployed in New Zealand by 1864 illustrated the continuing truth of David Syrett's comment on late eighteenth-century naval power; it "conferred upon the British army...a strategic importance and striking power far greater than the mere size of the force alone warranted."[15] To be sure, the Australian squadron, comprising six to eight ships in these years, had to manage that deployment and maintain supply and resupply from the Australian mainland. Its task, however, did not end there. Maori strength lay not in numbers—by sucking in so many imperial soldiers the colonists achieved overwhelming numerical superiority—but in geography and terrain. Colonists clung to North Island's edges while the indigenes defended themselves within the central region of rugged, densely forested hills. The underlying cause of the war was the Maori effort to establish a king whose ultimate sovereignty not only challenged that of the British but also formed a block to the alienation of individual tribes' lands. To defeat the royalist movement the British had to penetrate inland, nearly always into dense forests and bush. They were able, from July 1863 to February 1866, to interpose themselves fairly effectively into three regions of disaffection: Waikato, Tauranga, and Taranaki-Wanganui.

Naval assistance underpinned the Waikato campaign because its success depended on river transport and on assailing the Maori *pas*, or forts, from both river and land. The naval brigade assisted in manning specially armed riverboats, in shelling *pas*, in reconnaissance, and in land assaults on the Maoris' intricately laid-out fortifications. From July 1863 to April 1864, sailors labored long and hard, sometimes within Maori musket range, to maintain supply lines. In combat, they contributed to turning the Maoris out of their forts at Mere Mere and Rangariri during October and November 1863. The Australian squadron's commodore, Sir William Wiseman, agreed with the army view that the "only way" of taking the forts without "a very heavy loss of life [was] to throw rapidly a large force of men on shore from the river bank, close under their pits, the landing being covered by the fire of as many guns as we can bring to bear from Gunboats, steamers, and from the advanced post of Whangamarino."[16] And, when fighting switched to the Tauranga region, the naval brigade furnished 150 officers and men of the 300-strong assault party at the final and bloody attack on Gate Pa on 29 April 1864. (Clowes gives prominent attention to the naval brigade's work at Rangariri and Gate Pa.[17])

By joining the fighting, the naval brigade showed its commitment and courage.[18] Commodore Wiseman was eager to participate in the campaign and accompanied the army commander, Lieutenant General Duncan Cameron, deep into the interior as well as at the attack on Gate Pa.[19] This was not unusual; senior naval officers went far inland, for example, in the Ashanti campaign in 1874, on the march to Tel-el-Kebir in 1882, and with the expedition to Peking in 1900.[20] Bluejackets may have been valuable in these incursions, given their reputation for flexibility, adaptability, and technical skill. Their navigation experience was absolutely essential to the fruitful conduct of the Waikato campaign. In addition, the squadron provided firepower in the shape of heavy guns. These were used against the riverine *pas* and for the assault on Gate Pa.[21]

Other attributes of naval power might be emphasized. The fundamental strategic achievement of the campaigning was the British ability not only to penetrate into Maori country but also to confine the rebellion to one district at any one time, to respond speedily when disaffection spread, and to bolster the morale of friendly Maoris and widely dispersed white settlers alike. This ability, in short, to limit the scene of conflict and choose the theater of operations flowed directly from the presence of six warships and their patrolling and policing.

A number of prominent examples may illustrate the range of such activity. In late February 1864 the five warships of the squadron actually in North Island were dispersed both at vital bases and to keep a watch on events. One was at Manukau Harbor, the naval station. Another, at Waikato Heads, had done energetic work in protecting workmen engaged there in building new river steamers as well as the Putataka dockyard from rebel attack. But the remaining three were at Auckland, to reassure the civilian population, and off the coast watching Tauranga and the Firth of Thames. Wiseman expressed confidence in his ability to deploy troops very rapidly at the first signs of rebellion elsewhere in North Island.[22] A month later, Captain J. F. C. Hamilton of the HMS *Esk*, who was to be killed in the storming of Gate Pa, conducted a three-week long series of negotiations supporting the resident magistrate in an effort to settle disputes and induce Maoris to surrender weapons in the Thames district. It is unlikely that these negotiations would have succeeded without gunboat support.[23]

As North Island continued in a very unsettled condition, this capacity to move swiftly to new trouble spots was vital to British success in the slow work of subjugating the Maoris.[24] In March 1865, when trouble arose in Tauranga, the dispatch of a warship reinforced the loyalty of the Arawas, who were able to hand over rebels they had captured trying to pass through their lands. On 7 April, another warship, responding immediately to a request from the civil commissioner, went to Kennedy's Bay with the commissioner and ten loyal chiefs to confront rebels. The commissioner ordered twelve leaders to leave the area because they were allegedly stirring up discontent. They had arrived in the locality only two weeks earlier. Threatened with a naval presence and the arrival of arms for the white settlers, they left within a few hours.[25] Later in the same month, the governor asked Captain John P. Luce to visit Te Kaha, Hick's Bay, Kawa Kawa, Waiapu, and Poverty Bay. This he did in the *Esk*:

> I believe this visit of a Man-of-War with a message from you to the East Coast tribes has had a very good effect. The loyal and faithful feel themselves strengthened and encouraged whilst the King Party and Pai Marines [*sic*], who latterly have in some places, closed the roads and shown marked incivility to Loyal Native and English travellers changed their tone directly our being on the Coast was known to them, and not only opened the roads but also invited into their Pa's myself and those who were on their way to see me.[26]

Early in the following year, for example, the *Eclipse* took Governor Sir George Grey to Napier, Poverty Bay, Awanui, and Opotiki to meet chiefs and discuss the general terms of a peace settlement.[27] All such activities showed how valuable naval effort was in preventing a general rebellion which, as was predicted before the new war started, would have made "a large proportion" of British settlements in North Island "untenable."[28]

Analyses of Maori warfare written in 1862-63 made only brief mention of the naval role in fighting so determined and well organized a foe. On one side, the need was for regular forces to break the elaborately fortified *pas;* on the other, the probing power of highly trained flying columns, dispersed throughout North Island, promised ready success.[29] Scarcely any contemporary thought was devoted to the naval squadron.

Ashanti War

The same neglect applied to the Ashanti campaign of 1873-74, even though that West African conflict differed signally from the Maori War. It was far shorter, a matter of months rather than years. It was less complex, because it was not connected with white settler pressures and politics, because the field of operations was an easy terrain, and because the Ashanti lacked the defensive capability and determination of the Maoris. It was vigorously celebrated, serving as it did as a vindication of the army following a period of controversial reform in 1868-71, and providing the booster rocket for the second phase of General Sir Garnet Wolseley's stellar career. Not only did Wolseley rely on the good offices of journalists who accompanied the British expedition,[30] but his reputation also sparkled in the accounts immediately written up by his subordinates.

One of them, Colonel Evelyn Wood, VC, had this to say in June 1874 at a meeting chaired by the secretary of state for war:

> As was said by Scott of Napoleon, "He was a Sovereign among Soldiers." His means were limited by time and circumstances; with a handful of men he was required to accomplish a hitherto unattainable feat. In six months, he had to re-establish our reputation lowered by successive humiliations and failures, and to read a lesson in letters of fire to the arrogant and blood-thirsty race who had defied us so long by their weapons of Distance, Disease, and Treachery.[31]

This hyperbole disguised the fact that Wolseley's command scarcely approached Napoleonic proportions: a total of 4,000 combatants by December 1873, from whom came 1,509 white troops and 708 blacks for the final advance on the Ashanti capital of Kumasi in early February 1874.[32] Nor did Wood show that the Ashanti were by October 1873 divided politically and debilitated militarily from their incursion toward the coast.[33] Finally, although Wood himself had started his career in the navy, he made no more than cursory mention of the naval squadron, a precedent largely followed since.[34]

Admiral Sir E. R. Fremantle, who served and was wounded in West Africa in 1873, offered this explanation some thirty years later:

> To the navy, as usual, had fallen the period of danger, of doubt, and uncertainty, when responsibility was involved in any step undertaken, while the forces available were inadequate. This is the normal position of a naval officer

when matters become suddenly critical, and it often receives scant consideration, as no campaign is on foot, and no correspondents are at hand to give glowing reports of the operations.[35]

While Fremantle's was a reasonable complaint, his contention skirted the truth—which was that the navy interpreted the Ashanti threat very differently from the Colonial Office and the War Office and thought it was quite capable of protecting British interests by itself in 1873. Campaign accounts written by army officers and correspondents accompanying the army in the first flush of military success deliberately excluded the squadron's work, presumably a reflection of the navy's doubts in that year over the very necessity for a land expedition.

The war began in January 1873 with a large, if lumbering, Ashanti army of perhaps up to 40,000 men moving southward into territories under British protection. The immediate occasion for this invasion was the Ashanti king's desire to assert his claims to the coastal town of Elmina, transferred in 1872 by the Ashanti, a trade the British were bound to suppress. But other factors included the personal ambitions of King Kofi Kakari, the traditional assertion of the Ashanti right to secure homage from Elmina, and the desire to challenge Britain's client Fanti confederacy that lay between the coast and the Ashanti domain. From January to October (when Wolseley reached Cape Coast Castle, the principal British base), the only forces that stood between the invaders and the coast were the Fanti allies (who were defeated in battle on 14 April), the naval squadron, Haussa police reinforced from Lagos, and 110 Royal Marines and a detachment of the West India Regiment, the latter dispatched by London in May and thrown into action immediately on their arrival in the second week of June. Yet, despite the paucity of resources, the British held Elmina and the coast; by the time Wolseley was prepared for his quick-step advance in December, the Ashanti army had been forced back across its borders and had been facing severe food shortages as early as June. The naval brigade of Royal Marines and bluejackets provided the backbone of British forces that fought three engagements at Elmina (13 June), Chamah (14 August) and, just after Wolseley's arrival, Essaman (14 October).[36]

The first of these, Elmina, was especially important since the small British force met 2,000 or 3,000 Ashanti very far forward on the outskirts of the town —their campaign's principal objective—and killed about 200 of them in a classic display of superior firepower. Fremantle, then a captain and the senior naval officer, reported: "I do not believe they will dare to face Englishmen again, at least in the plain."[37] And years later he asserted that the most frightening aspect of the encounter for the Ashanti was that they had never before seen so many men killed so quickly.[38] The army view was far less flattering. Writing in 1874, in a history described nearly a century later as the "best account of the campaign,"[39] Captain Henry Brackenbury delivered this verdict:

> The Ashantis suffered severely; but in no action of the war did any officer in command of troops get so splendid an opportunity of punishing the enemy as did Colonel Festing [Royal Marines] on this occasion. It is the only time on which the Ashantis were ever encountered on open ground, where the enormous superiority of the Snider rifle had full opportunity of displaying itself;

and one almost wonders that during an action lasting on open ground for some hours, not more than 200, out of the reported 3,000 engaged, should have been placed *hors de combat.*

Brackenbury served as Wolseley's military secretary, and his exposition of what happened before the general's arrival clearly was intended to justify the larger strategic conclusion. "As the enemy had not been pursued into the bush," he wrote, "the Ashantis retained the opinion, they were known previously to possess, that the European troops dare not advance after them into the bush."[40]

The army view was repeated as late as 1924 when Major General Sir Frederick Maurice, another member of Wolseley's staff, published a biography of his former chief. Credit was given to the defense of Elmina, but the naval squadron was only very briefly mentioned, and the theater assessment was one of imminent collapse. Maurice insisted, "it was clear that nothing less than a British occupation of Kumasi would impress the Ashantees with the reality of British power."[41] Colonel Wood in June 1874 also depicted the situation following Elmina as a stalemate lasting for three and one half months.[42] Army officers did not even deign to point out how Elmina illustrated very dramatically the naval brigade's flexibility, adaptability, and rapidity in being diverted from other duties. After all, the Royal Marines had been brought to Cape Coast Castle in the paddle steamer, *Barracouta,* lying at Gibraltar and keeping an eye on dangers to British interests threatened by civil war in Spain. It had been bound for Australia. Instead, it proceeded to Lisbon, picked up the marines sent from Plymouth, and its commander and crew participated in the fighting only slightly over a month after the decision to reinforce had been taken in London.[43] This episode showed how quickly small, but significantly potent, forces could be assembled and deployed by the navy.

More generally, the squadron covering West Africa, the Cape of Good Hope squadron, responded very effectively to the Ashanti incursion. When news of that advance reached the commodore in early February, Edmund Commerell was in Sierra Leone, on a trip to trouble spots created by indigenous warfare. One of his warships was trying to sort out further internecine rivalries at Secondee. Another was supporting the consul at Old Calabar in efforts to get rulers on the Bonny and Oporto rivers to adhere to recently concluded trading treaties. Commerell saw nothing in the local situation during February to deflect him from his original plans to proceed to the River Congo, to check on slave trading, and to Cape Town.[44] He did not return to Cape Coast Castle until 5 July.[45]

In the meantime, ships of the squadron busied themselves in efforts to contain the Ashanti advance. By 21 March three warships were at Cape Coast Castle, or about to be there, and a fourth was at Lagos. This presence enabled the British to put pressure on their allies and neighbors. For example, when the king of Elmina declined to sign an oath of allegiance to the British, he was brought to Cape Coast Castle in the *Seagull* to discuss matters with officials.[46] Until the main battle of 14 April the British relied on their Fanti allies to halt the enemy advance. Once that battle was lost, naval activity became even more important. Fremantle later emphasized, "constant visits of our ships were of good service in reassuring the loyal inhabitants of such coastal towns as

Secondee, Dix Cove, and Axim." Where friendly encouragement failed, chastisement often followed; on 28 August, for instance, Fremantle shelled Tacoraddy and Aboaddi.[47] When the *Rattlesnake* reduced the town of Chamah to "a heap of burning ruins" after two hours of shelling, the report argued: "It is not possible many Natives were killed by these measures but the lesson will be severely felt, and those who have gone to the bush will spread far and wide the punishment their disloyalty and treachery has so deeply merited." To ram the point home, a palaver was staged the next day at Secondee to inform loyal chiefs that they had nothing to fear if they proved constant.[48]

Following the Fanti defeat, the government in London decided on 10 May to send 110 marines and detachments of the West India Regiment as well as a great deal of ammunition. This deployment was effected by 7 June, entirely because naval vessels were variously available. By 20 June the six warships concentrated at Cape Coast carried thirty-one guns and 759 sailors.[49] As the senior naval officer, Captain Fremantle noted later: "It does not sound a very formidable force, but it represented much under the circumstances."[50] The bluejackets and marines were used to assert the British presence along and just beyond the coastal strip at Elmina, Chamah, and Essaman between 13 June and 14 October, the first and last being set-piece engagements.

Given this ability to repel the Ashanti—who, by 16 November, were retreating toward the Prah River[51]—Commodore Commerell on his return to the Gold Coast on 5 July naturally took an optimistic view of affairs. He concluded that Elmina and Cape Coast Castle "are in no danger, and have not been in any." He noted that the Admiralty "specifies 'that no expedition in the Interior was to be contemplated, . . . and that the Forts only were to be held,'" instructions that made good sense, for the rainy season then prevailed, and that Commerell was confident of fulfilling. Plunging into the interior seemed unappealing to him anyway, since raising native troops had proved difficult and the Fantis failed to impress with their fighting abilities—"it appears to me difficult to help a Nation unwilling to help itself." Although intelligence gathering frustrated the British, Commerell believed that Ashanti numbers were falling, perhaps to only about 10,000 to 12,000, in their main army by late July, and that he comfortably could prevent Ashanti replenishment of their contracting food stocks by controlling Elmina.[52]

These impressions from the naval commander displeased the Colonial and War offices. At the very time Commerell drew his reassuring conclusions about the safety of British coastal interests, Lord Kimberley, the colonial secretary, and Edward Cardwell, the secretary of state for war, were planning Wolseley's expedition to Kumasi. Kimberley worried that public opinion would not countenance the continuing Ashanti occupation of the protectorate inland; "all the trade of our protectorate is practically destroyed by the presence of the invading force," a fact that would make the settlements "merely a heavy burden on the Imperial Treasury."[53] Kimberley objected to Commerell's indifference to the protectorate's fate and also to his attitude: "I don't at all like the tone of Commerell's despatches. It is vexatious to have the naval officer commanding pooh-poohing the whole affair, when we are treating it as a very serious business, which it most certainly is."[54]

As preparations for the punitive expedition unfolded, the Admiralty continued to express doubts. On 12 September, Cardwell wrote to First Lord George J. Goschen:

> But what course do you recommend? Could Kimberley leave a state of things in existence, in which his Revenue is destroyed by a Barbarian invader and the people whom he assumes to govern are butchered or enslaved? Is he to eat humble pie & withdraw? Is he, like Captain Commerell, to wait in the hope that perhaps the savages may think better of it? Like the man in the play who when his house was on fire, did not send for the engine, because he thought that perhaps the fire would go out of itself?[55]

The Admiralty gave way under the weight of such remonstrances. Perhaps its resolve was weakened by Commerell's departure on 22 August for Cape Town; the commodore had sustained severe injuries in the skirmishing at Chamah on 14 August.[56] His departure removed a highly skeptical voice from the West African scene, but the doubts he repeatedly raised about the seriousness of the Ashanti threat may well explain why the army accounts of the war compiled in 1874 were so grudging toward the naval contribution during "the period of danger" from April to August 1873.

In fact, Wolseley's punitive expedition, which had to complete its task by March 1874 and the onset of the rainy season, depended on the naval squadron for three things: coastal protection and a mobile base off a littoral notoriously dangerous to Europeans' health; a blockade to prevent the enemy from securing any additional weapons and ammunition; and hospital ships and a seaborne ambulance service to keep down casualties, which might have been high and therefore politically damaging to an already ailing Liberal government in London. The first of these tasks was easily achieved. But the success of Wolseley's expedition and its low casualty levels depended on keeping the troops on board ship until they could be landed and immediately marched into the Ashanti kingdom, along roads prepared by Africans under British supervision and stocked amply with supply depots and resting places.[57] The second task, the blockade, was condoned by the colonial administrator, Colonel Robert W. Harley, on the senior naval officer's advice after Commerell left. The blockade applied to the whole Gold Coast and provoked controversy at home because of its dubious legality. Its justification was that much smuggling of powder, lead, and weapons occurred, effected by, for example, Dutch ships and the connivance of unfriendly tribes controlling parts of the coast. A general blockade was easy to operate; the alternative, of meticulously searching suspect ships on which materiel of war would be very carefully concealed, promised to be merely time consuming. In the navy's view supplies were indeed cut down, creating shortages in the main Ashanti camp. More generally, Captain Fremantle, its firmest advocate, argued that the blockade "has made the Coast tribes feel our power, and, if not relaxed, it alone will in time make them sue for peace and forgiveness." Wolseley (who took on civil as well as military power over the protectorates) decided on 11 December, following inquiries from London, that some blockading had been invalid. The coast westward from Elmina to the boundary of French territory remained under blockade, however, for it offered too convenient a supply route to the Ashanti for the general's liking.[58]

The third naval contribution was a practical and largely overlooked one. The hospital and ambulance service planned and provided by the navy helped make Wolseley's expedition both a shining contrast to, say, the Crimean winter of 1854–55, and a legend for its modest casualties. The pride of the naval contribution was the *Victor Emanuel*, a 79-gun screw steamship launched in 1855 and completely refitted as a hospital vessel from 15 September to 30 November 1873. The very closest planning went into its design, layout, and furnishings. It had a capacity for 250 patients. Between sailing for the Gold Coast on 30 November and leaving for the return journey on 26 February 1874, the ship accommodated a total of 565 invalids, of whom only thirteen died on board. In addition, three naval transports furnished a total of 300 places off shore.[59] For a planned force of 1,500 European troops and 1,000 soldiers of the West India Regiment, there were 550 places immediately available at the coast.

Moreover, careful preparations ensured that steamship lines' vessels could assist in the removal of invalids direct to Britain or to Porto Grande on St. Vincent, Cape Verdes, where the *Simoom*, described as a "commodious and well ventilated hospital,"[60] provided 100 more places for men unable to be sent home immediately. Packets of the British and African Company called twice per month and could take twelve to twenty patients home from Cape Coast. Three steam vessels specifically were detailed to provide a service every ten days from Cape Coast to the *Simoom*. From there packets of the Union Company, returning from the Cape of Good Hope, and of the Royal Mail Company, returning from South America, could pick up small numbers of invalids. Between them these companies would furnish five visits per month to St. Vincent.[61] Altogether, these arrangements worked satisfactorily. It appears all the more curious that this well-planned naval contribution to Wolseley's campaign should have been overlooked.

In these various ways, the naval squadron, though small, helped contain the Ashanti thrusts to the coast, galvanize African allies, defeat Ashanti forces in the field, deploy British troops, and keep British casualties low. But the value of naval power lay not simply in its support role, however manifold and persistent that was; it lay also in the effect that the holding operation of April–October and the engagements of those months had on Ashanti strength and morale. The Ashanti retreat began before any imperial soldiers had arrived and was completed before Wolseley set off for Kumasi. This was a contribution to the success of Wolseley's expedition and the projection of British power that the politicians and the army, frustrated by the navy's skepticism over the need for a campaign inland, made no effort to recognize in the prolific writings on the war.

In the twenty-five years between the end of the Ashanti War and the beginning of the second Anglo-Boer War, naval squadrons and brigades variously were called upon to assert British interests or influence. The most prominent example of a diplomatic demonstration of British power was the Mediterranean fleet's passage of the Dardanelles in 1878. The principal example of the military use of naval power was the bombardment of Alexandria in 1882 and the conveyance of the British army that triumphed at Tel-el-Kebir in the same year. The use of naval brigades for inland operations was very well illustrated by the campaigning on the Nile from 1883 to 1885 and in the Burma

War of 1885.[62] But it is worth concluding this discussion with a brief look at a far larger conflict.

Boer War

The Anglo-Boer War of 1899-1902 was a conflict of a totally different order from the Maori War or the Ashanti campaign. Despite its scale and the attention lavished upon it at the time and by historians since, the naval role has been neglected or played down.[63] Briefly, that role may be defined as transporting the British armies to South Africa, blockading the coast north of Durban to stop the Transvaal from gaining access to foreign arms supplies, and providing naval brigades for land operations. Each of these contributions was most important in 1899-1900, before the guerrilla phase of the war began.

The Admiralty supervised and organized the transporting of 396,311 soldiers to South Africa from the United Kingdom, India, and the white settler colonies.[64] Colonel Calwell saw this concentration of force as a shining example of what could be achieved, given command of the seas.[65] Others, including historians since 1902, simply have assumed the inevitability of such an operation. According to the *Times History*, "it is as well to remember that any other result would have been utterly discreditable to the greatest naval and maritime power in the world."[66] Yet the colossal transport operation—involving, for example, the passage of 197,000 men and 90,000 horses and mules in 351 vessel-arrivals, essentially between the beginning of October 1899 and early May 1900[67]—showed that the Admiralty coped effectively with an unprecedented job of coordinating an array of private steamship companies. This efficiency deserves a somewhat more positive recognition than the *Times* accorded it. And, clearly, without the Admiralty's promptly organizing transport on this scale from so many places, the British recovery from the battlefield reverses of December 1899 and their steamroller advance into the Transvaal during 1900 would have been impossible.

On a more minor level, but one overlooked by Clowes, was the Cape squadron's blockade of the coast north of Durban. A Delagoa Bay and Natal division was formed in November 1899 with three ships. By 20 June 1900 those three vessels each had spent between 126 and 138 days at sea, blockading. The HMS *Magicienne*, the divisional senior naval officer's vessel, cruised for about 12,000 miles in this period. By June, the division totaled ten warships. Although it reported capturing only two prizes, bearing the delightfully and appositely contrasting names *Bundesrath* and *Matabele*, this fact may have shown the blockade's effectiveness in preventing vessels with supplies for the Transvaal from approaching, let alone entering, Delagoa Bay.[68]

The third naval contribution to the South African war was the provision of small naval brigades armed with the latest artillery. Although these brigades' land operations were not as significant in relation to the total British war effort as were similar contributions against the Maoris and the Ashanti, they still made important local impacts. This was especially the case with the swift and flexible deployment of naval gunnery. The most dramatic instance of adaptability was the well-known conversion by Captain Percy Scott of 12-pounder,

12-hundredweight guns from the cruiser *Terrible* for use on land. Scott called at Cape Town on 14 October 1899 on his route to China. By 3 November and just in the nick of time, his ship's guns provided the only long-range defense of the besieged garrison at Ladysmith.[69] In addition, two naval brigades served with the army in its drive into the Transvaal and in Natal outside Ladysmith. Their participation ended in October 1900, but they brought very heavy guns to bear far inland during the "formal" period of the war against the Boers.[70] One unit under Commander W. L. Grant, RN, covered over 966 miles in sixty-seven days of actual marching between January and early October 1900; its rate of progress on land rivaled that of any troops in South Africa.[71]

Thomas Pakenham, however, has wondered, like the *Times History* before him, quite how valuable the heavy guns were, and his history of the Boer War gives little weight to the mobile naval brigades of 1900.[72] His question merits extended technical assessment beyond the scope of this paper. But it might be stressed here that the big guns primarily countered Boer long-range artillery. They prevented the enemy from gaining an advantage rather than according one to the British. More dynamically, the naval guns helped discomfort and dislodge Boer emplacements and so removed impediments to the British advance. Enemy guns were pinned down or driven back; enemy soldiers were sometimes scared off hills; occasionally, distant enemy laagers were broken up. If the naval brigades did not claim to inflict direct hits or heavy casualties, they believed themselves, with good reason, to be vital in maintaining the momentum of British progress against a foe who possessed long-range artillery that had to be neutralized if British objectives were to be secured.[73]

It is fitting to end this brief discussion with a consideration of the naval brigade in the Transvaal, for Clowes concluded in 1903 his monumental seven-volume history of the world's proudest, largest navy with accounts of the expeditions in 1900 to Pretoria and Peking. The latter, an international relief operation led by Vice Admiral Sir Edward Seymour, is better known than the small brigade at work on the high veld. The point made by these two expeditions, however, was the same one. Clowes regretted "the frequency, previously unparalleled, with which the officers and men of the service, either with troops or alone, have been employed to do what should be purely landmen's work, all over both hemispheres, sometimes fighting hundreds of miles from the sea."[74] In the years to follow, the Admiralty and the intellectuals alike were to concentrate even more determinedly than hitherto upon European waters and European challenges, leaving one recurrent role of Victoria's navy to languish uncelebrated in obscurity.

From these three examples, it is possible to offer a more general statement of how the Royal Navy contributed to the projection of British power in the late nineteenth century. Not only did the navy make the application of British force possible by offering or organizing transport, but it also sustained campaigns by supplying food, materiel, and, very important in West Africa, both hospitals and a long-distance ambulance service. In North Island, mobility within the theater of war depended wholly on the navy; and in South Africa, there were occasions when naval transport moved troops quickly from the Natal front to Cape Colony and thence up by rail into the Orange Free State. Once fighting began, the naval brigades proved to be fruitful sources of heavy artillery and of shock troops. The campaigning in North Island in 1863-64 would have been even slower than it was, if not impossible, without naval navigational expertise and assistance and without the heavy naval guns. The British position on the Gold Coast in 1873 would have collapsed without the naval squadron and the energetic defense of Elmina. And the severe weakening of the Ashanti offensive—which allowed Wolseley to attack a defensive, debilitated, and politically divided enemy—was the result of the naval presence and the encouragement afforded by that presence to Fanti and other allies. Without the introduction of naval guns (from a cruiser en route to China), it seems likely that Ladysmith would have fallen to the Boers in 1899. The wider use of naval artillery far inland in South Africa helped the British counter the Boers' initial advantage in weaponry.

More generally, the navy provided surprise. Unexpectedly large forces could be brought to bear quickly, even suddenly, by the tempo of nineteenth-century campaigning beyond Europe. The 110 marines from Portsmouth reaching Cape Coast Castle in three weeks, partly through the good offices of a paddle steamer destined for Australia, furnished one minor example. And the enormous concentration in South Africa of men, horses, and mules from Britain, Southern Europe, North America, Argentina, Australasia, and India furnish the most spectacular case. The Maoris, Ashanti, and Boers could not have predicted the sheer scale of force that the British, courtesy of the navy, were able to project. Rapid and reasonably substantial deployment also enabled the British to maintain the "spirit of the offensive," the belief in which was especially vital to their performance in colonial warfare. As Calwell asserted: "The lower races are impressionable. They are greatly influenced by a resolute bearing and a determined course of action."[75] Naval power afforded the springboard for launching offensives and the support, supplies, and even shock troops to sustain them. But it also gave the British a more subtle instrument to exert power.

During the South African war, the Delagoa Bay blockade was an insurance against the Boers' replenishing their military materiel and against their expanding upon a European diplomatic offensive. During the Ashanti campaign, the squadron blockaded part of the coast and enabled the British to keep their allies up to the mark; gunboat diplomacy contained the Ashanti by making it difficult for them to extend their influence politically among the coastal tribes. Finally, the campaign in North Island depended heavily upon the Australia squadron's work in boosting Maori allies' morale and in limiting the spread of rebellion. Pinpointing major objectives against which to launch decisive military blows was thus signally assisted by naval activity in limiting the extension of enemy influence or power. In these various ways, the Royal Navy contributed to the success of three important campaigns in which its role largely has been overlooked or neglected.

NOTES

1. Brian Bond, ed., *Victorian Military Campaigns* (London, 1967), 26-27.
2. Anthony Preston and John Major, *Send a Gunboat! A Study of the Gunboat and its Role in British Policy, 1854-1904* (London, 1967), 185.

3. Ronald Hyam, *Britain's Imperial Century, 1815-1914: A Study of Empire and Expansion* (London, 1976), 20-25, 125-26; Bernard Porter, *The Lion's Share: A Short History of British Imperialism, 1850-1983* (London, 1984), 13, 123-25; T. O. Lloyd, *The British Empire, 1558-1983* (Oxford, 1984), 138-39, 229, 275; James L. Stokesbury, *Navy and Empire* (London, 1984), 222-26, 235-36, 253-57, 278-80, 287-89. An excellent study of an earlier period, C. J. Bartlett, *Great Britain and Sea Power, 1815-1853* (Oxford, 1963), concentrates on policymaking and European threats. As one naval historian said of the nineteenth century: "The influence of sea power upon the British Empire is a subject which deserves far greater attention than it has hitherto received." Colin S. White, "The Bombardment of Alexandria, 1882," *Mariner's Mirror* 66 (1980): 31.

4. As may be seen in Paul Kennedy, *The Rise and Fall of British Naval Mastery* (London, 1983), 177-202, and Arthur J. Marder, *British Naval Policy, 1880-1905* (London, n.d.).

5. P. H. Colomb, *Naval Warfare: Its Ruling Principles and Practice Historically Treated* (London, 1891), viii, 415-16; Gerald S. Graham, *The Politics of Naval Supremacy* (Cambridge, 1965), 107.

6. George S. Clarke, *The Navy and the Nation of Naval Warfare and Imperial Defence* (London, 1897), passim.

7. Hew Strachan, *European Armies and the Conduct of War* (London, 1983), 76, 89.

8. C. E. Calwell, *Small Wars: Their Principles and Practice* (London, 1896), 37-39; C. E. Calwell, *The Effect of Maritime Command on Land Campaigns since Waterloo* (Edinburgh, 1897), 328-31; C. E. Calwell, *Military Operations and Maritime Preponderance: Their Relations and Interdependence* (Edinburgh, 1905), 22, 148-49, 178-80, 193-94.

9. G. G. Aston, *Letters on Amphibious Wars* (London, 1911), vii-viii, 360.

10. Geoffrey Callender, *The Naval Side of British History* (London, 1924), 234-37.

11. Sir W. Laird Clowes, *The Royal Navy: A History from the Earliest Times to the Death of Queen Victoria*, 7 vols. (London, 1897-1903).

12. Preston and Major, *Send a Gunboat!*, 122-23.

13. None of these wars is mentioned in Graham, *Politics of Naval Supremacy*. There is only a trivial reference to the Boer War in D. M. Schurman, *The Education of a Navy: The Development of British Naval Strategic Thought, 1867-1914* (London, 1965), indication enough of their lack of impact on contemporary naval analysis.

14. James Cowan, *The New Zealand Wars: A History of the Maori Campaigns and the Pioneering Period*, 2 vols. (Wellington, 1922); M. P. K. Sorrensen, "Maori and Pakeha," in *The Oxford History of New Zealand*, ed. W. H. Oliver (Oxford, 1981), 174-77, 182-84.

15. David Syrett, "The Methodology of British Amphibious Operations during the Seven Years and American Wars," *Mariner's Mirror* 58 (1972): 269-80.

16. Wiseman to Secretary of the Admiralty, 30 October 1863, London, Public Record Office (hereafter PRO), (Admiralty Records) ADM1/5817.

17. Clowes, *Royal Navy* 7:177-86.

18. Officers also gained promotions and honors from their zeal in these campaigns. Clowes lists the promotions won in the first year of this Maori war. Far more honors were obtained from the Ashanti and Boer wars. The effect of service in gunboat actions may be illustrated from one incident in 1878. Vice Admiral G. T. Phipps Hornby, who had not been in action since 1840 (although he held a high administrative reputation), commanded the Mediterranean fleet when it entered the Dardanelles in a demonstration of British power. Both his second in command, Rear Admiral Sir Edmund Commerell, and one of his six battleship captains, Sir William Hewitt, already held the KCB, secured for their services as commodores of the Cape of Good Hope squadron during the Ashanti War. Both men also held the VC from the Crimean War. Ibid., 181, 186, 262, 291, 295, 471, 476. For South Africa, see *A Supplement: The Names of the Following Officers Appear in the Reports of the Naval Commander-in-Chief*, PRO, ADM1/7453.

19. Clowes, *Royal Navy* 7:179-82; Wiseman to Secretary of the Admiralty, 28 February, 3 April 1864, PRO, ADM1/5868.

20. Clowes, *Royal Navy* 7:260, 522-23; Leigh Maxwell, *The Ashanti Ring: Sir Garnet Wolseley's Campaigns, 1870-1882* (London, 1985), 213.

21. James Bellich, "The New Zealand Wars, 1845-1870: An Analysis of Their History and Interpretation" (D.Phil. dissertation, University of Oxford, 1982), 274-79, expertly questions the military effectiveness of these bombardments.

22. Russell to Grey, 1 February 1864, enclosed in Sir George Grey to Commodore Wiseman, 3 February 1864; Wiseman to Secretary of Admiralty (2 letters), 28 February 1864, PRO, ADM 1/5868.

23. Captain J. F. C. Hamilton to Wiseman, 19 April 1864, enclosed in Wiseman to Secretary of Admiralty, 4 May 1864, ibid.

24. Wiseman to Secretary of Admiralty, 7 December 1864, ibid.

25. Wiseman to Secretary of Admiralty, 7 March 1865; E. R. Fremantle, letter of proceedings, enclosed in Wiseman to Secretary of Admiralty, 22 May 1865, PRO, ADM 1/5925.

26. Captain J. P. Luce to Sir George Grey, 11 May 1865, enclosed in Wiseman to Secretary of Admiralty, ibid.

27. Wiseman to Secretary of Admiralty, 26 April 1866, PRO, ADM 1/5969.

28. Captain Pasley, RE, "The War in New Zealand," *Journal of the Royal United Services Institution* 6 (1862): 584.

29. Ibid., 583–88; Colonel H. J. Ware, "New Zealand—Its Occupation and Defence against Native Aggression," *Journal of the Royal United Services Institution* 7 (1863): 154–56.

30. Lucy Brown, "The Treatment of the News in Mid-Victorian Newspapers," *Transactions of the Royal Historical Society* 27 (1977): 38.

31. Colonel Evelyn Wood, "The Ashanti Expedition of 1873–74," *Journal of the Royal United Services Institution* 18 (1875): 357.

32. John Keegan, "The Ashanti Campaign, 1873–74," in *Victorian Military Campaigns*, ed. Brian Bond (London, 1967), 185, 190.

33. Ibid., 177, 182. One irony of the conflict is that just as the British Cabinet in October 1873 still hesitated to authorize the dispatch of 1,500 imperial troops, so the Ashanti Council took the first steps to withdrawal. After Gladstone's ministry decided on 17 November to send three battalions, the Ashanti Council, appalled by heavy losses earlier in the year, then decided formally to retreat. By 29 November the main Ashanti force had crossed the Prah back into Ashanti territory; it entered Kumasi on 22 December only five days after the three British battalions had arrived at Cape Coast Castle. W. David McIntyre, "British Policy in West Africa: The Ashanti Expedition of 1873–74," *Historical Journal* 5 (1962): 36–38, 45; Maxwell, *Ashanti Ring*, 45; Ivor Wilkes, *Ashanti in the Nineteenth Century: The Structure and Evolution of a Political Order* (Cambridge, 1975), 82–83, 505–8.

34. Wood, "The Ashanti Expedition," 331–57; Keegan, "The Ashanti Campaign," 163–98; Maxwell, *Ashanti Ring*, 19, 22, 23, 26, 29, 35, 58, 73, 74.

35. Sir E. R. Fremantle, *The Navy As I Have Known It: 1849–1899* (London, 1904), 214.

36. Keegan, "The Ashanti Campaign," 168–74, 177–79, 182; Wood, "The Ashanti Expedition," 331–39; Clowes, *Royal Navy* 7:247–57.

37. Captain Fremantle to Commodore Commerell, 17 June 1873, enclosed in Admiralty to Colonial Office, 13 July 1873, *Further Papers Relating to the Ashantee Invasion*, PRO, (Colonial Office Records), CO 879/4.

38. Fremantle, *The Navy As I Have Known It*, 198.

39. Bond, *Victorian Military Campaigns*, 315.

40. Henry Brackenbury, *The Ashanti War: A Narrative. Prepared from the Official Documents by Permission of Major-General Sir Garnet Wolseley*, 2 vols. (Edinburgh, 1874), 1:76–77. Brackenbury mentions naval activity very much by way of background and without further analysis (73–77, 83–84, 86, 93–96). The action on open ground almost certainly was far briefer than Brackenbury's "some hours" implied, and the naval brigade had been in the field for twelve hours by the time that final engagement occurred! Fremantle to Commerell, 17 June 1873, enclosed in Admiralty to Colonial Office, 13 July 1873, *Further Papers*, PRO, CO 879/4.

41. Major General Sir F. Maurice and Sir George Arthur, *The Life of Lord Wolseley* (London, 1924), 61, 65.

42. Wood, "The Ashanti Expedition," 335–36.

43. Fremantle, *The Navy As I Have Known It*, 183.

44. Commodore Commerell to Secretary of Admiralty, 4, 20 January, 1, 12 February, 2 March, 14 April 1873, PRO, ADM 1/6260.

45. Commerell to Secretary of Admiralty, 12 July 1873, ibid.

46. Commander Ernest A. Stubbs to Secretary of Admiralty, 21 March 1873, enclosed in Admiralty to Colonial Office, 15 April 1873, *Copies and Extracts...*, PRO, CO 879/4.

47. Fremantle, *The Navy As I Have Known It*, 200-1, 203-5.
48. Commerell to Secretary of Admiralty, 15 August 1873, PRO, ADM 1/6260.
49. Admiralty to Colonial Office, 26 June 1873. *Further Papers*, PRO, CO 879/4.
50. Fremantle, *The Navy As I Have Known It*, 189.
51. Commodore Hewett to Secretary of Admiralty, 16 November 1873, PRO, ADM 1/6260.
52. Commerell to Secretary of Admiralty, 8, 22, 24 July, 3, 5 August 1873, ibid.
53. Kimberley to Cardwell, 26 July 1873, Edward Cardwell Papers, PRO, P.R.O. 30/48, file 33. The politics of the preparations for war are well described in W. David McIntyre, "British Policy in West Africa," 26-46, and in W. David McIntyre, *The Imperial Frontier in the Tropics, 1865-75* (London, 1967), 143-50. There also are some excellent points in Freda Harcourt, "Gladstone, Monarchism and the 'New' Imperialism, 1868-74," *Journal of Imperial and Commonwealth History* 14 (1985): 20-51. This emphasizes that Gladstone's ministry had been discredited in the field of foreign policy in 1872. It was divided and precarious in itself and was faced with mounting and parliamentary pressure for action, with press coverage of Ashanti affairs becoming very prominent from September 1873 (ibid., 38-41). It should be noted, however, that the Cabinet did not decide to give Wolseley imperial battalions until 17 November and had been very reluctant to commit British troops (McIntyre, "British Policy in West Africa," 36-38). None of the existing accounts scrutinizes the naval opposition to the Kumasi campaign, except to mention the First Lord of the Admiralty's lack of enthusiasm for it. The significance of the dispute over policy also is missed by Thomas J. Spinner, Jr., *George Joachim Goschen: The Transformation of a Victorian Liberal* (Cambridge, 1973), 41-42.
54. Kimberley to Cardwell, 21 August 1873, Cardwell Papers, PRO, P.R.O. 30/48, file 33.
55. Cardwell to Goschen, 12 September 1873, Cardwell Papers, ibid., 30/48, file 27. Goschen had noted that the Ashanti appeared to be retreating, not advancing, and that an expedition to a region with so harmful a climate would not be worth the high costs. Commerell's assessment was a "strong" one. The First Lord felt "so uncomfortable" and "so doubtful" about the expedition that he was "bound to unburden myself of my views." Goschen to Cardwell, 8 September 1873, ibid.
56. Commerell to Secretary of Admiralty, 22 August 1873, Commander Thompson to Secretary of Admiralty, 14 October 1873, PRO, ADM 1/6260.
57. Keegan, "The Ashanti Campaign," 195.
58. Fremantle, *The Navy As I Have Known It*, 107-8; Fremantle to Kimberley, 27 November 1873, enclosed in Colonial Office to Foreign Office, 19 January 1874, and Wolseley to Hewett, 11 December 1873, enclosed in Wolseley to Kimberley, 16 December 1873, *Further Correspondence Respecting the Ashantee Invasion*, PRO, CO 879/6.
59. Vice Admiral A. P. Ryder, "The Fitting of Her Majesty's Ship, 'Victor Emanuel' As a Hospital Ship during the Late Ashantee Campaign," *Journal of the Royal United Services Institution* 18 (1875): 383-400.
60. Commerell to Secretary of Admiralty, 20 August 1873, PRO, ADM 1/6260. The *Simoon* then was stationed off Cape Coast Castle.
61. Director of Transport to Admiralty Board, 9 October 1873, Admiralty to Commodore Hewett, 21 November 1873, PRO (Ministry of Transport Records), MT 23/38. I.T. 3798/73. I am grateful to Dr. Andrew Porter for advice concerning this source.
62. Clowes, *Royal Navy* 7:292-99, 323-46, 350-71, 375-84.
63. Thomas Pakenham, *The Boer War* (London, 1982), 161, 203, 217-30 passim, 267, 274-75, 363. He refers briefly to naval guns and naval brigades in various battles and sieges. Peter Warwick, ed., *The South African War: The Anglo-Boer War, 1899-1902* (London, 1980), offers no discussion of the naval contribution. These are the two preeminent modern accounts.
64. L. S. Amery, ed., *The Times History of the War in South Africa, 1899-1902*, 6 vols. (London, 1909), 6:279, 282-96. See Table 1.
65. Calwell, *Military Operations and Maritime Preponderance*, 190.
66. Amery, *Times History* 6:282.
67. I use the term vessel-arrivals because some vessels made repeat journeys.
68. Captain W. B. Fisher to Rear Admiral Sir Robert Harris, n.d., enclosed in Harris to Secretary of Admiralty, 2 July 1900, PRO, ADM 1/7454A.
69. Clowes, *Royal Navy* 7:463-71; *A Supplement*, PRO, ADM 1/7453.

70. Their activities are very fully recounted in Clowes, *Royal Navy* 7:471–518. No mention is made of blockading or of transporting.

71. Commander W. L. Grant to Captain J. E. Bearcroft, 9 October 1900, *London Gazette*, 12 March 1901, 1756. The figures given here do not tally with those in Clowes, *Royal Navy* 7:492.

72. Pakenham, *Boer War*, 203, 267.

73. Grant to Bearcroft, 1 June 1900, *London Gazette*, 12 March 1901; Amery, *Times History* 6:487. It was pointed out that the Boers fired 20,000 shells into Ladysmith during a period of four months and inflicted only 300 casualties by such long-range fire. Shelling parapets and entrenchments generally achieved nothing. However, it could be said that just as the Boer shelling of Ladysmith disrupted the defenders' organization and pinned them down effectively, so British long-range shelling in their major advances disrupted enemy lines and reserves. Ibid., 476–78, 483–85, 487.

74. Clowes, *Royal Navy* 7:vii. Calwell, *Military Operations and Maritime Preponderance*, 156, while praising sailors' versatility, stressed that their proper place was on ships.

75. Calwell, *Small Wars*, 62.

The Diplomat versus the Sailor: Armed Intervention in Taiwan, 1867

DAVID F. LONG

Diplomatic relations between naval officers and civilians, which often determined the success or failure of nineteenth-century American foreign policy, are a long-standing source of controversy and debate. In this essay, Professor Long examines the dealings between an American admiral and a consul concerning atrocities committed against westerners by native tribes on Formosa's southern coast in 1867. While in many instances the naval officer outshines the diplomat, such was not the case here.

****

To those engaged in shipping along the south China coast, the shores of Taiwan (Formosa) were known as a graveyard for merchantmen.[1] Between 1850 and 1869, thirty-two vessels were shattered upon the rocks; of that number, sixteen were looted and three had all their survivors massacred.[2] The local assailants had nothing to fear from any official reprisals, for the island's extreme south was an administrative no-man's-land. Legally, Taiwan was part of China, an extension of Fukien Province. Chinese authority, however, was restricted to Taiwan's western coast, but even there it ended some twenty miles above the southern tip.[3] That area and more remained in the hands of the indigenous aborigines, joined in a loose confederation under "Tok-e-Tok, chief of the eighteen tribes," among them his own Koaluts.[4]

During early March 1867 the American bark *Rover*, commanded by Captain Joseph W. Hunt, sailed from Swatow, China, north for Newschwang (now Yinkow) in Manchuria. Three days out, a storm drove the ship on the rocks called "Vele Rete" just off Taiwan's southern extremity. The foundering *Rover* was abandoned. The captain, his wife, the European second mate, and three Chinese hands took to one boat, the American first mate and six Chinese to the other. After almost a full day of rowing, Hunt came into Lang Ch'iao Bay, about eleven miles above the southern tip. It is impossible to reconstruct what happened from the testimony of the *Rover*'s only survivor and later evidence provided by the tribesmen responsible for the attack. Mrs. Hunt came upon an aboriginal woman, gave her some money, and sent her for help. Instead, the woman reported the presence of the newcomers to her fellow Koaluts whose warriors came boiling out of the thick underbrush, killing Mrs. Hunt before dispatching her husband and the others coming to her aid.

Tek-kwang, a Chinese sailor, managed to hide out temporarily and eventually escaped. A little later those in the second boat arrived at the same spot and were quickly murdered.[5]

Tek-kwang made his way to Taiwan-fu (Tainan) and told his story to resident British Consul Charles Carroll and to Commander George Broad of the sloop HMS *Cormorant*. They agreed to investigate the matter and steamed south immediately to see if any of the *Rover*'s people might still be alive. But when thirty-seven sailors tried to go ashore at Lang Ch'iao late in March, they were met by a steady rattle of gunfire from the heavy growth behind the beach. The entire party was hurriedly recalled after one Briton had been wounded by "a spent slug in the abdomen." The *Cormorant* lobbed "a few shells" into the bush before returning to Taiwan-fu. Broad had called off his expedition, realizing that it would have been folly "to risk the lives of his men in pursuit of an invisible enemy in the jungle, where every advantage would have been on their side."[6]

As no U.S. diplomat was stationed on Taiwan, that island was considered under the jurisdiction of the Amoy consul. He was Charles W. LeGendre, French-born and University of Paris-educated, who married an American girl and became a naturalized citizen. He served as an officer in the Union army during the Civil War, and after being twice wounded (losing an eye in the process), was brevetted a brigadier general. His Amoy appointment was in part a recognition of his able service. When his consulship ended in 1872, he became an adviser to the Japanese government for three years and encouraged his employers to occupy temporarily southern Taiwan during 1874. He remained in Japan, engaging in private business from 1875 to 1890, and advised the king of Korea from then until his death in 1899.[7]

As soon as LeGendre heard about the *Rover* atrocity, he went at once to Foochow where he asked Li Fu-t'ai, governor of Fukien Province, to order his subordinates on Taiwan to rescue any survivors of that vessel and "to inflict just punishment, with the utmost rigor," on the murderers. He justified his request by referring to Articles XI and XIII of the Sino-American Treaty of Tientsin (1858), by which the Chinese government granted to U.S. citizens within its boundaries the same protection as that guaranteed for its own subjects. The governor agreed to act, but he notified his officials on Taiwan that should the impulsive American personally visit them and try to start anything on his own initiative, "please invite him not to do so, for those savages might give him more trouble than he thinks."[8]

Li's apprehensions were warranted, for LeGendre was determined to apply some on-the-spot pressure to accelerate a Chinese response in the matter. He sailed on that errand with Commander John C. Febiger in the gunboat USS *Ashuelot*. Arriving at Taiwan-fu in mid-April, they conferred with Wu-t'ing, the Tao-t'ai (superintendent of customs at a treaty port, among other duties), and General Liu Ming-teng, commanding Chinese forces on the island. Febiger offered to aid Liu's military operations by using the *Ashuelot* to tow his soldiers into action against the tribesmen. The general replied that he was not yet ready to move. When the Americans offered to wait for him, they were told politely but firmly that he must act unilaterally. The meeting ended with LeGendre and Febiger repeating that U.S. rights under the Treaty of Tientsin must be upheld. Actually, there was little likelihood at this time of any vigorous Chinese endeavors to avenge the *Rover*'s victims. Liu and the Tao-t'ai looked with dread upon a plunge into the forbidding interior on what they deemed a hopeless mission, having already turned down a similar appeal from British Consul Carroll. Their negativism was reinforced by their belief that China had no jurisdiction over the aborigines in the extreme south. They admitted as much when they said that "those savages are like animals... like Monkeys.... Their territory is not on our Maps, they do not obey our laws."[9]

Following a stopover at Takao (now Kaohsiung), LeGendre and Febiger decided to look into the scene of the massacre. They took the *Ashuelot* to the southernmost Chinese village, picked up some pilots, and went on the few miles to Lang Ch'iao Bay. There they mulled over their options. With only a gunboat's personnel available, no landing in force could be seriously considered, nor could they expect any Chinese cooperation. LeGendre informed Secretary of State William H. Seward that he and Febiger "feared by interfering in the least way with the Chinese officials, they might claim as a redeeming point of their inaction our own intervention." Under these intelligent considerations, departure seemed the only sensible course to adopt. The *Ashuelot* weighed anchor on 24 April and reached Amoy two days later.[10]

Febiger reported to his superior, Rear Admiral Henry H. Bell, commander of the navy's Asiatic Squadron, outlining the difficulty of a hostile incursion into the area where the *Rover* tragedy had occurred and emphasizing in particular the terrain. The hills were "well-wooded, with thick undergrowth coming down close to the water." Because of the damp climate and the prevailing winds, this heavy cover could not be burned off. He concluded that landings under the protective fire of heavy guns would be no problem, but even with as many as 150 to 200 men in an attack force, penetrating any distance inland would be most troublesome and could accomplish nothing.[11]

Bell undoubtedly perused Febiger's letter, but he might as well have filed it unread in his wastebasket, for he paid no attention to anything it said. This is surprising, for he had had a praiseworthy career. A North Carolinian by birth, Bell had been commissioned in 1823, first campaigning against pirates in the West Indies and then progressing slowly but steadily up the chain of command. He had been with Commodore James Armstrong and Commander Andrew H. Foote at Canton in 1856; after the Chinese had fired upon American ships trying to reach the city, sailors and marines stormed and razed the four huge stone barrier forts guarding it. Despite his Southern background, Bell sided with the Union in 1861 and served with distinction throughout the war, especially as Rear Admiral David G. Farragut's fleet captain during the capture of New Orleans in 1862. Three years later he was rewarded with his Far East post.[12] The navy's old East India Squadron had been allowed to disintegrate from 1861 to 1865, and the Asiatic Squadron had been established at the end of hostilities to replace it.

Late in June Secretary of State Seward gave Anson Burlingame, U.S. minister to Peking, the following instructions in reference to the *Rover*. He was: 1) to ascertain the facts in the case; 2) to find out whether China actually ruled southernmost Taiwan, and if so, "to demand investigation and punishment" of those responsible for killing American citizens; 3) if outside Chinese jurisdiction, to suggest what alternatives might be "adopted with a view to obtain redress and to prevent such transactions in the future"; and 4) to realize that "you are advised that in no case do the United States desire to seize and hold possession of Formosa or any part of said island."[13]

Although Bell would assault the Koaluts long before Seward's letter reached him, his reasoning processes during mid-1869 could hardly have been more opaque. No instructions were forwarded to him from Washington authorizing him in any way to conduct forcible operations in Taiwan, whether in league with the Chinese or not. Even more to the point, during April Burlingame had asked him to do no more than to investigate the matter and to "cooperate with the Chinese" on the *Rover* incident.[14] Nothing in the records suggests that Bell ever approached a single Chinese bureaucrat on that subject.[15] Furthermore, he utterly disregarded the experiences and recommendations of Febiger and LeGendre. He shrugged off the commander's report about the discouraging prospects of any worthwhile offensive at Lang Ch'iao Bay. LeGendre later recalled that he also had thought that it would be "perfectly useless" for an invader to attempt to coerce the Koaluts into compliance without Chinese assistance. He forecast that unilateral efforts there would "very likely not only fail, but would also meet with severe reverses." He asserted that "I requested the Admiral to cooperate with me in carrying out these views, which were endorsed by Capt. [*sic*] Febiger. But my advice was not listened to." Indeed, Bell behaved throughout as if he were unaware that his two compatriots already had visited the exact locale into which he would soon intrude. Although both could have joined him quickly in Shanghai, he issued no such invitations.[16]

On 7 June Bell headed for Taiwan in his flagship, the *Hartford*, accompanied by the corvette *Wyoming*, and picked up en route guides and interpreters at Takao. A week later the Americans came into Lang Ch'iao Bay, and at once it became clear that any landing would be resisted. The admiral reported to Washington that, "soon after we anchored, the savages, dressed in clouts and with their bodies painted red, were seen, through our glasses, assembling in parties of ten or twelve on the cleared hills about two miles distant, their muscles gleaming in the sun."[17] Shore operations were placed under the direction of Commander George W. Belknap, the *Hartford*'s chief executive officer, who decided to divide his sailors and marines from both ships into two prongs. He and his second in command, Lieutenant Alexander S. Mackenzie, would proceed inland with about half of his 181 men. Lieutenant John J. Read would go ashore with the rest some three-quarters of a mile to the east. The two detachments were supposed to rendezvous atop the crests mentioned by Bell, thereby closing a pincers movement.[18]

The expedition immediately plunged into an inferno. One officer wrote that after his invaders had incinerated a few nearby huts, they began a "very... circuitous, and toilsome" march into "rocks, bushes, dense jungle, and rugged ravines which afforded facility and shelter to the savages, and gave us no hope in getting at them." As the twin columns wound slowly toward one another, the tropical sun commenced exacting its toll. In their reports, officers referred to the temperature and humidity as "killing," "burning," "oppressive," and "scorching." In the early afternoon Mackenzie was shot from ambush and died a few minutes later. The landing parties finally reassembled on the hills, straggled back to the beach, and returned to their vessels. Mackenzie was the only fatality, but the *Hartford*'s chief surgeon itemized fifteen men as "sunstruck," four "dangerously" so. Bell lost no time in canceling further operations and steamed that night for Takao and then back to Shanghai.[19]

There were eight other armed American interventions in Asia during the nineteenth century, pirate chasing and the quelling of brief local disturbances excepted: two in Sumatra (1832 and 1839), three in China (1854, 1856, and 1859), two in Japan (1863 and 1864), and one in Korea (1871). On either tactical or strategic grounds, Bell's incursion into Taiwan must be considered the most ill conceived and poorly handled of all. His tactical planning was doomed from the start. LeGendre and Febiger had warned him about the practically impenetrable terrain into which he would go, and he should have realized the high temperatures to be expected in southern Taiwan during June. Even if his reunited two columns had occupied some ground for a couple of days, they could have done no more than kill a Koalut or two and burn some thatched-roof hovels that could have been rebuilt in a matter of hours, for there were no settlements there, not even a hamlet. One historian has tried to defend Bell's landing by comparing it to the Prussian warship *Elbe* in 1860, but the two cases are not identical. After the Germans had been shot at from a coastal village north of Lang Ch'iao, they dashed ashore and torched it.[20] The destruction of a settlement might have composed some sort of an object lesson; Bell, on the other hand, went into country occupied by only isolated hut-dwellers.

In explaining his failure, Bell informed Secretary of the Navy Gideon Welles that "sailors are not adapted to that kind of warfare against a skilled enemy, and they could be fitted for it only by a lengthened experience."[21] That should have been clear to any intelligent layman, but Bell had already disdained his own sensible observation. Rather than the censure that he deserved, Welles in his *Annual Report for 1867* did little more than paraphrase the admiral's apologia for his inept campaign, and he probably excused this delinquency in view of that officer's previously estimable career.[22] (One reason for this criticism of Bell is that before coming to a final conclusion about his tactics, the author visited Lang Ch'iao Bay in 1974. Its environs lack any natural feature that might aid assailants or work against defenders, and it is hard to visualize a more hopeless landscape for the successful conclusion of a pincers movement.)

The local stringer for the *New York Times* made a point that might have exonerated Bell, at least partially. He wrote in 1867 that Bell's offensive at the bay could solidify the Chinese hold on the island; he stressed that "an occasional warlike demonstration would force the Chinese government to move into a vacuum in southernmost Taiwan lest the United States or some other power do it for them."[23] The *Times* man was perceptive, for as engineered later by LeGendre, matters turned out that way. But one seeks in vain for a word in the admiral's correspondence that this keen observation ever occurred to him, so he must be evaluated by his own rationalizations. Later that year Bell was replaced as Commodore of the Asiatic Squadron, although there is no evidence that his Taiwanese bungling was responsible for it. In January 1868 he was drowned when his barge overturned in a river near Osaka. His entry in the

Dictionary of American Biography describes him as "distinguished by high technical skill" in his profession.[24] Granting that this summation is well deserved, it could not be for his actions at Lang Ch'iao Bay.

It remained for LeGendre to pick up the pieces. Back in Amoy he received a note from Tao-t'ai Wu and General Liu full of excuses as to why they had not gone south to punish the Koaluts. Even more aggravating to the consul was the placid assumption by the two Chinese that the people of the *Rover* had not been killed in their territory but at a locale "beyond the limits of our jurisdiction." Therefore, the 1858 Sino-American treaty "did not apply" in this instance.[25] LeGendre was so infuriated by this disavowal that he dashed off a fourteen-page letter in reply, emphasizing that if China forfeited its police power in southern Taiwan, a European nation, Japan, or the United States might be obliged to act in its stead. He clearly implied that this could lead to foreign annexation of part or even all of the island, although he did not think that his country would "retain any portion of the territory acquired."[26]

The consul's angry missive lit a fire under the previously lackadaisical Chinese officials. Governor Li acceded to LeGendre's request that the Tao-t'ai and the general be ordered to cooperate with the American against the Koaluts, telling him that troops on Taiwan were readying themselves to proceed to Lang Ch'iao Bay. LeGendre soon received equally good news from Wu and Liu, who had surrendered to the arguments contained in his long letter and confirmed that an army would be sent south. He then suggested to the governor that his subordinates on the island should build and garrison a fort in Koalut territory. The *Times* reporter's forecast that a vacuum there soon would be filled was corroborated, although Chinese documentation shows that these ostensibly pro-American decisions were designed primarily to avert a second U.S. invasion of the south.[27]

LeGendre remained so dubious about how effectively General Liu would execute his mission that he insisted on going to Taiwan-fu and accompanying him on his expedition, but he faced a transportation problem. He asked Bell to provide him with a ship for that purpose but was refused on the questionable grounds that none could be spared. Later, he sourly noted that "our Admiral, who was even then lying in Hong Kong with his whole fleet, permitted me to remain in these wilds unsupported by the presence of our flag." Perhaps nothing shows better the persuasiveness that LeGendre could exert when he wished to than his talking Governor Liu into lending him a steamer in place of "the gunboat which my admiral had refused."[28]

On 4 September LeGendre sailed for Taiwan-fu. Arriving there two days later, he was pleased to find that General Liu was prepared to march with a small detachment. The expedition tramped into the bush behind the shoreline, following LeGendre's advice that they hack out a road of sorts as they went along. En route, William Pickering, a Scottish resident who had been available as Bell's interpreter in the *Hartford* on 13 June, joined them. Almost four weeks dragged by before they came to the bay, where Pickering managed to arrange a meeting between the consul and the leader of the aborigines. Tok-e-tok, chief of the Koaluts and the seventeen other tribes, impressed LeGendre with his bearing and intelligence. The attack on the *Rover*'s people was justified by the explanation that, years before, Tok-e-tok's tribesmen had been decimated by foreigners; since then, they had hated and feared interlopers. LeGendre promised that no Koalut would be punished for the atrocity but rather that they would be protected from invaders in the future. This cleared the way for the oral understanding called the "LeGendre-Tok-e-tok Treaty." The Koaluts pledged that shipwrecked sailors—provided that by flying a red flag they identified themselves as peaceful refugees—would be escorted to safety.[29]

In a book published thirty-one years later, Pickering narrated a yarn that one hopes but doubts is true. He claimed that at one point in these negotiations matters became logjammed, but he thought of a ruse to get them under way by taking advantage of one of LeGendre's Civil War wounds. He intoned to the Koaluts:

> "Come, my brothers... we must trifle no longer. This great man grows angry. We must get to work. Beware of his displeasure; he is no ordinary man; he can do things you have never seen before." I looked intelligently at General LeGendre, whereupon he spoke American phrases in a mighty voice, stamped his foot, and, taking out his glass eye, he cast it on the table before them. The savages were absolutely dumfounded [sic]. They gave us very little troubles, and the treaty was signed [sic] forthwith.[30]

LeGendre himself makes no mention of this engrossing little episode. If it happened, possibly he was too ashamed of such theatrics to admit it. More likely, Pickering trumped up the incident to make a good story.

LeGendre continued his productive efforts and induced General Liu to construct a temporary fort near Lang Ch'iao Bay. Although this was soon abandoned, LeGendre on later visits during his tenure as Amoy consul kept pressing the Chinese to control more effectively southern Taiwan. Eventually, a lighthouse was built and a garrison maintained there off and on. These, in conjunction with improvements on the road he started, brought the area under visible Chinese occupation.[31]

At this point, issue must be taken with George W. Carrington and Ernest N. Paolino, both eminent scholars in their respective fields. In his monograph, Carrington has a lengthy analysis of the *Rover*'s victims and the aftermath.[32] Many of his conclusions are similar to those above, especially about LeGendre's able work. Where his opinions differ is over Bell's invasion at Lang Ch'iao and the sources used. While Carrington has absorbed well the pertinent State Department correspondence and has used the secretary of the navy's *Annual Report for 1867*, his notes give no evidence that he consulted Bell's Asiatic Squadron letters or the even more essential LeGendre's "Notes of Travel in Formosa."[33] Most of his account is based upon the works by James Davidson and Sophia Yen.[34] Since he does not mention the warnings of Broad, Febiger, and LeGendre, earlier visitors to Lang Ch'iao Bay, he thus is able to be kind to Admiral Bell.

In his work on Secretary of State Seward and American foreign policy, Paolino summarizes the relationship between Seward and LeGendre: "Throughout the *Rover* affair Seward had avoided being stampeded into violent action by his impetuous Consul at Amoy." He also says that LeGendre praised Bell's landing, for it would "greatly add to the prestige of our flag in the East."[35] The first statement is wrong, and there are serious reservations about the second. Conceding that LeGendre was naturally truculent and often seemed on the verge of exploding, the essential fact is that he never lost his self-control in dealing with the Chinese either on the mainland or the island. Rather, the secretary of state was the more belligerent. While the consul used pacifist means throughout, Paolino even admits that Seward

> clung firmly to his announced policy of patience and forbearance toward the Chinese, and aside from diplomatic pressure would use no force against them. Towards the Formosans, however, he felt no such tolerance. They lay outside the pale, and other measures would be needed to deal with them.[36]

It is more difficult to explain LeGendre's remark that Bell's invasion would enhance the status of the United States in the Orient. He may have said it, but certainly it did not reflect his real opinion, for he held the admiral in considerable contempt and accurately predicted his failure of 13 June. Paolino, similar to Carrington, looked into neither naval records nor the consul's "Notes," either of which would have given a clearer picture than those based essentially upon commendations to and from the State Department.

In assessing the efficacy of LeGendre and Bell, the diplomat outclassed the sailor, and the former proved himself perceptive and persistent. He activated governors or governors general, the Tao-t'ai, and the general, maneuvering them all to his and his nation's advantage without resorting to compulsion. His negotiations with the Koaluts averted another *Rover* tragedy. Indeed, during 1869 he met again with Tok-e-tok, whose brother asked that the verbal understanding be put in written form. LeGendre was surprised by the sophistication of the request, but he was happy to comply. A year later the value of the treaty was underlined when refugee Chinese seamen were treated well by the same Koaluts who had so ferociously handled the Hunts and their shipmates.[37]

LeGendre's diplomacy also worked well, not merely for endangered sailors but indirectly to avoid possibilities of national embarrassment. Such men as Commodore Matthew C. Perry and U.S. Commissioner to China Peter Parker had advocated the need for a U.S. naval foothold on Taiwan. Isaac F. Allen, American consul at Hong Kong, upon learning about the *Rover*, urged Seward to set up a "port or station" on the island, for that would be "the greatest boon that our Government could confer upon our national commerce in the East."[38] Purchaser of Alaska though he was, the Secretary made short shrift of Allen's appeal in the fourth point of his letter to Burlingame.[39] In this he was continuing the mid-nineteenth century American insistence that no overseas possession should be acquired. Nonetheless, there was always the possibility, remote though it was, that some hot headed U.S. naval officer might, emulating Bell's incursion, take and hold on to an unauthorized seizure. Washington could be presented with a fait accompli from which it would be difficult or humiliating to disengage. For all practical purposes, at least in southern Taiwan, such a contingency was obviated by LeGendre's facile diplomacy rather than by Bell's ineffectual landing.

In addition, the consul's work had prodded the Chinese authorities to take a much more active role in an area which initially they were not even sure that they wanted. He disclosed to them the power vacancy revealed by the *Rover* incident and its follow-ups. He persuaded them to move into the Lang Ch'iao

Bay environs to guarantee that no further atrocities would be committed against foreign sailors which might lead to punitive naval occupations, temporary at first, but then perhaps hardening into permanency. In short, the events during and after the *Rover*'s sorry end enabled LeGendre to devote his efforts toward aiding the Chinese to expand their hold on more of Taiwan and to retain that island for almost a generation, before losing it to Japan in 1895.

NOTES

1. Manaspas Xuto, "United States Relations with Taiwan, 1850-1895" (Ph.D. dissertation, Fletcher School of Diplomacy, Tufts University, 1961), 106.
2. James W. Davidson, *The Island of Formosa, Past and Present* (London, 1903), 180-82.
3. Hsieh Chaio-min, *Taiwan—Ilha Formosa: A Geography in Perspective* (Washington, 1962), 154.
4. Thomas F. Hughes, "Visit to Tok-e-tok, Chief of the Eighteen Tribes, Southern Formosa," *Royal Geographical Society Proceedings* 16 (1871-72): 265.
5. "Statement of Tek-kwang," 9 April 1867, *Papers Relating to the Foreign Relations of the United States* (hereafter *FRUS*), 1867, vol. 1, 495; Charles W. LeGendre, "Notes of Travel in Formosa," vol. 3, 152-53, Manuscript Division, Library of Congress, Washington, DC; Febiger to "Taotai of Taiwanfu," 17 April 1867, enclosed in Bell to Welles, 3 June 1867, U.S. Navy Department, Letters Received by the Secretary of the Navy from Commanding Officers of Squadrons (hereafter ASL), M 89, roll 252, National Archives, Washington, DC.
6. Broad to LeGendre, 29 April 1867, *FRUS*, 1867, vol. 1, 496-97.
7. Augustus E. Ingram, "Charles William LeGendre," *Dictionary of American Biography* (hereafter *DAB*), 22 vols. (New York, 1928-44), 11:145-46.
8. LeGendre to Seward, [?] May 1867, *FRUS*, 1867, vol. 1, 498; "Taotai and Prefect of Foochow to the Prefect of Formosa," 10 May 1867, ibid., 493. There is confusion about which Chinese official LeGendre met on the mainland. He calls the one whom he visited "Li Fu-t'ai, Governor of Fukien Province." But Sophia Su-fei Yen in *Taiwan in China's Foreign Relations, 1836-1874* (Hamden, CT, 1965), 132-33, does not mention him. She refers instead to "Governor-General of Min-che [Fukien and Chekiang Provinces] Wu T'ang," who was quickly succeeded by "Ying-kuei," as the ones concerned. Li and Wu are mentioned in Arthur Hummel, *Eminent Chinese of the Ch'ing Period, 1644-1912*, 2 vols. (Washington, DC, 1943-44), 1:90, 89, 465; their dates are applicable, but they are not specified by what offices they held in 1867. Possibly LeGendre conversed with both, but Ying does not appear in Hummel. In the Chinese political system of that time a governor general of two provinces could have a governor under him in each.
9. LeGendre to Seward, [?] May 1867, *FRUS*, 1867, vol. 1, 492; Leonard D. H. Gordon, "Formosa as an International Prize in the Nineteenth Century" (Ph.D. dissertation, University of Michigan, 1961), 92-93; "General, Taotai, and Prefect" to Febiger, 16 April 1867, enclosed in Bell to Welles, 3 June 1867, ASL.
10. LeGendre to Seward, [?] May 1867, *FRUS*, 1867, vol. 1, 492.
11. Febiger to Bell, 26 April 1867, ASL.
12. Edward Breck, "Henry Haywood Bell," *DAB*, 2:154-55.
13. Seward to Burlingame, 20 June 1867, *FRUS*, 1867, vol. 1, 498.
14. Burlingame to Seward, 23 April 1867, ibid., 477.
15. Bell to Welles, ASL, passim.
16. LeGendre, "Notes," vol. 3, 158-59.
17. Bell to Welles, 19 June 1867, 40th Cong., 2d sess., 1867-68, *Executive Documents of the House of Representatives: Report of the Secretary of the Navy, 1867*, vol. 4, no. 1 (hereafter SN's *Report*), 54-56.
18. Belknap to Bell, 15 June 1867, ibid., 56-57.
19. Read to Belknap, 17 June 1867, ibid., 59-60; Dr. Beale to Bell, 13 June 1867, ibid., 62; Bell to Welles, 19 June 1867, ibid., 54-56.
20. George W. Carrington, *Foreigners in Formosa, 1841-1871* (San Francisco, 1971), 151.

21. Bell to Welles, 19 June 1867, SN's *Report*, 55.
22. SN's *Report*, 7-9.
23. *New York Times*, 15 August 1867.
24. "Henry Haywood Bell," *DAB*, 2:154-55.
25. General Liu and Taotai Wu to the U.S. Consul at Amoy, 3 June 1867, U.S. Department of State, Consular Despatches, Amoy, M 100, roll 3.
26. LeGendre to Liu and Wu, 22 June 1867, ibid.; LeGendre, "Notes," 174.
27. LeGendre to Li, 6 August 1867, Consular Despatches, Amoy; Gordon, "Formosa as an International Prize," 101-2.
28. LeGendre, "Notes," 174.
29. LeGendre to Burlingame, 8 November 1867, Consular Despatches, Amoy; Yen, *Taiwan*, 135-36.
30. William A. Pickering, *Pioneering in Formosa* (London, 1898), 200.
31. Carrington, *Foreigners in Formosa*, 169-71.
32. Ibid., 152-76.
33. LeGendre, "Notes," passim.
34. Davidson, *Island of Formosa*, passim; Yen, *Taiwan*, passim.
35. Ernest N. Paolino, *The Foundations of American Empire: William Henry Seward and U.S. Foreign Policy* (Ithaca, 1973), 167 n. 49.
36. Ibid., 167-68.
37. Yen, *Taiwan*, 139.
38. Allen to Seward, 7 April 1867, *FRUS*, 1867, vol. 1, 500.
39. Seward to Burlingame, 20 June 1867, ibid., 498. See note 13 above, 89.

Tirpitz: Architect of Modern German Naval Power

GARY E. WEIR

Alfred von Tirpitz provided the Imperial Navy with formidable leadership, definite purpose, and the relentless drive to become the instrument of Germany's world power. However, as Dr. Weir argues, an important part of Tirpitz's strategic "Risk Theory" actually had collapsed as early as 1902, and Tirpitz failed to recognize it. Furthermore, his devotion to battleship technology really retarded other technological developments as well as hindered an effective naval-industrial complex in Germany during its growing estrangement with Britain.

****

"Fleet development... later possibly... against England... maintain Tradition."[1] This quote from an abbreviated marginal note penned by Admiral Erich Raeder in 1934 testifies to the strength of a tradition born many years earlier, when Kaiser Wilhelm II appointed Alfred von Tirpitz to the post of state secretary of the German Imperial Navy Office (RMA). This essay will demonstrate that, in this capacity from 1897 to 1916, Tirpitz molded the German navy in fact and spirit as no other figure before or since.

Upon assuming office, the new state secretary found fertile ground for his ideas on the reform and development of the navy. Wilhelm II wanted to follow an expansionist course politically and economically, emulating the success of British and French overseas ventures. Impatient with the failure of the former RMA chief, Admiral Carl Eduard Heussner, and the incumbent, Admiral Friedrich von Hollmann, to convert the imperial dream into reality, the kaiser turned to Tirpitz in the hope of finding the strategic philosophy, political skills, and managerial ability his predecessors at the RMA had lacked.[2]

Three years earlier, in 1894, Tirpitz set forth his personal strategic doctrine in the context of a commentary on the navy's fall fleet maneuvers. *Service Memo IX*, as it was called, proposed a direct challenge to Great Britain and a vast increase in German naval power via the battleship.[3] Discarding the option of commercial war against Germany's potential enemies, Tirpitz suggested building a formidable naval force which would drastically increase the risk for anyone contemplating conflict with Germany on the high seas. This "Risk Theory" suddenly made naval war, even with Britain, an acceptable game of chance that Germany might win. In other circumstances a strategic theory proposed by a person primarily responsible for politics and construction might have gone unnoticed. However, when the kaiser appointed Tirpitz to direct the RMA, the new state secretary's own strategy became the blueprint for RMA policy and governed the character of naval expansion for the next seventeen years. Over the objections of Admiral Eduard von Knorr, selected to govern the Admiralty staff simultaneously with Tirpitz's appointment to the RMA, the kaiser gave the latter the right to determine the types of contracts awarded to the naval shipyards. This allowed Tirpitz to compose a fleet suited to his concept of how Germany should wage war.[4]

For Tirpitz, *Service Memo IX* served not only as a statement of his Mahan-like philosophy of strategy but also as a political and professional move to enhance his own reputation. In one stroke, he both satisfied the kaiser's desire to emulate British naval might and created a professional platform of considerable credibility and strength which supported him both in the service and in the Reichstag until the advent of World War I.

As a proponent of direct confrontation and the decisive battle, Tirpitz also personified the antithesis of the *Jeune Ecole*, or "Young School," of strategy popularized by Théophile Aube, French naval minister from 1886 to 1887. Many of Tirpitz's opponents agreed with Aube that the best way to challenge Britain's awesome superiority was to avoid the decisive battle between capital ships. Rather, an attack by cruisers and torpedo boats on Britain's overseas trade routes could significantly impair its ability to wage war. French success with submersible vessels like the *Gustave Zédé*[5] as early as 1899 only strengthened the argument for this approach.[6]

A commercial war "à l'Aube" required vessels with speed and power, or at least the element of surprise, and would cost considerably less in hardware and lives. However, western nations historically relied on their ships of the line as the foundation of their naval power. This tradition, considerably reinforced after 1890 by the works of Alfred Thayer Mahan as well as by Tirpitz's activity in Germany, proved too much for the Aube challenge.

In spite of the fact that he had little to fear from the Young School by 1897, Tirpitz did not ignore the fact that these ideas still had supporters among his colleagues in the German navy. As Tirpitz's authority and influence increased, he ruthlessly attacked proponents of cruiser and U-boat strategies like Captain Curt von Maltzahn, and he made sure other outspoken partisans of commercial warfare, such as Lieutenant Commander Franz Rust and Captain Lothar Persius, had short careers in the Imperial Navy.[7]

Tirpitz's response to opposition betrays two significant weaknesses in his position that bear discussion in order to understand his actions and thus German naval affairs at the turn of the century. In the first place, he felt obliged to react swiftly and decisively against opponents because his political credibility depended completely on the validity of the Risk Theory and its alluring promise of a naval force to rival Great Britain's. This philosophy of strategy brought Tirpitz to power and formed the foundation for his exceptionally well-organized and documented arguments in favor of the battleship and fleet construction. As a contemporary political analysis put it: "Admiral von Tirpitz's strength lay chiefly in this, that he knew exactly what he wanted and why he wanted it."[8] How long would this strength endure if the premise upon which the entire structure rested came into question? One can easily understand the admiral's sensitivity on this point and his tendency toward a strictly dogmatic and intolerant treatment of those holding differing viewpoints. Unfortunately, this personal attitude and his utter devotion to a battleship strategy earnestly supported by Naval Leaguers, heavy industry, and some fellow officers deprived the navy of the opportunity to profit from a positive exchange of ideas on both strategy and technological innovation.[9]

The other major flaw in Tirpitz's design was the "Danger Zone." Although he wanted potential opponents to believe otherwise, he intended from the beginning that the High Seas Fleet should challenge Great Britain. At what point, then, would the intended adversary realize the plan and react? The gap between realization of German intentions and the actual completion of the fleet formed Tirpitz's Danger Zone.

In his analysis of *The Tirpitz Plan*, Volker Berghahn offers the currently favored interpretation that Tirpitz kept the navy within the Reich's financial means and avoided extraordinary price and tonnage until 1905.[10] In this way, the admiral successfully concealed his true intentions from both the Reichstag and the British.

After 1905, however, when construction of the HMS *Dreadnought* commenced, Tirpitz could not hesitate to follow suit. After all, most of the world's major naval powers already had all big-gun designs on the drawing board. Some plans, like those for the American *South Carolina* and *Michigan* classes, actually predated their British counterpart by a few months. Moreover, Britain's First Sea Lord, Admiral Sir John Fisher, had moved swiftly, and the *Dreadnought* came off the slip only 130 days after the laying of its keel on 2 October 1905.[11] Berghahn insists that when events forced Tirpitz to take quick action in copying the British he betrayed his intention not only to exceed his proposed capital ship expenditure but also to challenge the British, thus thrusting the navy into the Danger Zone. In addition, the new British commitment to innovative battleship designs and technology after 1905 definitely affected the duration of the zone and the navy's potential to survive it.

Even though current research places German entry into the Danger Zone in 1905, a closer examination of the international situation suggests that Tirpitz's plans began to go awry much sooner. As early as 1902, Great Britain's worldwide fortunes improved markedly and its attentions changed focus. The naval treaty with the Japanese in that year stabilized the British position in the Far East and gave London greater freedom to become more involved in the European political situation. Prompted by the successful stand made by the British at Fashoda in 1898, France took the first step toward the Entente of April 1904 by suggesting closer cooperation regarding matters of continental and colonial policy. Conflict with the United States seemed less likely than ever with the signing of the Hay-Pauncefote Treaty in 1901 and the Alaskan Boundary Settlement of 1903. Internally, Britain engaged in extensive army reforms and drastically increased the naval budgets of 1900 and 1903. The latter eventually took concrete form as ten new battleships and eighteen armored cruisers.[12]

The German service attachés in London sent back ominous reports regarding the treatment of German naval expansion in the British press. An article in *Vanity Fair* recalled the 1807 "copenhagening" of the Danish fleet and suggested that the same technique used against the Germans would guarantee world peace for two generations.[13] As Paul Kennedy observed, Britain was "clearly looking very carefully at the expansion of the German fleet, which, due to the agitation of the *National Review, Spectator,* the *Times* and other journals, had entered the 'danger zone' much earlier than Tirpitz suggested was likely."[14]

Thus, the intense activity at Germany's shipyards certainly encouraged Britain's renewed interest in continental affairs during the 1902–04 period. Keeping German tonnage and expenditure down to disguise his intentions from the Reichstag worked, but Tirpitz failed completely to obscure his goals from the British. With London's first step toward a European focus, the Naval Treaty with Japan in 1902, Tirpitz lost the initiative and the navy passed into the Danger Zone without the state secretary fully appreciating it. Admiral Fisher's decision to pursue the type "H" battleship design and the launching of the *Dreadnought* two years later forced Tirpitz to react and checkmated his efforts to challenge the Royal Navy. Germany and Britain did not pass into the Danger Zone in 1905. Actually, they initiated something very different; namely, the first of the twentieth century's armaments races, a war of hardware development with high technology as the most important weapon and without definite duration or endpoint. After 1905, Britain and Germany tested one another to see which would collapse first from financial and perhaps physical exhaustion. Thus, Tirpitz's political success at home combined with major revisions in British attentions abroad after 1902 to render the Danger Zone permanent, while significantly changing its character.

How, then, did Tirpitz manage to achieve the dramatic success at home that prematurely propelled Germany into an arms race with Great Britain? Upon taking office in 1897, Tirpitz embarked on a plan to tie the Reichstag to a long-term building commitment as the groundwork for a step-by-step increase in ship numbers, size, and power. His political and organizational talents suited the task perfectly.

The admiral chose to present his 1898 naval estimates to the Reichstag in the form of a law, not merely an appropriations bill. This would commit the parliament to naval spending and allow Tirpitz to tailor future supplementary measures according to need or in response to political advantage. In spite of the obstacles confronting him in the Reichstag, Jonathan Steinburg believes that it "was precisely because Tirpitz behaved as if Germany had a parliamentary regime that he was so successful."[15] He took the politicians seriously. He talked, negotiated, and argued with them, and thus became one of them. This often represented the opinion of naval colleagues as well, for "he was generally viewed by the other admirals as an essentially political figure."[16]

If Tirpitz often exhibited a ruthless attitude toward potential rivals among his follow officers, another side of his political personality handled influential members of the Reichstag with a seasoned grace. He sent the parliamentary leaders thorough memoranda to keep them well informed on naval affairs, frequently engaging in personal conversations or encouraging his deputies, Harald Dahnhardt and Eduard Capelle, to do so.[17] The RMA responded to questions posed by the Reichstag members and even arranged for tours of the naval yards for some of the more important deputies.[18]

Moreover, in every step of the fleet program, from the laws of 1898 and 1900 establishing the national financial and materiel commitment through the supplementary laws of 1906, 1908, and 1912, Tirpitz relied heavily on propaganda and information to achieve political success. The RMA News Bureau controlled the flow of fleet information to the news media and cultivated support among journals and periodicals. Tirpitz changed the technical journal *Marine-Rundshau* into a popular magazine and founded *Nauticus*, the naval annual. The RMA also encouraged intellectual support for the fleet within the academic community and promoted nautical activities and enthusiasm among the general population through the Naval League. Consequently, with every successive step in Tirpitz's plans the RMA could apply a great deal of preliminary pressure on the Reichstag.[19]

Tirpitz's political and administrative talents, his appreciation for the power of propaganda, his very able deputies, and an unassailable professional position produced a string of five legislative victories for the navy between 1898 and 1912. Through a step-by-step process, he nearly quadrupled Germany's naval budget and proposed to build a High Seas Fleet consisting of forty-one battleships, twenty heavy cruisers, forty light cruisers, and numerous auxiliary vessels.[20]

Tirpitz and his associates were just as effective managing appropriations as they were in obtaining these resources from the Reichstag. The RMA responded to the problems of construction with a very effective system of regulations, which this author calls the "Protocol System." It began to take form during Admiral Hollmann's tenure (1891–97), with Tirpitz refining it into the single most important lever possessed by the RMA in its relationship with industry.

The origins of the Protocol System extend back to the navy's formative years in the decade before 1900. Under Construction Chief Alfred Dietrich, predecessor to the first head of the RMA's Construction Department, Admiral Rudolph von Eickstedt, naval construction experts attended numerous international congresses, such as those at Zurich in 1895 and at Stockholm in 1897,[21] on testing methods and engineering. Here they accumulated the best and latest information applicable to warship construction. This laid the basis for various editions of the *General Guidelines* for naval projects, first published in 1894. These regulations stipulated routine construction site inspections and strict adherence to technical specifications.[22] The *General Guidelines* also required a weekly accounting of man-hours, work accomplished, and the amount and type of materials used. The yard or subcontractor took responsibility for plant space, tooling, and working conditions. The RMA Construction Department received quarterly financial reports, and any requests for RMA assistance became part of the monthly reports submitted by civilian project directors.[23]

All shipyards experienced the same routine supervision and review. The RMA Technical Department had resident experts at each yard overseeing the more sophisticated aspects of a project. As components arrived at the yard for installation, already inspected by Purchasing Office personnel at the production site, Technical Department people supervised and often assisted in the actual assembly.

The ultimate authority in all phases of ship construction at the yard, however, was the Construction Inspectorate. Usually one naval official functioned as a resident inspector at the shipyard for each project, whether German or foreign. He determined the maximum amount of hours and output the RMA could expect from a shipyard's work force. It also fell to him to pinpoint and remedy any technical complications in construction in order to avoid falling behind schedule. The Construction Department allowed its inspectors a great deal of freedom so they could react quickly to any problems without always having to contact the RMA in Berlin. In addition, all shipyard correspondence went to the RMA via the resident inspector. Thus, he could comment on any communication to the benefit of his superiors while repeatedly confirming Construction Department support in his relationship with the shipyard.[24]

The most important element of the valuable RMA Protocol System was the *Lieferantenverzeichnis,* or Suppliers' List. This directory was a roster of all firms, great and small, allowed to work on naval projects. Without appearing here a company could not act as a subcontractor to a shipyard working for the Imperial Navy.[25] The Suppliers' List became the ultimate screening procedure used by the RMA. If a firm had once qualified and the Purchasing Office or Construction Inspectorate later found its products to fall below standard, it was removed from the list. Unless it requalified, further contracts with the RMA were out of the question.

When Tirpitz took office in 1897, he expanded the Protocol System as needed and made it work effectively in a wide variety of situations. If businesses wanted to work on naval projects, they had to follow the RMA's regulations. With the exception of certain technological innovations, this procedure assured the RMA of a strong position in its relations with industry.

Why, then, should technology pose a problem in an otherwise very efficient system of turning Reichstag appropriations into lethal naval hardware? Constantly in a state of flux and development, technology spelled increased expenditure and change, neither of which Tirpitz found appealing. Thus, he consistently restricted RMA commitments to research and development. He maintained a hands-off policy from the beginning of his tenure as state secretary that kept naval research almost exclusively in the domain of the private sector. Furthermore, if some promising product of naval research posed a challenge to the Risk Theory, he would quickly try to minimize its importance.

For Tirpitz, the U-boat represented just such a challenge. While his professionalism prompted him to keep abreast of the technology, personal dogmatism led him to argue against the submarine's usefulness before thoroughly probing the weapon's possibilities. Budget constraints and his imperative to build rather than to explore may have played a role in Tirpitz's restricted commitment to research and development. However, by the time Krupp produced the U-1 in 1906, Tirpitz already had committed the navy to his plan of battleship construction, supported in the same year by the first new supplement to the 1900 Naval Law. The sheer inertia of RMA construction plans and Tirpitz's unwillingness to explore the submarine's promise severely curtailed early U-boat development.

Along with the U-boat, German conversion to the turbine engine became another rare and therefore instructive example of RMA mismanagement. With the turbine engine, neither the price nor the character of the innovation conflicted with Tirpitz's plans, and he freely pursued his policy of noninvolvement in the research and development of naval technology. The RMA merely kept track of Charles Parsons's 1884 invention and the subsequent testing of the machine in the HMS *Turbinia,* until an RMA commission could witness successful turbine trials in Great Britain.[26] Then Tirpitz quickly advocated introducing the new propulsion system into German ships, but he refused to allow the RMA to become involved in this process, even when German efforts at duplicating Parsons's technology became diffuse and only minimally successful. By insisting that the navy initially employ only the tested Parsons model, Tirpitz might have brought turbine power to the navy much earlier. Firms with such funds, like Krupp or Siemens, could have improved the system in conjunction with the RMA, later providing the navy with a truly domestic and perhaps better variation of the original. Instead, the period between 1884 and 1914 witnessed a wasteful duplication of effort involving M.A.N., Siemens-Schuckertwerke, Brown und Boveri, and seven other firms.[27] Here Tirpitz imitated his predecessors in that he did nothing to improve Germany's technological independence.[28] Thus, the RMA was prohibited from coordinating and channeling industrial efforts by the very man whose talents were so well suited to the task.

Tirpitz's efforts experienced a major setback with the Social Democratic party's success in Germany's 1912 elections. The last naval supplement, presented to the Reichstag in that year, encountered considerable opposition from a vastly more powerful left wing than the RMA faced in 1906 and 1908. In addition, Chancellor Theobald von Bethmann-Hollweg and Treasury Secretary Adolph Wermuth thought that Germany's true protection lay with the army. The consequences of this point of view were not lost on Tirpitz, and they possibly contributed to the admiral's unbending position in arms control conversations with British emissary Viscount Haldane in 1912. However, by this time it had become clear that the naval building program was fast approaching its political zenith.

When the war began in 1914, the High Seas Fleet remained embarrassingly inactive. The kaiser had no wish to commit his capital ships to an early surface battle with the British, and Tirpitz did not have tactical command of the fleet his strategic philosophy had designed. Moreover, he had failed to guide the navy successfully through the Danger Zone. Indeed, Tirpitz never fully comprehended that the navy had entered the zone as early as 1902. To make matters worse, the Reich's narrow revenue base prohibited the RMA from competing on an equal footing with Great Britain in the naval arms race launched by First Sea Lord Fisher's decision to build the *Dreadnought* in 1905. Only the U-boat, that product of independent research rejected by Tirpitz, proved useful in consistently bringing the naval war to Britain's doorstep.

The admiral's strategic rigidity deprived the Imperial Navy of the chance for a greater degree of success against Great Britain in wartime. Flexibility and adaptability must exist while a fleet is designed and built. Only in an atmosphere of this sort can naval experts produce an instrument best suited to exploit not only the strengths of domestic innovations and engineering but also the weaknesses of potential enemies. Unfortunately, Tirpitz's choice of weapons played directly into the strength of his chosen adversary.

As the value of the U-boat increased and the High Seas Fleet remained relatively dormant, Tirpitz's reputation and position declined. The Risk Theory obviously failed to discourage Great Britain from entering the war against Germany. Raids on the British coast and the Dogger Bank encounter of January 1915 represented the best Tirpitz's much vaunted surface fleet could manage.

As Admiral Hugo von Pohl replaced Friedrich Ingenohl as chief of the High Seas Fleet in February 1915, Tirpitz suddenly suggested the possibility of a cruiser war. Coming as it did from Germany's longtime proponent of the battleship, this statement certainly undermined his credibility. This, combined with his growing advocacy of unrestricted U-boat warfare, gave Tirpitz the appearance of an opportunist and called into question the strategic philosophy upon which his career and the fleet rested.[29]

On 30 August 1915 the state secretary lost both his position on the General Headquarters staff and his advisory post at the Admiralty. Although Tirpitz continued to defend his past policies, the tide had clearly turned against him. The kaiser accepted his resignation on 17 March 1916, just two months and fourteen days before the only major surface battle of the war off Jutland. Admiral Capelle succeeded him as state secretary of the RMA.

Alfred von Tirpitz provided the Imperial Navy with independent identity, formidable leadership, definite purpose, and the relentless drive to become the instrument of Germany's world power. He produced spectacular political success for the RMA and exercised surprising control over the firms rushing to profit from the fleet when the 1898 Naval Law opened the Reichstag's purse.[30]

The admiral does not qualify as a naval revolutionary. Rather, he reflected his time and brought to his task an acute sensitivity for domestic politics, a firm belief in the value of propaganda, and an unbending faith in the validity of his strategic philosophy. This combination allowed him to provide Germany with a strong naval tradition, firmly impressing his professional ambitions and spirit upon the officer corps.

His failure to appreciate the potential value of research and innovation removed him from the company of more receptive contemporaries such as Aube, Wolfgang Wegener, Karl Galster, or Sir Percy Scott. In the final analysis, these attitudes probably brought the admiral's remarkable career to an end quicker than any other consideration. Nonetheless, he radically changed the navy's concept of itself and its role, and in so doing he created a tradition that still held Admiral Raeder and many of his colleagues in its grasp nearly one half-century later.

NOTES

1. Wilhelm Deist, *The Wehrmacht and German Rearmament* (Toronto, 1981), 75. Not every historian of Weimar naval affairs agrees with Professor Deist's assertion that these comments reflected Raeder's thoughts and plans for the navy. Both Michael Salewski and Jost Duelffer believe that the note actually reflected an aggressive intention toward England voiced by Adolf Hitler. Neurath (Foreign Office), War Minister Blomberg, and Hitler were present at this June 1934 meeting with Raeder when the admiral wrote the note which read: "Entwicklung Fl. spaeter ev. gegen E.... Tradition Hochhalten. Ich: vor 1936 an gr. Schiffe mit 35 cm. Wenn Geld ja Bundnis 1899. Lage 1914?"

For further information on this issue and the navy in the early Nazi period refer to Jost Duelffer, *Weimar, Hitler und die Marine: Reichspolitik und Flottenbau 1920 bis 1939* (Düsseldorf, 1973), and Michael Salewski, "Marineleitung und politische Fuhrung 1931-1935," *Militaergeschichtliche Mitteilungen* 10 (February 1971): 113-58. (Salewski's suggestion in footnote 158 that the "E" in Raeder's note is actually a poorly rendered "F" which could change the complexion of things considerably [England or France?].)

2. Refer to Keith W. Bird, *Weimar, the German Naval Officer Corps and the Rise of National Socialism* (Amsterdam, 1977), 26-27, taking note of the passage which begins at the bottom of p. 26.

3. The full title of *Service IX* was: "Allgemeine Erfahrung aus den Manovern der Herbstubungsflotte" (1894).

4. The kaiser's Supreme Cabinet order of February 1898 which gave Tirpitz the advantage in matters of construction is discussed in Jonathan Steinberg, *Yesterday's Deterrent: Tirpitz and the German Battle Fleet* (New York, 1965), 136-40.

5. Bundesarchiv-Militaerarchiv (BA/MA) RM3/3685 *Daily Graphic* clipping from 3 February 1899. Tirpitz's policy toward submarines receives a detailed exposition in Gary E. Weir, "Tirpitz, Technology and Building U-boats, 1897-1916," *International History Review* 6 (May 1984): 178ff.

6. BA/MA RM3/1050 Naval Attaché, Paris, to State Secretary of the RMA, Berlin, 10 April 1906. The navy planned to acquire forty-two defensive and eighty-two offensive submarines over the next decade.

7. Holger Herwig, *"Luxury" Fleet: The Imperial German Navy, 1888-1918* (London, 1980), 38-39. Weir, "Tirpitz, Technology and Building U-boats," 180-81.

8. Archibald Hurd and Henry Castle, *German Seapower: Its Rise, Progress and Economic Basis* (London, 1913), 195.

9. For a detailed discussion of this issue see Weir, "Tirpitz, Technology and Building U-boats," 178ff.

10. Volker R. Berghahn, *Der Tirpitz Plan: Genesis und Verfall einer Innenpolitischen Krisenstrategie unter Wilhelm II* (Düsseldorf, 1971).

11. Herwig, *"Luxury" Fleet*, 54-57.

12. Paul M. Kennedy, *The Rise of Anglo-German Antagonism, 1860-1914* (London, 1980), 265.

13. J. Lipsius and A. Mendelssohn-Ba, eds., *Die Grosse Politik der Europaeischen Kabinette*, vol. 19/2, no. 6149 (Berlin, 1922-27): Coerper, Naval Attaché in London, to Kaiser Wilhelm II, 18 November 1904.

14. Kennedy, *Rise of Anglo-German Antagonism*, 265.

15. Steinberg, *Yesterday's Deterrent*, 186.

16. Samuel P. Huntington, *The Soldier and the State* (Cambridge, MA, 1957), 102.

17. Admiral Capelle: entered the German navy on 18 April 1872; captain (1900); director of the Administrative Department, RMA (to 1906); admiral (1913); assistant state secretary of the RMA (1914-16). Admiral Dahnhardt: entered the navy in April 1879; captain (1905); director of the Budget Division of Capelle's Administrative Department; vice admiral (1914); director of the RMA Budget Department. Source: *Rangliste der kaiserlichen deutschen Marine 1880-1913* (Berlin, 1880-1913); refer to appropriate annual volume according to date desired.

18. Paul M. Kennedy, "Fisher and Tirpitz: Political Admirals in the Age of Imperialism," in *Naval Warfare in the Twentieth Century*, ed. by Gerald Jordan (London, 1977), 52.

19. For further information on RMA propaganda work see Wilhelm Deist, *Flottenpolitik und Flottenpropaganda. Das Nachrichtenbureau des Reichmarineamtes 1897-1914* (Stuttgart, 1976); Wolfgang Marienfeld, *Wissenschaft und Schlachtflottenbau in Deutschland 1897-1906* (Berlin, 1957); Herwig, *"Luxury" Fleet*, 40.

20. Herwig, *"Luxury" Fleet*, 1, and Table 17.

21. BA/MA RM3/2098 "Bericht ueber die Verhandlungen der internationalen Konferenz zur Vereinfachung einheitlicher Prufungsmethoden...," 9-11 November 1895.

22. Every shipyard contracting with the RMA also received specifications, called the *General Construction Guidelines*, which varied according to the ship in question.

23. BA/MA RM3/11564 *Allgemeine Bedingungen*, 1894.

24. BA/MA RM3/421. See, for example, KI, KII, and KIV Construction Dept. interoffice correspondence.

25. BA/MA RM3/2210 Consideration of a firm for the Suppliers' List (1910).

26. BA/MA RM3/2108 "Bericht nach Schottland und Ingland zum Studium der Parsonsturbinen ensandten Kommission" to State Secretary of the RMA, Berlin, 16 May 1902.

27. Tirpitz refused to buy the Parsons patents when offered: BA/MA RM3/2112, 2113 (1906-7). Brown und Boveri acquired the exclusive rights to use the Parsons system in Germany: BA/MA RM32107 Brown und Boveri, Mannheim to RMA, Berlin, 23 August 1900. M.A.N. is the abbreviation commonly used for Maschinenfabrik Augsburg Nurnbert.

28. The RMA did not see the Parsons turbine as the last word in turbine technology. Take note of the comments made by Construction Dept. head Admiral Rudolf von Eickstedt: BA/MA RM3/2112, 2113, especially the press clippings from the *Daily Telegraph*, 23 November 1906, sent to the RMA by the German Foreign Office.

29. Carl-Axel Gemzell noted in his *Organization, Conflict and Innovation: A Study of German Naval Strategic Planning, 1888-1940* (Lund, 1973), 211, 232, that Tirpitz's critics, like Wolfgang Wegener, now began to criticize him with greater regularity.

30. For a detailed discussion of this topic see Gary E. Weir, "The Origins of German Seapower: Military Industrial Relationships in the Development of the High Seas Fleet, 1897-1912" (Ph.D. dissertation, University of Tennessee, 1982).

Choosing among Technologies in the Anglo-German Naval Arms Competition, 1898-1915

CHARLES H. FAIRBANKS, JR.

The Anglo-German naval arms race leading up to World War I has produced various interpretations by modern scholars, especially in regard to whether the British or the German navy was superior. By examining technological changes and how they related to the two navies from the pre-Dreadnought period to the war, Dr. Fairbanks contends that the great difference between British and German battleship designs was triggered by the dreadnought revolution.

****

The Anglo-German naval arms competition between 1898 and 1914 is, as Bernard Brodie remarked, "the most celebrated arms race in history [and] stands out as the stereotype of the modern arms race."[1] This case is important to historians because of the way in which it affected the agenda of German domestic politics, shifted the European coalitions, and perhaps engendered war between Britain and Germany. It remains important to understand whether the German navy was a danger to Britain (and thus an opportunity for Germany) or only a scare.

For the student of defense policy and arms control, this is the most famous example of a quantitative arms race, or a competition in numbers, which was transformed into a qualitative race in which the two sides strove to build superior ships. This transformation occurred when Admiral Sir John Fisher, the great reformer of the Royal Navy, built in 1905 two radically new types of battleship, the *Dreadnought* and the *Invincible* (originally called an armored cruiser). While for decades almost all battleships mounted four big guns, the *Dreadnought* had ten and the *Invincible* eight; where most battleships steamed at 18 knots, the *Dreadnought* sped at 21 knots and the *Invincible* at 25, using turbine engines for the first time in large warships. The British thus resorted to "breakthrough technology," as the United States often has in its competition with the Soviet Union.

In the Anglo-German naval competition, unlike many others, the advantages gained by each side were weighed in the balance of war. The outcome was one that neither side had anticipated in the course of the competition. Great Britain had inaugurated the dreadnought revolution with superior technology. At the Battle of Jutland in May 1916, however, German battleships revealed themselves to be superior technologically in a number of important respects.

This essay, which is part of a larger inquiry into the nature of arms races,[2] first asks why the arms competition took this course. Technological developments and their logic are an aspect of arms races that is understood much less well than action-reaction mechanisms, bureaucratic politics, and international power relationships. Second, what accounted for the differing technological choices to which the German ships' superiority at Jutland is often traced? The answer focuses on the British emphasis on offense (speed and guns), the German on defense (armor, stability, damage control).

British and German Battleship Design Priorities

The priority dominating British battleship design was formulated in the early years of the century by Admiral Fisher, who stated: "The guiding principle in the construction of a ship of war should be that she is a floating gun carriage."[3] Speed was a more personal obsession of Fisher himself, and its priority over armor was to a great extent his personal work. Typical of his outlook was this exposition of the need for speed: "There is no question whatever that the first desideratum in every type of fighting vessel is *speed* [Fisher's italics].... Strategy demands it... and tactics... demands it.... It is absolutely impossible to exaggerate the supreme importance of speed."[4] Armor was not opposed for any specific reason but rather was taken care of as an afterthought.

The German approach was very different. Admiral Alfred von Tirpitz, the architect of the Imperial Navy, argued: "The supreme quality of a ship is that she should remain afloat, and by preserving a vertical position, continue to put up a fight.... In naval warfare, the main object is... the annihilation of the enemy; since the introduction of steam power and modern guns this is... effected... only by sinking him. So long as a ship is afloat, she retains a certain fighting value and can afterwards be easily refitted."[5]

These divergent paths led to rather different designs in practice. British ships generally had larger guns and more advanced fire-control equipment than German vessels. On the other hand, British armor plate was consistently thinner than German. The disparity between British and German protection was particularly great in battle cruisers. These designs are especially interesting because they embodied the ideas of Admiral Fisher in a purer form than contemporary battleships.[6] Disregarding the huge areas of British ships unprotected by armor or with 4- or 5-inch armor, we find that six British battle cruisers of the nine available in August 1914 relied on 6-inch armor to protect their vitals. The remaining battle cruisers relied entirely on 9-inch armor, as the majority of British battleships which had 9-inch barbettes relied on this thickness, to protect their magazines from explosion.

Military Consequences of Technological Choices

British 6-inch armor was penetrated by German 11-inch shells at 17,000 yards (as in the *Lion* at the Dogger Bank in 1915). Since the extreme range of the 12-inch guns in the *Invincible* class with the shells supplied in 1914 was 16,350 yards,[7] these ships could be riddled by the enemy at the limit of the range at which they could make any reply. British 9-inch armor was pierced by German 12-inch shells at about 14,400 yards (blowing up the *Queen Mary*) and was damaged (resulting in flooding, a 10-degree list, and loss of all electric power) in the *Lion* (at the Dogger Bank) at 18,000 yards.

The ranges at which British admirals expected to fight are a fair test of the adequacy of their armor as designed. The Grand Fleet Battle Orders, issued by Admiral John Jellicoe on the outbreak of the war, called on the British ships with 13.5-inch guns to open fire at 15,000 yards, the 12-inch ships at 13,000. Before the war Jellicoe had considered 12,000 to 13,000 yards the best range and sought to avoid going within 7,000.[8] The distance of actual fighting at the Dogger Bank, at Jutland, and in the Black Sea varied from 20,000 to 5,500 yards, with 3,000 yards down to point-blank range in the night encounters at Jutland. It follows that the vital parts of all the British battle cruisers could be penetrated at the ranges where the British commander in chief sought to fight, risking the sudden destruction of these ships. Some important parts of all the British battleships completed in 1914 (especially the barbettes wholly or partially armored with 9-inch plate) also could be penetrated at these ranges.

The debility of British armor was a more serious problem because the penetration of one turret or barbette by one German shell could—and did—destroy entire ships by blowing up the magazines. It has been argued that this, rather than the priority for offense over defense, was the real problem of British battle-cruiser designs.[9] But the purpose of armor is to keep out enemy shells. If British armor was not thick enough to keep enemy shells out of vital parts of the ship at the ranges expected, what was it for? In fact, the propellant explosion problem converted a major defect of British designs into a potentially catastrophic vulnerability.

Underwater Protection

British ships were far less well protected against underwater damage by torpedoes or mine explosions than German ones. The only way to afford protection against this damage is (in simplified terms) to provide space (at least 12 feet) for the gases to expand before striking an inner torpedo bulkhead of relatively thin armor. To reach this solution required a knowledge of physics and a series of careful experiments to determine the size of the vital expansion space. Before World War I, only Germany, as will be seen, carried out a systematic series of experiments.

As a result of these tests, all the dreadnought battleships built by Germany after 1906 were constructed with the fundamentally correct system of underwater protection, improved as the years went on, along the side. In addition, these ships were divided into a large number of watertight compartments. The major underwater compartments were unpierced by doors or other passages, which tended to leak. Moreover, German ships were provided with powerful pumping equipment to empty flooded compartments. To ensure that injured ships would not capsize, they were designed with a larger beam and metacentric height than British battleships so as to be stable even when damaged.

Royal Navy battleships displayed far less attention to underwater protection. The British showed some awareness of the need by adopting unpierced, transverse bulkheads in the *Lord Nelson* class (1904). In the *Dreadnought* itself and in the first battle cruisers, longitudinal armored screens were added at the sides of the heavy gun magazines only. In the *Bellerophon* of 1906 a continuous bulkhead was adopted, although it was not part of a scientifically designed system and was so far inboard, forward and aft, that it only protected the magazines. But after this beginning, much inferior to contemporary German battleships, British underwater protection actually became worse. In the *Neptune* class of 1909 unpierced transverse bulkheads were abandoned. The following *Colossus* class reverted from a continuous if inadequate armored bulkhead to protection over the magazines only. Only in the *Queen Elizabeth* class, which entered service after the war began, did the British return to a continuous torpedo bulkhead, and even then it was somewhat incorrectly designed. None of the prewar battle cruisers was ever protected.

As a result, Germany entered the war with seventeen dreadnought battleships and battle cruisers carefully protected against mines and torpedoes, while Britain entered it with no ships properly protected, seven ships with a complete but inadequate bulkhead, and twenty-two with protection only over the magazines. In addition, British ships were built with a narrower beam and a smaller metacentric height, to fit existing docks and to make them steadier gun platforms. However, this made them more likely to capsize if damaged. While more vulnerable to flooding, the British warships were less able to reverse it: the *Queen Elizabeth* could pump out 950 tons of water per hour, the contemporary German ship *Bayern*, 5,400 tons.[10]

Many of the measures discussed here, such as internal compartmentation and pumping, were useful in dealing with flooding from shell hits as well as from mine and torpedo explosions. Combined with better training in damage control, they made German ships much more able to resist all types of damage and less "sinkable." German capital ships, such as the *Seydlitz* and *Derfflinger*, survived degrees of damage that surely would have sunk comparable British ships.

Design and the Test of War

The British choice to give priority to the offensive (guns and speed) and the German choice to give priority to the defensive (armor and resistance to sinking) were both guesses. Lack of war experience and the rapidity of technological change meant (as they may today) that both sides were working in the dark. The war showed the German guesses to be more broadly correct. It is worth briefly asking why. In part, it was because the conditions of naval combat diverged from British expectations.

The value of underwater protection was affected by the fact that torpedo and mine attacks loomed larger in the minds of naval officers than the British had anticipated. This put a premium on the highly developed German systems of protection.

In regard to armor, wartime naval battles were fought at long ranges, often at 14,000 to 20,000 yards. Admiral Fisher's designs of 1904-05 were based on the expectation of long-range fighting, but it is important to recognize that at this time "long-range" meant 5,000 yards, not 15,000 to 20,000 yards. At these extreme ranges there were few hits, this putting a premium on absolute protection against catastrophic loss (such as magazine explosions) rather than on average protection against the gradual accumulation of damage.

Fisher's emphasis on speed was vindicated by war experience, but it failed to fulfill the expectations he had of it. The admiral had argued that speed was the key advantage both strategically and tactically. Strategically, the advantage of the dexterity given by speed was reduced by the presence of slower pre-dreadnoughts in both fleets during much of the decisive period, by the fear of underwater attack which chilled most adventurous strategic moves, and by the need, in the British case, to coordinate separate squadrons operating from widely separated bases (Scapa Flow and Rosyth). The resulting clumsiness greatly reduced opportunities to exploit the reach of the battle cruisers.

The tactical advantages of speed were understood by Fisher to be the ability to decline or force battle and to choose one's range. These advantages, theoretically enormous, were substantially nullified by a combination of factors: enormous fleets (an unstudied aspect of Fisher's North Sea concentration), poor reconnaissance, and bad North Sea weather. These factors combined to make even a summer battle, such as Jutland, extremely disorganized and confused. Because the fleets tended to encounter one another only briefly and by accident, it was difficult to use a speed advantage to "cross the T," attack detached forces, or cut off the enemy's line of retreat. Fisher, who had commanded smaller fleets (eight to twelve battleships was normal for the Mediterranean) in Mediterranean and West Indian climates, was not intellectually prepared for these conditions.

Finally, the tactical value of speed was affected by the rapid escalation in fighting ranges in a way that is usually not understood. Fisher and the other Royal Navy reformers were accustomed to the assumption that battles would be fought at 1,000 to 2,000 yards. Fisher hoped that his ideal capital ship (the *Invincible* type) would have a 7-knot speed advantage over ordinary fleets (25 to 18, plus the advantage of turbines in sustained sea-speed) and thus would overtake or pull away from another ship at 14,000 yards per hour. If 1,000 yards is the most lethal range and 3,000 yards out of effective range, a ship with this speed advantage could pull out of range or close with the enemy in some eight minutes. The resulting flexibility confers an enormous advantage. Even at 5,000 yards, the kind of range Fisher considered long when the *Dreadnought* and *Invincible* were designed, most of this advantage remains. But if the maximum range is 14,000 yards it will take an hour to cover the same distance, at 21,000 yards an hour and one half—within which time a ship could sustain crippling damage. While these examples are abstract, given the unpredictable circumstances in which real ships and fleets encounter each other, they show how the vast increase in expected fighting ranges between 1905 and 1914 diminished the premium conferred by speed.

Roots of German Technological Choices

The difference between German and British technological priorities so far described is well known. But how did it come about? In order to understand the design priorities on the eve of the dreadnought revolution, it is necessary to compare the armor protection of the last predreadnoughts. The last German predreadnought class, the *Deutschland*, had 9.4-inch armor in the belt, as compared with the 9 inches of the British *King Edward VII* class (1902–04) and 12 inches in the *Lord Nelson* (1905). Against the *Deutschland*'s 10- and 11-inch barbette and turret armor, the two British classes had 12-inch armor in both places.

An important conclusion follows from these figures: German predreadnoughts were generally less well protected than their British contemporaries. The German shift in design priorities followed the transition to dreadnoughts, as did the increase in displacement necessary to reconcile heavy protection and substantial armament. In moving from the *Lord Nelson* to the *Dreadnought*, Britain decreased armor thickness by one inch; in moving from the *Deutschland* to the *Nassau*, Germany left the turret armor the same but increased the belt by 2.6 inches (at its thickest) and the barbettes by one inch. The best indication of design priorities is the fractions of displacement devoted to the major weight groups: armament, armor, machinery, fuel, and hull. Here, a major shift in German design took place within a few years after the dreadnought revolution. The share of displacement devoted to armor rose from 33 percent in the *Deutschland* to 35 percent in the *Nassau*, then to 37 percent in the *Ostfriesland* class, and to 40 percent in the *Koenig* class.[11]

What about "unsinkability" in a more general sense—stability, compartmentation, and underwater protection? A number of authors (including Tirpitz) have tried to give the impression that the qualities displayed by German dreadnoughts during the war go back to the predreadnought period.[12] This impression is misleading. A number of German predreadnought battleships and armored cruisers were damaged by mines and torpedoes during World War I, and they sank with the same celerity as British ships. The most famous case is the *Pommern*, one of the latest classes of German predreadnoughts. When torpedoed at Jutland the *Pommern* blew up, broke in two, and sank with all hands.

To understand what caused the very different design priorities of Britain and Germany, so important in determining the technical superiority of German battleships in 1914, it is crucial to determine at exactly what point the Imperial Navy's design priorities changed. This key turning point is particularly clear for underwater protection. Careful study of the evidence provided by H. Burkhardt discloses that the experiments necessary to devise an efficient system of underwater protection for battleships began in 1906. The original German dreadnoughts, the *Nassau* class, were the first ships to be protected in this way.[13]

The shift in constructional priorities with the *Nassau* class was not confined to the new side protective system. This system was only one sign of a general attempt to rework German battleships to make them harder to sink.

Such a change involves so many elements of design (some so small and utilitarian as ventilation and drainage systems) that it tends to elude observation; the shift made by the naval architects between the *Deutschland* class—the last German predreadnoughts—and the *Nassau* class has in fact largely escaped notice both at the time and since. But one good indication of the importance given to resistance to sinking in an overall design is the metacentric height (GM), a number that is the product of many technical characteristics of the design.[14]

The GM measures the ship's resistance to capsizing when damage causes flooding. Paradoxically, a ship's resistance to capsizing does not go along with resistance to rolling; a good gun platform tends to be at the same time a ship easier to sink, and vice versa. Thus, the naval architect has to buy resistance to sinking, in the form of a high GM, at a real price. The GM of battleships is therefore a real test of relative priorities in ship design. In German dreadnoughts of the decade before World War I, it was substantially higher than in British dreadnoughts. Of the world's naval powers, Germany alone designed battleships with a GM similar to those of all countries in the period before World War II, when much more attention was given to controlling damage.[15]

This great metacentric height was a change for Germany. The GM in the five successive classes of German predreadnoughts laid down between 1890 and 1905 was 1.05, 0.917–1.18, 0.966, 1.02, and 0.98 meters. In the *Nassau*, it rose to 2.33 meters, then in the next four classes to 2.60, 2.59, 2.59, and 2.53 meters.[16] The sharp discontinuity in GM is the sign of a comprehensive transformation in the technical and military qualities asked of the ships by the designers.

What emerges from the study of the designs themselves is that a massive reassessment of battleship design, including the new program of experiments, was triggered by the construction of the HMS *Dreadnought*. This radically new and far more powerful ship disrupted all earlier canons of warship design, permitting naval architects to rethink the problem from the ground up. It is clear from Burkhardt's testimony above that this occurred in the area of underwater protection, and it can probably be assumed that the same cause lay behind the general shift of design priorities that happened at this point. As Hans Hallmann explains:

> Once the great step of the *Dreadnought* had been taken, against [our] original desires, and now freed from considerations of harbor and canal dimensions, [we] also wanted to achieve the utmost possible and build a ship containing the highest measure of battle qualities, seaworthiness, unsinkability, and efficient exploitation of available weight. It was worth the effort to allow several months for this, which gave the German ship construction program that systematically thought-through foundation that so advantageously differentiated it from the British.[17]

Hallmann and other writers on the period do not note that another precondition of the comprehensive design reassessment must have been the substantially greater displacement available once the size limits imposed by finance and by the docks and Kiel Canal were disrupted. All warship designs are constrained by the money available to buy them and by less familiar factors such as the size of the available docks and of shallow harbors and canals. But among all navies of the period, German battleship size was perhaps most constrained by a number of factors that reinforced each other. Financial limits were much less elastic because of the political constraints that stood behind them. These political constraints were inherent in the very enterprise of building a great navy for Germany. Before 1898 efforts to build a major fleet had been crippled by the interaction between Kaiser Wilhelm's impulsive initiatives and the Reichstag's caution and desire for economy; these two political forces, reacting to each other, became increasingly exasperated and intolerant on naval matters and blocked any possibility of coherent fleet development.

Tirpitz was the man who saw a way out of this impasse by a twenty-year naval building program, with a fixed number of ships and a fixed cost set in advance, which would simultaneously reassure the Reichstag as to the rationality and economy of the process and restrain the whims of the kaiser. If the Reichstag would vote such a long-term building program—as it did in 1898—the development of the fleet would be made immune to the fluctuations of German domestic politics. The key to this scheme was to lay down a fixed number of battleships and armored cruisers in each year. Its great vulnerability, however, was the possibility of a qualitative increase in the size and cost of ships that would render it impossible to provide the planned number for the budgeted cost, thus reopening the contentious political issues of just how large a fleet Germany required and just how much it should cost. This complex political situation, unique to Germany, meant that the displacement of capital ships was highly constrained.[18]

A second specific factor limiting size was the Kiel Canal, linking the Baltic and the North Sea, completed in 1895. The canal enabled the German battle fleet to operate on interior lines against forces in two seas; it was taken for granted that Imperial Navy warships should be small enough to pass through the canal. The canal was 72 feet (approximately 22 meters) broad at the bottom and 29 feet, 6 inches (approximately 9 meters) deep.[19] These dimensions rigidly constrained the beam (width) and draft of German warships, and thus their total displacement. With the *Braunschweig* class of predreadnoughts, laid down in 1901, the limits of battleship beam permitted by the canal had already been reached.

These constraints on displacement had a very important effect in limiting technical innovation by German naval architects. Design displacement increased only from 11,087 metric tons in the *Kaiser Friedrich III* class, designed in the utterly different situation prevailing before Tirpitz's Naval Law was conceived, to 13,191 metric tons in the *Deutschland* class, the last German predreadnoughts. For practical purposes, these figures meant that major technological innovation would have to have taken place by shifting weight among various weight groups, such as armament, protection, and machinery, and not by substantially increasing the weight. Here the psychological climate that surrounds weapons development, both in the public and the bureaucratic contexts, becomes important. With a more or less constant displacement ceiling, a change in priorities to enhance "unsinkability," for example, could only be purchased by fewer guns or less speed. A ship that embodied such a change in qualities would inevitably be decried as a "weaker" ship. This mechanism must have powerfully reinforced the bureaucratic tendency toward merely incremental change from year to year, as long as the predreadnought era lasted.

In the end Germany was forced to break through all these constraints and follow Britain's jump to the *Dreadnought* type. Against his will Tirpitz accepted a great rise in displacement, a corresponding rise in cost, and the necessity to widen and deepen the Kaiser Wilhelm Canal to fit wider and deeper ships.

Freedom from these constraints had a great impact on design. The latitude for designers became much greater; there was less opening for the accusation that a new design synthesis had produced a "weaker" ship. The freedom of designers from displacement constraints was compounded by the fact that battleship size was not to stabilize, as in the 1890-1904 period, but to grow very rapidly in design displacement, from the 18,873 metric tons of the *Nassau* (1907) to the 28,530 tons of the *Baden* (1913).[20]

To summarize the argument up to this point as it sheds light on arms races: Germany responded to the British initiative of the *Dreadnought* by imitation in broad outline. It built its own dreadnoughts and battle cruisers. But the British action triggered a rethinking of German battleship design that was in no way imitative of the Royal Navy. The resulting designs were superior to Britain's, a fact that gained significance from Germany's ability to "start the quantitative arms race over again," counting battleships again beginning with one. None of these indirect effects of the *Dreadnought* was anticipated by British planners, nor would it have been easy to anticipate most of them. The dreadnought revolution shows the great complexity of arms interactions in the real world and their substantial incalculability.

Roots of the German Turn to Protection

It is very clear that the *Dreadnought* sparked the reordering of German design priorities; it is less clear why the result was an emphasis on protection rather than on armament and speed. To answer this question definitively would require a new look at the documents in the light of contemporary culture and technology, but four forces leading in this direction can be identified from the available evidence. First, the freeing of design by the challenge of the *Dreadnought* and the rise in displacement was particularly liberating for protection, because it tends to be an afterthought. During the prolonged deliberation that went on within the *Reichsmarineamt* (the Imperial Naval Office) about whether to imitate the dreadnought type with its increased size and cost, the documents exchanged between Tirpitz and his staff seem to have designated alternative ship designs by displacement, armament, speed, beam, draft, and cost, not by armor protection.[21] In the case of underwater protection, the size and armament of German battleships had been nearly settled when the *Kaiser Friedrich III* class was designed, around 1894, and there seems to have been little awareness anywhere of the need for protection against torpedoes and mines until the late 1890s, when the first side protective systems, the French

Henri IV and the Russian *Tsarevich*, were designed. As explained earlier, any need for better underwater protection that began to be felt after this point would have been difficult to accommodate within the limits of the available displacement.

Second, the breaching of the constraints set by the Kaiser Wilhelm Canal had a particularly great impact on underwater protection. Because of the basic physics of explosions, an efficient system of underwater protection requires many feet of a battleship's beam; the absence of this depth cannot be compensated for in any other way. As already noted, German battleships had attained the maximum beam permitted by the canal well before 1905. Given bulky reciprocating engines and the German belief in the protection against shellfire afforded by coal bunkers, there was scarcely any way of squeezing a side protective system into the ships. When the canal limits were set aside, protection against torpedoes and mines suddenly became a practical possibility. The beam of the *Nassau* class, the first German dreadnoughts, grew by 15.42 feet (4.7 meters), and the same ships incorporated the first scientific system of underwater protection.

It was easier for protection to grow because of a third factor: the elements of design that might have competed with it had less claim on German than on British planners. In the case of armament this was a matter of design tradition; German battleships had had smaller main armaments than those of most countries since the early 1890s. This tradition was probably a relic of the period when the small quickfirer was widely seen as the decisive weapon. In the case of speed it appears that German designers consciously rejected British design priorities. German professional opinion was well aware of the British priority for speed and armament over protection, which emerged with particular clarity when the *Dreadnought* and *Invincible* types appeared.[22] The Germans did rethink their own attitudes, but the outcome was to revalue the worth of speed not upward but downward. In 1904 an authoritative German source said that speed and "fighting strength" (armament and armor) should be equally valued.[23] By 1907 the view had shifted:

> Speed stands behind other strategically more important factors. It should not be overvalued strategically. It is indefensible for strategic reasons to sacrifice fighting power.... Speed is no weapon. It remains, even after Tsushima, what it always was: only a means to carry weapons into battle.[24]

The reasoning behind the depreciation of speed is quite visible in the German professional literature. An important article in the 1911 *Nauticus* makes three arguments that, taken together, do tend to discourage giving priority to speed.[25] First, as the speed rises, the horsepower (and therefore the share of total weight) required to get additional speed rises much more steeply. Second, to possess greater speed than the enemy ship or fleet does confer an advantage, but this advantage diminishes steadily as speed rises: a ship with 19 knots speed has a greater advantage over a ship with 18 knots speed than a ship with 28 knots has over one that goes 27 knots. Third, the Germans seem to have understood that, as argued earlier, increased ranges reduced the value of speed:

The sharp increase in expected battle ranges has a considerable influence on the tactical value of the speed advantage. The expansion of distances predicted for modern combat acts to reduce this value. For example, the danger of being enveloped is smaller now than earlier, and, consequently, one cannot as easily drag one's opponent off course in order to put him in a disadvantageous artillery firing position.[26]

To be sure, none of these arguments in itself refutes Fisher's position that speed conferred an advantage. Taken together, however, they had an impact like that of Colonel Glenn Kent's "damage limiting" studies on American ballistic missile procurement in the 1960s: they show that as speed rises, one has to pay more and more in terms of weight for less and less advantage. The effect of these analyses, more careful than anything done in England, was to dampen impulses toward giving priority to speed.

A fourth and very important factor in the emphasis on protection was the bureaucratic structure of the defense establishment. In Britain the basic features of ship design were settled by the lords of the Admiralty, that is, by sea officers and politicians. During the vital transition to the *Dreadnought* and *Invincible* types, First Sea Lord Fisher (a sea officer) shaped the designs himself through the pliant Committee on Designs. In Germany, on the other hand, the *Reichsmarineamt* and its head, Tirpitz, were responsible for ship design and completely separated from the sea officers under the *Admiralstab* and the fleet high command, who had to operate the ships produced. This bureaucratic separation gave the naval constructors, who were technicians with academic training and not sea officers, an unusual degree of authority and independence in determining ship designs.

The organizational position of German naval constructors at this time gave greater freedom to the design outlook latent in their professional role. While it is a complicated subject, there has been a tendency for sea officers to emphasize guns in design and for naval architects to emphasize protection. Naval architects E. J. Reed, Nathaniel Barnaby, and Emile Bertin, for example, were prominent proponents of heavy protection during the predreadnought era. After all, if a ship wins a battle by good gunnery, it is due to the officers; if it wins by heavy protection, it is due to the naval architect. More generally, there is a certain tendency of professional military men to discount purely passive weapons such as naval mines and civil defense, and underwater protection is a "weapon" of this type. The bureaucratic structure of the German navy countered this tendency.

The bureaucratic situation was reinforced by the fact that the building of the *Dreadnought*, the most recent naval event, gave the constructors great authority. As Walther Hubatsch remarked, the building of the *Dreadnought* brought a new age in which political and strategic considerations receded and the new maritime weapon gained the spotlight, enhancing in the process the authority of the *Reichsmarineamt*.[27] The climate of naval policy in the years before World War I was the opposite of the climate in the period after the Washington Naval Treaty (1922), when the freezing of battleship design by arms control made American and Japanese naval officers concentrate on how actually to fight a naval war if one broke out.[28]

The most recent war experience, that of the Russo-Japanese War of 1904–05, probably did not itself provoke any innovations, but it did facilitate the constructors' arguments about the importance of underwater protection. In this war the initial surprise torpedo attack of 8–9 February 1904 had temporarily eliminated the Russian margin of superiority in battleships, resulting in the prolonged passivity of the Russian fleet. When it became active again under the leadership of Admiral Makarov, a Japanese mine destroyed the Russian flagship, *Petropavlovsk*, and the remaining initiative of the Port Arthur squadron (13 April 1904). The Japanese were very lucky that it was a month later when Russian mines reduced their battleship strength by one-third in a single day (15 June 1904). Thus, it was a correct inference from the Russo-Japanese War that every other advance in battleship design could be negated by vulnerability to underwater attack. As a German author wrote in 1911:

> The development of underwater protection can be divided into two great periods... by the Russo-Japanese war with all its lessons. From the present standpoint, the development of underwater protection was in all navies in a bad state in the first period. Today it appears to us wholly unsatisfactory.[29]

Even if the British had not viewed the Russo-Japanese War through the lens of their existing military doctrine,[30] the mere timing of events put them in a much worse position to incorporate the lessons of the war in their battleship design. Admiral Fisher had decided the basic lines of the *Invincible* and *Dreadnought* types before information was available from the war, and the detailed designs were drawn up while the attaché reports were being received from the Far East some four to five months afterward.[31] The consternation into which the German building program was thrown by the *Dreadnought* allowed them some two years to remold their designs in the light of the wartime experience of February–May 1904: the first German dreadnoughts were laid down only in 1907.

Everything the German naval constructors did was facilitated by the greater prestige in their country of expertise (*Wissenschaft*) and of natural science, which tended again to enhance the authority of the naval architects, to encourage them in producing careful, tightly integrated designs, and to help them in securing funds for careful experimentation rather than to rely on traditional or intuitive designs. This facet of Wilhelminian culture was liberated by the shock of the *Dreadnought*. The British tendency, on the other hand, was toward improvisation and amateurism. It was three months before the outbreak of war when an official of the Admiralty plaintively noted: "So far as Admiralty records show, it does not appear that any official statement exists as to the principles which should govern the provision and distribution of armor in warship design."[32] The British were bound to be in deep trouble if German *Wissenschaft* ever got thoroughly to work on battleship design. It did so as an unforeseen result of a British initiative, the *Dreadnought*.

V. R. Berghahn has described very well the depth of the disruption in Germany's naval programs caused by the *Dreadnought*,[33] but he does not tell something even more important: that the very disruption of routines was the source of a new superiority in German designs. Such is the strange and unpredictable character of arms races in real history.

Roots of British Technological Choices[34]

British ships gave priority not to protection but to armament and, to a lesser extent, to speed. Increased speed, the real enthusiasm of Admiral Fisher, can be treated briefly because it was his individual passion and because it proved to be an abortive revolution. After the *Dreadnought* and *Invincible*, battleship and battle-cruiser speed stabilized on a new plateau (at least until 1912). All the other naval powers followed British battleship speed, and Germany followed the battle-cruiser type.

The emphasis on speed was in part, as Arthur J. Marder remarks, an aspect of the emphasis on guns, since the faster ship could choose its best range.[35] But Fisher had broader reasons, which he explained in 1901 when asked by the Admiralty about design priorities for battleships. "The British naval policy is to take the offensive," wrote Fisher, thus raising the problem (as in the French wars) of bringing the enemy's ships or fleets to action. The solution was "speed and coal endurance which are the first two essentials of every type of British fighting vessel simply because they permit an admiral to choose his own time of fighting."[36] Generally, the dominant position of the Royal Navy, as channeled by the seriousness and intensity of Fisher, conduced to unbalanced designs, while the inferior position of the German navy led to anxiety, caution, and balanced designs that left no weaknesses for the enemy to exploit. The quest to eliminate weaknesses in design, exacerbated by the uncertainty that came with the dreadnought type, tended in practice toward repairing weaknesses usually neglected, such as survivability in battle.

Fisher defined the Royal Navy's task as "instant readiness for war," and his design concepts were thus keyed not only to keeping pace with the enemy but also to gaining a decisive advantage. It seemed as if speed might confer such an advantage. As discussed earlier, this may have been more true around the turn of the century than it was in 1914, and "cultural lag" may have played a certain role in the priority given by the British to speed as to armament.

The priority to armament was a reflection of an emphasis on the gun that pervaded the entire naval profession in Britain. As Marder says: "Guns, big guns, long ranges..., good shooting—these were the articles of faith of the naval officer, and to the proper development of this method of attack all systems of tactics were directed and subordinated."[37] This spirit was embodied by Fisher and his protégés such as Jellicoe, Sir Percy Scott, and Admiral Bacon, but it was also shared by his opponents. On the eve of the war one of the most violent members of the anti-Fisher faction, Admiral Sir Reginald Custance, contributed to *Brassey's* an article urging not thicker but thinner armor. He said of British battle cruisers as compared with battleships that "the reduction in armor represents no loss of fighting power and might even be carried further, but the loss of guns is very serious and prepares defeat."[38]

The source of this pervasive spirit is not usually identified, but it must be the great gunnery reform begun by Scott in 1898. During that great campaign the preparation of the navy for war became identified with the improvement of shooting. The obsession of Scott, the other reformers, and their biographers with the stupid conservatism of the Admiralty and of unprogressive fellow officers has tended to hide how widely and quickly good shooting became a preoccupation in the Royal Navy. This success of the gunnery crusade must have been assisted by something in the institutional life of the navy. In fact, good shooting filled an important professional function by giving the keen officer a way to distinguish himself. In this respect it filled the same place as sailing exercises, the close-order ship maneuvers practiced during the 1880s, and the cleanliness of brass and paintwork—except that it was more substantive, more visibly related to efficiency in war. Thus, the priority of armament in ship design was intimately linked to the daily life and career goals of British naval officers. The same was not true of protection.

The development of the German navy was very different. Germany had not possessed a serious blue-water navy before the 1890s. There was no "old" navy with the grandeur of the British, and no decline from the grandeur to the sleepy decay of the Victorian age. The Imperial Navy did improve its gunnery somewhat as the British did but without the weight of the past; good gunnery was not particularly seen as a reaction against past folly and certainly did not bear the weight of being seen as the escape from that past folly. Thus, it is reasonable to expect that gunnery, and armament as a design element, would have been better integrated into the whole professional activity of the German navy, even if its bureaucratic organization had not drawn designs away from the preponderance of armament. It is profoundly ironic that the force that pushed the British navy into readiness for war—the gunnery revolution—also prepared that navy's most dangerous vulnerability when war began.

Why German Advantages Were Never Used

The final irony was one that prevented Britain from paying the price for its technological choices, because it discouraged the Germans from using the magnificent weapon Tirpitz had forged. There are many reasons why the Imperial Navy, built up in a spirit of such truculence, did not want to fight in 1914. In all navies the fear of new, untested technologies such as submarines and long-range gunnery encouraged passivity. The German navy, for its part, lacked the confidence that came from a long, victorious tradition. It had been built up for reasons of Great Power status and as a lever to achieve political goals (the explicit purpose of the Risk Theory), not to win a war.

The very twofold bureaucratic structure, however, that resulted in such superior designs was also a potent cause of the passivity of the fleet. To start with, the concentration of power in the *Reichsmarineamt* meant that more intelligence and energy were expended on organizing a fleet and designing ships than on how to fight a war. Moreover, it becomes apparent that even those officers who wanted in 1914 to use the fleet more vigorously, such as Franz Hipper, did not know how good their ships really were. They proposed more imaginative courses out of impatience, as a risk, or from a sense of honor, not because they believed they would prevail.[39] This was the effect of secrecy about the technical features of German ships; the character and rationale of the underwater protection system, for example, were largely unknown to German sea officers.[40] This secrecy arose from the separation between design and use, between the *Reichsmarineamt* and the sea officers, the latter had not suggested or developed these features or trained extensively in their use, because they were "passive" protection. As a result, the power of German technological choices was not unveiled until Jutland, when it was too late. That changed history.

NOTES

1. Bernard Brodie, "On the Objectives of Arms Control," in *The Use of Force: International Politics and Foreign Policy*, eds. Robert J. Art and Kenneth N. Waltz (Lanham, MD, 1983), 432.

2. For a preliminary report of the overall conclusions, see Charles H. Fairbanks, Jr., "Arms Races: The Metaphor and the Facts," *The National Interest* 1 (Fall 1985): 75-90. For an analysis of the U.S.-Soviet arms race, see Charles H. Fairbanks, Jr., "Do Arms Races Exist?" Occasional Paper no. 69 of the International Security Studies Program, Woodrow Wilson International Center for Scholars, 1985.

3. Quoted in Ruddock Mackay, *Fisher of Kilverstone* (Oxford, 1973), 98.

4. P. K. Kemp, ed., *The Papers of Admiral Sir John Fisher*, 2 vols. (London, Navy Records Society, vols. 102 [1960], 106 [1964]), 1:28; compare letter of 19 December 1900 in Mackay, *Fisher*, 269.

5. Alfred von Tirpitz, *My Memoirs*, 2 vols. (London, 1919), 1:133, 131.

6. This was rediscovered by Jon Tetsuro Sumida, "British Capital Ship Design and Fire Control in the *Dreadnought* Era: Sir John Fisher, Arthur Hungerford Pollen, and the Battle Cruiser," *Journal of Modern History* 51 (June 1979): 207n4, passim.

7. N. J. M. Campbell, *Battle Cruisers: The Design and Development of British and German Battlecruisers of the First World War Era* (London, 1978), 5.

8. A. Temple Patterson, ed., *The Jellicoe Papers*, 2 vols. (London: Navy Records Society, vols. 108 [1966], 111 [1969]), 1:59, 24.

9. See especially Arthur J. Marder, *From the Dreadnought to Scapa Flow: The Royal Navy in the Fisher Era, 1904-1919*, 5 vols. (London, 1961-70), 2:173-75.

10. For British underwater protection see Oscar Parkes, *British Battleships "Warrior" 1860 to "Vanguard" 1950: A History of Design, Construction, and Armament* (New Haven, 1970); Siegfried Breyer, *Battleships and Battle Cruisers, 1905-1970*, trans. Alfred Kurti (New York, 1973), 113-48; Campbell, *Battle Cruisers*, passim; N. J. M. Campbell, "German Dreadnoughts and Their Protection," *Warship* 1 (October 1977): 19; N. J. M. Campbell, *Queen Elizabeth Class* (London, 1972), 10-11.

11. Heinrich Evers, *Kriegsschiffbau: Ein Lehr- und Hilfsbuch für die Kriegsmarine*, 2d ed. (Berlin, 1943), 105, Table 3. These figures are prepared on a different basis than comparable English figures. Gratitude is extended to David Wurmser, Eugene Beye, and Duncan Moore for assistance with these materials and to Jon Sumida for British documents.

12. On German underwater protection in this period see Heinrich Evers, "Alfred Dietrich: Dem ersten Chefkonstrukteur der Marine zum Gedachtnis," *Marine Rundschau* 48 (July 1943): 487-90; compare John Leyland, "The Progress of Foreign Navies," *Naval Annual* (1901): 48.

13. For the experiments and the resulting German system of underwater protection see the recollections (from memory at the age of eighty) of one of the designers: H. Burkhardt, "Die Entwicklung des Unterwasserschutzes in der Deutschen Kriegsmarine," Part I, *Marine Rundschau* 58 (June 1961): 151-69; for the date see p. 153. The application of this system to the first German dreadnought battleships, the *Nassau* class, is clarified in Evers, *Kriegsschiffbau*, 41. See also Tirpitz, *My Memoirs* 1:131-33.

14. For a nontechnical explanation of GM, see Norman Friedman, *Battleship Design and Development* (New York, 1978), 49-53.

15. See figures in ibid., 165-73.

16. Erich Groener, Dieter Jung, and Martin Maass, *Die deutschen Kriegsschiffe, 1815-1945*, 2 vols. (Munich, 1982), 1:36-52.

17. Hans Hallmann, "Vor dreissig Jahren: Die Anfange des deutschen Dreadnoughtbaus 1905 bis 1908," *Marine Rundschau* 43 (December 1938): 915. Hallmann's account made it clear, as Berghahn since has shown very ably, that the dreadnought type was forced on Germany and was not an independent German initiative, as Hubatsch and other writers had implied.

18. For the best explanation of the logic of the Naval Law and how it constrained German designs, see V. R. Berghahn, *Der Tirpitz-Plan: Genesis und Verfall einer innenpolitischen Krisenstrategie unter Wilhelm II* (Düsseldorf, 1971), 448–49, 452–53, 466–70.

19. *Encyclopaedia Britannica,* 11th ed., s.v. "Germany, Waterways."

20. Tonnage (as before) and dimensions are from Groener, Jung, and Maass, *Die deutschen Kriegsschiffe,* passim.

21. See the examples quoted in Berghahn, *Der Tirpitz-Plan,* 455, 460–61, 466–72.

22. "Geschwindigkeit und Gefechtskraft," *Nauticus* (1907): 232–47; "Die Entwicklung des Modernen Kampfschiffes," *Nauticus* (1911): 219–20.

23. "Militarisches Wert der Schiffsgeschwindigkeit," *Nauticus* (1904): 89–101.

24. "Geschwindigkeit und Gefechtskraft," *Nauticus* (1907): 238–39, 246. The analysis also deprecates the tactical advantage conferred by speed.

25. "Die Entwicklung des Modernen Kampfschiffes," *Nauticus* (1911): 207–42.

26. Ibid., 216, 218.

27. Walther Hubatsch, *Der Admiralstab und die obersten Marinebehörden in Deutschland, 1845–1945* (Frankfurt, 1958), 215.

28. See especially Michael Vlahos, "Wargaming, an Enforcer of Strategic Realism: 1919–1942," *Naval War College Review* 39 (March–April 1986): 9, 13, 15–16.

29. "Die Entwicklung des Unterwasserschutzes," *Nauticus* (1911): 189.

30. See Philip Towle, "The Evaluation of the Experience of the Russo-Japanese War," in *Technical Change and British Naval Policy, 1860–1939,* ed. Brian Ranft (London, 1977), 65–79; Admiral Sir Cyprian Bridge, "The Russo-Japanese Naval Campaign of 1904," *Naval Annual* (1905): 118–19, 143, 164, 167–68, 171.

31. Towle, "Experience of the Russo-Japanese War," 68; Marder, *From the Dreadnought,* 1:59–60.

32. London, Public Record Office, Minute Third Sea Lord, 1 June 1914, in Admiralty Confidential Print.

33. V. R. Berghahn, "Zu den Zielen der Deutschen Flottenbaus unter Wilhelm II," *Historische Zeitschrift* 210 (February 1970): 86–93; Berghahn, *Der Tirpitz-Plan,* 419ff.

34. These conclusions should be taken as provisional. Professor Jon Sumida's forthcoming book on British naval policy will clarify many of these issues.

35. Marder, *From the Dreadnought,* 1:414.

36. London, Public Record Office, Letter to the Secretary of the Admiralty, 25 June 1901, (Admiralty Records) ADM 1/7521.

37. Marder, *From the Dreadnought* 1:414.

38. Admiral Sir Reginald N. Custance, "The Principles Governing the Use of Armour and Guns in Ships of the Line," *Naval Annual* (1913): 122–31.

39. For example, see Tobias Philbin III, "Reflections on the Strategy of a Continental Commander: Admiral Franz Hipper on Naval Warfare," *Naval War College Review* 30 (Fall 1977): 77; Holger Herwig, *The German Naval Officer Corps: A Social and Political History, 1890–1918* (Oxford, 1973), 177–80.

40. See Burkhardt, "Die Entwicklung des Unterwasserschutzes in der Deutschen Kriegsmarine," Part II, *Marine Rundschau* 58 (August 1961): 204, 211.

Admiral Nelson and the Concept of Patriotism: The Trafalgar Centenary, 1905

GERALD JORDAN

The centenary on 21 October 1905 of Nelson's death at the Battle of Trafalgar gave the Navy League the opportunity to arouse popular support for the Royal Navy. Nelson as hero was to be seen as the personification of national pride and purpose. Concentrating on the Trafalgar Day ceremonies, Dr. Jordan suggests that the attempt to create a popular cult of the admiral and revive interest in the navy was a failure.

****

Heroes long have served to inspire national unity and spirit in times of great crisis. The centenary on 21 October 1905 of the death of Vice Admiral Lord Nelson at the Battle of Trafalgar marked the apogee of a long campaign to arouse patriotic feeling and mass support for the Royal Navy in the face of apparent national decline and foreign threats to Britain's maritime hegemony. Part of the campaign, spearheaded by the Navy League, focused upon the admiral as the personification of national greatness and purpose. Nelson, proclaimed the *Daily Chronicle,* was needed "in time of unrest and materialism, decadence and inefficiency."[1] His image became an important element of the widespread but loose-knit campaign to bring efficiency to the nation by imposing on the lower classes both inflexible bourgeois standards of morality and elitist notions of duty to the state. "The Nelson celebrations," noted *The Globe,* "are said to have created the impression in Japan that we are imitating Admiral Togo's example, and adopting the worship of ancestors."[2] The impression was not far from the truth.

Focusing on the Trafalgar Day ceremonies, this paper examines the attempts to create a popular cult of Nelson and to assess its reception. The working classes were a major target for navalist propaganda and, since they constituted nearly 75 percent of the population in 1900, it seems reasonable to concentrate mainly upon them. This is not to suggest, however, that they were the only, or even the main, object of navalist attention.

Historians have shown little interest in public attitudes toward the navy. Although considerable research has been devoted to naval administration, technology, and the colorful personalities of the Tyron-Beresford-Fisher era, claims in organs of naval interest groups, particularly the Navy League, of widespread and vocal support for expansionist maritime policies generally have been taken at face value. It is no wonder, because these claims were made and accepted without question by most of the upper classes from within whose ranks navalist pressure emanated and who saw the Royal Navy as the principal guardian of free trade and empire. They created a myth of popular support for the navy which historians since have not questioned. Naval history has been written from the point of view of the middle-class nation for whom the question of popular appeal appears to have only passing relevance. Seen in the wider context of the nation as a whole, however, the issue assumes greater importance.

The three decades before the Great War saw challenges to British trade, industry, and sea power unparalleled since the Napoleonic era. As they had one hundred years earlier, fears of a nation divided within itself and threatened from outside by ambitious European powers spawned a myriad of middle- and upper-class organizations aimed at creating national unity and efficiency. The Royal Navy was only one element of society which appeared to fall short of national needs. To many, however, it was the most important. The country could survive, perhaps even thrive, without a large army, but naval supremacy was considered essential by imperialists and radicals alike. Hence, the need for strongly applied public pressure seemed great.[3]

The Navy League was founded in 1895 with Admiral of the Fleet Sir Geoffrey Phipps-Hornby as first president. A portrait of Nelson was at the center of its crest. Its leaders were entirely upper class, as were those of other patriotic organizations. Among the vice presidents were Field Marshal Lord Roberts, who a decade later became president of the National Service League, and the earl of Minto, future governor general of Canada and viceroy of India, together with the dukes of Devonshire, Hamilton, and Westminster. Rudyard Kipling became vice president in 1898. The earl of Meath, founder of the Lads' Drill Association, the Duty and Discipline Movement, the Empire Day Movement, and a leading member of the National Service League, was vice president in 1909.

Ordinary membership was almost entirely bourgeois: naval officers, members of Parliament, headmasters of public and grammar schools, journalists, Church of England clergymen, businessmen, and university lecturers. By 1900 the league claimed 14,000 members. London had four branches: the prosperous areas of Belgravia, Hyde Park, South Kensington, and Kentish Town-Northwest London. Provincial branches were at Bristol, Windsor, Brighton, Birmingham, Plymouth, Oxford, Cambridge, Liverpool, Sydenham, Southampton, Worcester, Torquay, Edinburgh, and Glasgow. Industrial Britain was underrepresented. The league spread more rapidly in the settlement empire than at home, and in 1914 membership throughout the empire was estimated at 100,000. The purpose, spelled out in the *Navy League Journal,* was to arouse public awareness that the protection of seaborne trade was "vital to the people of this country, and especially to the working classes"; to enlist "the support of all classes" for naval supremacy; and to impress upon the British people that the unity of the empire could be maintained only by the navy.[4]

On the face of it, the league's tactics for gaining working-class support were logical. Believing that mass enthusiasm would be aroused more by slogans, dramatic ceremonies, and the theater of the heroic than by bourgeois arguments of two-power standards and economics, the league resurrected England's greatest fighting seaman. Nelson's valor and his devotion to duty, king, and country would, they hoped, become watchwords for the working classes. The league's secretary, Sir Patrick Hannon, summed it up:

> In religion, in art, in adventure, and in all departments of human life the tendency of the populace is to personify a principle by a human being.... So Nelson's life and death, it was foreseen, might be utilised to personify British sea power to the children, if not the veterans, of British democracy throughout the world.[5]

Trafalgar Day was central to the league's plans. Their objective was to make the anniversary of the hero's glorious death an annual public observance which would act as both a focus and definition of patriotism. It would become part of a national cult which would inculcate bourgeois values, foster loyalty to state rather than to class, and thus be a means of overcoming class antagonisms without destroying class barriers. For the upper classes the occasion would mark a reaffirmation of the existing social order. The lower middle class also would reaffirm its allegiance to that structure in an assertion of its respectability and superiority over the members of the working class, who in turn would be impressed by Nelson's heroic virtues and thus come to identify with the values of their social superiors.[6] The laying of wreaths from the HMS *Excellent* and the Navy League in London at the foot of Nelson's column in Trafalgar Square on 21 October 1895 was, the *Daily Mail* observed a year later, "much commented on at the time as a new departure in the teaching of historical events to the masses."[7]

The late nineteenth-century calendar lacked the unity of earlier counterparts, but many of the old conventions of festive life and ritual remained important. Upper-class Britain was not without its moments of theater, its symbolic representations of power and prestige which legitimized the political order. The London civil calendar still contained occasions that stretched back to Tudor and Stuart times: the solemn majesty of the law at the opening of Old Bailey, royal largesse with the distribution of Maundy Money, the controlled exuberance of beating the bounds on Ascension Day, charity school processions oozing paternalism, and, best of all, the magnificent Lord Mayor's Show, an expression of civic pride and merchant wealth. Although old national celebrations like Oak Apple Day were losing significance and London's festive Bartholomew Fair had been abolished in 1855, they were being replaced by a new and full calendar of patriotic occasions like Lord Meath's Empire Day and royal jubilees and other anniversaries, when services of thanksgiving linked sovereign and nation and empire with divinity.

Trafalgar Day was to be part of this new pattern. "The Navy League," commented the *Daily Mail*,[8] "thinks it has good reason for its belief that the practice of commemorating the day will yearly grow more general, and that soon Trafalgar Day will be a big national festival." It would, the league hoped, fit into the ritualized calendar and become part of the annual workingclass rhythm which still included Pancake Tuesday, hot cross buns on Good Friday, and bonfire night. As Guy Fawkes Day had long been an outlet for traditional anti-Catholic prejudices and insularity, so Trafalgar Day would provide the focus for displays of patriotism and national solidarity. Indeed, it might draw attention away from Guy Fawkes festivities, only two weeks later, which in many towns had become a classical day of license marked by a breakdown of the customary order and riotous clashes between bonfire societies, crowds, and the authorities, reminiscent of eighteenth-century pope-burning revelries.[9] With these factors in mind, the Trafalgar Day celebrations were to be staged with appropriate ceremony—special church services, naval and military parades, patriotic levees, illuminations—to remind the nation of its special heritage by recalling the momentous events of 1805 and to define that heritage in a particular way. Pageantry would be melded with explicit didacticism to sanctify the social order and elevate the status of one of its principal guardians, the Royal Navy.

Until 1905 the Trafalgar commemorations, held annually since 1896, attracted little attention. The centenary ceremonies at Trafalgar Square, however, were the most elaborate public function ever undertaken by the Navy League. Nelson's column, entwined with forty tons of bay and laurel and 20,000 chrysanthemums, was topped with the national flags of France and Britain. An immense wreath tied with the French and Spanish colors was laid by the league in memory of gallant former enemies. One hundred twenty-six wreaths and other floral tributes from the colonies, League branches, and descendants of officers and men who fought at the battle adorned the monument.[10]

Saturday, 21 October, was cold and gray with occasional showers. But by 10:30 that morning the crowd was so large that the police had to form the people into queues to view the decorations. Souvenir vendors did a brisk trade and "for the most part, all was good humoured and peaceable."[11] The children of the prince and princess of Wales drove by on their way to Sandringham and were observed giving the military salute. Miss Weston's Naval Boys' Brigade paraded. Crocodiles of school children were led around the column in homage. "Several little mites eager to lay a posey . . . were carefully guided through the crowd by police."[12] Twelve survivors of the Battle of Balaclava laid a wreath. A poem in praise of "the immortal Nelson," sent by an octogenarian lady whose father had fought on the HMS *Victory*, was affixed to a wreath of yellow, white, and pink chrysanthemums and geraniums. By 2:30 in the afternoon, when the formal ceremony commenced, the crowd was estimated at between 12,000 and 15,000. On the plinth with Lord Drogheda, the president of the Navy League, were the current Lord Nelson as well as Lords Ranfurly, Strathcona, and Cottesloe, the agents general for Natal and Tasmania, Admiral and Lady Fremantle, and Bishop Welldon with his chaplain. The mayor of Westminster, Lord Chellesmore, resplendent in robes and chain of office, was attended by the town clerk, the mace bearer, and the members of the Westminster City Council.[13]

The service was solemn and brief. The Queen's Westminster Volunteers band struck up "The Death of Nelson," the ensigns on the column were dipped to half-mast, Bishop Welldon said a prayer to the hero's memory, Mr. Alexander Watson recited Kipling's "Recessional," and trumpeters sounded reveille. The ensigns were hoisted, and the ceremony concluded with two verses of the national anthem led by Mr. Robert Hilton, who had sung the anthem in Westminster Abbey on the occasion of Queen Victoria's Jubilee in 1887. About 4 o'clock, almost at the hour of Nelson's death, the sky darkened and there was a heavy rain shower.[14]

Elsewhere in London there were other ceremonies. The London Society of East Anglians laid a wreath on Nelson's tomb in the crypt of St. Paul's Cathedral. Following the Trafalgar Square ceremonies, the ladies' branch of the Navy League held a patriotic musical celebration in the Royal Agricultural Hall, Westminster. Admiral Sir Clements Markham addressed the boys of Westminster School. The Anglo-French entente was applauded that evening at a Navy League dinner in Piccadilly's Criterion Restaurant. In the Royal Albert Hall, Lord Brassey presided over a distinguished gathering organized by the British and Foreign Sailors' Society, at which the speakers included Viscount Hayashi, the Japanese ambassador. Captain Kaburaki, the imperial naval attaché, accepted a bust of Nelson on behalf of Admiral Togo and was "cheered for several minutes." When the kaiser was mentioned, "there were hisses from the stalls."[15]

Provincial towns and villages held their own celebrations. At Burnham Thorpe, Nelson's birthplace in Norfolk, a dinner of roast beef and plum pudding was provided for the villagers. Large crowds turned out at Liverpool and Birmingham for ceremonies similar to those of Trafalgar Square. Norwich, Portsmouth, and Bristol also mounted elaborate civic observances. Commemoratory services, preceded by corporate and military processions, were held at the cathedrals of Manchester, Liverpool, and Ripon; the bishop of St. Albans preached at St. Mary's Portsea, and Nelson's call to duty was stressed in sermons across the country.

On the face of it, the observances appeared to be a great success. The Navy League's efforts received widespread support from the mainstream press, naval and military officers, and among the upper and middle classes in general. The press had mounted a sustained effort to foster a spirit of consensual celebration long before the occasion. As early as October 1895, *The Observer* was confident that "landsmen and seamen of British birth will henceforth remember Trafalgar Day as one sacred to the Empire and the race."[16] John Leyland, writing for Brassey's *Naval Annual* in 1897, predicted that:

> When the history of Her Majesty's reign comes to be written, without doubt, one of the most significant things to be recorded will be the vastly increased interest taken by Englishmen in the question of naval defence.... We should go very far to find a parallel for this awakening of public opinion.[17]

By 1905, Nelson mania appeared to be sweeping the country. Even C. P. Scott's *Manchester Guardian* had adopted a navalist stance. Indeed, that radical mouthpiece vied with the *Times* in the bulk and hyperbole of its tributes to the hero. Naval exhibitions focusing upon Nelson at Greenwich, the British Museum, the Royal United Services Institution, and other centers across the country combined with lengthy articles in service and literary journals, didactic Nelson biographies, and boys' stories to achieve what a later generation would call media saturation.

Evidence indicates, however, that public interest in and knowledge of the navy was neither so widespread nor so "vastly increased" as Leyland and others claimed. "The Nelson Centenary," said the *Manchester Guardian,* "has apparently sent no thrill through the nation." Although the *Daily Chronicle* mentioned "some remarkable demonstrations of popular enthusiasm," several reports suggest that the general public was singularly uninformed about the significance of the occasion. When a bystander asked a policeman in Trafalgar Square a few days before the event "what was to do?" he received the startling reply: "Wellington, Sir, anniversary next Saturday." A servant woman who had lived forty years in central London confessed to a reporter that before that day she had never noticed Nelson's column. "I bin [sic] often to Charing Cross... but I never set eyes on that pole before." She had never heard of Nelson except for a piece of information she had picked up in the crowd: "that the gentleman had been dead for a hundred years." She thought the "long pole" was the monument to the Great Fire of London.[18] Even the imperialist *Daily Mail* departed from its usual sanguinary tone to report that the Nelson Exhibition at the Royal United Services Institution had, since its opening in May, attracted many French and American visitors but "hardly a Londoner has crossed the door."[19]

The picture from the provinces was no brighter. Centenary observances were of a similar didactic and elitist nature to those held in London. Special church services, military parades, processions of town notables in full regalia, and mayoral and private banquets were recorded at length in the press, but there are no indications of any favorable working-class response. In many towns the elites did not stage public celebrations. The Cambridge Corporation, for example, was afraid "of the probability of any ensuing disturbance by the undergraduates."[20] The weekly *Southend Standard* made only passing reference to the centenary, and no celebrations were seen to have taken place in the Thames estuary town often visited by naval vessels. In North Wales, the occasion "was not very generally celebrated.... The only celebrative sign of Llandudno was a flag flying over Trinity Church.... Colwyn Bay did nothing in the way of celebrating the centenary."[21] No public ceremonies were held in Nottingham or Sheffield, although the latter observed Temperance Sunday on 22 October with some seventy sermons preached in the city's churches on the subject. In Scotland, a subscription for the Navy League received a total of twelve shillings and sixpence.[22] Even naval dockyard towns displayed a lack of enthusiasm. Portsmouth showed "little interest in the business... the event of the day was undoubtedly the Welsh football match." At the Sheerness dockyard church, a special appeal by the naval chaplain raised only one pound, eighteen shillings.[23]

By 1909, when the Anglo-German naval race was at full flood, even some Navy League writers were admitting failure. J. Alex Mitchell lamented in the *Navy League Annual*:

> For the last fourteen years the Navy League has endeavoured by means of lantern and other lectures, the formation of branches and excursions to dockyards, to create an interest in the Navy, and may take credit unto itself for having done good work; but every one engaged in the work has been met with the "birthright" attitude and with almost complete apathy.... The large majority of us have but the dimmest notion of what the Navy really represents.[24]

On the eve of war, Arnold White, a founding member of the league and originator of the Trafalgar Day celebrations, observed despairingly that "fifteen million children of Great Britain are not taught one line on the subject of the Navy, and there is no school book used to impart to school teachers and their pupils a knowledge of the place of the Navy in the British scheme of existence."[25]

What had gone wrong? Why had the manufactured ritual struck so few chords among the mass of Britons? Part of the answer lies with the reincarnation of Nelson which was presented in the press and in league publicity. The admiral failed to survive industrialization and its attendant hardening of class lines. The public hero of 1805 could not exist in an urban class-ridden society.[26] The Nelson of 1805 reflected a society in which the realities of class had still to solidify. The Nelson of the Nile huzzahed in the streets had popular characteristics which were genuine, not manufactured by an elite struggling to stem democratic trends. And, perhaps realizing the basis of Nelson's appeal, many of the elite saw something dangerous in the attempted reincarnation. By 1900 the patriotic organizations were unable to reconstruct the old popular image of Nelson. Instead, they constructed a remote aristocratic figure whose virtues were those of the public school, far removed from the realities of urban working-class life.

To form the patriotic image, the facts must be so selective that the full truth, or the unwholesome facts, must be suppressed. Basic to the idea of heroism is that the hero can be emulated, his virtues are human, and he becomes the model for the common man. The late Victorian hero embodied upper-class virtues of courage, resourcefulness, self-sacrifice, and a high-blown morality, all included in the overriding concept of duty to king and country. The new Nelson possessed all of these to the point where the hero of 1905 was scarcely recognizable as the hero of 1805. "Personal character," declared the *Pall Mall Gazette*, "is in the last resort everything."[27] Many of the factors which helped to make Nelson an object of popular veneration in his own lifetime were distasteful to the evangelical spirit of the late Victorian upper classes who organized the resurrection.

The national hero of 1905 could not be known to have flaunted his lower-class mistress to the world, fathered an illegitimate child, or turned his back on his wife. He could not be vain or take a childish delight at his decorations. Neither could he be pictured as a short, rather ridiculous-looking figure who took great and obvious pleasure in the adulation of the crowd. He had to be a virtuous, modest man whose heroic proportions were carried within a frail frame. Above all, he had to be guided by a firm, unswerving sense of duty and love of country. And so the popular hero whose carriage had been dragged by the common folk through the drizzle of Yarmouth and Ipswich and Colchester in 1801 was replaced by a serious, staid, and aloof muscular Christian. A figure of rectitude with little appeal for the masses, he was molded in the Victorian concept of Havelock and "Chinese" Gordon rather than that of the eighteenth-century Nelson.[28] One hundred years earlier, Nelson's popularity with the crowd had been partly due to his ability to blend paternalism with a distinctly common touch. Now, his totally upper-class image evoked no spontaneous demonstrations of working-class affection. There are few reports from October 1905 of street decorations or illuminated windows among the tenements of Whitechapel or Sheffield or Manchester.[29]

From the beginning, the Navy League's attempts to enlist working-class support met with a wide range of opposition from within the established orders. The deification of Nelson exasperated even some league leaders. E. T. Jane, an authority on the navy and member of Parliament for Portsmouth, thought that their efforts were misdirected and insisted that they would be better occupied grappling with problems of technology and strategy.[30] The Liberal party, especially its radical wing, was generally opposed to the league's activities. In October 1896 the first anniversary celebrations sponsored by the league aroused the ire of the increased Armaments Protest Committee, made up mostly of Liberal radicals, who denounced the use of Trafalgar Day "for the general purposes of jingo imperialism" and called for "the progressive reduction of armaments."[31] Echoing a similar sentiment in 1905, Scott's *Manchester Guardian*, although declaring that "a little more ancestor worship would do us as a nation no harm . . ., regretted that the public Nelson celebrations should have depended so much on an organisation identified in the public mind with indiscreet and often unintelligent advocacy of increased naval expenditure."[32]

Even before the Entente Cordiale of 1904, fears were expressed that the celebrations would damage relations with France. One observer in 1896 quite missed the point of it all when he proposed that a more suitable memorial to the great admiral would be a public subscription to look after Nelson's needy descendants. Festooning a "stone statue" with laurel could, he believed, "only wound the susceptibilities of a friendly nation."[33] Robert Blatchford, owner-editor of the usually nationalistic weekly, *The Clarion*, wrote on 13 October 1905 that the forthcoming festivities would "hardly be complimentary to the *entente*" and that he was "glad that the Corporation of the City of London have refused to vote a grant in aid of the proposed commemoration."[34] A member of the London Common Council, Mr. Stapley, objected to the use of a religious service to rake up unpleasant memories. Nelson's memory, he said, needed no "repulsive" celebrations.[35] The Admiralty believed that "nothing should be done to mar the *Entente Cordiale*" and refused to sanction official ceremonies at Portsmouth and Devonport or to take part in those at Trafalgar Square.[36]

In the event, such fears proved groundless. The Navy League was sensitive to the problem and staged the anniversary not as an aggressively anti-French occasion but as one which embodied Britain's national spirit and naval prowess in terms attractive to its allies. The Tricolor flew along with the British flag from Nelson's column. Members of the Paris City Council, visiting London, were pleased to accept mementos of the occasion, and the French press and government were as anxious as the British to avoid any embarrassment. According to one report, a party of French naval officers, including Admiral Gaillard, riding through Trafalgar Square some weeks before the celebration, "turned and gazed at the statue of Nelson, and many of them gravely saluted the column, keeping their hands at salute till the carriage had passed."[37]

The organization of the ceremonies came in for some criticism. A *Manchester Guardian* leader writer thought that, across the country, the arrangements were unworthy of a great national celebration and that the Navy League had "not shown a great deal of its own special virtue—efficiency—in organising the affair."[38]

Official responses to the celebrations were curiously obstructive. In October 1896 the *Daily Mail* thundered: "There can be no mistake about the fact that the British government frowns upon the observance of trafalgar day."[39] George Goschen, First Lord of the Admiralty in Salisbury's Conservative ministry, refused to permit a naval guard of honor in Trafalgar Square or to consider a fleet review to mark the occasion. The band of the Queen's Westminster Volunteers were refused permission to play in the square that day. The situation had not changed much in 1905. Although the Westminster Volunteers took part in the centenary ceremonies, the occasion was marked by Admiralty disapproval and the absence of any official naval contingent. The commissioner of works would not allow Nelson's column to be floodlit after dark for fear that "nervous horses might be startled."[40] The Tory government, about to collapse, provided no backing, financial or otherwise. It refused to sponsor a committee to consider beautification of the square, and it advised the league that it would consent to alterations only if the Office of Works approved the design and the Navy League raised the money before work commenced.[41] King Edward would not express an opinion until he heard the view of the government.[42] Prime Minister Arthur Balfour spent Trafalgar Day with his brother Gerald, the Irish secretary, on the golf course at North Berwick.[43]

Ultimately, the success of Trafalgar Day depended on the existence of more permanent dependencies linking the ruling classes with the governed and upon a high degree of political consensus. The ceremony could not be a basis for class mutualities; it could only reinforce them. In the fifty years before the Great War the old, essentially preindustrial dependencies had broken down. Urban society had become highly class conscious, and the social distance between classes in 1900 was far wider than it had been a century earlier. As society became more rigidly defined, so patriotic ceremonials were less able to fulfill their integrative function. Working-class unrest was great and labor was organized, politicized, and militant as never before.

In 1905 the Labour Representation Committee (LRC) was preparing to field candidates in the upcoming general election. Although an electoral agreement had been reached with the Liberal party, the LRC's objectives were class oriented. Much of organized labor had been permanently alienated by the Taff Vale decision of 1902, the culmination of a decade of harsh official repression of trade union activities. It is notable that the celebrations of 1905 were more evident in areas where the old ties remained important—in rural East Anglia rather than the North Country, in Central London rather than the East End, in small towns rather than large industrial centers. A majority of the celebrations took place south of a line from Bristol to Hull. Here, trade unionism was least powerful and the patriotic element of popular festivals more persistent.

The central location of the London ceremonies is significant. The Navy League was determined to turn Trafalgar Square into a shrine. The square long had been the object of complaints as a gathering place for "loafers alive with vermin... nominally unemployed... Eastenders, roughs, casuals and tramps," who made the area unsafe for decent people to frequent.[44] In 1899 the league protested against the "systematic desecration" of the memorial by "politicians, Socialists and professional agitators" and called upon the commissioner of works to forbid such meetings.[45] Far from being symbolic of elite hegemony and imperial glory, Trafalgar Square since the 1860s had been a forum for popular protest and official repression. "To the mass of Londoners," declared the *Daily Mail,* the name [Trafalgar] is better known in

> connection with the Square, where many not altogether bloodless fights have taken place, than it is with the great sea-fight where Nelson secured for us that "command of the sea" so absolutely essential to an island dependent for the existence of its workers upon the regular supply of food and the commerce borne upon its waters.[46]

In working class minds, the square was associated with Bloody Sunday, 13 November 1887, when 1,500 police, backed by 350 mounted Life Guards and a detachment of Grenadier Guards with fixed bayonets, attacked with clubs and rifle butts a peaceful free-speech demonstration. Two hundred people were treated in hospitals, three of whom later died of their injuries. R. B. Cunninghame-Graham, Radical member of Parliament for Northwest Lanark, who had been arrested that day "with a violence and brutality... shocking to behold," later told the House of Commons:

> It was bad taste of the people of London to parade their insolent starvation in the face of the rich and trading portions of the town. They should have starved in their garrets, as he had no doubt members of Her Majesty's Government and most of the upper classes would have wished them to.[47]

The *Times,* on the other hand, called the demonstration "the revolt of dull brutality against the rule of law."[48] The following Sunday, as crowds again gathered in the square, the mounted police, "trying to imitate the heroes of Balaclava," charged through the demonstrators.

One of them, Alfred Linnell, was trampled to death by a police horse.[49] The metropolitan police commissioner's refusal to allow Linnell's funeral cortege "to pass the Square or any of the streets adjoining" moved William Morris to observe bitterly: "The Square is a place where the police may kill a man with impunity. It is no longer a place from which we may bury our dead."[50] A crowd estimated at tens of thousands lined the streets and followed the martyr's hearse, starkly inscribed "Killed in Trafalgar Square," to Bow cemetery. For several weeks after the funeral, Morris traveled to working-class centers across England and Scotland, lecturing on "Trafalgar Square" to trade unions and Socialist meetings. Cunninghame-Graham and John Burns, then a member of the Marxist-leaning Social Democratic Federation, were arrested and each received six weeks' imprisonment for leading the Bloody Sunday demonstration. On leaving prison, Burns is alleged to have declared that "Trafalgar Square [was] their revolutionary square; Pentonville their Bastille."[51]

In October 1892 the new Liberal government lifted a five-year police ban on public meetings and issued the first Trafalgar Square Regulations, by which four days' written notice of intended gatherings had to be given to the commissioner of police. Two weeks later, on 12 November, the Metropolitan Radical Federation organized a demonstration to mark the fifth anniversary of Bloody Sunday. In November 1893, following an Anarchist demonstration in the square, Home Secretary H. H. Asquith told the House of Commons that he regarded such "outpourings of a very foolish and very ignorant people as having, at any rate, this advantage—that to use a vulgar expression 'they let off steam' and act as a kind of safety valve to feelings and opinions which are only dangerous as long as they are held in suppression and not properly looked after."[52]

If it is unlikely that working classes were drawn to the Trafalgar centenary ceremonies out of patriotic fervor, how can one account for the thousands of people who filled the square on that occasion? What led most of the press and the Navy League to judge the celebrations to be a massive explosion of popular patriotism? Navalist belief in mass support was probably substantiated by the misconception of jingoism as a working-class phenomenon. Jingoistic patriotism was seen as an emotion that swelled up from the masses. A. G. Gardiner thought it was a "stirring up of all the foul dregs of the coarsest and rankest material among us."[53] However, as Richard Price has shown, flag-waving patriotism appealed most to the lower middle class, anxious to display its solidarity with the ruling elite and to assert its own superiority over the working masses.[54] From the crowds who celebrated in Trafalgar Square Victoria's Diamond Jubilee in 1897 and the relief of Mafeking in May 1900, both imperialists and anti-imperialists drew wrong and similar conclusions: that the mass of workers had become imperialistic. It is reasonable to speculate that the same holds true for the Trafalgar Day celebrations. There is no evidence to suggest that the crowd on that occasion was any different from those of only a few years earlier. The *Manchester Guardian,* almost alone in seeing the event as a failure, detected an "unmistakable reaction against jingoism... people are beginning to feel that the name of patriotism is too often profaned."[55] But *Punch* was probably closer to the meaning of the centenary for the working-class men and women who crowded into Trafalgar Square:

> Just now they pipe a patriot tune;
> Anon they'll wonder why they spent
> A precious football afternoon
> Mafficking round a monument.[56]

On the few occasions when Socialist organizations noticed Nelson, they applied the imagery to their own millennarian tradition. The reaction of J. Bruce Glasier in the Independent Labour party's *Labour Leader* is typical. Glasier believed that, although the commemorations stemmed from the "oppressors of the people and filchers of public freedom," working men and women could learn from Nelson's example. The call to give their utmost efforts, even their lives, for something that would never be theirs was a lesson all Socialists should take to heart. Their duty was to strive "not each for himself, not for money, not for present happiness, but for... the dawning radiance of the future commonweal endowed by our deeds and sacrifice."[57]

No attempt was made to draw the lower orders into the ceremonials. The working classes were neither the instigators nor the participants; they were simply spectators. Thus, Trafalgar Day did not fulfill the safety-valve function with which Asquith had attributed the Bloody Sunday commemoration in 1892. For the working man, there was no sense of the relaxation of the inhibitions of class, no sense of inversion of the normal rules which even protest marches provided and, hence, no release of the tensions which build up in a vastly unequal, highly stratified society. Neither did it provide him with any sense of community with the upper classes. The working classes were not apathetic. For most of them the Nelson message was simply irrelevant in the daily struggle for survival. To them, the plea that "to preserve our national life, we must each be ready like Nelson, to pass, if need be, through the baptism of suffering and self-denial" was meaningless.[58] The distinct working-class culture which had developed during the nineteenth century was little affected by bourgeois sentiment. It is impossible to apply successfully bourgeois standards to working-class life.

Trafalgar Day was not the embodiment of a shared consensus. As part of the upper-class onslaught to change working-class attitudes and behavior, it was a failure. For the Navy League, as for other patriotic organizations, the closed nature of working-class society constituted a major barrier which they were unable to overcome. Although the anniversary was commemorated annually until the Great War, it never again attracted the crowds of 1905. In 1916, after the battle of Jutland, the league proposed that the event be renamed Jutland Day, but that inconclusive engagement had been fought in May and the proposal was quietly dropped. It does indicate, however, that even the league members were aware that their attempt to reincarnate Nelson as a popular hero had failed.

NOTES

1. *Daily Chronicle* (London), 21 October 1905.
2. *The Globe* (London), 19 October 1905.
3. For example, see H. W. Wilson, "A Plea for the Navy League," *United Service Magazine* 11 (April 1895): 78-85.
4. *Navy League Journal*, July, December 1895, March 1898; W. Mark Hamilton, "The 'New Navalism' and the British Navy League, 1895-1914," *Mariner's Mirror* 64 (February 1978): 37-44.
5. London, House of Lords Records Office, P. J. Hannon MSS, Box 1/2.
6. For a discussion of a similar idea, see Elizabeth Hammerton and David Cannadine, "Conflict and Consensus on a Ceremonial Occasion: The Diamond Jubilee in Cambridge in 1897," *Historical Journal* 24, no. 1 (1981): 111-46.
7. *Daily Mail* (London), 10 October 1896.
8. Ibid., 21 October 1896.
9. For a discussion of the civic calendar see Robert D. Storch, "Please to Remember the Fifth of November: Conflict, Solidarity and Public Order in Southern England, 1815-1900," ed. Robert D. Storch, *Popular Culture and Custom in Nineteenth-Century England* (London, 1982).
10. *Daily Chronicle* (London), 23 October 1905.
11. Ibid.
12. *The Observer* (London), 22 October 1905.
13. Almost all of the London and many provincial newspapers covered the ceremonies in Trafalgar Square. A very few Socialist organs, like the *Labour Leader*, hardly reported the celebrations but did suggest some lessons for the working man which might be drawn from Nelson's example.
14. *Daily Chronicle* (London), 23 October 1905.
15. Ibid.
16. *The Observer* (London), 20 October 1895.
17. T. A. Brassey, ed., *The Naval Annual* (Portsmouth, 1897), 209.
18. *Manchester Guardian*, 21 October 1905; *Daily Chronicle* (London), 23 October 1905.
19. *Daily Mail* (London), 11 September 1905.
20. *The Observer* (London), 22 October 1905.
21. *Liverpool Courier*, 23 October 1905.

22. *Nottingham News,* 21 October 1905; *Sheffield Weekly Independent,* 21, 28 October 1905. The *Sheffield Daily Telegraph* (21 October 1905) lamented that there were no observances and that "Sheffield is without a monument to the memory of the hero of Trafalgar."

23. *Sheerness Guardian and East Kent Advertiser,* 28 October 1905. *Sheerness Times and General Advertiser* (21 October 1905) made no mention of the centenary.

24. J. Alex Mitchell, "The Popularisation of the Navy," ed. Alan H. Burgoyne, *The Navy League Annual, 1909-10* (London), 139-41.

25. [Arnold White], *The Views of "Vanoc"* (London, 1913), 327.

26. Neither could an eighteenth-century Nelson exist in the Royal Navy of 1905. Fisher was grooming Jellicoe to an image that was impossible to achieve.

27. *Pall Mall Gazette* (London), 21 October 1905.

28. For example, see Arnold White's letter to the *Daily Express* (London), 14 October 1905.

29. One exception was Birmingham where, according to a report in the *Birmingham Weekly Mercury* (28 October 1905), flags flew from all public buildings and from "many humble tenements." In 1802, Birmingham saw a particularly boisterous and unplanned popular demonstration when Nelson visited the city.

30. *Navy League Journal* (January 1904).

31. *Daily Mail* (London), 24 October 1896.

32. *Manchester Guardian,* 23 October 1905.

33. *Daily Mail* (London), 22 October 1896. An editorial on the same page expressed the view that "deference to others may be carried too far."

34. *The Clarion* (London), 13 October 1905.

35. *Daily Chronicle* (London), 20 October 1905.

36. *The Observer* (London), 22 October 1905. Nelson's flagship, the *Victory,* was illuminated for the occasion.

37. *Daily Express* (London), 14 October 1905.

38. *Manchester Guardian,* 21 October 1905.

39. *Daily Mail* (London), 22 October 1896.

40. *Daily Chronicle* (London), 21 October 1905.

41. *Daily News* (London), 21 October 1905.

42. London, Public Record Office, Lord Windsor to Cabinet, 27 June 1905, CAB 37/78/113.

43. *Sunday Times* (London), 22 October 1905.

44. *Times* (London), 18, 27 October 1887.

45. London, Navy League Archives, Minutes of the Executive Committee, 10 October 1899.

46. *Daily Mail* (London), 10 October 1896.

47. Sir E. Reed, "Remember Trafalgar Square," *Pall Mall Gazette* (London), "Extra," quoted in E. P. Thomson, *William Morris* (New York, 1976), 490.

48. *Times* (London), 14 November 1887.

49. Eyewitness description, quoted in Rodney Mace, *Trafalgar Square* (London, 1976), 192.

50. William Morris, *Alfred Linnell, Killed in Trafalgar Square, November 20th, 1887,* 2, passim, quoted in Mace, *Trafalgar Square,* 193.

51. Ibid., 196.

52. Great Britain, Parliament, *Parliamentary Debates* (Commons), 4th ser., 18 (c.889-90): 14 November 1893.

53. A. G. Gardiner, *The Life of Sir William Harcourt,* 2 vols. (London, 1923), 1:346.

54. Richard Price, "Society, Status and Jingoism: The Social Roots of Lower Middle Class Patriotism, 1870-1900," ed. Geoffrey Crossick, *The Lower Middle Class in Britain, 1870-1914* (London, 1977); Richard Price, *An Imperial War and the British Working Class: Working Class Attitudes and Reactions to the Boer War, 1899-1902* (London, 1972).

55. *Manchester Guardian,* 21 October 1905.

56. *Punch* (London), 25 October 1905.

57. *Labour Leader* (London), 27 October 1905.

58. Rev. John White, *The War Hero of Our Country* (Glasgow, 1916), a reissue of a centenary lecture, 26.

The Imperial Russian Navy's Pioneer Efforts in Arctic Aviation

WILLIAM BARR*

In the summer of 1914 an extensive search was mounted by the Russian government for three expeditions missing in the Arctic. As part of the search effort, a naval officer made the first successful attempt at operating an aircraft anywhere in the Arctic. During the same time, another Russian naval pilot made history with his airplane, this time, however, on the ground. Professor Barr examines the circumstances of these two aviation pioneers in the Russian Arctic.

****

By what can only be described as a remarkable twist of fate, three separate expeditions were missing in the Russian Arctic in the summer of 1912. One of these was attempting to reach the North Pole, while the other two, independently and without collaboration, were trying to effect a passage of the Northern Sea Route from west to east.

The North Pole attempt was being made by an expedition led by Lieutenant Georgiy Yakovlevich Sedov, a thirty-seven-year-old officer in the Imperial Russian Navy, aboard the wooden *Svyatoy Foka*.[1] While bark-rigged, the ship also had a 100-horsepower steam engine and was strongly built for work in ice. The total complement of the expedition was twenty-seven men.

Due to shortage of funds, the ship's coal reserves were lamentably low, sufficient for only three- to four-weeks' steaming. If all went according to plan, however, these should have been adequate since it was not intended that the ship would winter in the Arctic; having landed the expedition as far north as possible on the shores of Zemlya Frantsa Iosifa, the *Sv. Foka* was to return to Arkhangel'sk in the fall. The provisions, consisting mainly of rusks, canned goods, salt beef, and salt fish, were far from suitable for arctic conditions. The expedition had no wireless equipment, and winter clothing was provided only for its fourteen members, not for the crew. The *Sv. Foka* sailed from Arkhangel'sk on 14 August 1912.

The second expedition was that of Lieutenant Georgiy L'vovich Brusilov.[2] With the financial support of his uncle, Lieutenant General B. A. Brusilov, the

---

*Thanks are extended to Keith Bigelow of the Department of Geography, University of Saskatchewan, for drafting the map, and to Dr. Michael Wilson for his expert advice on early aircraft. Gratitude is also owed to the staffs of the Baker Library and the Department of Geography, both at Dartmouth College, Hanover, New Hampshire, for their assistance and hospitality extended to a visiting researcher. The photographs reproduced as Figures 3 and 4 were generously made available by the Arctic and Antarctic Research Institute in Leningrad, through the cooperation of the Arctic Institute of North America.

younger Brusilov had bought the *Blencathra* and renamed it the *Svyataya Anna*. His plan was to take the ship through the Northern Sea Route from the Atlantic to the Pacific, anticipating that he would be able to cover his costs, even in the event of a wintering, by hunting along the way. The total complement on board was twenty-four. The *Sv. Anna* was well stocked with a good variety of provisions designed to last eighteen months. The expedition sailed from St. Petersburg on 10 August 1912 and from Yekaterinskaya Gavan' (now Murmansk) on the 28th. The ship was last seen pushing boldly through the ice in Karskiye Vorota on 16 September 1912.

The third expedition was that of Vladimir Aleksandrovich Rusanov.[3] A geologist with considerable experience of arctic fieldwork obtained on Novaya Zemlya, Rusanov had been commissioned by the Russian government to explore the coal resources and to stake claims on Svalbard. The vessel chosen for the job was the little Norwegian sealer, *Gerkules,* of only sixty-three tonnes displacement. The expedition personnel totaled fourteen, and apart from Rusanov, the scientists aboard were geologist R. L. Samoylovich and zoologist Z. F. Svatosh.

Having completed a successful summer's fieldwork on Svalbard, Rusanov announced his intention to attempt the Northern Sea Route to the Pacific. Svatosh, Samoylovich, and the boatswain declined to participate and left the ship at Grønfjorden. With the remaining eleven people on board, the *Gerkules* sailed from Grønfjorden eastbound in mid-August 1912. Calling at the settlement of Matochkin Shar on Novaya Zemlya, Rusanov left a telegram dated 31 August which was to be relayed to St. Petersburg. In it he indicated that he planned to reach the Kara Sea by rounding the northern tip of Novaya Zemlya, then push eastward. None of the expedition members was ever seen again.

Search Efforts

As early as the spring of 1913, some public anxiety began to be expressed in St. Petersburg as to the whereabouts and safety of all three expeditions. Specifically, a group of members of the Imperial Russian Geographical Society put forward a proposal that searches be mounted.[4]

Some light was cast on one of the expeditions when N. P. Zakharov, the *Sv. Foka*'s captain, arrived at Arkhangel'sk on 1 October 1913 with four members of his crew aboard the regular mail steamer from Matochkin Shar.[5] Zakharov was able to report that Sedov had been forced by heavy ice conditions to winter at Poluostrov Pankrat'yeva on the northwest coast of Novaya Zemlya. Inevitably, the *Sv. Foka*'s crew also had been forced to winter, causing a heavy drain on the expedition's reserves of food and fuel. Nevertheless, Sedov was still determined to reach the Pole; when Zakharov and his group had left the ship in June, Sedov's intention was still to push north to Zemlya Frantsa Iosifa as soon as breakup had released his ship, although this would mean using driftwood and seal blubber to fire the ship's boilers.

Even this rather disturbing news about Sedov was more than was received concerning either Brusilov's or Rusanov's expeditions. They had simply disappeared without a trace. Nonetheless, three more months were to pass before any official moves were made to mount any search efforts. In January 1914 the vice president of the Russian Geographical Society, Dr. P. O. Semenov-Tyan-Shanskiy, sent a petition to the Ministry of Internal Affairs to request that the government mount a search expedition.[6] That same month the Council of Ministers yielded to the growing pressures and ordered the Naval Ministry, in collaboration with the Ministry of Internal Affairs, to set in motion a search operation aimed primarily at Sedov's expedition. In view of the fact that all three expeditions were private ventures, mounted without official sanction, and in view of the almost total lack of clues as to where searches should be concentrated in at least two cases, the government's reluctance to become involved is to some degree understandable.

Ultimately, four ships took part in the search for the missing expeditions in the summer of 1914, the selection having been made after consultation with the famous Norwegian explorers, Fridtjof Nansen and Roald Amundsen. Two ships, the *Eclipse* and the *Gerta,* were purchased, and another two, the *Pechora* and the *Andromeda,* were chartered. Conditions of the *Andromeda*'s insurance stipulated that it was unable to proceed farther north than Poluostrov Pankrat'yeva on Novaya Zemlya; for the same reason, the *Pechora*'s northern limit was set at Krestovaya Guba.

Since both the *Gerkules* and the *Sv. Anna* had planned to attempt the passage of the Northern Sea Route, it was proposed that a search for both could best be concentrated in the eastern part of the Kara Sea. The *Eclipse* was chosen for this task, and the veteran Norwegian arctic explorer, Otto Sverdrup, was engaged to take charge of the operation.[7] The *Eclipse* was a good ship for the task. A three-masted whaler, it had been built in Aberdeen in 1867 and, sailing first out of Peterhead and later Dundee, had made annual voyages to either Greenland or the Davis Strait whaling grounds until 1906, when it had been sold to Norwegian owners. The ship loaded the supplies for the expedition in Christiania (now Oslo) in June 1914. Apart from provisions for sixteen months, thirty-one dogs, sledges, and normal arctic equipment, it also took on a number of unusual-looking wooden crates that contained a disassembled aircraft. Their stowage was carefully supervised by a Russian naval pilot, Yan Iosifovich Nagurskiy (Figure 1).

Nagurskiy and the Voyage North

A Pole by nationality, Nagurskiy was born on 27 January 1888 and grew up in the village of Shpetal' Dol'ny on the Vistula.[8] In 1906 he applied for entrance to the Odessa Infantry College and was accepted in October of that year. There followed three years of military training in the Crimea. He graduated on 6 August 1909. As a sublieutenant he was posted to the 23d East Siberian Infantry Regiment, stationed at Khabarovsk.

After two years in the Far East, Nagurskiy applied in late 1910 for entrance to the Naval Engineering College in St. Petersburg and was accepted. At this time, like most of the rest of the world, Russia was in the grip of flying fever; to set this situation in context, one recalls that the Wright brothers had made their pioneer flight in December 1903 and Louis Blériot had flown across the English Channel in 1909. In February 1909 the *Silver Dart* with John McCurdy at the controls had taken off from the ice of Bras d'Or Lake at Baddeck, Nova Scotia, and had flown about 800 meters.

Figure 1. Yan Iosifovich Nagurskiy at about the time of his Arctic flight.

Nagurskiy found that flying was a favorite topic of conversation among his fellow students at the Naval Engineering College. Of even greater significance in terms of his career was a meeting with an old friend, Lebedev, who was a member of a flying club and invited him to watch the planes in action. It was not long before Nagurskiy decided to learn how to fly. Under a scheme whereby the government subsidized officers to take flying lessons, Nagurskiy joined the Imperial All-Russian Aero Club at Novaya Drevnya in 1911. Some months later he passed the exam for his pilot-aviator's diploma, a civilian qualification.

In 1911 the Officers' Airship School at Gatchina had initiated an aviation section, and it now became Nagurskiy's dream to take the requisite course and attain the qualification of *voyenniy letchik*, or military pilot. In June 1912 he officially enrolled in the school.[9] He passed the necessary exams and was awarded the *voyenniy letchik* early in 1913. Despite these considerable demands on his time, Nagurskiy had continued his studies at the Naval Engineering College and graduated as a naval engineer in July 1913.[10]

On graduation he joined the Chief Hydrographic Administration, the oceanography branch of the Russian navy, although he still continued to fly regularly on an amateur basis. Naturally, he was fully aware of the excitement caused by the disappearance of the Sedov, Brusilov, and Rusanov expeditions in 1912, and since the administration had been assigned to coordinate the searches in 1914, he was more knowledgeable about the topic than most.

Early in 1914, therefore, Lieutenant General M. Ye. Zhdanko, head of the Chief Hydrographic Administration, asked Nagurskiy whether, in his opinion, aircraft might profitably be used in the search.[11] After some deliberation Nagurskiy expressed the opinion that aircraft would be of enormous help in an operation of this kind. Zhdanko then asked him to prepare a proposal on the topic, specifying the type of machine and the support facilities that would be required. Two days later Nagurskiy had assembled the data; to his surprise and delight, not only was his recommendation to use aircraft accepted, but he also was nominated as one of the pilots who would participate. He was put in charge of all the arrangements.

The choice of aircraft was left entirely up to him.[12] He decided that he needed a floatplane with a speed of up to 100 kilometers per hour and an air-cooled engine. This was a period when Russian designers such as I. Sikorskiy, D. P. Grigorovich, I. Gakkel', S. V. Grizodubov, N. P. Lobanov, and V. V. Dybovskiy were in the forefront of aircraft design. Russian factories such as Russko-Baltiyskiy at St. Petersburg were producing a wide range of aircraft types.[13] According to M. V. Vodop'yanov,[14] Nagurskiy's first choice was a Grigorovich M-5 flying boat, but in this he was overruled by the authorities. Hence, he opted for the French biplane produced by Maurice Farman as next best suited to his needs.

Another pilot, P. V. Yevsyukov, was chosen to fly the aircraft that was to accompany the *Eclipse* on its search of the Kara Sea.[15] His choice was a Henry Farman, but due to the outbreak of World War I, the aircraft became held up at Bergen and the *Eclipse* proceeded without aerial support. Yevsyukov and his mechanic returned to St. Petersburg from Aleksandrovsk.[16]

Nagurskiy left for Paris on 21 May 1914 to supervise the assembly of his machine and spent the next few weeks at the Maurice Farman factory and at the Renault engine works.[17] The machine he had selected was a biplane, mounted on floats, with a 70-horsepower air-cooled Renault engine. It had a payload of 300 kilograms and was capable of almost 100 kilometers per hour. Its fuel tank contained enough gasoline for five or six hours of flying. An open cockpit could accommodate a crew of two. The engine was a "pusher type," mounted aft of the cockpit, and it drove a walnut propeller whose leading edges were sheathed in brass.

Nagurskiy studied every aspect of the assembly and operation of the machine and its engine and established amiable relations with the French mechanics and factory workers.[18] Up until then he had been serving in the *Pogranichnaya strazha* (Border Guards), but as of 9 June he was transferred to the navy.

By 14 June Nagurskiy's machine was reasdy. After eighteen test flights he supervised disassembly of the machine. On his instructions the cockpit and wings had been painted red for maximum visibility against snow and ice. Packed in eight crates, the aircraft was shipped to Christiania with a guaranteed delivery date of 22 June.[19] Nagurskiy was ordered to Christiania to be on hand for supervision of the loading of the plane on the *Eclipse*. He duly reached Christiania by the 22d and saw his machine safely stowed aboard.

To his dismay Nagurskiy was given a very discouraging reception by the expedition leader, Captain I. I. Islyamov, who considered aircraft to be useless toys that would only occupy valuable space on the ships and contribute nothing to the search.[20] But fortunately during this final period of preparations, Nagurskiy also met Amundsen, who was in overall charge of fitting out the search expedition, and Sverdrup; both men were much more encouraging.

The send-off of the expedition on 30 June was a major event in the Norwegian capital: Sverdrup was heading for the Arctic once again. On hand were

Amundsen, Nansen, the Russian ambassador, the mayor of Christiania, cabinet ministers and politicians, and a crowd of several thousand. After a series of toasts and speeches, the *Eclipse* finally put to sea.[21]

After calling at Bergen, Trondheim, and Vardø, the *Eclipse* reached Aleksandrovsk-na-murmane on 1 August. Meanwhile, as the *Eclipse* steamed north along the Norwegian coast, Zhdanko had been trying frantically to locate a mechanic to accompany Nagurskiy. Finally, Yevgeniy Kuznetsov, an experienced aircraft mechanic stationed with the navy at Sevastopol in the Crimea, was signed on. Kuznetsov left Sevastopol on his long journey north on 9 July.[22]

The day after the *Eclipse*'s arrival at Aleksandrovsk, Nagurskiy and his aircraft were transferred to the steamer *Pechora*, captained by P. A. Sinitsyn.[23] Nagurskiy's final orders from Islyamov were to conduct an aerial search of the coast of Novaya Zemlya from Krestovaya Guba north to Poluostrov Pankrat'yeva for any sign of the missing expeditions. The *Pechora* put to sea on 13 August.

Once the ship was at sea Nagurskiy met Kuznetsov for the first time. He was impressed by the mechanic's enthusiasm and obvious competence but found his traditional, stiff attitude to a superior officer somewhat unusual after the relatively informal relations that tended to prevail among the flying fraternity.[24]

On 16 August the *Pechora* reached Krestovaya Guba on the west coast of Novaya Zemlya (Figure 2) at 9:00 P.M. to find the *Andromeda* already lying at anchor.[25] It had arrived just the previous day, having earlier been as far north as Poluostrov Pankrat'yeva. Late that evening, the *Andromeda*'s captain, G. I. Pospelov, gave an account of his northern foray. The *Andromeda* had been stopped by ice between the Krestoviye Ostrova, Yuzhniy, and Severniy; prolonged whistle blasts had evoked no response from shore. Pospelov had taken a party ashore since he knew this was where the *Sv. Foka* had wintered. There, in a cairn, he found a note left by Sedov written in Russian, German, French, and English. It indicated that after the breakup, the *Sv. Foka* had sailed again, bound for Zemlya Frantsa Iosifa in August 1913, and that a cache of provisions had been left at a cairn on Ostrov Pankrat'yeva some twelve kilometers to the north.

Following this lead, Pospelov had next landed on Ostrov Pankrat'yeva. Here he had found a wooden cross with an inscription, but no depot. Then, on the northwest end of the island, he had found a cairn with a hollow inside for a depot, but it contained only a can of engine oil and a bucket. In sealed cans at all three locations Pospelov had left notes that read: "A party from *Andromeda* found a cairn with the following note at the cape on Ostrov Pankrat'yeva."[26] But he had had to be content with this less-than-satisfactory achievement; by the terms of the ship's insurance, he could not push any farther north. He had headed south, therefore, to Yugorskiy Shar from where he had reported by wireless to St. Petersburg. He then had been ordered back north to Krestovaya Guba to rendezvous with the *Pechora*.[27]

Nagurskiy had wanted to establish his base at Ostrov Pankrat'yeva, but in this he was frustrated by the *Pechora*'s terms of insurance. Nor could he use the *Andromeda* to reach his goal, since the crates containing the plane and spare parts were simply too bulky for that small vessel to handle. Hence, he had to resign himself to making Krestovaya Guba his base.

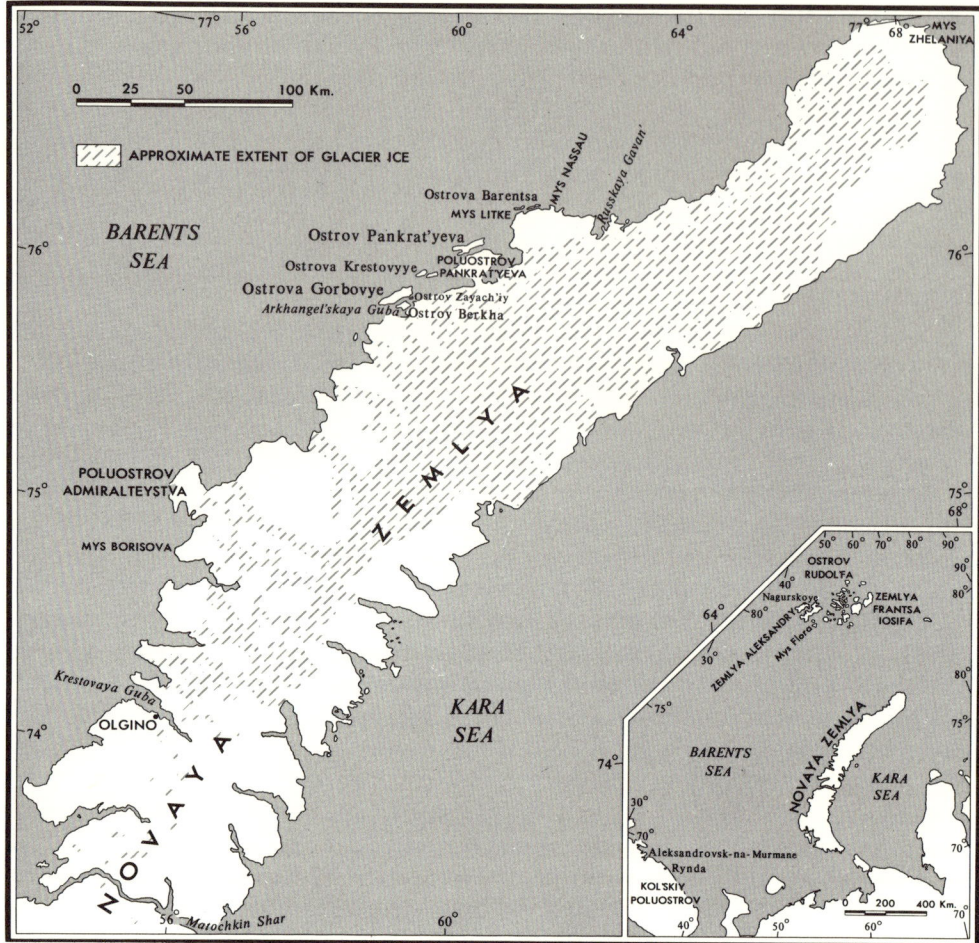

Figure 2. Map of the north island of Novaya Zemlya, indicating the area of Nagurskiy's flights. The inset shows the site of operations of Sedov's expedition.

The plane was assembled on the beach at the settlement of Ol'gino. With the *Pechora* lying offshore, a willing group of officers and men assisted Nagurskiy and Kuznetsov in their task. By then the weather had deteriorated; rain alternated with snow and the temperature barely reached 1°C during the day, dropping below zero at night. Altogether it was a challenging task. Figure 3 depicts the assembly of Lieutenant Aleksandrov's Henry Farman aircraft, allocated to the *Taymyr* and the *Vaygach* expedition,[28] on the beach at Bukhta Emma in Chukotka at almost exactly the same time. Although the locations lie several thousand kilometers apart, the aircraft were almost identical, and the conditions for the assembly of the two machines scarcely could have been more closely matched.

Figure 3. Aleksandrov's Henry Farman aircraft being assembled on the beach at Bukhta Emma, Chukotka, in late July 1914.

Nagurskiy's Aerial Search

After two days of work, Nagurskiy's Maurice Farman was assembled, fueled, and ready to be tested. A driftwood launching ramp was quickly constructed, and the plane was slid down it tail-first into the sea. Early in the morning of 21 August, Nagurskiy took off, and after a couple of test circuits, landings, and takeoffs, he declared himself satisfied with the machine's performance. Anxious not to lose any time, he fueled the plane to capacity, stowed aboard a ten-day supply of food, a rifle, ammunition, skis, and sleeping bags, and with Kuznetsov in the passenger seat took off to fly north to Ostrov Pankrat'yeva. Flying at speeds of 100 to 105 kilometers per hour and at an altitude of 800 meters, Nagurskiy enjoyed fine weather and visibility for this maiden arctic flight.

But then the weather began to deteriorate; long tatters of fog appeared beneath the plane, and soon the coast had entirely disappeared. Only the mountain tops projected above the fog bank. A serious incident threatened when the factory-installed compass ceased to function. Fortunately, Nagurskiy had brought a boat's compass as a spare, and he was able to maintain his course. When the fog thinned again, he managed to recognize the Gorbovye Ostrova. The straits between the islands were still full of broken ice, but soon Ostrova Pankrat'yeva drifted below the plane's red wings and Mys Litke appeared ahead. Checking the time, Nagurskiy decided to fly over and examine the Barentsovye Ostrova before heading back; he planned to make a landing somewhere near Ostrova Pankrat'yeva, where he had arranged for the *Andromeda* to meet him with fuel, oil, and provisions.

After some considerable apprehension over a landing site owing to the lack of open water, the presence of ridged and rafted ice, and the extensive fog banks covering much of the area, Nagurskiy finally brought his plane down close to the place prearranged with the *Andromeda*. The first arctic flight in aviation history had lasted four hours, twenty minutes, and had covered about 450 kilometers. As the plane taxied toward shore, it suddenly jarred to a halt as one of the floats hit an unseen rock. Fortunately, the water was only knee-deep, and the two men were able to push the plane off the rock and tow it ashore. Having secured the aircraft, they lit a fire, brewed some tea, had a quick meal, and then fell asleep. They had been awake for some thirty-six hours.

On waking, the two men set about hauling the aircraft ashore and repairing the punctured float. That evening the *Andromeda* hove into view. After dropping anchor it ferried fuel to the plane. Meanwhile, Nagurskiy reported to Captain Pospelov on the ice conditions to the north. Realizing the significance of this pioneer flight and the value of aerial ice reconnaissance, Pospelov produced a bottle of cognac to celebrate the auspicious occasion. He then requested that on his next flight Nagurskiy investigate ice conditions around Ostrov Zayach'iy, where he was supposed to leave an emergency food depot in a trapper's hut.

After a short rest Nagurskiy and Kuznetsov took off again early on 22 August in clear, sunny weather. Heading north toward the Gorbovye Ostrova, Nagurskiy spotted several discrepancies between the coastline as plotted on the chart and the reality unfolding beneath him, noting particularly glaring mistakes on his chart. The plane was soon over Arkhangel'skaya Guba with the Gorbovye Ostrova to port; the sound and straits between Ostrova Berkha, Lipotina, and Zayach'iy were all still covered with ice. Spotting a little hut on Ostrov Berkha, Nagurskiy landed, completing a flight of one hour, forty-five minutes in duration. By this stage Kuznetsov was shivering and had a pounding headache; Nagurskiy unrolled the sleeping bags, and the two men caught up on sleep.

Late that evening, 22 August, the *Andromeda* again appeared at the ice edge near to the fliers, who were soon taken aboard, Kuznetsov packed off quickly to sick bay. Meanwhile, Nagurskiy, Pospelov, and three seamen went ashore to examine the trapper's hut. It contained only a stove, some remains of food, and some Norwegian magazines. Messages on the wall indicated that the last Norwegian had been there five years previously. There were no signs of Sedov's expedition. The party next walked across to the cairn on Ostrov Zayach'iy where Sedov had said in his note that he would leave food and copies of his maps but which Pospelov had already found to be empty. On reaching it, Nagurskiy decided to leave some gasoline and oil for possible future emergencies. Soon a work party had hauled food, gasoline, and lubricating oil to the depot. To mark its position Nagurskiy left a note at the massive cairn, crowned with a cross that Sedov had left on Ostrov Pankrat'yeva.

Recovered from his illness, Kuznetsov joined Nagurskiy on 25 August to investigate again by air the ice conditions around Gorbovye Ostrova. They discovered that a gale had broken up the ice and driven it out to sea, thereby freeing the north and west sides of Ostrov Zayach'iy. That evening Captain Pospelov asked Nagurskiy to take him on a flight to reconnoiter ice conditions in the direction of Russkaya Gavan. Agreeing, Nagurskiy took off and climbed to about 500 meters, setting a course for Mys Nassau in excellent visibility. Suddenly, a sharp crack in the engine prompted him to cut his engine and begin a long glide down to the sea, fortunately still within sight of the ship. Both Nagurskiy and the captain were only too conscious of what might have happened if the mishap had occurred at a later stage in their flight.

Owing to the conditions, the plane could not be repaired on the spot and was subsequently dismounted and ferried out to the *Andromeda*, where Kuznetsov began the repairs. The broken connecting rod in one cylinder and the bent main shaft were owing to negligence at the factory. For over two weeks the aircraft was immobilized, initially because Kuznetsov had the engine in pieces and later because of a series of blizzards. During this period Nagurskiy and a group of sailors found another trapper's hut on Ostrov Zayach'iy. Inside was a cache of supplies, maps, and a note from Sedov written just before the *Sv. Foka*'s departure for Zemlya Frantsa Iosifa on 25 August 1913.

The *Gerta* arrived from the north and dropped anchor close to the *Andromeda* in the early morning of 3 September 1914. Captain Islyamov congratulated Nagurskiy on his successful flights and had the decency to confess that he had been wrong in his predictions. He then went on to report that the *Gerta* had reached Zemlya Frantsa Iosifa. Three days previously, at Mys Flora on Ostrov Nortbruka, he had found a message, dated 25 July 1914, from Dr. P. G. Kushakov, deputy leader of Sedov's expedition. In it the doctor reported that Sedov had died in a forlorn attempt to reach the North Pole and that the *Sv. Foka*, though desperately short of fuel, was now southward bound to Arkhangel'sk.[29] Although a month had elapsed since the discovery of the message, there had been no sign of the *Sv. Foka*, nor had the *Gerta* received any wireless messages to say that it had reached Arkhangel'sk or any other port. In fact, the *Sv. Foka* had encountered heavy ice that, since the ship now was entirely dependent on its sails, had proved impassable; indeed, it was solidly beset for almost a week.[30] It finally reached the little port of Rynda on Kol'skiy Poluostrov on 4 September, the day after Islyamov's conversation with Nagurskiy.

Islyamov's instructions to the aviator were to make a wide sweep out to sea from Ostrova Pankrat'yeva in the hopes of spotting the *Sv. Foka*, to call at Russkaya Gavan in case it had taken refuge in that anchorage, and to leave a note there to the effect that coal and provisions would be left for the *Sv. Foka* on Ostrov Zayach'iy. But first Nagurskiy and Kuznetsov had to finish the repairs on the plane. Pospelov took them south in the *Andromeda* to Krestovaya Guba for the necessary spare parts, then back to Arkhangel'skaya Guba, finally arriving on 6 September.

Having quickly reassembled, reinstalled, and tested the engine, Nagurskiy was fully aware that winter rapidly was approaching and that a substantial dark period every night imposed further restrictions on flying. This time flying solo, Nagurskiy left early on 12 September and headed west-northwest out to sea at about 1200 meters. The weather then began to deteriorate; snow, falling heavily, cut visibility almost to zero. Realizing that his chances of spotting the overdue ship, already slim, were almost infinitesimal under these conditions, Nagurskiy returned east toward land, about 100 kilometers away. The snow then ended, and the coast of Novaya Zemlya in the vicinity of Mys Litke loomed ahead. From there Nagurskiy swung back southwest again to where the two ships lay in Arkhangel'skaya Guba. Noting that the heavy ice over which he had been flying was heading south, endangering the anchored ships, he reported the situation to Captain Islyamov as soon as he landed. The *Andromeda* and the *Gerta* immediately weighed anchor and headed south to avoid being beset, having first arranged a rendezvous with the aircraft at Krestovaya Guba.

With Kuznetsov again in the passenger seat, Nagurskiy took off early in the afternoon of 13 September into a westerly wind. There was a great deal of low cloud cover, and at one point Nagurskiy was unable to see the ground for a considerable period. When the clouds cleared, he found himself over the mountainous, glacier-covered interior of Novaya Zemlya with the Kara Sea clearly visible a short way to the east. The steady westerly wind had drifted the biplane well off course before Nagurskiy corrected the error. Finally, after three and one-quarter hours in the air, the little plane landed at Krestovaya Guba where the *Pechora* was still at anchor. Thirty-six hours later the *Andromeda* appeared. On orders from Captain Sinitsyn, Nagurskiy and Kuznetsov dismantled the plane, packed it in its crates, and supervised its stowage aboard the *Pechora*.

During his five major flights totaling ten hours and forty minutes in the air, Nagurskiy had flown a total of 1,060 kilometers. Although he had found no traces of the missing expeditions (apart from the cairns and the note by Sedov), he had been able to make numerous corrections to the charts and had provided invaluable ice reports to the search ships. Most significantly, he had clearly demonstrated the feasibility of flying in the Arctic, despite some extremely dangerous flying weather.

During his voyage south Nagurskiy compiled a report for Lieutenant General Zhdanko of the Chief Hydrographic Association. Having summarized the major events of his search, he added a series of recommendations for the guidance of future arctic pilots, based on his own experience, including the taking of spare floats and flares to attract attention in case of accident.[31] Nagurskiy submitted this report on his return to St. Petersburg on 14 October 1914. In a personal interview Zhdanko congratulated him warmly and told him that he was to be awarded the Order of St. Stanislav. After answering all of Zhdanko's questions, Nagurskiy put forward a proposal for flying to the North Pole.[32] He proposed a main base on Ostrov Rudol'fa, the most northerly island of Zemlya Frantsa Iosifa, as being accessible by sea in a normal year. From there to the Pole he proposed establishing support bases every 200 kilometers, each with two airstrips with food and fuel depots. Three such intermediate depots would be required. (This plan bears a striking resemblance to that adopted for the establishment of I. D. Papanin's group at the North Pole in 1937.[33]) Zhdanko was genuinely intrigued by the idea but tactfully suggested that, since there was a war on, it would have to be postponed.

Aleksandrov's Contemporaneous Activities

Also in the summer of 1914, while Nagurskiy was making aviation history over Novaya Zemlya, at the other end of the Russian Arctic an attempt was being made by another Russian pilot to use his aircraft in support of a different arctic expedition, also mounted by the Imperial Russian Navy. The pilot was Captain D. N. Aleksandrov who, with a Henry Farman aircraft and accompanied by a mechanic, A. G. Firdarov, had been attached to the icebreaker *Taymyr*. Along with its sister ship, the *Vaygach*, the *Taymyr* was engaged in a long-term survey of the arctic coast of Siberia in an operation known as the Arctic Ocean Hydrographic Expedition, 1910–15.[34] During each of the navigation seasons between 1910 and 1913, the two icebreakers had pushed progressively farther west along the arctic coast from the Bering Strait, returning to Vladivostok each winter. But in 1914 the intention was to complete the through-passage to Arkhangel'sk.

The two icebreakers sailed from Vladivostok on 7 June 1914 and reached Bukhta Emma in Chukotka on 28 July. With the assistance of a party of sailors, Aleksandrov and Firdarov ferried their aircraft ashore and assembled it on the beach (Figure 3) under conditions almost identical to those with which Nagurskiy had to cope on Novaya Zemlya. By the morning of 2 August the plane was ready to fly (Figure 4). The weather was clear and calm, and the sea mirror-smooth. On Aleksandrov's second attempt at taking off, a part of the rudder assembly broke. The damage was sufficiently serious that he could not repair it in the field, and the plane was towed ashore and disassembled.

Figure 4. Aleksandrov's Henry Farman ready for its first test flight. Apart from having a rotary engine, a much higher mounted stabilizer, and a single rather than a double rudder, this machine is essentially the same as Nagurskiy's Maurice Farman.

The remainder of the voyage must have been extremely frustrating for Aleksandrov and Firdarov. The two icebreakers successfully negotiated Proliv Vil'kitskogo, but in mid-September they became icebound off Mys Mogilniy on the west coast of Poluostrov Taymyr and were forced to winter. During March 1915, Aleksandrov, who by now had abandoned any hope that his machine might fly again, decided to try to operate it as an aerosled, initially without any significant modifications. Presumably the idea was simply to taxi across the sea ice and the snow-covered land surface. This idea was less than successful. The plane managed to crawl only a very short distance before several of the major wing struts broke from jolting. Undaunted, Aleksandrov and Firdarov removed the engine and mounted it on a solidly built sledge to produce what was almost certainly the world's first aerosled.

It was a complete success. Pulling the sledge at speeds of up to forty kilometers per hour on firm, level snow, the aerosled was used to support a field party that completed a survey of Zalov Gafnera between 1 and 11 June 1915.[35] Dr. L. M. Starokadomskiy, A. M. Lavrov, and N. I. Yevgenov were able to map the inlet for the first time and also to carry out geological and zoological studies. Thus, while far from being as successful as Nagurskiy's arctic operations, Aleksandrov's contribution is in its own way quite significant.

NOTES

1. N. Pinegin, *Georgiy Sedov* (Moscow-Leningrad, 1948); W. Barr, "Sedov's Expedition to the North Pole, 1912-1914," *Canadian Slavonic Papers* 15, no. 4 (1973): 499-523; S. A. Seleznev, *Pervaya russkaya ekspeditsiya k Severnomu polyusu* (Arkhangel'sk, 1964).

2. G. L. Brusilov, "Extract from the Log of the Sailing Ship *Svyataya Anna*," *Izvestiya Imperatorskago Russkaga Geograficheskago Obshchestva* 59, no. 3-4 (1914): 193-237; V. I. Al'banov, *Podvig shturmana Al'banova* (Moscow, 1953); W. Barr, "South to Zemlya Frantsa Iosifa! The Cruise of *Sv. Anna* and Al'banov's Sledge Trip, 1912-1914," *Canadian Slavonic Papers* 17, no. 4 (1975): 567-95; W. Barr, "The Drift of Lieutenant Brusilov's *Svyataya Anna*," *The Musk-Ox* 22 (1978): 3-30.

3. W. Barr, "Rusanov, *Gerkules*, and the Northern Sea Route," *Canadian Slavonic Papers* 16, no. 4 (1974): 569-611; W. Barr, "The Fate of Rusanov's Expedition aboard *Gerkules* in the Kara Sea: Further Details and Recent Developments," *Polar Record* 22, no. 138, (1984): 287-304; S. P. Petrosov and M. S. Derzhavin, "The Life and Heroic Feat of V.A. Rusanov: A Biographical Account," in *Vladimir Aleksandrovich Rusanov: Stat'i, lektsii, pis'ma*, ed. by A. N. Tsvetkova (Moscow-Leningrad, 1945), 5-59.

4. D. M. Pinkhenson, *Problema severnogo morskogo puti v epokhu kapitalizma. Istoriya otkrytiya i osvoyeniya Severnogo morskogo puti*, vol. 2 (Leningrad, 1962).

5. Pinegin, *Georgiy Sedov*; Seleznev, *Pervaya russkaya*.

6. Pinkhenson, *Problema*.

7. O. Sverdrup, *Under Russisk Flag* (Oslo, 1928).

8. For information on Nagurskiy's life see M. B. Chernenko, "The Biography of the First Polar Pilot, Yan I. Nagurskiy," *Letopis' Severa* 2 (1957): 150-54; Yan I. Nagurskiy, *Perviy nad Arktikoy* (Leningrad, 1960); and Gal'perin, *On byl pervym. Byl' o polyarnom letchike Yane Nagurskom* (Moscow, 1958).

9. Ibid.

10. Nagurskiy, *Perviy nad Arktikoy*.

11. Gal'perin, *On byl pervym*; Nagurskiy, *Perviy nad Arktikoy*.

12. Gal'perin, *On byl pervym*.

13. H. J. Nowarra and G. R. Duval, *Russian Civil and Military Aircraft, 1884-1969* (London, 1971).

14. M. V. Vodop'yanov, *Na kryl'yakh v Arktiku* (Moscow, 1954).

15. Chernenko, "Biography of the First Polar Pilot."

16. Pinkhenson, *Problema*.

17. Yan I. Nagurskiy, "Report of Naval Pilot Lieutenant Nagurskiy to the Head of the Chief of the Hydrographic Administration," *Letopis' Severa* 1 (1949): 222-26.

18. Gal'perin, *On byl pervym*.

19. Nagurskiy, "Report."

20. Nagurskiy, *Perviy nad Arktikoy*; Gal'perin, *On byl pervym*.

21. Sverdrup, *Under Russisk Flag*; Nagurskiy, "Report"; Nagurskiy, *Perviy nad Arktikoy*.

22. Gal'perin, *On byl pervym*.

23. Nagurskiy, "Report."

24. Gal'perin, *On byl pervym*.

25. Nagurskiy, "Report"; Gal'perin, *On byl pervym*.

26. Ibid.

27. Seleznev, *Pervaya russkaya*.

28. L. M. Starokadomskiy, *Charting the Russian Northern Sea Route: The Arctic Hydrographic Expedition 1910-1915* (Montreal, 1976).

29. For further details see Barr, "Sedov's Expedition."

30. Al'banov, *Podvig.*
31. Nagurskiy, "Report."
32. Gal'perin, *On byl pervym.*
33. I. D. Papanin, *Zhizn' na l'dine* (Leningrad, 1938).
34. Starokadomskiy, *Charting the Russian Northern Sea Route.*
35. Ibid.; Pinkhenson, *Problema.*

"World Wide Wireless":
The U.S. Navy, Big Business, Technology, and Radio Communications, 1919-22

JOHN P. ROSSI*

In order to develop a global radio communications system to serve post-World War I security and commercial needs, the Navy Department entered into close cooperation with corporate interests, as seen with the formation of the Radio Corporation of America. Mr. Rossi explores the complex relationships among technology, the modern corporation, and the state in expanding American wealth and power abroad by way of radio communications.

****

In October 1919 one of the great American industrial giants—the Radio Corporation of America (RCA)—was born. The creation of this new communications firm was the result of a direct request by the U.S. Navy. As one of its founders, Owen D. Young, then a vice-president of the General Electric Company (GE), later would relate:

> One day Admiral Bullard [director of Naval Communications] and Commander... Hooper came to see me. It was at that time when President Wilson was in Europe [at the Paris Peace Conference], and Admiral Bullard had come all the way from Paris at his request to talk about the radio. On that day, for the first time, radio made an indelible impression on my mind. Here was something so important that the President of the United States, in the very midst of the peace negotiations, had sent one of his admirals from Paris to New York to talk about it.[1]

The youthful GE vice-president went on to say that Woodrow Wilson had sent Admiral William H. G. Bullard to confer with the company's officers because of the concerns he had developed at the peace conference about international communications. During the war and its immediate aftermath, Britain utilized its dominance of international communications through its worldwide cable network to promote its political and economic interests, often at American expense. At Paris, Wilson had learned that the British were attempting to maintain their control over world communications by purchasing a key GE radio patent on the Alexanderson alternator.[2]

"So," Young continued, "the President asked Admiral Bullard to say that in the interest of America he hoped we [GE] would not transfer exclusive rights to

---

*I wish to thank John Chambers, Paul Clemens, and Lloyd Gardner of Rutgers University for their comments on various drafts of this essay. In this paper and at the time, 1919-23, radio communications referred to the transmission of telegraph signals over radio waves. The technical term for this was radio telegraphy, in contrast to radio telephony or broadcasting, which is the transmission of voice patterns over radio waves.

the alternator to any other country. He based his appeal quite frankly on patriotic grounds. Here was history in the making. Admiral Bullard warned me that the decision might change the whole trend of world affairs."[3]

Young's story about the formation of RCA is more than an amusing anecdote. It speaks volumes about the rivalry between the United States and Great Britain in international politics, the new position of the United States in the post-World War I world, and the importance of communications and technology in that new postwar order. A key factor in determining the U.S. position in this order was the relationship between corporate capital and state power.

The recent historiography on the 1914-33 period has outlined several major themes, two of which this paper examines: U.S. economic and political expansion abroad, and the transformation of the American political economy by the large, technologically driven modern corporation. Historians writing on the growth of American influence in the international arena have concentrated mostly on the efforts of the State and Commerce departments working in close, yet informal, cooperation with American businessmen to create an international political economic order along liberal capitalist lines.[4]

In contrast, historians concentrating on the rise of the large modern corporation, led by Alfred Chandler, have emphasized the role of technological and bureaucratic innovation in this rise and its restructuring of American economic life.[5] Chandler's managerial capitalist school usually has dismissed the state as inconsequential, having little impact on the corporate reconstruction of the national economy.[6] Ironically, the scholars examining American efforts to construct a liberal capitalist world order have focused primarily on U.S. government policy. While acknowledging the role of economic interests, these historians have largely ignored the tremendous impact that the technology/market-driven modern corporation has had on American foreign relations.[7]

Unfortunately, there has been little cross-fertilization between the study of liberal corporate political economy and the modern corporation. This paper will attempt to bridge this gulf by exploring the complex relationships among technology, the modern corporation, and the state in expanding American wealth, influence, and power abroad during the early post-World War I period by way of radio communications.

In their efforts to develop radio communications, Admiral Bullard and President Wilson hoped private capital would serve the public interest by creating an American international wireless system. The creation of a private firm to handle international radio communications, however, came hard on the heels of British efforts to establish domination over the industry. When the United States entered the war, the Navy Department took over and operated the country's limited network of privately owned radio stations.[8] The large majority of these stations was owned by the British Marconi Company. With vigorous support from the London government, British Marconi had undertaken an aggressive campaign to ring the world with wireless stations and establish a monopoly over international radio communications.

By World War I the firm was the world's largest radio company, and its U.S. subsidiary, the American Marconi Company, was the largest radio firm in North America. Nonetheless, the dominant position of British Marconi in international radio communications was threatened. The Marconi companies possessed an inferior technology; their Time Spark system of transmission was more expensive and less efficient than emerging American technologies.[9] What the British did not have in the way of technology, they sought to purchase. In 1915 "the leading radio apparatus in the world," the Alexanderson alternator, was developed by GE scientist Dr. E. F. W. Alexanderson. The alternator had performed successfully in transoceanic radio communications during the war. Indeed, it worked so spectacularly that the alternator was credited with hastening the end of the war by broadcasting Wilson's Fourteen Points to the Central Powers.[10]

The Navy Department was fully cognizant of the implications of British Marconi's postwar attentions toward GE and its alternator patents.[11] The Bureau of Steam Engineering, which was responsible for the purchase of radio equipment for the Navy Department, commented on the prospective sale of the alternator:

> To have this control transferred to a Company under the combination of foreign capital, especially a Company as powerful as the British Marconi Company, would entirely preclude the competition of American Companies, and in the opinion of the Bureau, be a grave menace to the safety of the U.S.... Should these negotiations be terminated to the satisfaction of the British Marconi Company, the communications of the world would be controlled completely by this foreign country, with all the dangers which would be sure to ensue from such a condition.[12]

The Navy Department was quick to recognize the commercial implications of the British threat as well. Commander S. C. Hooper, who headed the Bureau of Steam Engineering's radio division, pointed out that Britain long had recognized that "communications" were one of "the handmaidens of commerce," a fact the United States "was slow to realize." It was clear, Hooper went on, that now "we would have to compete with Europe in the world markets, and that international communications and commerce would become of great importance to us."[13]

Commercial considerations, however, were not the only reason for the initiative to organize an American-controlled worldwide radio communications network. In a confidential wartime memorandum Captain D.W. Todd, director of Naval Communications, outlined the military dimensions:

> Communications are such an important feature of all Naval Strategy that the Navy Department is keenly interested in their development whether primarily intended for military purposes or not.... Any cable or radio communications whatever ... would be of the utmost value during the twilight period immediately proceding [sic] the beginning of a war, and afterwards, as long as they were not interrupted.[14]

For these reasons, the navy moved to block the British by keeping the Alexanderson alternator in U.S. hands. With control of superior technology, private corporations could build a worldwide network. Anchored by the Alexanderson alternator, American radio would counter the British dominance in cables and foil their efforts to establish a monopoly over international communications.[15] With these considerations in mind, Hooper and Bullard went calling on GE.

In the first GE-navy conference Admiral Bullard "strongly urged" the company's officers, "as patriotic Americans," not to sell the alternator to the Marconi interests. Bullard "suggested that the Navy Department would be sympathetic with the formation by the General Electric Co. and other clearly American interests of an American-owned, world-wide, radio-operating Co., which would be strong enough to deal with the Marconi Companies as an equal." Bullard also intimated that the Navy Department would release patent rights which it held to the firm "and generally that the Government would cooperate in assisting the New Company to obtain [foreign] concessions and otherwise."[16]

A. G. Davis, Young, and other GE officers were quite familiar with the advantages of controlling innovative technologies through patents. GE also was aware that the navy itself was a major purchaser of radio equipment, and its explicit support promised fat contracts. These men doubtless were tantalized by the prospect of vast opportunities held out by a world wide communications system, cemented with patent control over the leading technology. To implement these prospects, Young and Davis for GE, and Bullard, Hooper, and Assistant Secretary Franklin D. Roosevelt for the Navy Department, drew up a contract which provided for the creation of a new radio corporation.[17]

The contract gave the proposed firm control over navy-held patents as well as a monopoly on all nongovernmental radio messages and all contracts for equipment with the navy. In return, the proposed company agreed not to transfer or sell its radio patents or equipment to foreigners without the written consent of the Navy Department or make any operating agreements with foreign companies without its approval. It also agreed to have a representative of the department sit on the new board of directors. The firm's primary obligation was to establish and operate "a chain of wireless stations intended to constitute a high grade international system of communication."[18]

Other members of the department, however, were not at all sanguine about granting a monopoly on radio to private business interests. Secretary of the Navy Josephus Daniels refused to sanction the proposed GE-navy contract. Daniels confided to his diary his fears that the new company would work with British Marconi. This would "give the English company too much power in world communications." Daniels also worried that the company would join with the cable companies to maintain the high cost of international communications.[19]

Despite Daniel's refusal to authorize the contract, GE forged ahead and organized RCA. The professionals in the Naval Communications bureaucracy did their best to support the new firm. They believed that this was the only way to create an American worldwide radio system and avoid a British monopoly over international communications. The officers in the Navy Department controlling radio communications hoped that private profit could be meshed with the national interest. A marriage of technology, patriotism, and profit would, they believed, produce an American-owned system of "World Wide Wireless" (RCA's early motto) serving the strategic and commercial interests of the United States.[20] To meet the objections of the department's officers who feared British domination, RCA's bylaws stated that the majority of stockholders (80 percent), all officers, and directors had to be American citizens, and only they would have corporate voting rights. To ensure further the navy's support, the bylaws also granted a seat on RCA's board of directors to a representative of the government.[21]

This Navy Department-RCA partnership was formalized with Wilson's appointment of Admiral Bullard to RCA's board of directors on 14 January 1920. Having the director of Naval Communications on RCA's board would ensure that the corporation performed in the national interest, or so the navy hoped.[22] As Commander Hooper would later point out before the Senate, the Navy Department held its new relationship with RCA in very high regard: "We thought we were doing a great thing, to help get up a great American company to compete with the British monopoly in communications."[23]

Ironically, while GE sought the navy's consent for a domestic radio monopoly to counter the British, it worked to eliminate competition in radio communications on the international level. In July 1919, Young sent Vice-President Davis, one of GE's patent experts, to England to negotiate traffic agreements and patent licensing with the British Marconi Company. These consultations resulted in November in the British Marconi-RCA traffic agreement.[24]

In fact a cartel agreement, it divided the world market and exchanged patents between RCA and British Marconi, including the all-important patent to the Alexanderson alternator. By the fall of 1921, RCA had added the major French and German radio concerns to the cartel under much the same terms of market division and patent exchange.[25] Thus, in its first major international transaction, the Radio Corporation gave its leading foreign competitor the right to use the Alexanderson alternator in much of the world for communications purposes. Moreover, this agreement was signed before Bullard was appointed to RCA's board.

Why did GE adopt this policy of cartelization, thus abandoning the principles of an American "world wide wireless," and the technology upon which it was based, to foreign competitors? The reason for this apparently anomalous behavior has to do with the interrelationship of the technological, economic, and political imperatives surrounding the operation of international radio circuits. The firm's primary revenue-producing functions were the transmission of messages and the sale of equipment. The purpose of its existence as a private corporation was to earn dividends for its stockholders—primarily large electrical manufacturers.

The means to earn these dividends, the establishment of a worldwide wireless system, required extensive capital investment. These capital expenditures were threatened by rapid obsolescence because the radio "art" was expected to undergo rapid technological advance. Because of the newness of the technology, radio firms faced great difficulties in doing a communications business, such as being unable to communicate between the northern and southern hemispheres. In addition, the radio communications companies had to compete with entrenched cable companies that had "piled up tremendous cash reserves" through years of profit and noninnovation.[26] Consequently, in order to make radio a paying proposition, there was great pressure on the international radio communications firms to share the costs of development through cross-licensing of patents.

RCA had other reasons to support international cartelization. When discussing the company's plans to build stations for international communications in 1919 before the Senate, Chairman of the Board Young would point out time and again: "Quite obviously before those stations were built we had to know that we had someone at the other end of the circuit with which to communicate... you only own half a circuit. You always have to have somebody to communicate with, else your property is valueless."[27] Not only was RCA concerned with having someone with whom to communicate, but it also was concerned about ensuring that both stations were technologically equal. Since a primary source of RCA's communications revenues was on paid words transmitted and received, the only way the firm could compete with the cable companies and pay its capital costs was by increasing the flow of paid messages through its facilities.[28] This meant that "the moment the American company [RCA] had contracts with these other countries it was greatly interested in having the other end of the circuit as efficient as its own." To create these efficient circuits, RCA signed cross-licensing agreements, including the Alexanderson alternator patent, with its British, German, and French competitors.[29]

While the international agreements sought to stimulate traffic and the development of radio communications, they had another purpose. That, according to Young, was "to protect" RCA against "potential competition." RCA's chairman held that in radio "the cost of competition" was "so great that we [Americans] cannot afford it." Should more firms enter the field, Young predicted dire results: "the competition will become ruinous, wages will be inadequate, capital will be lost, and ultimately services will be demoralized." To avoid such demoralization, the chairmen of RCA and GE embraced cartelization; cartels were necessary to uphold wages and profits, even at the expense of the ultimate object of RCA's organization.[30]

It is perhaps unfair to criticize Young for pursuing a policy of international patent pooling. In the case of either countries organizing their radio communications around state ownership or private firms operated with government assistance, RCA was unable to build and operate stations. Given the large capital outlays essential to construct long-distance radio stations and the need to liquidate these capital costs by traffic through the facilities, it was absolutely essential to have long-term agreements ensuring traffic and circuit efficiency. Although RCA controlled the patents for efficient radio communications, other countries and/or foreign companies held the rights for radio communications.

To open circuits it was much easier for RCA to work with the foreign companies that held radio communications concessions than it was to compete with them. RCA purchased cooperation through cross-licensing patents and exclusive long-term traffic agreements. These were seen as essential both to ensure earnings and to protect capital investment.[31] This line of reasoning seems to have made sense to the Naval Communications Service, for there is no record of protest against this early set of traffic agreements, world market divisions, and patent pools.

Although RCA failed to gain the navy's contractual sanction for its monopoly, government support played a large part in the formulation of its initial business strategy. This was noted in RCA's early (1920 and 1921) *Annual Reports*:

> As our Company expands and its operations extend into various foreign territories, the harmonious working arrangements between the Company and our Government become more and more essential. It will therefore continue to be the policy of your officers and directors to strive to merit and retain the good will and cooperation of our Government.[32]

With the prospect of government support, RCA's management was optimistic about its future. "The expansion of your Company into a world-wide wireless communication system... presents commercial possibilities that can scarcely be calculated."[33]

RCA's early optimism, however, proved to be misplaced. In organizing the company, GE's officers simply did not realize just how expensive radio communications were going to be. In January 1920, RCA's Commercial Manager David Sarnoff prepared for Chairman Young an evaluation of the business situation in radio and the prospects of the new firm. In a lengthy report he pointed out that wartime experiences had created a large demand for maritime and high-power radio. But the technology to meet that demand was lacking: "The problems involved in connection with the development, manufacture and sales of radio devices are made more difficult by reason of the rapid changes of the art; that no sooner had a particular device been developed when it was obsolete by some improvement which has made the sale of the earlier device impractical."[34]

This rapid obsolescence of capital investment was not the only problem confronted by RCA's founders. As Sarnoff reported to President E. J. Nally, the distances RCA planned to cover in its radio program were in some cases between 4,000 and 6,000 miles. "No successful continuous commercial radio service over so great a distance," continued Sarnoff, "has yet been maintained by anybody."[35] He concluded that it was only after RCA had "obtained actual commercial experience" over these distances that the company would "be in a position to map out and execute a World-Wide Wireless program that should place our Company in a prominent position of World Leadership. Our Company should be the first to acquire such experience and data, even though we may have to pay substantially for this education."[36]

Substantial payment in radio meant a multimillion dollar investment in capital equipment. In high-power transoceanic radio, the average station in the early 1920s cost about $1,500,000. And as radio developed, as it would in this new and internationally competitive industry, RCA would be faced with a tremendous capital drain if it was to keep pace with its foreign and domestic rivals.[37]

Nonetheless, GE believed it could profitably establish RCA as a leading communications firm, and it was willing to put up considerable sums. To this end, on Long Island RCA constructed Radio Central, the world's most powerful radio station. The station, built around Alexanderson alternators for transmission, cost an estimated $10,000,000 and was designed to communicate between distances of 4,000 and 6,000 miles.[38]

These efforts only served to plunge RCA into a sea of red ink. In addition to the investment in Radio Central, the firm spent an equal amount on other facilities. Plagued by technical problems and competition from the cable companies, RCA suffered "only deficits" in its first years of operation.[39] Naturally, these losses put tremendous pressure on RCA to minimize costs and maintain capital investment at levels necessary to keep up with the cable competition. The strategy chosen by Young to raise additional capital and reduce costs was combination at home. Following its foreign experiences, RCA sought to end domestic competition in the radio communications industry. This was done through a manufacturers' cartel cemented through patent pooling. In this effort, the Naval Communications bureaucracy proved of indispensable assistance.

One of the key problems in radio faced by the Navy Department during the war and by RCA afterward was the patent situation. Any attempt to manufacture efficient radio apparatus in quantity confronted a welter of competing patents.[40] To solve the problem during the war, the Navy Department pooled the patents and promised that it would take responsibility for possible infringement cases. Fearing widespread legal problems, the department canceled this responsibility at the war's end. Naval Communications, however, recognized that the cancellation of the patent pool would mean an end to production of state-of-the-art radio equipment. To ensure a continued supply of up-to-date equipment, Hooper wrote to the companies involved suggesting that they exchange patents.[41]

Young seized the opportunity provided by the navy to corral support for an anemic RCA. Through the vehicle of cross-licensing, Young, with navy backing, enticed firms owning important radio patents—American Telephone and Telegraph (AT&T), United Fruit in 1920, and Westinghouse in 1921—into the RCA combine. This policy of combination brought RCA an infusion of badly needed capital. It also resulted in the cross-licensing of patents among the leading radio equipment manufacturers—AT&T, United Fruit, GE, and Westinghouse—within RCA.[42] By uniting the leading American electrical manufacturing firms (GE, Western Electric, and Westinghouse), competition in the domestic radio industry was substantially reduced. And, through cartelization, RCA achieved the ability to produce virtually any type of radio apparatus without fear of patent litigation.[43]

While it may have been good for the corporate bottom line, Young's strategy of combination at home and abroad created strains in the Navy Department-RCA partnership. By uniting most of the major manufacturers of radio apparatus within the RCA "combine," Young raised concerns among government policymakers about the wisdom of the monopoly he openly advocated.[44] In addition, RCA's relative inactivity in international communications served to undermine the Naval Communications bureaucracy's confidence in RCA as a promoter of the national interest.

Although the navy officers involved apparently approved the traffic agreements and license exchanges for European communications, they wanted RCA to set up American or American-dominated radio stations in the undeveloped areas of the world. In May 1920, Bullard had attempted to get RCA's board to adopt a "Wireless Monroe Doctrine" for South America. In Bullard's corollary to the Monroe Doctrine, "control of radio communication in the Western Hemisphere" would "remain in the hands of citizens or subjects of that hemisphere." The admiral urged RCA's directors to "exclude the participation of European companies" and build a South American station equal to the $10,000,000 Radio Central on Long Island.[45]

The admiral's efforts, however well intentioned, threatened to disrupt the international cartel Young had so painstakingly constructed. Of equal importance, the international communications side of RCA's business proved a tremendous drain of capital, generating only losses. By 1922 only one of RCA's six international radio communications circuits was producing a profit, despite the fact that the firm had "more long distance circuits" and "more high powered radio stations than any other country in the world."[46]

Such a financial track record made RCA's officers particularly anxious to share the costs of developing international communications with other companies, even at the expense of American control. In South America, Young organized the radio companies of France, England, and Germany into the AFEG Consortium to develop the region's radio communications. The navy grudgingly went along with the scheme because RCA had promised that the consortium would be dominated by Americans and use American equipment.

To avoid embroiling itself further in potentially embarrassing controversies with the Navy Department, like the Wireless Monroe Doctrine, RCA simply elected not to replace Bullard on its board. Such action, however, only served to discredit further RCA in the navy's eyes. In 1921 the Naval Communications Service produced several studies on international radio communications that were highly critical of RCA. One analysis pointed out that RCA, "to date, has no station in operation on foreign territory." Indeed, it only had concessions in Poland and Argentina, and the Argentine station was to be absorbed by the AFEG Consortium. Naval Communications also learned that RCA would not dominate the South American cartel nor would American equipment be used in its stations. Thus, for the navy, RCA's cartel had proved unproductive; it failed to deliver the promised worldwide wireless system for which it had been created.[47]

The navy's growing dissatisfaction with RCA emerged in an acrimonious debate over the issue of radio communications with China in the winter of 1921–22. In January 1921 the Federal Telegraph Company signed a contract with the Chinese government's Ministry of Communications for the construction of a high-power station at Shanghai for transpacific transmissions. This plunged the United States into a web of conflicting radio contracts held by the British and the Japanese. The British Marconi Company and the Mitsui Company both had "exclusive" contracts with the Peking government for external and internal radio communications. In addition, both firms possessed the full backing of their governments for these Chinese contracts.[48]

To make matters worse, both British Marconi and Mitsui had invested a substantial amount in securing and attempting to fulfill these contracts. Neither company, however, had the technology required to complete them. Although RCA recognized the British contract with Peking, China was one of the areas where the 1919 traffic agreement allowed competition; it was not covered by the patent pool. Thus, RCA could not contract for the Chinese government's radio communications and British Marconi could not use the alternator technology in its Chinese stations. This gave an opening for Federal Telegraph, which did possess the technology, to supply the Chinese with the radio communications that their foreign competitors were unable to provide.[49]

The Navy Department, anxious to gain a China-U.S. radio circuit, had been unhappy with RCA's lack of action in China. Because of its overall unsatisfactory relationship, the department sought an American competitor to RCA in radio communications and equipment manufacturing. The navy chose Federal Telegraph for this role and attempted to use the Chinese government's contract to promote the firm's fortunes. To encourage the contract's implementation and strengthen Federal Telegraph, the Navy Department gave back to the firm all the rights, patents, and licenses it had purchased during the war, free of charge. This was done through a contract negotiated by President Warren G. Harding's newly appointed secretary of the navy, Edwin Denby, in late March 1921.[50]

Despite the Navy Department's support for Federal Telegraph's Chinese radio contract, the British and Japanese interests managed, by the fall of 1921, to block its implementation by placing tremendous pressure on the Peking government.[51] With the Chinese international radio communications situation locked in a bitter stalemate, RCA (with an eye to the upcoming Washington Conference) attempted to move in as arbiter. In an open letter to one of RCA's directors, Chairman Young recommended cooperation along the lines of the AFEG South American radio consortium to solve the Chinese radio tangle. Young held that the recently created South American radio consortium had replaced the competing American, French, English, and German interests with cooperation, and the same could be done for China. Under this proposal, RCA would cooperate with Federal Telegraph in providing a comprehensive solution to China's radio communications by bringing the firm into the RCA combine. In this way China's radio needs would be served, and all major competition would be ended in the American radio communications business.[52]

Instead of solving the Chinese radio tangle, Young's proposal only served to bring the navy's conflict with RCA into the open. A nasty exchange regarding the nature of U.S. radio communications policy and the problem of China-U.S. radio ties took place between the two antagonists. In a letter to Secretary of State Charles Evans Hughes (with a copy to RCA), Secretary of the Navy Denby responded to Young's suggestion for a Chinese radio consortium. Denby first outlined the department's grievances with RCA. He then attacked RCA's monopolistic practices by arguing that:

> Maintaining free and open competition in the matter of radio communication in the U.S. is as equally important as correction of the present chaos in China resulting from an endeavor to create monopolies, and [the Navy Department] believes that every endeavor to correct the latter condition should in no wise prevent a tendency towards the former condition.... [The] Navy Department fears that any commitment on the part of the Government to an arrangement favorable to a monopoly by a single commercial company, though limited to a particular service, would but lend a means towards extending that monopoly to other services such as development and distribution of apparatus in general, and this is considered absolutely undesirable.[53]

In his letter to Hughes, the secretary of the navy portrayed RCA as a bad monopoly, concerned only with maintaining high prices and profits by squelching technological development. To keep prices low and to ensure the continued development of the art, the Navy Department held that competition abroad was essential to prevent monopoly at home.[54]

Strategic considerations were another important, although publicly unstated, reason for the department's opposition to an international Chinese radio consortium. Federal Telegraph's contract called for stations operated primarily by Americans, for twenty years. This American control, held Captain S. W. Bryant, director of Naval Communications, was of "very considerable importance to the United States' Fleet" in the case of conflict in the Pacific. This was true "especially during a period preceding the outbreak of hostilities." Bryant concluded that it was in the "best interest of the Navy, and the Nation in general to assist in every way practicable the carrying out of the Federal contract with China."[55] Clearly RCA's worldwide cartel threatened American strategic communications interests, as well as innovation and low prices for radio equipment. For these reasons the Navy Department opposed Young's proposal for Great Power cooperation in Chinese radio.

RCA responded to Denby's criticism with bitter complaints that the government was impossible to deal with in regard to radio. Young wrote a lengthy reply to Denby defending monopoly in American external radio communications. He also alleged that RCA had been unable to "ascertain any uniform policy of the Government [on external radio communications] and there is not a department of the Government authorized to formulate or execute a policy."[56]

Young's efforts to shift the blame on the broken partnership to Washington only served to underline the reasons for the navy's disillusionment with the company. It was RCA which had not requested the appointment of another governmental representative to its board after Bullard's reassignment, and the company had not kept Naval Communications informed of its plans for extending U.S. external radio ties.[57]

The department's dissatisfaction with RCA was stated explicitly in several Naval Communications' postmortems on the Denby-Young exchange. The director of Naval Communications noted in one memo that:

> The object to be accomplished by American private radio companies [that is, RCA] would appear to be not the acceptance of equality, but the attainment of superiority over foreign companies. The Radio Corporation's letter [proposing the China radio consortium] accepts as an objective equality or superiority. In the specific case of the cables referred to as British controlled,—if equality with England in radio is accepted, then we should, by accepting radio equality, deliberately place the United States in an inferior position as regards combined radio and cable communication facilities. This cannot be accepted.[58]

Thus, the underlying basis of Naval Communications' conflict with RCA was not the firm's domestic monopoly in manufacturing but rather its forsaking the objective for which the company was formed: "the attainment of superiority" in international radio communications. From the Navy Department's perspective, RCA's plans for an *American* worldwide wireless system had been scrapped for monopoly profits. Consequently, the department was forced to turn to competition to promote its communications-related security objectives.[59]

The disintegration of the Navy Department-RCA cooperative relationship illustrates some of the difficulties faced by the military in trying to harness the profit motive to the national interest. In creating RCA, officers of both the

Navy Department and GE underestimated the difficulty and expense of establishing a profitable worldwide wireless system. The technological and economic imperatives of long-distance radio communications—heavy capital investment, the need for a high volume of traffic at low cost to amortize investment costs, continuous research and development, rapid obsolescence of expensive capital equipment, and competition from cables—ensured that the business would have minimal profits and high costs.

RCA responded to these conditions by following the logic of profit-maximizing organizations; it sought to reduce its costs by cooperating, rather than competing, with other firms in the field, including foreign companies. This came, however, at the expense of RCA's original objective: the creation of an American worldwide wireless system. To facilitate this move, RCA reduced its level of contact and cooperation with Naval Communications policymakers who would have opposed this change in the firm's strategy.

The Navy Department responded to RCA's turn to monopoly by using its power within the government to promote competition in the radio industry. The navy refused to sanction RCA's monopoly and sought to ensure competition domestically between radio communications and manufacturing firms. It worked to promote competition between U.S. radio companies and those of other countries in Chinese external radio communications, and it specifically rejected RCA's plan to promote cooperation with foreign radio firms in China.

Wilson and Bullard's original vision of an American business cooperating closely with the government to construct and operate a chain of radio stations around the world that would rival the British system of cables had failed. Instead, RCA developed its own independent strategy for expansion abroad based on cooperation with foreign interests. This policy was antithetical to the government's policy of competition with foreign communications interests. It is important to note, however, that both RCA and the Navy Department were committed to expanding U.S. communications interests abroad. And this expansion assumed a world political economy which was safe and profitable for American business.

The conflict between the Navy Department and RCA was over the best means to expand privately owned American communications interests abroad. As the department relied on corporate interests to promote its own objectives, these interests were the partnership's controlling hand. As seen, RCA opted to dissolve the partnership for more lucrative relations with foreign and domestic firms. While this proved more profitable for RCA, the navy was left to turn to other, less competent, domestic competitors to achieve its international communications objectives. Ultimately, neither RCA nor its competitors would establish a worldwide wireless system to rival British cables and meet the navy's radio communications requirements.

NOTES

1. U.S. Cong., Senate, Committee on Interstate Commerce, *Hearings on S. 6: Commission on Communications,* 9 December 1929, 73d Cong., 3d sess., 1100-01 (hereafter *Hearings on S. 6*).

2. Ibid.; Anson W. Burchard, Vice President, General Electric, to Owen D. Young, 17 May 1919, Young MSS, File 11-14, Box 72, Owen D. Young Papers, Owen D. Young Library, Van

Hornesville, New York (hereafter Young MSS); Admiral W. S. Benson, Chief of Naval Operations, to Josephus Daniels, Secretary of the Navy, 29 May 1919, File 21, Record Group 38, Records of the Office of the Chief of Naval Operations, Series 35, Division of Naval Communications, Confidential Correspondence, 1917-1926 (hereafter RG38/35), National Archives and Records Service, Washington, DC (hereafter NARS).

3. *Hearings on S. 6*, 9 December 1929, 1100-01.

4. See William Appleman Williams, *Contours of American History* (Chicago, 1966); Ellis W. Hawley, *The Great War and the Search for a Modern Order: A History of the American People and Their Institutions, 1917-1933* (New York, 1979); Carl P. Parrini, *Heir to Empire: U.S. Economic Diplomacy, 1916-1923* (Pittsburgh, 1969); Lloyd C. Gardner, *Safe for Democracy* (New York, 1984); Melvyn Leffler, "Expansionist Impulses and Domestic Constraints, 1921-1933," *Economics and World Power: An Assessment of American Diplomacy since 1789*, eds. William H. Becker and Samuel F. Wells (New York, 1984); Michael J. Hogan, *Informal Entente: The Private Structure of Cooperation in Anglo-American Economic Diplomacy, 1918-1928* (Columbia, MO, 1977); Thomas McCormick, "Drift or Mastery? A Corporatist Synthesis for American Diplomatic History," *Reviews in American History* 10 (December 1982).

5. Alfred Chandler, *Strategy and Structure: Chapters in the History of American Industrial Enterprise* (Cambridge, MA, 1962); Alfred Chandler, *The Visible Hand* (Cambridge, MA, 1977); Mira Wilkins, *The Maturing of Multinational Enterprise: American Business Abroad from 1914 to 1970* (Cambridge, MA, 1974); David Noble, *America by Design: Science, Technology, and the Rise of Corporate Capitalism* (New York, 1977).

6. Chandler, *Visible Hand*, 374-76.

7. There are several notable exceptions to this trend. William H. Becker's *The Dynamics of Business-Government Relations: Industry and Exports, 1893-1921* (Chicago, 1982) and Emily Rosenberg's *Spreading the American Dream: American Economic and Cultural Expansion, 1890-1945* (New York, 1982) are two provocative works on the role played by business and the government in American expansion abroad. Philip T. Rosen's *The Modern Stentors: Radio Broadcasting and the Federal Government, 1920-1934* (Westport, CT, 1980) discusses the connections between the radio industry and the government during the formative years of broadcasting. Rosen offers an astute account of the nature of this relationship and the role of technology in defining it.

8. Captain L. S. Howeth, *History of Communications—Electronics in the United States Navy* (Washington, DC, 1963), 253-59, 118, 221-25; Woodrow Wilson, Executive Order No. 2585, 6 April 1917, File 28761, Record Group 80, Records of the Office of the Secretary of the Navy, Series 19, General Correspondence (hereafter RG80/19), NARS; undated, unsigned paper, c. 1918, "Naval Communications Service," File ZD, RG45 Naval Records Collection of the Office of Naval Records and Library, Subject File, 1911-1927, NARS; R. S. Griffin, Chief, Radio Division, Bureau of Steam Engineering, Memorandum to Navy Department (Material), 12 October 1914, File C-29-44, Record Group 80, Records of the Office of the Secretary of the Navy, [no series number], Secret and Confidential Correspondence, 1917-1919 (hereafter RG80/Secret and Confidential Correspondence, 1917-1919), NARS.

9. U.S. Cong., Senate, *Hearings on S. 4301: A Bill to Prevent the Unauthorized Landing of Submarine Cables in the U.S.*, 66th Cong., 3d sess., 11 January 1921, Owen D. Young, Testimony, 353 (hereafter *Hearings on S. 4301*); *Hearings on S. 6*, 22 May 1929, Captain S. C. Hooper, Director of Naval Communications Service, Testimony, 310; Admiral W. S. Benson, Chief of Naval Operations, to Secretary of the Navy Josephus Daniels, 29 May 1919, and Walter S. Rogers, communications expert, Committee of Public Information, to Woodrow Wilson, 27 May 1919, both in File 21, RG 38/35, NARS; Minutes of an American Marconi Company Conference Held in David Sarnoff's Office, 16 September 1919, "David Sarnoff Papers" I (a boxed set of bound papers), David Sarnoff MSS, RCA Labs, Sarnoff Library, Princeton, New Jersey (hereafter Sarnoff MSS); Howeth, *History of Communications*, 147, 151-52, 313-14.

10. *Hearings on S. 4301*, Young, Testimony, 333; 1937 Interview with Young, quoted in Gleason L. Archer, *The History of Radio to 1926* (New York, 1938), 194-95.

11. *Hearings on S. 6*, Lieutenant Commander Harold W. Dodd, Patent Section, U.S. Navy, Judge Advocate Section, 1012-14; Owen D. Young to Franklin D. Roosevelt, Assistant Secretary of the Navy, 29 March 1919, File 21, RG38/35, NARS.

12. Acting Director, Bureau of Steam Engineering, Memorandum to Secretary of the Navy Josephus Daniels, 4 April 1919, File 21, RG38/35, NARS.

13. *Hearings on S. 6*, Hooper, Testimony, 321.

14. Captain D. W. Todd, Director of Naval Communications, Confidential Memorandum Regarding Transpacific Communications, 29 August 1918, File unnumbered, Box 17, RG38/35, NARS.

15. Josephus Daniels, Secretary of the Navy, to Senator Duncan U. Fletcher, 19 May 1917, File 2876 (1-92), RG80/19, NARS; Howeth, *History of Communications*, 353-56.

16. Albert G. Davis, Vice President, GE, to Owen D. Young, Vice President, GE, 30 June 1919, File 11-14, Box 72, Young MSS; Federal Trade Commission (FTC), *Report on the Radio Industry* (Washington, DC, 1924), 15-17.

17. Anson W. Burchard, Vice President, GE, to Young, 17 May 1919, Paris, File 11-14, Box 72, Young MSS; Josephine Young Case and Everett Needham Case, *Owen D. Young and American Enterprise* (Boston, 1982), 181-82; Noble, *America by Design*, 9-10; Contract for the Establishment of High Power Radio Service, Draft of 1 May 1919, File unnumbered, Box 8, RG38/35, NARS.

18. Ibid.; Davis to Young, GE, 30 June 1919, File 11-14, Box 72, Young MSS.

19. Admiral W. S. Benson, Chief of Naval Operations, to Daniels, 29 May 1919, File 21, RG38/35, NARS; E. David Cronon, ed., *The Cabinet Diaries of Josephus Daniels, 1913-1921* (Lincoln, NE, 1963), 416.

20. Davis to Young, 30 June 1919, File 11-14, Box 72, Young MSS; Minutes of an American Marconi Company Conference..., 16 September 1919, and E. J. Nally, Letter to the Stockholders of the Radio Corporation of America, 4 May 1920, in Sarnoff MSS; RCA, *Annual Report* (1920).

21. Albert G. Davis, Vice President, GE, to Rear Admiral William H. G. Bullard, 16 September 1919, Box 1, Record Group 38, Records of the Office of the Chief of Naval Operations, Series 38, Personal Files of Director of Naval Communications, Rear Admiral Bullard (hereafter RG38/38), NARS; Minutes of an American Marconi Company Conference..., 16 September 1919, Sarnoff MSS; RCA's bylaws cited in FTC, *Report*, 18-20. For FTC statement on Bullard see ibid., 19.

22. Davis to Bullard, 16 September 1919, Box 1, RG38/38, NARS; Minutes of an American Marconi Company Conference..., 16 September 1919, Sarnoff MSS; E. J. Nally, President, RCA, to Woodrow Wilson, 3 January 1920, and Thomas Washington, Acting Secretary of the Navy, to Woodrow Wilson, 12 January 1920, File 26509 (283-98), RG80/19, NARS.

23. FTC, *Report*, 14, 24, 25; *Hearings on S. 6*, Hooper, Testimony, 315, 329, 317, 319.

24. Young to A. G. Davis, 22 August 1919, cited in Case and Case, *Owen D. Young*, 187-88; Exhibit DD, 21 November 1919, Articles I-VI, in FTC, *Report*.

25. Ibid.; Exhibits HH, II, and SS in FTC, *Report;* Case and Case, *Owen D. Young*, 188-89; RCA, *Annual Report* (1919).

26. Bullard to RCA's Board of Directors, 6 May 1920, File 11-14-65, Box 147, Young MSS; *Hearings on S. 4301*, Young, Testimony, 344-47, 354; Sarnoff to Nally, 16 February 1920, Source Books I, and Sarnoff to Young, 30 January 1920, quoted in E. E. Bucher, "Radio and David Sarnoff," I (unpublished manuscript), 227-28, Sarnoff MSS.

27. *Hearings on S. 6*, Young, Testimony, 1133.

28. Ibid., 1140-43, see Chandler, *Visible Hand*.

29. Ibid., 1143, 1138; *Hearings on S. 6*, Young, Testimony, 1143, 1138, Senator C. C. Dill, 1142.

30. Ibid., Young, Testimony, 1133, 1084, 1087, 1088.

31. *Hearings on S. 4301*, W. S. Rogers, Testimony, 46.

32. RCA, *Annual Report* (1919).

33. RCA, *Annual Report* (1920).

34. Sarnoff to Young, 30 January 1920, quoted in Bucher, "Radio" I:229, Sarnoff MSS.

35. Sarnoff to Nally, 16 February 1920, David Sarnoff, "Source Books for Early Reports" I, Sarnoff MSS.

36. Ibid.

37. A. A. Isabel, General Superintendent, Pacific Division, RCA, to Owen D. Young, 1 April 1921, File 11-14-47, Box 125, Young MSS; *Hearings on S. 6*, Clarence H. Mackay, Chairman of the Board of Postal Telegraph and Cable Corporation, Testimony, 1670.

38. Bucher, "Radio" I:246, 241; "To Wireless 1,000 Words a Minute," *New York Times*, 16 May 1920.

39. *Hearings on S. 6,* Hooper, Testimony, 321; "Public Liberally Capitalized Radio's Possibilities," *Wall Street Journal,* 2 May 1922; "Radio Corporation to Reduce Capital," *New York Times,* 3 May 1924; "Radio Corporation," *Wall Street Journal,* 18 August 1928.

40. *Hearings on S. 6,* Hooper, Testimony, 315; FTC, *Report,* 25.

41. *Hearings on S. 6,* Hooper, Testimony, 315; Young to J. R. Geary, GE representative, Tokyo, 26 August 1920, File 11-14-47, Box 124, Young MSS.

42. Admiral A. H. Hepburn to GE, Attention A. G. Davis, 5 January 1920, cited in Case and Case, *Owen D. Young,* 209–10; RCA, *Annual Report* (1920); *Hearings on S. 6,* Hooper, Testimony, 328; E. E. Bucher, "Radio and David Sarnoff" I:278-D, Sarnoff MSS.

43. RCA, *Annual Reports* (1920), (1921); E. E. Bucher, "Radio and David Sarnoff" I:278-D, Sarnoff MSS.

44. *Hearings on S. 4301,* Young, Testimony, 334-35, 351; Howeth, *History of Communications,* 366–69; undated, unsigned Memorandum by W. S. Rogers, U.S. Delegate to International Communications Conference, to Undersecretary of State, 8 June 1921, 574.D1/511, Record Group 59, Records of the Department of State, Decimal Files 1910–1929 (hereafter RG59), NARS; A. E. Kennelly, Commerce Department Radio Expert, to Herbert Hoover, Secretary of Commerce, 7 April 1921, enclosing Minutes of a Conference between representatives of the State Department, War Department, Navy Department, and Commerce Department on U.S. Government radio policy, 7 April 1921, File 67032/3, Record Group 40, General Correspondence of the Office of the Secretary of Commerce (hereafter RG40), NARS.

45. Admiral Bullard to the Board of Directors, Radio Corporation of America, 6 May 1920, File 11-14-65, Young MSS.

46. A. G. Davis, Vice President, GE, to Young, 24 March 1922, File 11-14-47, Young MSS; RCA, *Annual Report* (1923).

47. Unsigned, undated, Naval Communications Service Memorandum of Communications Policy, c. 2 April 1921, File 574.D1/618, RG59, NARS; unsigned Naval Communications Service Memorandum, "Effect of the Preponderating Control of Radio by any One Nation," 22 November 1921, File 211-15, Record Group 80, Records of the Office of the Secretary of the Navy, [no series number], Secret and Confidential Correspondence, 1919–26 (hereafter RG80/Secret and Confidential Correspondence, 1919–26), NARS; Captain S. W. Bryant, Naval Communications Service Memorandum, 3 January 1922, File 26509-283:23, RG80/19, NARS.

48. Charles R. Crane, U.S. Minister to China, to Secretary of State, 29 November 1920, 893.74/48; Crane to Secretary of State, 16 December 1920, /52; Paul S. Reinsch, Minister to China, to Secretary of State, 14 January 1919, /10.2451; Nelson T. Johnson, State Department, Division of Far Eastern Affairs Memoranda, 26 May 1919, /20.2658, 11 June 1919, /14.2145; Crane to Secretary of State, 26 May 1919, /132, all in RG59, NARS.

49. Reinsch to Secretary of State, 27 March 1919, 893.74/18.2638, RG59, NARS; M. A. Oudin, Vice President, International General Electric Co., to Young, 27 March 1920, File 11-14-47, Box 124, Young MSS; Exhibit DD, Articles I–VI in FTC, *Report.*

50. *New York Times,* 17 November 1921; *Hearings on S. 6,* Lt. Commander Harold Dodd, Testimony, 1015-16; Contract between U.S. Government, represented by Secretary of the Navy Edwin Denby, and the Federal Telegraph Co., 19 March 1921, File 34, China 5, RG38/35, NARS; unsigned Naval Communications Service Memorandum, "Effect of the Preponderating Control of Radio by any One Nation," 22 November 1921, File 211-15, and S. W. Bryant, U.S. Asiatic Fleet Intelligence Officer, to Commander-in-Chief, U.S. Asiatic Fleet, 5 July 1920, File 108-10, RG80/Secret and Confidential Correspondence, 1919–27.

51. Crane to Bainbridge Colby, Secretary of State, 20 January 1921, 893.74/59; Crane to Colby, 9 February 1921, /91; A. B. Ruddock, Chargé d'Affaires, U.S. Legation, Peking, to Charles E. Hughes, Secretary of State, 8 August 1921, /179, all in RG59, NARS.

52. Owen D. Young, Chairman of the Board, RCA, to James Sheffield, 7 December 1921, 893.74/550, RG59, NARS; Young to Elihu Root, 12 December 1921, File 11-14, Box 72, Young MSS.

53. Edwin Denby, Secretary of the Navy, to Charles E. Hughes, Secretary of State, 16 December 1921, 893.74/204, RG59, NARS.

54. Young to Bullard, 6 March 1922, File 11-14-65, Box 147, Young MSS.

55. Captain S. W. Bryant, Director of Naval Communications, unsigned Memorandum, 5 January 1922, File 74, RG38/35, NARS.

56. Young to Denby, 22 December 1921, File 6320, (279-336) RG80/19, NARS.

57. Captain S. W. Bryant, Director of Naval Communications, Naval Communications Service Memorandum, 3 January 1922, File 26509-283:3, RG80/19, NARS.

58. Bryant, unsigned Naval Communications Service Memorandum, 10 January 1922, File 74, RG38/35, NARS.

59. Ibid. Given this commentary on RCA's practices, the recent historiography on the subject of government-RCA ties is somewhat anomalous. Michael J. Hogan's discussion of New Era radio communications policy in *Informal Entente* is a case in point. A useful corrective to Hogan's overemphasis on cooperation in radio is Brady Alexander Hughes, "Owen D. Young and American Foreign Policy, 1919–1929" (Ph.D. dissertation, University of Wisconsin, 1969). Hughes notes that the Navy Department was extremely critical of RCA and sought to ensure competition in the domestic radio industry.

U.S. Naval Air Expeditions in the Arctic in the 1920s

NANCY FOGELSON

Navy flights in the Arctic in the 1920s addressed three issues: the role of a peacetime navy, the increasing importance of aviation, and the value of the Arctic for U.S. airways and naval bases. Dr. Fogelson shows how these flights demonstrated the strategic importance of transpolar air routes between Europe and Asia and the advantage to the United States of participating in Arctic development.

****

U.S. Navy air expeditions in the Arctic during the 1920s contributed to the development of Arctic air routes and aided in determining the sites of air bases that could be used by the military. Explorers' reports from the late nineteenth century onward had described rich mineral deposits and charted shortened water routes between Europe and North America, but it was the use of aircraft during and immediately after World War I that caused the government to consider the Arctic as a path for commercial and military air routes.

This emphasis on the Arctic as a route for airways began in 1920 with a round-trip flight between New York and Nome, Alaska, organized by William Mitchell as part of his campaign for a unified air force. The flight's success focused attention on the Arctic, and it became clear that air routes across northern latitudes could shorten shipping time between the United States and Europe and Asia. Shortened trade routes also could be used for military purposes and, as the government began to employ a polar perspective, the proximity of Russia, Japan, England, and Germany to the United States and Canada stimulated interest in establishing an American presence in the Arctic. Expeditions were sent out to explore territory that might be suitable for air bases, to test the ability of aircraft to function successfully in Arctic conditions, and to collect environmental data that could be useful to shipping interests and the new aviation industry.

Numerous articles and editorials describing the economic and strategic importance of the Arctic appeared regularly following Mitchell's Alaskan flight and made it difficult to ignore the possibility of utilizing polar regions for air routes and air bases.[1] The navy's Bureau of Navigation decided to expand into Arctic exploration as a way of promoting its peacetime role, as a stimulus for scientific and industrial achievement, and to establish a position of leadership in aviation technology.[2] In order to accomplish these objectives, an air expedition was scheduled for 1923 with orders to locate land and chart the one-million square mile area between Europe and Japan.[3] The dirigible *Shenandoah*, whose size and range of operation were unexcelled at the time, was chosen as the lead aircraft.[4] The airship, an example of "American skill, ingenuity, and engineering ability," also was an example of a future-oriented navy: it was designed by the Navy Department, fabricated at the naval aircraft factory in Philadelphia, assembled at the Lakehurst Naval Air Station, and manned by navy officers and personnel.[5]

In addition to the *Shenandoah*, plans called for a support system of airplanes to transport equipment and supplies. The department considered using six seaplanes then under construction. Although all were capable of cruising the required range of some 2,200 miles, there was considerable argument about allocating these planes to the Arctic project. Questions were raised about their usefulness when it became evident that scientific instruments and supplies would have to be limited because of space needed for fuel. Even if this problem were resolved by improving cruising speed and altering flight plans, including these planes in the expedition would necessitate modifying naval strategy. Initially, they had been scheduled for duty in the Pacific and, if diverted to the Arctic, maneuvers in the Pacific and Caribbean would be delayed for a year or more. If, however, the planes were assigned to the expedition and the Arctic experiment succeeded, a three-pronged defense perimeter through the Pacific, Caribbean, and Alaskan Arctic could be developed which would protect the three strategic and commercial sea approaches to the United States while establishing future air routes.[6]

To gain support for the operation, naval authorities described the Arctic as "destined to become the Mediterranean of the future," and they emphasized that the navy had an obligation to contribute to the exploration and development of this area in order to further international communications.[7] Secretary of the Navy Edwin Denby promoted the expedition's importance to American national interests and warned that another power "would and could win" the race to find new land if the United States did not undertake an expedition before the year was out. He added that he believed the area was "certain to be of high strategic value if we look forward to warfare and commerce in the future." He acknowledged that the possibility of finding new land was slim, but he supported the search: "whether there is land out there or not it should be the property of the United States." On hearing of the proposed expedition, Captain Robert A. "Bob" Bartlett (ship's captain on the Peary expeditions) gave his hearty approval, commenting: "What are we going to do with the *Shenandoah* if we don't fly to the Pole? I want to see the Stars and Stripes carried to the North. Don't read American history! Make it!"[8]

Congressional committee hearings on the proposed expedition began in December 1923. Denby, testifying in the House of Representatives, reviewed scientific studies indicating that a continent or land mass could be present in the area directly north of Alaska.[9] He believed it was highly desirable that the United States discover any such land because of its "contiguity to the United States and its strategic value." The material value might not be realized immediately, but because the area would be used for bases for planes in flight between Europe and Asia, he could not "view with equanimity any territory of that kind being in the hands of another power." He reminded the committee that "beyond the Pole there [was] territory in the hands of another power, the more reason why something in that Arctic Circle, if there is anything there, should be in the hands of the United States."[10]

The expedition plans provided for systematic aerial photography, extensive reconnaissance, mapping, and the establishment of bases capable of servicing airplanes and dirigibles.[11] The airplanes assigned to accompany the dirigible were to gather aerological data during short flights and test weather conditions, which then would be broadcast to the *Shenandoah*.

The National Geographic Society, historically a supporter of naval Arctic exploration, offered to help promote the project. Gilbert Grosvenor, one of its directors and a member of the congressional committee, suggested that the society contribute $40,000 to help defray costs, adding that the contribution would not affect the navy's control of the project. He recommended launching a careful publicity campaign to stress the expedition's scientific value, in order to avert adverse public opinion that might arise if the project were considered some kind of stunt. He also offered the assistance of the society's scientists in preparing a statement on the value of exploring polar regions by air, an offer that was readily accepted. Although the committee argued over every aspect of the plan from the route it would take through the type of gas the *Shenandoah* would use, all members did agree that the dirigible would be capable of returning with valuable economic, military, and scientific information.[12] The importance of the mission was described by Bartlett:

> The flying route across the Pole is the aerial Panama Canal of the future. It is absolutely essential that, for trade and military purposes, the United States should control the area on the American side of the Pole—just as essential as that the United States should control the Panama Canal.
>
> To have some other nation find this land would cause endless trouble for future generations, when flying from the American to the European side of the Pole is going to be so valuable commercially that military control of the area between the American flag already planted by Peary at the Pole and the American territory of Alaska will be essential.[13]

Speculation over national benefits that could materialize from the *Shenandoah* flight reflected a growing public acceptance of political and economic expansion. The *Literary Digest* justified the possibility of annexing the Arctic by claiming that sovereign rights could be established, based on discovery of territory while exploring by air. Annexation would secure any possible economic advantages from access to coal deposits, such as those in Spitsbergen, and it would provide the United States with military advantages from air routes traversing the general Arctic area. The *New York World* echoed Secretary Denby's enthusiasm over possible land claims, adding that "we need the North Pole to strengthen our defenses" and warning that, after annexation, the Pole and adjacent ice fields would have to be covered with long-range guns to protect the area and secure it for bases for a flying fleet, ice cruisers, and destroyers.[14]

Lieutenant Commander Fitzhugh Green also stressed the potential strategic importance of the Arctic, describing Europe and Asia as "two great reservoirs of trade... connected by long thin pipes of traffic via Panama and Suez." Commercial traffic between the two continents could be greatly increased with transpolar trade routes adequately defended by the navy.[15]

American bases in Alaska were important but not sufficient for adequate defense of the general area. "From a military point of view," the United States should establish a "terrestrial oasis somewhere between Alaska and the Pole. That there is such an oasis we have excellent reasons to believe. But it will not be ours unless we get there first."[16]

Despite the many disclaimers, Arctic flying in 1924 was hazardous. Winter flights were not practical because of the lack of equipment necessary for night flying, and summer flights, while able to take advantage of the long daylight, had to contend with dangerous fog.[17] Economic advantages were real, but the ability to exploit natural resources was still many years away. Not only was transportation unreliable, but also the machinery and technology necessary for cold-weather mineral extraction were insufficiently developed. The potential was there; the tools were missing.

Arguments advanced by Secretary Denby and those who testified at the hearings did not persuade Congress to allocate sufficient funds for the operation. The expense was too great and the hearings continued for too long, leaving too little time to complete preparations for the expedition that year. The expedition was canceled, and the *Shenandoah* was assigned to regular naval duty.[18]

Cancellation of the *Shenandoah* flight, however, did not deter the navy from continuing with plans to explore the Arctic with aircraft. On learning that the National Geographic Society was organizing an Arctic expedition for 1925, the new secretary of the navy, Curtis Wilbur, suggested that the two organizations cosponsor the operation. When Richard E. Byrd (who had tried for a post on the aborted *Shenandoah* flight) heard of the proposal, he contacted Wilbur to recommend that the expedition plans include an airplane flight over the North Pole. Wilbur expressed interest and presented the plan to President Calvin Coolidge as well as to Donald MacMillan, expedition commander.[19] (MacMillan, a U.S. Navy Reserve officer, had been a member of Peary's 1909 team and had gone on to lead numerous Arctic expeditions.)

Coolidge conferred with MacMillan about his proposed voyage, and the two men agreed that the United States should make a major effort to claim additional territory near the North Pole. MacMillan reminded the president that Denmark already had a foothold in the Arctic with Greenland, a situation MacMillan thought could prove embarrassing to the United States if landing fields for airships and airplanes were needed in the North.[20]

The expedition, organized with MacMillan as commander of the entire operation and Byrd in charge of naval personnel and aircraft, was scheduled to sail from Wiscasset, Maine, on 17 June 1925, with MacMillan's ship the *Bowdoin* leading the way and the *Peary*, a converted trawler, carrying the navy's planes.[21] The area to be investigated extended over one million square miles of previously unexplored territory northwest of the Canadian Archipelago. Additional exploration was planned for Ellesmere Island, the northern part of the Greenland ice cap, northern Labrador, and the interior of Baffin Island. Main headquarters were to be established at Etah, Greenland. Gas and supplies would be relayed to Cape Thomas Hubbard on Axel Heiberg, and from there the men would proceed to the center of the unknown area.[22] Byrd, in charge of leading the aerial excursions, planned to land planes and supplies on the east side of Smith Sound near Cape Sabine and then fly two Loening amphibian planes to set up the next depot at Cape Columbia, 300 miles north, making two or three trips with each plane. When a sufficient supply of fuel was established, one plane would fly north as far as possible over the Polar Sea and, on returning, then fly to Axel Heiberg.[23]

The *Bowdoin* and *Peary* arrived at Etah on 1 August in the middle of a snowstorm. MacMillan planned to remain in the North until 25 August, but if it were necessary, the departure date could be extended to, but no later than, 1 September. This was because the expedition carried only enough provisions for the thirty-nine-man crew for a maximum of three months. Should any mishap occur, wintering over by one or both ships would be dangerous. Because of concern over weather, the entire project—landing and assembling planes, establishing food and fuel depots on Ellesmere, and flying at least 2,000 miles—had to be accomplished in an orderly and efficient manner. By 3 August the preliminary work was finished, and the first flight was able to survey part of Greenland.

All planes were operational and engaged in flights by 5 August, but unfortunately none was running satisfactorily. Minor engine trouble and unusually heavy fog, rain, and low-flying clouds kept the flights short and hindered attempts to set up supply depots. On 8 August a successful flight was made over Smith Sound, which was covered with ice pans. Flying over Ellesmere, the planes reached altitudes of 5,500 and 7,000 feet, but the flights were abruptly shortened when heavy storm clouds appeared and all attempts at landing to cache supplies were abandoned.[24] By 18 August the planes had covered 6,000 miles despite technical problems and constant poor weather.[25] MacMillan, aware that all spare parts were then in use and that the weather appeared to be getting even worse, recommended that no further attempts be made to establish aircraft bases and that the expedition abandon original flight plans to explore Baffin, Greenland, and Labrador.[26] Byrd protested the decision and expressed his disappointment to the Navy Department, but he made no attempt to do other than follow orders.

Although the 1925 expedition was cut short, flights made during the few days when weather was favorable surveyed 30,000 square miles of territory in just a few hours, compared to the months of backbreaking effort necessary to cover the area on land and water. MacMillan, on his return, described the Arctic as a "strange and wonderful place" that had aroused the curiosity of men continually from the time of Norse voyages to the present, and it would continue to attract explorers until "every square foot of this little world of ours will be explored." He believed polar studies, aside from measurable benefits for commercial interests, added to the "sum total of human knowledge."

MacMillan had hoped aviation would provide the means to accomplish a full investigation of the Arctic area in question. After reviewing maintenance problems that arose during the 1925 expedition, however, he was skeptical about the degree of success that could be expected. He thought planes had been given a fair trial, but he was "convinced that far northern work [would] never be done at least with a single engine airplane" because of the difficulties in landing and taking off. He also thought three-engine planes might be useful but preferred dirigibles at that time. He reasoned that, although dirigibles needed better design and construction to withstand low temperatures and gale winds, the necessary improvements could be made within the next few years.[27] MacMillan's forecast of improvements in aviation technology in the immediate future was quite accurate. In 1925, Byrd's flights had been canceled because the planes could not be flown in bad weather, but by the next year dirigibles and planes would both be used to cross the Arctic without incident. In 1926, Roald Amundsen completed the first successful transpolar dirigible flight, and Byrd made the first successful flight from Spitsbergen over the North Pole in a trimotor airplane.

Byrd began planning his North Pole flight as soon as he returned from the MacMillan expedition in 1925. He believed that the flight was important for testing the ability of airplanes to fly at high altitudes and that, if successful, the flights would increase chances of finding unexplored land since planes had a wider viewing range than dirigibles. He also thought a successful flight across the Pole might stimulate public interest in aviation. Byrd hoped the navy would provide four Wright air-cooled motors and the necessary spare parts, meteorological and camping equipment, and two aviation machinist mates, and in return he offered to submit a report on engine and equipment performance.[28] Admiral William A. Moffett endorsed the plan in the "interest of science" and sent it on to Secretary Wilbur. Although the navy was enthusiastic about the idea, there was little support for so expensive and large an expedition.[29] Failure to have completed the flights during the MacMillan expedition could have been an important factor in rejecting Byrd's proposal.

Although there was no financial support from the navy, Byrd and his machinist mate, Floyd Bennett, were granted leave for the expedition which was scheduled to depart from New York early in April 1926.[30] Byrd then went to the National Geographic Society and a number of his wealthy friends for funding, all in the tradition of earlier explorers. The society made a substantial contribution, and Edsel Ford, Vincent Astor, and John D. Rockefeller each contributed $20,000. The Federal War Shipping Board leased Byrd a 4,000-ton steamer, the *Chantier,* for a token fee of one dollar per year.

Byrd stressed that the venture was an all-American expedition, staffed with forty-six adventure-seeking volunteers.[31] Using a Fokker trimotor plane equipped with air-cooled 200-horsepower Wright motors, Byrd planned to fly from King's Bay, Spitsbergen, crossing 375 miles to Cape Bridgeman, Greenland, where bases would be established while he explored the area. If the region proved impractical for landing, he still would be able to explore 40,000 square miles of unknown territory during the flight. In addition to the flight, he planned to sail to Etah in September and freeze-in the ship for the winter.[32] Byrd emphasized that his object was not to find the North Pole; Peary had already done that. Rather, he hoped to prove the airplane safe for Arctic travel and demonstrate the commercial value of Arctic aviation. Byrd believed the area was becoming crowded; there was a need to act quickly and not to wait "while foreigners locate and take over land that probably is in the Polar Sea and that may within twenty-five years be of value to the United States as a landing base for transpolar flights of a commercial or a military nature."[33]

When he found that Amundsen's dirigible flight was scheduled to leave from Spitsbergen at the same time, Byrd cancelled all aspects of his own flight except the dash to the Pole. The plane took off on 9 May 1926, with Bennett as aviator and Byrd as navigator, and followed a straight line to the area of the North Pole, circled, and returned to Spitsbergen. It was a triumph for Byrd, an example of his able preparation and audacity, and a triumph for Americans who then were able to claim that the first conquests of the Pole had been made by American naval officers.[34] Despite great acclaim, the actual value was minimal because the flight had been too short and too brief to test the plane's ability to withstand prolonged flight in the Arctic. Flying over the polar area required skilled navigation, but the information brought back was too little to be of much scientific or technical use. Byrd's flight was both praised and severely criticized, and because the North Pole is only a theoretical point, his success could not be documented.[35]

The press described Byrd's flight as characteristic of the United States, a country that had achieved major feats in the Arctic. The flight had added a "golden page to the history of aviation and exploration" and was acclaimed as a "first" for the United States, a country that accomplished things first and better. The flight was more than a heroic gesture; it was an "example of technology defeating nature." Commander Byrd may have added no new territory to the nation's possessions and he may not have made a great contribution to science, but he was accorded a hero's status because he had "written a brilliant chapter into the history of Anglo-Saxon pioneering."[36]

In January 1927, Byrd was awarded the Congressional Medal of Honor for "distinguishing himself conspicuously by courage and intrepidity at the risk of his life in demonstrating that it [was] possible for aircraft to travel in continuous flight from a now inhabited portion of the earth over the North Pole and return." The next month, Bennett also received this award as a member of the Byrd Arctic expedition and for "contributing largely to the success of the first heavier aircraft flight to the North Pole." Byrd and Bennett were congratulated for promoting "peaceful relations between the nations of the world" through the use of aviation. Byrd, Bennett, and Charles Lindbergh had contributed significantly to the view of airplanes as peace advocates rather than as instruments of destruction.[37]

Byrd had not been able to secure the information nations had been so eager for, evidence of the existence of land in the region north of Alaska, but his flight over the North Pole, coupled with MacMillan's annual sea excursions, established an American presence in the eastern Arctic. The importance of the Arctic was summed up by a navy representative who explained that control of lands in the north polar region was a valuable asset to the United States or to any country from a "commercial and expansion standpoint." He believed that the land above Point Barrow could become the "junction point of commercial aviation," as airliners from Russia and the East passed near the Pole and those flying from the opposite direction did the same.[38] Aircraft had not, in 1926, developed enough for regular use in Arctic regions, but American navy expeditions from 1923 to 1926 had demonstrated that U.S. economic and strategic interests could and would expand into the Arctic with improvements in aviation technology and the development of air routes.

NOTES

1. *Annual Report of the Navy Department* (1921), 3.
2. Office of Naval Intelligence, *The United States Navy in Peace Time* (Washington, 1931), iv, 48.
3. "Arctic Exploration by Air," Navy Department Records RG 80, 111-99 (hereafter RG 80, 111-99), National Archives, Washington, DC (hereafter NA).
4. "Star Trip of the Stars' Daughter," *Literary Digest* 79 (29 December 1923): 12-13. The *Shenandoah* was as large as an ocean liner (680 feet long and 78 feet wide). It was powered by six engines and had a cruise radius of 4,000 miles.
5. *Annual Report of the Navy Department* (1923), 47. Gas capacity was 2,150,000 cubic feet. Helium was used because it was nonflammable and nonpoisonous.
6. "Memorandum," 25 November 1923, RG 80, 111-99, NA.
7. "*Dixmude*'s Lesson to *Shenandoah*," *Literary Digest* 80 (12 January 1924): 15; *New York Times*, 4 January 1924.
8. *New York Times*, 17 January 1924; D. M. LeBourdais, "The Aerial Attack on the Arctic," *The Nation* 118 (1924): 60.
9. "Arctic Exploration by Aircraft," RG 80, 111-99, NA.
10. Hearings before the Committee on Naval Affairs of the House of Representatives, 1923-24, 68th Cong., 1st sess., House Report, 149, 78-108 (hereafter Naval Hearings), NA.
11. RG 80, 111-99: 1-105, NA; Naval Hearings, 5 December 1923, NA.
12. Ibid., 3; Naval Hearings, 7 December 1923, NA.
13. Naval Hearings, 11 December 1923, 61, NA.
14. "To Annex the Arctic by Air," *Literary Digest* 80 (23 February 1924): 18.
15. Fitzhugh Green, "The Navy and the North Pole," *Proceedings of the U.S. Naval Institute* 50 (March 1924): 373-85.
16. Fitzhugh Green, "Over the Top of the World," *Outlook* 135 (19 December 1923): 681-83.
17. "Polar Perils Await the *Shenandoah*," *Current Opinion* (3 March 1924): 344-46; Vilhjalmur Stefanson, "Arctic Air Routes to the Orient," *The Forum* (December 1924): 721-32.
18. *Annual Report of the Navy Department* (1924), 31, 616, 167.
19. Byrd, never one to submit easily to routine protocol, was irked and regretted "extremely that the Secretary finds it necessary to take such a small matter up with the President." Byrd to Bartlett, 24 February, 30 March 1925, Robert A. Bartlett Papers, Bowdoin College Library, Brunswick, Maine.
20. *New York Times*; 31 March 1925, Department of Marine, RG 42, v4623, f84-1-1, Public Archives of Canada, Ottawa (hereafter PAC); clipping from *Washington Star*, 30 March 1925.
21. Memorandum by Secretary of the Navy to Byrd, 15 June 1925, State Department Records, RG 59, 842.014, NA.
22. "To Seek the Unknown in the Arctic," *National Geographic* 47 (June 1925): 673-75.
23. Byrd to J. A. Wilson, May 1925, Northern Affairs Program, RG 85, v59, f831, PAC.
24. "1925 MacMillan Arctic Expedition with Airplanes," unpublished manuscript, Box 20, Donald B. MacMillan Papers, Bowdoin College Library, Brunswick, Maine.
25. D. H. Dinwoodie, "Arctic Controversy: The 1925 Byrd-MacMillan Expedition Example," *Canadian Historical Review* 53 (March 1972): 51-65.
26. RG 80, Sc11-99:3, NA.
27. "Arctic Exploration from the Air," n.d., Box 17/1, MacMillan Papers, Bowdoin College.
28. Edwin P. Hoyt, *The Last Explorer: The Adventures of Admiral Byrd* (New York, 1968), 100.
29. The expedition was estimated to cost $140,000. Northern Affairs Program, RG 85, v764, f5052, PAC.
30. *Annual Report of the Navy Department* (1926), 37.
31. *New York Times*, 2 April 1926.
32. Hoyt, *Last Explorer*, 97-100.
33. *New York Times*, 3 April 1926, quoted in Hoyt, *Last Explorer*, 100.
34. "The Byrd Flight to the North Pole," *Aviation* 20 (24 May 1926): 780-82. The flight, described as a technical triumph particularly for the Wright engines, took nine hours, three minutes for the round trip and covered 1,200 miles.

35. For a critical appraisal of Byrd's flight see Finn Ronne, *Antarctica, My Destiny* (New York, 1979), 182–89.
36. "Crowding the North Pole," *Literary Digest* 89 (22 May 1926): 8–11.
37. Microfilm Reel 179, #3580, Calvin Coolidge Papers, University of Cincinnati Library, Cincinnati, Ohio.
38. Northern Affairs Program RG 85, v584, f571-6, PAC; see clipping in *Washington Post*, 28 May 1926.

Admiral Mahan, "Narrative Fidelity," and the Japanese Attack on Pearl Harbor: The Rhetorical Interaction between Discourse and Corroborative Events

RONALD H. CARPENTER

Japan's strategy and tactics at Pearl Harbor were influenced by a sense of history. What Japanese naval commanders "knew" as history, however, evolved in part from interaction among events, their nation's earlier experiences at sea, and the writings of Alfred Thayer Mahan. In his essay, Professor Carpenter explains the influence of Mahan's rhetoric on Japanese strategic planning in 1941.

****

The name recurs in analyses of America's emergence as a world power as well as in the course of international affairs generally: Alfred Thayer Mahan. In the United States, this naval historian's discourse influenced decisions favoring imperialism; Germany and Great Britain used his doctrine to justify naval growth, colonial expansion, and actions during both world wars; and recent Russian naval building "might almost have been inspired by the prophetic writings of...Alfred Thayer Mahan."[1] To Theodore Roosevelt, "he was one of those men who leave a permanent mark on history and literature, aside from their profound and far reaching influence on contemporary thought."[2] For many people, Mahan articulated "man's role in society" during "widening uncertainty and chronic stress" when "the historian's voice is most needed, the more so as the others seem inadequate, often absurd."[3] His message was part of the "communication mosaic" about military might during the turn of the century.[4] Mahan was heeded because he made compelling historical sense to guide future action.[5]

While nominally a U.S. Navy officer and Naval War College lecturer, Mahan contributed prolifically to periodicals and wrote several volumes on naval history. His reputation rests most securely on *The Influence of Sea Power upon History*, published in 1890. The book won acclaim not only for its content but also for its form and style.[6] Letters from his readers pointed to a persuasive "paramessage" from his style in discourse "quite apart from the representational meaning of the message itself."[7] For readers of English, carefully qualified periodic sentences evinced a prudent, cautious writer not given to rash assertions or overstatement, and a stylistic counterpoint of epigrammatic generalizations projected exceptional wisdom and powers of insight.[8]

The concern here is with Japanese readers of translations who praised "the great principles herein set forth by your forcible pen." With Japan's "Naval and Military College having adopted it as their textbook," *The Influence of Sea Power upon History* also was in "every middle, higher middle and normal school in Japan."[9] Ronald H. Spector identifies sources of Japanese decisions about Pearl Harbor as ranging from "the British Royal Navy to the histories of Alfred Thayer Mahan."[10] And other historical research offers diaries, interviews, and correspondence indicating that Admiral Yamamoto, his planning staff, and attack commanders were "true disciples of Mahan."[11] Those rich primary sources facilitate rhetorical analysis of how the course of Japanese strategy and tactics at Pearl Harbor was vectored in part by an American's historical narrative.

Characterizing historians as "rhetorical agents" who "are always in search of those proofs that are able to explain the past to the present in the most persuasive terms," E. Culpepper Clark asks: "What makes certain explanations more satisfactory than others?" For him, historical writing is an analog of an oration's *narratio*, or "statement of facts," wherein "stylistic devices...to emplot the story...transform the warrant from its status as a general inferential rule to a connector between thought and action that is grounded in experience and appeals to common sense."[12] It is true that discourse does not function in isolation from other discourse.[13] But in Japan, Mahan's historical narrative superseded other stories about sea power.

For Japanese naval personnel who planned and executed the Pearl Harbor raid, Mahan's writing became increasingly influential; its message became doctrine as it was corroborated by events. To help account for decisions by the planners of the Pearl Harbor attack and the commanders at sea and in the air on 7 December 1941, Walter R. Fisher's concept of "narrative fidelity" will be used. His construct is appropriate here because it views human communication "as historical as well as situational, as stories competing with other stories;...and as rational when they satisfy the demands of narrative probability and fidelity."[14] Thus, those events will be explicated which made Mahan's story ring true for the Japanese prior to the attack on Pearl Harbor.

Although rhetorical interaction between discourse and corroborating events is integral to attaining narrative fidelity, Mahan's credibility complemented the process. His reputation among Westerners caused the Japanese to read him as they entered the twentieth century with a catch-up mentality about naval warfare. They found enticing statements from a distinguished historian who seemed to write directly about their nation and to advocate models of behavior. Readers so persuaded are drawn to such models initially because they perceive real or imagined similarities to people whose behavior should be emulated.[15] To Kenneth Burke such identification is *"acting together."*[16] But, as Fisher also observes, "any story, any form of rhetorical communication, not only says something about the world, it also implies an audience, persons who conceive of themselves in very specific ways. If a story denies a person's self-conception, it does not matter what it says about the world.... The only way to bridge this gap, if it can be bridged through discourse, is by telling stories that do not negate the self-conceptions people hold of themselves."[17] Mahan's "story" appealed forcefully to Japan's self-conceptions.

The most significant part of *The Influence of Sea Power upon History* was the opening chapter, "Discussion of the Elements of Sea Power." Preceding over four hundred pages of historical narrative about naval engagements from 1660 to 1783—typically won by British naval prowess—these first fifty-five pages identified and explained six sources of a nation's greatness at sea and thereby in the world: geographical position, physical conformation, extent of territory, population, national character, and character of government.[18] Mahan's model was the British Isles (rather than continental France or Holland), but he could have been writing about Japan. That island nation shared several British sources of sea power.[19] Perceiving bases of similarity with Great Britain, Japanese naval personnel also read Mahan's extensive, patent praise for "men and deeds of the British Navy."[20]

Great Britain's naval prowess was emulated by Japan. During the Russo-Japanese War of 1904–05, Captain William C. Pakenham of the Royal Navy was with Admiral Togo throughout the war as an observer and firm friend. He was aboard ship for fourteen months, during which Togo consulted Pakenham and another British naval attaché, Captain Thomas Jackson. Samuel Eliot Morison observes that Japanese naval "training methods and organization were on British models."[21] And after Pearl Harbor, Navy Day in Japan (27 May 1942) was celebrated with parades, ceremonies, and this proclamation published in English:

> This year, Navy Day is not a day of mere remembrance, not a mere reminder; it is a day of *fulfillment*. The Japanese Navy has not only duplicated the exploits of 37 years ago, but it has repeated it [sic] time and time again and on an unbelievably greater scale.... This is the moment of culmination, the moment of *fulfillment*.
>
> Today, *Britain's control over the seas has vanished*, thanks to the work of the German and Italian submarines and more to the work of the Japanese Navy. Britain's auxiliary, the United States, has likewise had her navy practically destroyed by the Japanese Navy. As a result, *Japan stands today as the premier naval power of the world*. It may well presage *the rise of Japan in the future history of the world to a position comparable to that which Britain has occupied in the past*.[22]

Japan's success in emulating the Royal Navy was made possible by learning the lessons taught in story after story within Mahan's broader historical narrative. That success also was made possible by an interaction between Mahan's discourse and an event which helped endow his stories with narrative fidelity for the Japanese: the battle of Tsushima.

In his "Introductory," Mahan argued that, "at a very conspicuous and momentous period of the world's history, Sea Power had a strategic bearing and weight." He immediately provided a supporting "story" of Rome's victory over Hannibal in the Second Punic War.[23] Moreover, Mahan's autobiography summarized his conception (in 1885 while reading Mommsen's *History of Rome*) and how it led him to "investigate coincidentally the general history and naval history of the past two centuries, with a view to demonstrating the influence of events of the one upon the other." "It suddenly struck me," he wrote, "whether by some chance phrase of the author I do not know, how different things might have been could Hannibal have invaded Italy by sea, as the

Romans often had Africa, instead of by the long land route; or could he, after arrival, have been in free communication with Carthage by water."[24]

Here was the historical analog of Japan and Russia at Tsushima in May 1905. After Japan's surprise attack on Russia's fleet at Port Arthur ("the first Pearl Harbor"), their mainland war was one of sieges, frontal assaults, and massive bodies of troops (at Mukden no larger forces had ever met in war's history). Hampered by a long, overland supply route for which the Trans-Siberia Railroad was inadequate, Russia sent an armada from Europe to interdict Japanese supplies and reinforcements to mainland operations. In the Straits of Tsushima between Korea and Japan, that fleet was destroyed decisively by Admiral Togo (with Captain Pakenham on the flagship *Mikasa*) after preparations "according to the best British traditions." According to Togo, "the fate of our empire was really settled within the first half hour" on 27 May (hence the date of Navy Day).[25] Tsushima brought the Russians earnestly to the conference table.[26] Japanese naval planning thereafter favored a "statutory Great All-Out Battle" because such "decisive victory" allowed the winner "to 'control the seas,' to cut off the enemy's seaborne supplies and reinforcements, and to ensure the arrival of one's own."[27] Rome against Hannibal paralleled Japan's experience with Russia, and Mahan's detailed chronicles of other "decisive" sea battles won by "men and deeds of the British Navy" corroborated what Japan believed already.

Mahan's eminence in Japan also is explained as "opinion leadership." For groups, some people's opinions expressed outside the group are especially potent. As described by Joseph Klapper, their influence is "expended often in favor of reinforcement" of group norms because the opinion leader is perceived as "characteristically more competent, within his specialty, than are his fellows," with "access to wider information" and "like everyone else only more so." From such a *"super-representative,"* that "guidance seems to be sought or accepted in specific areas partly—or perhaps largely—because it provides his followers with the sort of satisfaction they seek in those areas."[28] Mahan's credibility in Western eyes demonstrated competence to the Japanese; his book's scope of detail evinced "access to wider information"; and the historian's praise of "elements of sea power"—which Japan shared with Britain—displayed similarity in values with Japanese naval personnel. And by "predicting" in 1890 the impact of Togo's naval victory at Tsushima in 1905, Mahan's narrative about the past offered guidance for those who planned and executed the attack on Pearl Harbor. The experience confirmed the veracity of Mahan's narrative and fulfilled the early expectation of Japanese leaders that his work could "awaken our nation and as in Moses' time may be the pillar of fire leading our nation in the century to come."[29]

Another persuasive aspect of Mahan's story was his terminology. "Sea Power" was such a term.[30] However, it was the expression *"fleet in being"* that had a decisive impact on Japanese minds and military strategy and tactics. This term referred to a concentration of warships sufficient to ensure offensive success. The narrative fidelity to the concept was confirmed for Japanese by events that occurred during the Spanish-American War.

First, there was the battle of Manila Bay. Two months before the formal outbreak of hostilities on 22 April 1898, Assistant Secretary of the Navy

Theodore Roosevelt cabled Commodore George Dewey, commanding the U.S. Navy's Asiatic Squadron, to be ready at Hong Kong for "offensive operations in Philippine Islands" upon the declaration of war against Spain. Therefore, in Manila Bay at 5:40 A.M. on 1 May, Dewey said to the *Olympia*'s commander, "You may fire when you are ready, Gridley"; at 7:35 A.M., after five passes at Spain's ships, the squadron withdrew to redistribute ammunition and have breakfast; at 11:16 A.M. Dewey resumed the attack; at 12:30 P.M. the Spanish surrendered. American casualties were "none killed and but six slightly wounded."[31] Thus, in a few hours—including a break for breakfast—America acquired a forward Philippine naval base from which the U.S. fleet could "dominate the Far East."[32] Second, consider America's naval triumph at Santiago de Cuba. Spain's fleet under Admiral Cervera left harbor shortly before 10:00 A.M. on 3 July 1898 to battle the blockading Americans; by 1:15 P.M. its last vessel was destroyed; one American was killed. With morale shattered, Spanish troops there surrendered and peace was proclaimed on 12 August. Moreover, the triumph at Santiago was witnessed by Lieutenant Akiyama Saneyuki of the Imperial Japanese Navy as an observer aboard Admiral William T. Sampson's flagship.[33]

Saneyuki became a pivotal figure who, between 1900 and 1912, exerted a "dramatic and comprehensive impact on Japanese naval thinking."[34] During duty in America (1897–99), he conferred with Mahan, who received him cordially and recommended readings for his professional education. Although denied admission to the U.S. Naval Academy and the Naval War College, Saneyuki's assignment on Sampson's flagship allowed him to be the first Japanese naval officer to witness Western sea power in action. His observations about Sampson's "bold initiatives" in using modern battleships became Secret Intelligence Report 108, the "classic source of information on the U.S. Navy for Japanese planners," and his analysis of the American blockade at Santiago guided Japan's successful blockade of Port Arthur six years later, described by Mahan in *Naval Strategy* (1911) as a model of a "fleet in being" engaged in offensive operations.[35] Assigned to Japan's Naval General Staff College in 1900, Saneyuki "brought a sense of authority to his lectures" founded upon readings and his status as Japan's only direct witness to what U.S. battleships could do.[36] Reflecting medieval Japanese treatises, such as *The Ancient Corsair Tactics of the Yashima School* written in the fourteenth century, his doctrine (like Mahan's) advocated "concentration of forces" but added that destroying the enemy's "will" was equally important, if not more so, than ships. By 1904, as his navy's "unrivaled tactical genius," Saneyuki was aboard Togo's flagship, drafting the battle plan for Tsushima and subsequently writing the report of the engagement, thus being both architect and scribe of victory. His impressions during the Spanish-American War helped to shape tactics for Japan's naval triumphs against Russia and the resultant doctrine favoring "concentrated fleets of battleships" to win "command of the sea" in decisive battles.[37]

Still another of Mahan's ideas ultimately helped shape Japanese naval planning. Two and one-half weeks before formal hostilities, Admiral Cervera's fleet sailed from Cadiz for the Western Hemisphere (the *Maine* disaster in Havana preordained war). While its location was unknown, that "fleet in being" caused panic along America's eastern seacoast. A Georgia congressman asked the Navy Department for a ship to defend Jekyll Island "because it contained the winter homes of certain millionaires," and an influential woman insisted that "a ship should be anchored off a huge sea-side hotel because she had a house in the neighborhood." The Atlantic Fleet remained concentrated, however, for offensive operations to blockade Cuba and then "force Spain to surrender by threatening a naval attack on her coast."[38] In *Lessons of the War with Spain*, Mahan explained why American battleships must not be detached as single units to be overwhelmed by larger forces:

> The Navy Department had... to keep in mind... that we had not a battleship in the home ports that could in six *months* be made ready to replace one lost or seriously disabled.... *If we lost ten thousand men, the country could replace them; if we lost a battleship, it could not be replaced.* The issue of the war, as a whole and in every locality to which it extended, depended upon naval force.... A million of the best soldiers would have been powerless in the face of hostile control of the sea.[39]

And in *The Influence of Sea Power upon History*, Mahan quoted "a most accomplished French officer of the day" about another war: "Behind the squadron of twenty-one ships-of-the-line... there was no reserve; not another ship could have been commissioned within *six months*."[40] For Japanese readers, "six months" became a potent frame of reference; it later constrained decisions about America's "fleet in being" of battleships. Again, events made Mahan persuasive.

The Washington Naval Treaty of 1922 did not favor Japan. Great Britain, the United States, and Japan could build battleships in a 5:5:3 ratio, respectively, for a 40-percent American superiority over the Japanese (and the London Naval Treaty of 1930 specified 10:10:7, respectively, for cruisers). Japan experienced a "ratio neurosis" about being outgunned in the Pacific.[41] Two "super battleships," the *Yamato* and the *Musashi,* were secretly built to offset the imbalance. With 18-inch guns and displacing 70,000 tons, these behemoths substituted "striking power per ship for number of vessels," and faith in "huge battleships and big guns" constituted "mainstream" and "conservative" thought in Japan's navy.[42] Even after the successful carrier air strike against Pearl Harbor, the Japanese Navy General Staff still said that "the battleship constitutes the nucleus of naval power."[43] As Raymond O'Conner concluded, "Japan, in keeping with her program of Westernization, emulated Great Britain and the United States in embracing the fleet concept with the battleship as the ultimate arbiter."[44] That battleship mentality was maintained by Rear Admiral Matome Ukagi, for instance, who as combined fleet chief of staff "had almost reverent faith in the lessons taught in the Naval General Staff College and in the concept of the Great All-Out Battle"; and Admiral Yamamoto, despite his pioneering efforts to foster development of aircraft carriers and naval aviation, was said to be "under the influence of Alfred Thayer Mahan" and "visualized the battleship as the queen of the fleet."[45] That orthodoxy became more significant, however, as Japan moved inexorably closer to attacking Pearl Harbor.

Bogged down since 1937 in war with China, Japan sought expansion in Southeast Asia for raw materials, especially oil. Holland and France were defeated by Nazi Germany in 1940, and Great Britain seemingly awaited only Hitler's final blow; their Asian empires were vulnerable. In July 1941, Japanese troops entered French Indo-China and secured the flank for a drive to obtain oil in the Dutch East Indies. Although many Americans were isolationists, despite Franklin Roosevelt's appeal in 1937 to "quarantine" aggressors, sentiment was turning against Japan due to pro-Chinese propaganda, including the widely published photograph of a Chinese baby crying amid rubble after a Japanese air raid.[46] The French Indo-China incursion prompted a stern warning from Roosevelt and an embargo on U.S. shipments of strategic materials to Japan, including high-octane gasoline and crude oil. Time was running out. The Japanese could not meet extensive oil needs with synthetics or purchases abroad; their navy "would be disabled in two years, and important industries paralyzed in less than half that time" (in another estimate, the navy "had enough oil for only eighteen months of operations under war conditions"); and military seizure of oil and raw materials in Southeast Asia "would almost certainly precipitate war with the United States."[47]

One American force was, in Yamamoto's words, a "dagger being pointed at our throat": the U.S. Pacific Fleet.[48] Formerly based on America's West Coast, those ships were sent to Hawaii in May 1940 as a "putative deterrent to Japanese aggression against British or Dutch possessions in Southeast Asia."[49] Their maneuvers were regarded in Tokyo as a "brandishing of the big sword," calling forth "vigorous protests," for those ninety-six vessels—including eight battleships—constituted a "fleet in being" which "created a *strategical* situation incomparably more tense and threatening to the Japanese than had existed when it was based on the Pacific coast."[50] An attack on Pearl Harbor, once only a possibility in Japanese planning, became a probability.

Japan thought about war with the United States as early as 1907 because of tensions over American discrimination against Japanese immigrants. The early plan was to seize Guam and the Philippines. Ships sent to recover U.S. possessions would be intercepted near Japan and destroyed in decisive battle. For thirty years, the Japanese navy's "long-cherished" posture was a "conservative," *defensive* one of "calmly remaining in waiting" in "seas adjacent to Japan" for "its sole imaginary enemy," the U.S. Navy.[51] In 1936, however, Japan's Naval War College produced an *offensive* view of "Strategy and Tactics in Operations against the United States," the surprise attack on Pearl Harbor.[52] At Japan's Naval Academy, cadets soon learned about "sudden attack" against "the United States fleet, the strongest in the world."[53] By 7 January 1941 events and the factor of time led Admiral Yamamoto as combined fleet commander to write to Navy Minister Admiral Koshiro Oikawa that "a conflict with the United States and Great Britain is inevitable." Therefore, Japan's navy should "fiercely attack and destroy the U.S. main fleet at the outset of the war, so that the morale of the U.S. Navy and her people" would "sink to the extent that it could not be recovered." Moreover, "we should do our very best at the outset . . . to decide the fate of the war on the very first day," with aircraft carriers launching a "surprise attack . . . on a moonlight night or at dawn" against Pearl Harbor. In late January, Yamamoto and Rear Admiral Takijiro Onishi agreed on "smashing the morale of the American people by sinking as many battleships as possible," for "most Americans—like most Japanese—still believed battleships to be the mightiest weapons of war. The sinking of one or, better yet, a number of these giant vessels would be considered a most appalling thing, akin to a disaster of nature."[54] So Mahanism, favoring bold, offensive applications of sea power against battleships, complemented Saneyuki's traditional doctrine advocating a decisive blow at the enemy's will; together, the two viewpoints began to modify Japan's conservative, defensive naval posture toward the United States.

In February 1941 an air officer on the carrier *Kaga* was ordered to develop the mission's operational concept. As "one of the most brilliant 'Young Turks' of naval aviation in Japan," Commander Minoru Genda completed his assignment quickly; and while differing from Yamamoto in that the main objective was the two U.S. aircraft carriers at Hawaii, Genda saw the raid as "difficult but not impossible."[55] Furthermore, "if Yamamoto was the father of the Pearl Harbor plan," Genda was a "spiritual and intellectual mother, coaxing it to life, nourishing it from the well springs of his own heart and mind, defending it against all comers."[56] As of April, however, the Navy General Staff thought that "Hawaii Operation" planning should be abandoned, but Yamamoto's staff of "very loyal" and "powerful supporters" now included Captain Kameto Kuroshima, who wrote that pivotal 1936 Naval War College paper.[57]

Yamamoto's forceful personality and his planners' loyalty resembled "groupthink," wherein "members use their collective resources to develop rationalizations supporting shared illusions about the invulnerability of their organization or nation." Along with their willingness to take extreme risks and their collective discounting of warnings to reconsider assumptions, such groups often achieve conformity by stifling counterarguments and adverse information that might undermine faith in their decision.[58] Yamamoto, whose "position and influence in the Japanese Navy were unique," threatened to resign if the Pearl Harbor raid was not approved by the Navy General Staff.[59] Illusions about invulnerability were evident in the planners' tabletop war games (as practiced at the U.S. Naval War College and introduced to Japan by Saneyuki).[60] During September 1941, Yamamoto stood "over the table" and "dominated" exercises wherein one team executed his plan "as faithfully as possible" and another team simulated various American responses. When attackers suffered heavy losses, games were replayed with new dice, or umpires decreed the Japanese fleet "was divinely aided by a squall just in time to permit it to leave the Pearl Harbor area without serious damage." In postwar interviews, participants characterized their procedures as "unrealistic" and "self-indulgent thinking" wherein umpires would "slant their decisions" to favor the attackers.[61]

Despite the planners' conformity and illusions of invulnerability, however, Japan wavered. By October 1941 torpedoes still were not perfected for Pearl Harbor's shallow waters (when dropped from aircraft they nosed down too sharply and hit bottom); practice bombing results still left doubts in planners' minds; and Admiral Nagumo, who would command at sea, remained unconvinced about the attack.[62] Serious reservations about the attack's feasibility also were held by Commander Mitsuo Fuchida, who would lead aircraft over Pearl Harbor.⁶³ Air crews stepped up training and increased proficiency, however. As of 18 October, the Navy General Staff still remained unconvinced about launching the raid; for, as Admiral Shigeru Fukudome recalled in 1950, "we in Tokyo were against the Pearl Harbor plan." Nevertheless, because of Yamamoto's threatened resignation if his plan was not accepted, the Navy General Staff acquiesced on 21 October, with Admiral Nagano as chief of staff saying: "If he has that much confidence, it's better to let Yamamoto go ahead."⁶⁴ But the Navy General Staff was not ready yet to endorse the plan put forward for Imperial sanction.

Japan could not attack Pearl Harbor because Yamamoto threatened resignation. In the psychology of groups, even those characterized by "groupthink," decisions often require "bolstering" before final implementation. *"Bolstering* is an umbrella term that includes a number of different psychological tactics that contribute to creating and maintaining the decision-maker's image of a successful outcome with high gains and tolerable losses"; when fostered by "strong deadline pressures along with little or no opportunity to shift responsibility," the "classic pattern of *selective exposure* becomes dominant, marked by active search and preference for supportive information and avoidance of discrepant information."⁶⁵ That "supportive information" was obtained promptly on 23 October 1941 when Lieutenant Commander Takeshi Naito lectured to Yamamoto's planning staff, which now included Fuchida. In 1940, Naito was assistant naval attaché in Berlin when British carrier aircraft launched a torpedo raid against the Italian fleet in Taranto Harbor. The Germans flew him to Taranto to appraise the damage. Back in Japan, Naito reported his direct observations to the planners, and Fuchida as a good friend "interrogated him extensively all the next day."⁶⁶ To bolster a group's decision in the face of "strong deadline pressures," Naito's news was superb.

On the evening of 11 November 1940, the British aircraft carrier *Illustrious* was 170 miles from Taranto where Italy's six battleships and three cruisers were lying. The carrier launched twenty-one aircraft, eleven of which carried torpedoes (the others carried bombs and flares to light targets and help pilots avoid barrage balloons with their steel cables). The first planes attacked at 10:56 P.M.; within sixty-five minutes the last planes turned back to their carrier. Two battleships were so heavily damaged that they were beached, another battleship and two cruisers were severely damaged, and two destroyers were damaged and two auxiliary vessels sunk. Losing only two aircraft, the *Illustrious* escaped unscathed. Italy withdrew its remaining major warships to safer harbors from which they never again conducted offensive operations. Just as Japanese supplies could flow unmolested to Asia's mainland after Tsushima, so British convoys to Malta, Egypt, the Suez Canal, and India beyond were no longer interdicted by Italy's "fleet in being." British naval prowess praised by Mahan again attained decisive victory, this time with aircraft carrier operations which Japan began imitating shortly after World War I.⁶⁷ But Britain's Fleet Air Arm used twenty-one Fairey *Swordfish* aircraft—fabric-covered, open-cockpit biplanes, affectionately known as "Stringbags," with a top speed of 138 miles per hour.⁶⁸ If Britain accomplished so much at Taranto with obsolescent biplanes, Japan should attain more by surprise on a Sunday morning, against Pearl Harbor at peace, with six carriers and 353 superior aircraft.

In late 1940, Genda was assistant naval attaché in London, reading British releases about Taranto which undoubtedly influenced his subsequent operational plan for Pearl Harbor.[69] But in late October 1941, Naito's eyewitness report about Britain's naval success against the Italians was more pertinent as Japan's Navy General Staff moved closer to its final decision, which was not reached until 5 November. Saneyuki's earlier eyewitness analyses stood the test of time and contributed to Japan's "self-conception" of its own naval prowess. In making a final decision, Naito's eyewitness report about a corroborative event was an important addition to interact with other input, including orthodox attitudes about Mahan's "fleet in being"—particularly when Yamamoto's plan was so pragmatic in its ultimate goals.

Despite bravado about deciding "the fate of the war on the very first day," Yamamoto really wanted six months. As a man who would avoid war with the United States if possible, he did not anticipate landing troops in California, fighting across a continent, and capturing Washington. Yamamoto's two primary goals were to protect the drive south for oil and other raw materials and to secure the sea-lanes by which these resources came home, for "the southern operations, unlike the operations in China, will determine the nation's rise or fall." By destroying or crippling the U.S. "fleet in being" threatening those operations and taking away the American forward base in Manila Bay (won by Dewey's "fleet in being"), Japan obtained time to seize and strengthen forward island bases behind which its new empire would be secure until the rebuilt U.S. fleet advanced to the "Great All-Out" naval engagement far in the Western Pacific. Thus in January 1941, as he wrote to Navy Minister Oikawa, Yamamoto saw the Pearl Harbor attack gaining "approximately six months" and thereby assuring success for Japan's primary objectives.[70] And to Premier Fumumaro Konoye, Yamamoto boasted that "in the first six months to a year of war against the U.S. and England I will run wild, and I will show you an uninterrupted succession of victories."[71] For, as Mahan proclaimed in *Lessons of the War with Spain,* America "had not a battleship in the home ports that could in six months be made ready to replace one lost or seriously disabled."[72]

The American "fleet in being" was Japan's target at Pearl Harbor. As Gordon Prange attests, "the Japanese were after the U.S. Pacific Fleet and Oahu's air power—not the military installations, the tank farms, the dry docks, the machine shops, or the submarine base." On 23 November, Admiral Nagumo convened task force commanders and finally announced that "our mission is to attack Pearl Harbor"; having solved the problem with their torpedoes, the raiders departed on 26 November. On the way Fuchida's airmen "drilled incessantly" on recognizing ships that were their targets, for Yamamoto's direct order was to "operate in such a manner as to destroy the U.S. Fleet at the outset of the war."[73] So strategy dominated Japanese naval planning, but tactics deserve consideration, too. As "a word which perhaps better than any other indicates the dividing line between tactics and strategy," Mahan recommended *"contact."*[74] Once the attackers made contact in the air over Pearl Harbor, decision making shifted from Yamamoto in Tokyo to Nagumo on his flagship *Akagi,* about two hundred miles north of Oahu.

In Tokyo, as reports came in, the Navy General Staff felt "intense joy and relief" as the attack "greatly exceeded its most optimistic expectations."[75] In under two hours, Pearl Harbor's battleship row became a disaster scene. The *Arizona* and *Oklahoma* were totally lost, as well as the target ship *Utah* and two destroyers; the *West Virginia, California,* and *Nevada* were sunk or beached (but salvageable); the *Tennessee, Maryland,* and *Pennsylvania* were damaged, as well as three cruisers and a destroyer. American air power in Hawaii was shattered: 188 army and navy planes were destroyed, and 159 damaged. Japan lost twenty-nine planes with their sixty-four crewmen, although seventy-four other planes suffered some damage.[76] Japanese pilots returned to their carriers "wild with joy." Upon landing, Fuchida hurried to Admiral Nagumo. As he reported "four battleships sunk" and "four battleships damaged," the task force commander interrupted with the question uppermost in his mind: "Do you think that the U.S. Fleet could come out from Pearl Harbor within six months?" Fuchida replied: "The main force of the U.S. Pacific Fleet will not be able to come out within six months." Then, although Fuchida pressed for a second strike against "dockyards, the fuel tanks, and an occasional ship," Nagumo dismissed him with a "few words of praise."[77] In the heat of the battle, while making a tactical decision, Nagumo was constrained by "six months" as a criterion for judgment.

A second strike was within Nagumo's capability. Despite higher seas, aircraft landed without incident, and over two hundred planes could have been refueled, rearmed, and launched again. Fuchida's plea for the return was endorsed by Lieutenant Jinichi Goto (commanding the *Akagi*'s torpedo planes), Lt. Saburo Shindo (commanding fighter aircraft), and Genda (who wanted to find and destroy the two American aircraft carriers *Lexington* and *Enterprise*, not in the harbor that morning), for Pearl Harbor was "the chance of a lifetime." After weighing alternatives, including possibilities that Japanese submarines also sent to Hawaii would sink U.S. carriers, Nagumo ordered "Preparations for attack cancelled." Upon seeing the *Akagi*'s signal flags sending the armada homeward, Fuchida rushed to the bridge and protested, "why are we not attacking again?" Before Nagumo could speak, his chief of staff, Rear Admiral Ryunosuke Kusaka, replied: "The objective of the Pearl Harbor operation has been achieved." Fuchida saluted, turned on his heel, and stalked out, "a bitter and angry man."[78]

A second strike would have altered the course of the war. In retrospect, Admiral Chester Nimitz "knew what a close thing Pearl Harbor had been" because the Japanese did not "complete the job" and destroy "the oil supply," which "would have prolonged the war another two years." Admiral Raymond Spruance agreed that "the Japanese could have done much more damage.... So long as anything was left, they had not completed the job."[79] Amid the disaster scene, even Admiral Kimmel saw "some positive aspects to his situation. His precious oil tanks had escaped destruction; so had his machine shops, his 'Navy behind the Navy.'" Indeed, he fully expected another strike against shipyards and docks still "relatively undamaged, and above all, the tank farms," for "if they had destroyed the oil which was all above ground at that time... it would have forced the withdrawal of the fleet to the coast because there wasn't any oil anywhere else out there to keep the fleet operating."[80] Now America's naval war in the Pacific would not be fought from the West Coast.[81]

Nagumo's tactical decision reflected several factors. He was not absolutely sure Hawaii's land-based air power was shattered (it was) and feared counterattack.[82] More important were American aircraft carriers whose location was unknown. Nagumo need not have worried. Japanese *Zeros* were superior to Grumman F4F *Wildcat* fighters or any naval aircraft Americans could put in the sky, and the U.S. Navy's torpedo bomber, the Douglas TBD-1 *Devastator*, was inadequate as a frontline aircraft (at Midway all of Torpedo Squadron 8 would be destroyed by *Zeros* or antiaircraft fire before achieving a single hit). Japanese pilots then were "among the best in the world," many with years of combat experience in China.[83] Aviators from the *Lexington* and the *Enterprise* likely could not have found and hurt Japan's ships appreciably, particularly when they believed the raid was launched from south of Oahu.[84] But the most significant factor affecting Nagumo's tactical decision was commitment to a strategic goal. As a doctrinaire, Nagumo from the outset insisted: "One Attack only! One attack only!"[85] He even considered aborting the raid as late as 6 December when intelligence from the Japanese consul in Hawaii (relayed through Tokyo) reported U.S. aircraft carriers absent from Pearl Harbor. But his chief of staff, Admiral Kusaka, argued: "We can't do anything about carriers that are not there. I think we should attack Pearl Harbor tomorrow."[86] As Admiral William Furlong concluded in 1962: "Nagumo followed classic naval doctrine in staying within the established boundaries of his task and refusing to be tempted into alluring side paths"; although "that mission may have been wrong," the tactical commander "stuck with it."[87] He gained "six months" by destroying battleships, the core of the U.S. "fleet in being." Mahanism could not have been served better, particularly when Nagumo's "fleet in being" remained intact for subsequent, "decisive" engagements and that statutory "Great All-Out Battle."

Mahan did identify shore installations as contributing to sea power. While discussing "the making and repairing of naval material," the historian lauded the "staying power, or reserve force, which is even greater than appears on the surface." The topic was treated, however, under "Number of Population," and the importance of destroying an enemy's dockyards was buried in commentary about "Character of Government."[88] Thus, clues to tactical targets were subordinated to strategic conceptualizations. As a reader suggested in 1892, "it seemed to me that there loomed up through the account of various naval engagements a vague suggestion of a right way and a wrong way to do the thing and I wondered whether anyone is looking up the question of tactics"; and for that specific advice from the world's authority on sea power, people needed to read the text carefully, even "two or three" times, to find "anything that suggests itself," exercising "patience and comprehensiveness" coupled with "time and iteration" to find "true meaning" for tactical consideration.[89]

In conclusion, Pearl Harbor served Japanese strategy. In addition to gaining the time deemed essential for success of the "southern operations," naval treaties under which Japan suffered a "neurosis" no longer mattered. By destroying the U.S. battleship "fleet in being," the Japanese navy was no longer "outgunned" in the Pacific, and Yamamoto believed the "balance of power" was tipped "in our favor."[90] That orthodox view was shaped in part by

Mahan's historical narrative. In final decisions about and at Pearl Harbor, however, that discourse could remain influential only as it told "stories that do not negate the self-conceptions people hold of themselves." Mahan had corroborated Tsushima and in turn was corroborated by Taranto. Within a narrative paradigm, that interaction between events and discourse had advantage to be rhetorically potent. And the magic of Mahan's "six months" remained evident to Japan as its own formidable "fleet in being" roamed with impunity from Pearl Harbor on 7 December 1941 until the American decisive naval victory at Midway on 4 June 1942, as history repeated itself for the Japanese—for a while.

In the predawn of 7 December 1941, as the *Akagi* turned into the wind to launch aircraft, a unique flag flew from its mast: Admiral Togo's banner from Tsushima.[91] In attacking Pearl Harbor, Japan's navy demonstrated faith in history. What Japanese naval planners knew as history, however, evolved from interaction between their nation's experiences and an American admiral's discourse. And because Mahan's narrative of sea power achieved fidelity from real events, his rhetoric about the past guided Japan's future, briefly but momentously.

NOTES

1. See Barbara Tuchman, *The Proud Tower: A Portrait of the World before the War—1900-1914* (New York, 1962), 130-37, 148-49, 248-53; Howard K. Beale, *Theodore Roosevelt and the Rise of America to World Power* (Baltimore, 1956); W. D. Puleston, *Mahan* (New Haven, 1939), 106-9, 159; William Livezey, *Mahan on Sea Power* (Norman, OK, 1947), 70; Louis Hacker's introduction to Alfred Thayer Mahan, *The Influence of Sea Power upon History, 1660-1783* (New York, 1957), vi; and "Reaching for Supremacy at Sea," *Time*, 31 January 1972, 29.

2. Theodore Roosevelt to Mahan's wife, 5 December 1914, Box 2, Alfred Thayer Mahan Collection, Library of Congress (hereafter ATM). Work was undertaken on these papers as well as on those of the Naval Historical Foundation Collection through a Social Sciences Institute Grant from the University of Florida.

3. See Barbara Tuchman, "The Historian's Opportunity," Address, American Historical Association, December 1966, published in *Saturday Review*, 25 February 1967, as well as in Tuchman, *Practicing History: Selected Essays* (New York, 1981), 51-64. See in particular 51-52.

4. Samuel Becker, "Rhetorical Studies for the Modern World," in *The Prospect of Rhetoric*, ed. Lloyd Bitzer and Edwin Black (Englewood Cliffs, NJ, 1971), 33.

5. For other discussions of persuasion through history see Ronald H. Carpenter, "America's Opinion Leader Historians on Behalf of Success," *Quarterly Journal of Speech* 69 (1983): 111-26; "Carl Becker and the Epigrammatic Force of Style in History," *Communication Monographs* 48 (1981): 318-39; and *The Eloquence of Frederick Jackson Turner* (San Marino, 1983).

6. This dichotomy between style and content, or how a person talks about something rather than what he talks about, reflects a viewpoint expressed in Rulon Wells, "Nominal and Verbal Style," and Charles E. Osgood, "Some Effects of Motivation on Style of Encoding," both in *Style in Language*, ed. Thomas A. Sebeok (Cambridge, MA, 1960), 215, 293.

7. See Paul I. Rosenthal, "The Concept of the Paramessage in Persuasive Communication," *Quarterly Journal of Speech* 58 (1972): 15-17.

8. See Ronald H. Carpenter, "Alfred Thayer Mahan's Style on Sea Power: A Paramessage Conducing to *Ethos*," *Speech Monographs* 42 (1975): 190-202.

9. M. Minikami, Naval Commanding Staff, Imperial Japanese Navy Department, to Mahan, 15 July 1899, and Secretary of the Oriental Association, Tokyo, to Mahan, 1 April 1897, both in Box 3, ATM. See also Puleston, *Mahan*, 106-9, and Livezey, *Mahan on Sea Power*, 70.

10. Ronald H. Spector, *Eagle against the Sun: The American War with Japan* (New York, 1985), 33.

11. Ibid., 293. In addition to other helpful sources, in particular see Gordon W. Prange, *At Dawn We Slept: The Untold Story of Pearl Harbor* (New York, 1981), as well as his *Miracle at Midway* (New York, 1982).

12. E. Culpepper Clark, "Argument and Historical Analysis," in *Advances in Argumentation Theory and Research*, ed. J. Robert Cox and Charles A. Willard (Carbondale, IL, 1982), 298-317.

13. Stephen Lucas, "The Schism in Rhetorical Scholarship," *Quarterly Journal of Speech* 67 (1981): 7.

14. Walter R. Fisher, "Narration as a Human Communication Paradigm: The Case of Public Moral Argument," *Communication Monographs* 51 (1984): 1-22. See in particular 2, 6-8, 10, 15. For another view of rhetorical narration see Thomas S. Frentz, "Mass Media as Rhetorical Narration," The Van Zelst Lecture in Communication, Northwestern University (Evanston, 1985). See in particular 6-7, 15.

15. See Jerome Kagan, "The Concept of Identification," *Psychological Review* 65 (1958): 304; and Walter Weiss, "Effects of the Mass Media of Communication," in *Handbook of Social Psychology*, 2d ed., by Gardner Lindzey and Elliot Aronson (Reading, MA, 1969), 98-100.

16. Kenneth Burke, *A Rhetoric of Motives* (New York, 1955), 19-23, 55-59.

17. Fisher, "Narration," 14.

18. For other indices of the potency of Mahan's generalizations see Carpenter, "Style on Sea Power," especially 195-99.

19. See Theodore H. White, "The Danger from Japan," *New York Times Magazine*, 28 July 1985, 19ff.

20. For further discussion of Mahan's praise of British naval prowess and Lord Nelson specifically see Julius W. Pratt, "Alfred Thayer Mahan," in *The Marcus W. Jernigan Essays in American Historiography*, ed. William T. Hutchinson (Chicago, 1937), 221-22. Or see Carpenter, "Style on Sea Power," 195, 201.

21. Samuel Eliot Morison, *History of United States Naval Operations in World War II*, 15 vols. (Boston, 1948), 3:21. See also Denis Warner and Peggy Warner, *The Tide at Sunrise; A History of the Russo-Japanese War, 1904-1905* (New York, 1974), 184.

22. *Japan Times and Advertiser*, 27 May 1942, in Prange, *Miracle at Midway*, 88. Italics are mine.

23. Mahan, *Influence of Sea Power*, 11-18.

24. Alfred Thayer Mahan, *From Sail to Steam* (New York, 1907), 227.

25. This discussion is based on Warner and Warner, *Tide at Sunrise*, particularly 494-520, about Tsushima. See also 3-20 on "the first Pearl Harbor" and 513 about Togo and Mahan.

26. For discussion of the impact of the Japanese victory at Tsushima see Eugene P. Trani, *The Treaty of Portsmouth: An Adventure in American Diplomacy* (Lexington, KY, 1969), 46, 56, 110. Trani also found evidence that the Japanese sought advice from Admiral Mahan for the final terms of settlement in the Treaty of Portsmouth. See 92.

27. Prange, *Miracle at Midway*, 116; Spector, *Eagle against the Sun*, 511.

28. Joseph T. Klapper, *The Effects of Mass Communication* (New York, 1960), 34-35. See also Carpenter's "America's Opinion Leader Historians on Behalf of Success."

29. Minikami to Mahan, 15 July 1899, Box 3, ATM.

30. See reactions in the *Boston Evening Transcript*, 14 May 1890; *New York Daily Tribune*, 18 May 1890; *Louisville Courier Journal*, 24 May 1890; *San Francisco Chronicle*, 1 June 1890; *Chicago Daily Inter-Ocean*, 7 June 1890; *Literary World*, 5 July 1890; *Royal United Service Institution Journal* 34 (1890-91): 1067; *London Times*, 23 October 1893; and *Le Journal* (Paris), 3 December 1914. Actually, Mahan predicted his evolving statement would be less about tactics and more about "great moral lessons" upon which moral sea power and thereby international strength were based, Mahan to Luce, 22 January 1886, Box 3, ATM.

31. G. J. A. O'Toole, *The Spanish War: An American Epic, 1898* (New York, 1984), 102-3, 136-37, 174-93. Dewey then held Manila under siege, not attacking the city itself but forcing its surrender on 13 August, the day after the peace protocol was signed by both countries.

32. See the discussion of Japan's concerns in Asada Sadao, "The Japanese Navy and the United States," in *Pearl Harbor as History: Japanese-American Relations, 1931-1941*, ed. Dorothy Borg and Shumpei Okamoto (New York, 1973), 243-44. See 650-63 for an indication of the extensive primary sources used in this analysis. Naval presence in the Philippines still is important to the United States. See analyses in *New York Times*, 23 February 1986.

33. For an account of the battle of Santiago de Cuba see O'Toole, *Spanish War*, 328-39. Saneyuki's role as observer also is noted in Spector, *Eagle against the Sun*, 43.

34. Mark R. Peattie, "Akiyama Saneyuki and the Emergence of Modern Japanese Naval Doctrine," *U.S. Naval Institute Proceedings* 103 (1977): 62-65.

35. Mahan's chapter on "Fleet in Being and Fortress Fleet: The Port Arthur Squadron in the Russo-Japanese War" is reprinted in *Mahan on Naval Warfare: Selections from the Writings of Rear Admiral Alfred T. Mahan*, ed. Allan Westcott (Boston, 1920), 256-75.

36. Prior to Saneyuki's experience, a few Japanese officers had visited sites of naval battles in the Sino-French War of 1884 and the Greco-Turkish War of 1897, but they only interviewed participants after the encounters. See Peattie, "Akiyama Saneyuki," 69. For other noting of Saneyuki as a student of Mahan see Warner and Warner, *Tide at Sunrise*, 500.

37. Spector, *Eagle against the Sun*, 18-19.

38. O'Toole, *Spanish War*, 194-95, 209, 223, 325.

39. Alfred Thayer Mahan, *Lessons of the War with Spain* (New York, 1899), 185. Italics are mine. As an indication of American commitment to a concentrated "fleet in being," Britain asked in the spring of 1941 that the United States divide its Pacific Fleet and detach some of those ships to help defend Singapore, but the request was denied because "it was fundamental that the Pacific Fleet be held intact." See Morison, 3:50.

40. Mahan, *Influence of Sea Power*, 39. Italics are mine.

41. See the discussion, based on Japanese naval documents, in Sadao, *Japanese Navy*, 240-43. See also Spector, *Eagle against the Sun*, 20-21, 39-40.

42. Sadao, *Japanese Navy*, 238-42; Spector, *Eagle against the Sun*, 47; Prange, *Miracle at Midway*, 15.

43. Captain Hideo Hiraide, in *Japan Times and Advertiser*, 27 May 1942; Prange, *Miracle at Midway*, 89.

44. See Raymond O'Conner's "Commentary" in *The Japanese Navy in World War II: An Anthology of Articles by Former Officers of the Imperial Japanese Navy and Air Defense Force* (Annapolis, U.S. Naval Institute, 1971), 136.

45. Prange, *Miracle at Midway*, 305, 334. For discussion of Yamamoto's efforts on behalf of naval aviation and aircraft carriers see Sadao, *Japanese Navy*, 238.

46. For public opinion poll data at this time see Morison, *History* 3:39, 58-61.

47. Prange, *At Dawn We Slept*, 169, 191; Shigeru Fukudome (rear admiral and chief of staff under Yamamoto at the time of Pearl Harbor), "Hawaii Operation," in *Japanese Navy in World War II*, 8-9. The Japanese navy wanted 500,000 tons of oil on reserve "for the Great All-Out Battle," but peacetime consumption was 300,000 tons per month. For similar conclusions based on the United States Strategic Bombing Survey see Morison, *History*, 3:36, 62-63, 70, 78. See also Spector, *Eagle against the Sun*, 75-76.

48. In Fukudome, "Hawaii Operation," 5, 8.

49. Spector, *Eagle against the Sun*, 1. In ordering those ships to Hawaii, the president reflected his own Mahanism, for "ever since his school days at Groton, Roosevelt had been convinced of Japan's long-range plans of conquest. He pored over Admiral Mahan's *The Influence of Sea Power upon History* until, according to his mother, he had 'practically memorized the book.' Later he corresponded with Mahan and learned that the admiral shared with him a strong concern over Japan as a major threat in the Pacific." See John Toland, *The Rising Sun: The Decline and Fall of the Japanese Empire, 1936-1945* (New York, 1970), 47. Toland also notes that "at Harvard, in 1920 [sic], a Japanese student told Roosevelt in confidence about his nation's hundred-year plan for conquest, drafted in 1889," which included Manchuria, China, and British and U.S. possessions in the Pacific, including Hawaii. In 1934, Roosevelt informed Henry L. Stimson of this "plot" and pointed out how "many of its particulars had already been verified."

50. Fukudome, "Hawaii Operation," 5. Italics are mine. See also Morison, *History* 3:42-43, and O'Conner, "Commentary," vi.

51. Fukudome, "Hawaii Operation," 4-5. See also the postwar testimony of Admiral Osami Nagano, chief of the Navy General Staff, in *What Happened at Pearl Harbor: Documents Pertaining to the Japanese Attack of December 7, 1941, and Its Background*, ed. Hans Louis Trefousse (New York, 1958), 254ff.

52. Spector, *Eagle against the Sun*, 44, 79. The Americans also devised their corresponding "Orange Plan" for war in the Pacific.

53. Kazuo Sakamaki, *I Attacked Pearl Harbor* (New York, 1949), 28. He had entered the Naval Academy in 1937 and graduated in 1940.

54. From Prange's interviews with Juji Enomoto and Shuichi Mizota, respectively the legal adviser to the Japanese navy and Yamamoto's translator, in Prange, *At Dawn We Slept*, 16-17, 19-21. According to Prange, the first time Yamamoto spoke about attacking Pearl Harbor was in March or April 1940, to Fukudome. See 14. For discussion of Onishi's role in planning the attack see Fukudome, "Hawaii Operation," 6.

55. See Spector, *Eagle against the Sun*, 79-80, as well as several primary sources cited in Prange, *At Dawn We Slept*, 20-27.

56. Prange, *Miracle at Midway*, 136.

57. See Fukudome, "Hawaii Operation," 6, and Prange, *At Dawn We Slept*, 226, 98, as well as 235 on Admiral Matome Ukagi's "shatterproof convictions of the loyalty a chief of staff owed to his commander in chief" (Yamamoto). See also Prange, *Miracle at Midway*, 69.

58. Irving L. Janis and Leon Mann, *Decision Making: A Psychological Analysis of Conflict, Choice, and Commitment* (New York, 1977), 129-31. For analysis of American unpreparedness at Pearl Harbor see Irving L. Janis, *Groupthink: Psychological Studies of Policy Decisions and Fiascos*, 2d ed. (Boston, 1983).

59. Prange, *At Dawn We Slept*, 297-303; Spector, *Eagle against the Sun*, 81-82; and Prange, *Miracle at Midway*, 23, about Yamamoto "threatening to resign if he did not get his way, and the Navy General Staff yielding to his polite blackmail."

60. Peattie, "Akiyama Saneyuki," 63-64. See also Spector, *Eagle against the Sun*, 43-44.

61. See especially Prange, *At Dawn We Slept*, 223-31, 234. See also Spector, *Eagle against the Sun*, 81-82.

62. Ibid.; and Prange, *At Dawn We Slept*, 225, 236, 258-60.

63. Mitsuo Fuchida, "The Attack on Pearl Harbor," in *Japanese Navy in World War II*, 18.

64. Fukudome, "Hawaii Operation," 8-9, as well as Prange, *At Dawn We Slept*, 295-303.

65. Janis and Mann, *Decision Making*, 91, 205-6.

66. Prange, *At Dawn We Slept*, 320.

67. O'Conner, "Commentary," vii. The success of the British air strike against Taranto had not gone unnoticed by U.S. Navy personnel, including Admiral Stark at Pearl Harbor. See Prange, *At Dawn We Slept*, 40, 45, 147, 159. But inertia worked to the Americans' disadvantage. As Spector concludes, "naval aircraft were improving rapidly during the late 1930s; they had performed impressively on maneuvers, but they had also proven to be highly dependent on good weather and visibility. Their carriers, meanwhile, had proven highly vulnerable to both surface and air attack. Tactics that were to prove decisive in the air-sea battles of the 1940s appeared impossible with the aircraft available in the 1930s. 'There was just not enough evidence [yet] that aircraft carriers had become the dominant ship type' to convince most of the navy's senior command to abandon the battleship as the basis of the combat fleet." See Spector, *Eagle against the Sun*, 23.

68. Ian G. Stott, *The Fairey Swordfish Mks. I-IV: Profile* #212 (Windsor, England, n.d.), 34-37, 43. See also A. B. C. Whipple, *The Mediterranean* (Chicago, 1981), 63-71.

69. John Dean Potter, *Yamamoto: The Man Who Menaced America* (New York, 1965), 55.

70. Prange, *At Dawn We Slept*, 10-12, 18, 549. A copy of the letter was obtained by Prange from Rear Admiral Teikichi Hori, close friend and confidant of Yamamoto. See also Morison, *History* 3:80-81.

71. From Prince Konoye's Memoirs, quoted in ibid., 46, and in Roberta Wohlstetter, *Pearl Harbor: Warning and Decision* (Stanford, 1962), 350.

72. Mahan, *Lessons of the War with Spain*, 185.

73. Fukudome, "Hawaii Operation," 11; and Prange, *At Dawn We Slept*, 27, 373-79, 415. During September 1941 the Yokosuka Air Group experimented with torpedoes to which a special stabilizing fin had been added. These proved satisfactory in tests conducted in shallow waters similar to those of Pearl Harbor. The Mitsubishi firm quickly adapted its Mark II torpedoes with this fin and delivered a sufficient quantity to the striking force just in time for their departure. Ibid., 321-23.

74. Mahan, *Influence of Sea Power*, 7.

75. Prange, *At Dawn We Slept*, 548-49.

76. Arthur Zich, *The Rising Sun* (Chicago, 1977), 72. See also Prange, *At Dawn We Slept*, 544-45.

77. Ibid., 541-43. Quotations from the Fuchida-Nagumo interchange are from Fuchida's recollections during an interview in 1963. In Fuchida's published account for the U.S. Naval

Institute, "six months" is not included as part of the dialogue. But after the report of the number of battleships sunk, Nagumo is quoted as saying: "We may then conclude that anticipated results have been achieved." Fuchida, "Attack on Pearl Harbor," 27.

78. Prange, *At Dawn We Slept*, 543-47. See also Fukudome, "Hawaii Operation," 12-14.

79. Prange, *Miracle at Midway*, 9 (from an interview with Nimitz on 4 September 1964); Prange, *At Dawn We Slept*, 550 (from an interview with Spruance on 5 September 1964).

80. Ibid., 549-50, 565, 575, 587. Even during the subsequent Naval Court of Inquiry into the Pearl Harbor disaster, Admiral Kimmel asserted his disbelief that the Pacific Fleet "would constitute the Prime target." He testified: "I thought it was much more Probable that the Japs would attempt a raid on Pearl Harbor if the Fleet were away than if it were there." Ibid., 627.

81. See Spector, *Eagle against the Sun*, 83-84, as well as Morison, *History* 3:125-26.

82. Prange, *At Dawn We Slept*, 546.

83. Spector, *Eagle against the Sun*, 46-47.

84. Morison, *History* 3:214-15, 218. Even when the Americans expected the Japanese at Midway, U.S. naval aviators almost missed finding the enemy's fleet. This was a time before airborne radar and its search capabilities.

85. Prange, *At Dawn We Slept*, 426, 545.

86. Fuchida, "Attack on Pearl Harbor," 21. See also Wohlstetter, *Pearl Harbor*, 378. For further discussion of Japan's battleship mentality, see Spector, *Eagle against the Sun*, 34, 88, 167, 319.

87. Prange, *At Dawn We Slept*, 549-50. For the subsequent defense of Nagumo's decision see Fukudome, "Hawaii Operation," 15.

88. Mahan, *Influence of Sea Power*, 40, 55, 62-63.

89. Captain C. F. Goodrich to Mahan, 14 May 1892; Thomas G. Bowles to Mahan, 14 January 1893, Box 3, ATM. See also an unidentified newspaper analysis of 2 December 1914, Box 1, ATM (although the date is evident, the name of the newspaper was cut off).

90. Prange, *At Dawn We Slept*, 202.

91. That beau geste is noted in several sources: Fuchida, "Attack on Pearl Harbor," 22; Prange, *At Dawn We Slept*, 472; Morison, *History* 3:93; and Warner and Warner, *Tide at Sunrise*, 20.

Prisoner in the Mediterranean: The Evolution and Execution of Italian Naval Strategy, 1919-42

BRIAN R. SULLIVAN

In June 1940 the Italian navy enjoyed considerable geographical and numerical advantages over the Royal Navy in the Mediterranean. However, it failed to seize fleeting opportunities and soon suffered stinging defeats. Professor Sullivan examines the origin of these reverses during the period from 1919 to 1942. He contends that, while learning from its mistakes and improving its performance markedly by late 1941, the Regia Marina made changes too late to win the war in the Mediterranean.

****

Italy is actually a prisoner in the Mediterranean. . . . Italian foreign policy can have only one watchword: to advance to the oceans.[1]
—Mussolini

On 10 June 1940, Benito Mussolini declared war on a mortally wounded France and a badly wounded Britain. Two weeks later, the French surrendered, while the British desperately prepared to defend their island against a German onslaught across the Channel. In the Mediterranean, Italy appeared ready to exploit its highly favorable strategic situation. The Italian fleet, in particular, enjoyed extraordinary geographic advantages. The armistice with France had eliminated the threat to the Italian Royal Navy, or Regia Marina, posed by enemy forces based in Tunisia, Corsica, and southern France. With Malta virtually stripped of offensive capabilities and Britain's Royal Navy prudently pulled back to its anchorages at the extreme corners of the Mediterranean, Italian lines of communication to North Africa seemed quite secure. Italian naval and air units could now use Sardinia, Sicily, Libya, Albania, and the Dodecanese Islands both to dominate the central Mediterranean and to strike the east and west.[2]

The balance of forces in the Mediterranean also favored the Regia Marina over the Royal Navy. True, the British deployed five battleships and two aircraft carriers in the Mediterranean area while the Italians possessed only two battleships and no carriers. But the Italian navy would receive between July and October 1940 four more battleships, two completely modernized and two new. Furthermore, the Italians enjoyed marked superiority over the British in every other category of warship: in heavy cruisers, seven to none; in light cruisers, twelve to ten; in destroyers, fifty-seven to thirty-five; in torpedo boats, seventy-one to none; in submarines, one hundred fifteen to twelve. Finally, the Regia Aeronautica outnumbered the Royal Air Force in the Mediterranean by a factor of nearly three to one: 1,796 Italian aircraft to 620 British.[3]

But the Italian naval leadership dismally failed to translate these strengths into dominion over the Mediterranean. Instead, between early June 1940 and late March 1941 the Regia Marina suffered a string of reverses that culminated in the disasters of Taranto and Matapan. More serious than the loss or damage of ships, however, were the blows to the self-confidence of the commanders. Some acquired such a sense of inferiority that, for example, during the encounter in the Gulf of Sirte on 17 December 1941, the admiral commanding three Italian battleships refused to engage six British light cruisers any closer than 29,000 meters and thus allowed his helpless targets to escape unscathed.[4]

Equally dramatic was the Italian navy's recovery from this series of humiliations. Just two days after the first battle of Sirte, Regia Marina frogmen penetrated Alexandria Harbor and severely damaged two British battleships with explosive charges.[5] For the next fifteen months, Italian aeronaval forces enjoyed a brief moment of sunset glory, though admittedly with considerable German assistance. During this period, the Italians finally held their own against the Royal Navy, while they defended successfully the supply lines to Libya and Tunisia.[6]

The vicissitudes of the Regia Marina in World War II were due not so much to the strength of its available forces as to the manner in which the Italian fleet had been employed. In short, it had been a question of alternative Italian naval strategies articulated long before the war had begun. The origins of the successive naval strategies of 1940–43 lay in the four years that followed World War I. The Regia Marina leadership had emerged from that conflict with no experience of its own in fleet operations and quite uncertain of the conclusions to be drawn from British and German surface and submarine actions in the North Sea and the Atlantic. By 1919–20, however, three schools of thought had emerged within the naval officer corps.

The "Innovators," inspired by the air war theories of Giulio Douhet, urged the virtual abandonment of large surface vessels in favor of a sizable fleet of submarines and a powerful naval air arm. The "Evolutionists" called for a balanced fleet, although they doubted the particular efficacy of submarines in the Mediterranean and stressed instead the value of torpedo boats. They also called for the development of a powerful naval air service and the acquisition of aircraft carriers while suggesting the delay of new battleship construction until the lessons of the Great War were clear. The "Diehards," who included most of the senior admirals, remained firmly wedded to the dreadnought, although they accepted the utility of light craft for screening, scouting, and attack missions. These conservatives rejected aircraft carriers, as well as the idea of cooperation with an independent air force, and looked at submarines with considerable suspicion. The Diehards argued that impoverished Italy could afford the fabulously expensive new superdreadnoughts only if it did not squander precious funds on unnecessary fads like aircraft and submarines. All three factions agreed, however, that Italy must dominate the Adriatic and expand its influence over the Mediterranean and Red seas. Furthermore, most naval officers expected war with France and Yugoslavia as the eventual result of these aspirations, but the Regia Marina leadership realized that the navy needed many years of preparation before it would be ready.[7]

Thanks to shortsighted British support, the Italian navy took a major step in that direction, while avoiding a hopeless naval construction race with the French, with its diplomatic victory at the Washington Naval Conference of 1921–22. As a result, Italy, which had possessed just 268,000 tons of warships in August 1914 compared to 689,000 tons for France, advanced to naval parity with its "Latin Sister."[8]

Within a year the Regia Marina gained another advantage when Mussolini became head of the government. His dream of Italian expansion in the Mediterranean, across Africa and the Middle East and toward the Atlantic and Indian oceans, was far more congruent with the navy leadership's geopolitical vision than with the Alpine-oriented strategy of the army. As Mussolini bluntly explained to the Army War College in October 1926: "A nation which does not have free access to the oceans cannot be considered a great power: Italy must become a great power."[9]

However, the Royal Navy's response to Mussolini's initial attempt to expand Italy's maritime frontiers—the seizure of Corfu in September 1923—had already revealed that Britain would be an even greater obstacle to such schemes than were France and Yugoslavia. Thereafter, Mussolini's admirals should have realized that they also had to prepare for a future naval confrontation with Britain.[10]

In the short run, however, it was realistic for Italy to attempt only to build up its paper naval parity with France. Even that limited goal heavily taxed national resources. But as Mussolini and the Regia Marina leadership assimilated what they perceived as the naval lessons of World War I, they drew encouragement from the German example. As Mussolini noted in August 1927 to Navy Chief of Staff Admiral Giuseppe Sirianni, "the goal [was] to construct a navy that will represent for France what the German Navy represented and will represent again for England: a nightmare and a threat."[11]

From 1925 onward, after Mussolini had reordered national finances (thanks to generous British and American loans), the Regia Marina began a serious effort at expansion. Despite their near monopoly on the best minds in the navy, however, the Evolutionists had little influence on the construction program. Mussolini had come to power, in part, due to a bargain with the Diehard admirals—their political support in exchange for a free hand in running the navy. At the same time, Mussolini considered it useful to cultivate the goodwill of the Innovators, since many of them were fervent Fascists. Once Mussolini had paid other political debts by establishing in January 1923 an independent air force under Douhet's followers, he ordered the transfer of all naval aviation to the new service and forbade aircraft carrier construction. Mussolini's admirals shaped the development of the Regia Marina accordingly.[12]

The navy first ordered cruisers and destroyers, specifically designed to engage French warships. But above all, it acquired submarines. Battleship designs were studied, but construction was postponed. Mussolini and his admirals wished to avoid providing models for the French to outbuild in quality and quantity, while Italian diplomats attempted to negotiate an even more advantageous naval treaty with their Mediterranean rivals. When even the new Nazi threat failed to persuade the French to reach an understanding with the Italians, Mussolini ordered the complete reconstruction of two of Italy's four dreadnoughts, beginning in October 1933. Five months later, Mussolini agreed to Sirianni's request for the construction of two modern battleships, which would secretly exceed the Washington Naval Treaty's limits by 20 percent.

Despite their construction program the Italian admirals still anticipated that they would meet a somewhat larger French navy in battle. Moreover, the Italians estimated that their French opponents could replace their losses more quickly than the Regia Marina could. Therefore, as they did for cruiser designs, they ordered naval architects to stress speed over armor for their battleships. In theory, therefore, Italian commanders always would have the option to choose or avoid combat.[13]

As the Italian fleet grew, so did the confidence of its commanders. Since they anticipated war with the French only after they had approached actual naval parity, they saw little reason for concern about Italian maritime traffic in the Mediterranean. Instead, the Regia Marina staff planned to blockade the Yugoslavs behind the Strait of Otranto and concentrate the battlefleet for a decisive surface action with the French in the western Mediterranean.[14]

After late 1933, however, as Mussolini made active preparations for the conquest of Ethiopia, he anticipated opposition from Britain to his East Africa adventure and planned accordingly. Sirianni's successor, Admiral Domenico Cavagnari, had been informed of such plans at least as early as February 1934, but he appears to have confronted the real possibility of a conflict between the Royal Navy and the Regia Marina only in March 1935.[15] With only two obsolete dreadnoughts at his disposal, Cavagnari decided that he enjoyed no chance of success against the British. When the Home Fleet entered the Mediterranean in August 1935, raising the strength of the Royal Navy there to five battleships and two aircraft carriers, Cavagnari came close to panic. He warned Mussolini that, in the face of such odds, the Regia Marina could do no more than conduct a brief delaying action using a "maritime guerrilla warfare," after which Italy's naval bases and coastal cities would be defenseless against naval and aerial bombardment.[16]

This attitude infuriated Mussolini, who knew from intelligence reports that the British would do everything possible to avoid war.[17] "Are you afraid of the British Navy?" he contemptuously asked a group of his admirals. "I can give the King of England a slap in the face and get away with it."[18]

Cavagnari was not so bold, but when the Mediterranean Crisis settled into a war of nerves between September 1935 and July 1936, the naval chief of staff did develop a strategy in the event that Italy and Britain would actually clash. The Regia Marina would rely on its cruisers, destroyers, and submarines to defend the coasts, make raids on the British fleet, and create opportunities for possible forays by the battlefleet. Ultimately more important, the navy agreed to cooperate with the air force in creating torpedo bomber squadrons, began development of light surface-assault craft and underwater assault techniques, and ordered a crash program of motor torpedo boat construction. Equally significant, however, Cavagnari made no preparations to secure the sea-lanes to Libya, despite army plans to invade Egypt in case of war with Britain. Moreover, when the confrontation with the British ended in the summer of 1936, Cavagnari suspended the navy's innovative experiments.[19]

That the Italian naval leadership had little interest in either cooperation with the other services or the development of new naval weapons was confirmed by the proposal it submitted to Mussolini in January 1936. Based on the premise that Italy henceforth should expect war with either France or Britain, the admirals urged the construction of an "Escape Fleet" to allow the Regia Marina to break out into the oceans. If built, the core of this great fleet would consist of nine battleships, three aircraft carriers, thirty-six cruisers, and eighty-four large submarines, all to be ready by late 1942. Such a force would enable the navy to drive enemy shipping from the Mediterranean and Red seas, to defend its new mare nostrum from outside by sweeps into the Atlantic and Indian oceans, to savage enemy shipping lanes, and to conduct joint operations with the new German Kriegsmarine against the common foe.[20]

Such a program would have strained Italian resources to the breaking point, even without the burdens subsequently imposed on the economy by Mussolini's participation in the Spanish Civil War and the unexpectedly high cost of conquering and pacifying Ethiopia. As it was, Mussolini could only reject the navy's program as well as a more modest proposal submitted in late 1937. Furthermore, Mussolini refused to break the Regia Aeronautica's monopoly over aircraft by authorizing carrier construction, but he did agree to the reconstruction of Italy's two remaining dreadnoughts and to the laying down of two more modern battleships and forty-three submarines between January 1936 and April 1939.[21]

During the same period, the successive European crises that followed the Anglo-Italian confrontation of 1935–36 drove the Regia Marina into grudging collaboration with the air force and army. The strangulation of the Spanish Republic by an Italian aeronaval campaign from August 1937 to March 1939 persuaded the navy that some form of cooperation with the air force was unavoidable, given the Regia Aeronautica's complete control over national air assets. The very success of the campaign, however, convinced the two services that little further development of aeronaval techniques was necessary. Also, during the Czech Crisis of September 1938, the army forcibly brought the navy's attention to its duty of protecting supply lines to Libya in support of a land offensive against Egypt.[22]

This cooperation was limited. Constant bickering between the staffs of the naval and air services over financial and operational responsibilities stymied the creation of torpedo bomber squadrons. The navy's leadership came away from its talks with its army counterparts believing that convoy escorts to Libya would involve a one-time commitment lasting no more than three to five months. Furthermore, the real thoughts of Cavagnari and his staff remained hidden from Mussolini and the other service chiefs. They revealed them to the Germans, however, during the staff conversations between the new naval allies in Friedrichshaven in June 1939.

Mussolini already had warned Adolf Hitler the month before that Italy could enter a general European war no sooner than the end of 1942; in effect, the spring of 1943. But despite the prospect of four more years of preparation, by which time the Regia Marina would possess eight rebuilt or completely new battleships, the Italian admirals dreaded an encounter with the Royal Navy. Even in the guarded language that they addressed to their German allies, they confessed their fear that "even a numerically inferior English fleet would have many advantages, because of its experience and traditions, over an Italian fleet superior in numbers." They saw no reason to venture into the eastern Mediterranean waters controlled by the Royal Navy in any case. The army's plans to launch an attack on Egypt made no sense, since even seizure of the Suez Canal "would gain nothing of decisive importance." Furthermore, the admirals expected Libya to be overrun by a French offensive from Tunisia.

Instead, the admirals planned the concentration of their battlefleet in the western Mediterranean where, with the enlistment of Francisco Franco's Spain and assistance from the German navy in the Atlantic, there was every chance of eliminating the French navy. Thereafter, the Regia Marina could steam proudly out into the ocean and have a "decisive influence on the outcome of the conflict."[23]

In some ways, it was clear that Italian naval strategic planning had changed little since 1920. But it also appears that the naval leadership had yet to inform the Duce of this fact. However, it was Cavagnari who suffered the most painful surprises over the next year: first, Hitler's perfidious initiation of the Second World War; then, Mussolini's decision to enter the conflict in the spring of 1940; and finally, the sudden disappearance of the French navy as an opponent, leaving the Regia Marina to face the Royal Navy alone.

What might have impressed another admiral as a heaven-sent strategic opportunity struck Cavagnari as a situation filled with danger. Already, in April 1940, the chief of staff had argued vigorously against Mussolini's orders for an all-out naval offensive once Italy entered the fighting. Given the Regia Marina's unpreparedness, he warned, such operations would mean that Italy would reach the peace table "without a fleet."[24] Although it would not become clear until June that the Regia Marina would have to face only the Royal Navy, Cavagnari feared an encounter with even a portion of the British Mediterranean Fleet. The admiral viewed the matter in geographical terms, as he blurted out during a meeting with his fellow service chiefs on 9 April: "One [British] fleet will station itself at Gibraltar and another at Suez, we will strangle inside the Mediterranean."[25]

After Italy entered the conflict on 10 June, Cavagnari managed to avoid a fleet action for a month. But, to their horror, the Italians discovered that their vaunted submarines were little more than steel coffins for their crews. Not only did their submarines prove seriously deficient in technology and tactics, but also the British were well aware of their weaknesses and took advantage accordingly. Extensive Italian submarine operations during the Spanish Civil War had revealed too much to Royal Navy observers. In the first twenty days of the war the Regia Marina lost ten boats. Thereafter, it severely curtailed submarine patrols.[26]

The other major arm of Cavagnari's fleet soon was crippled psychologically as well. On 9 July, off Calabria, Italian and British battleships clashed during convoy escort operations. Long-held fears by the Regia Marina about the inferiority of their gunnery proved true when the two Italian ships failed to score a single hit. A 15-inch hit from the *Warspite* on the *Cavour*, however, sent the Italians scurrying for home. There then followed a series of hopelessly uncoordinated attacks by Italian high-level bombers on both fleets. Little damage was inflicted.[27]

Cavagnari avoided the third possibility for a major naval operation—an amphibious assault against Malta—by arguing that the island was too heavily defended. Such a landing probably would have led to a fleet encounter and also involved the distasteful prospect of close coordination with the army and the air force. Instead, Cavagnari persuaded the other service chiefs that the island could be "sterilized" by air attacks.[28]

In late August, however, Mussolini commanded Cavagnari to send to sea his two new battleships, the *Littorio* and the *Vittorio Veneto*, in order to interdict reinforcements for Malta and Alexandria. But the admiral ordered a withdrawal before contact. With a German invasion of Britain apparently imminent and the consequent withdrawal of the Royal Navy from the Mediterranean therefore inevitable, it seemed pointless to risk the loss of such fine ships.[29]

Operation Sea Lion, however, never took place. When the Regia Marina, six battleships strong in October 1940, refused to venture out of its base at Taranto, the Royal Navy came in after it on the night of 11–12 November. This attack, which the British first contemplated in 1935–36, cost the Italians half their battleships. It also cost Cavagnari his position. Admiral Arturo Riccardi replaced him as chief of staff.

Only ferocious German pressure on Riccardi forced the Italian fleet out in late March 1941. But the circumstances under which, at Matapan, the Regia Marina lost three heavy cruisers and nearly the *Vittorio Veneto* as well, confirmed its inferiority. Lack of aircraft carriers, of radar, and of night-fighting capability explained the immediate tactical defeat.[30] The far greater strategic defeat, however, which the Italians already had suffered, had been impending from the moment they entered the conflict in the Mediterranean. For twenty years, the Italian navy mistakenly had been preparing for the wrong war with the wrong enemy in the wrong ways. After Matapan, Mussolini ordered Riccardi to engage in no further actions out of range of land-based fighter aircraft. He also directed the air force and the navy to develop effective methods of aeronaval cooperation.[31]

The following months brought only fresh humiliations for the Regia Marina. The British Mediterranean Fleet bombarded Tripoli with impunity in April 1941. In August, "Force H" from Gibraltar launched carrier air strikes against northern Sardinia and withdrew without opposition. Meanwhile, the losses suffered by Italian convoys to Libya rose steadily until they reached 60 percent in November.[32]

Necessity and a lack of alternatives now forced Mussolini and the Regia Marina leadership to adopt previously ignored, slighted, or neglected strategies, operational techniques, equipment, and weapons. Mussolini lifted his ban on aircraft carrier construction. Italian ship designers projected greatly improved submarines and escort vessels. Combined air force-navy teams organized torpedo bomber squadrons. The Regia Marina gave its underwater assault teams proper support. Aeronaval cooperation was greatly enhanced beginning in late 1941 by intensive interservice training, the creation of an effective radio communications system, and the belated installation of radar on Italian vessels. More significantly, Riccardi relaxed the strict centralized controls that Cavagnari had imposed on naval commanders. Thereafter, the man on the spot could exercise greater initiative.[33] Perhaps most important, the navy leadership recognized from mid-1941 that protecting the sea-lanes to Libya was its essential task. The Regia Marina staff even began pressing for a landing on Malta.[34]

The degree of Italian success in transforming the Regia Marina into an effective fighting force should not be exaggerated. During the second battle of Sirte on 22 March 1942 an Italian force of one battleship, two heavy cruisers, and one light cruiser failed to destroy a British convoy escorted by only four light cruisers. Once again, the Regia Marina exhibited many of its weaknesses— lack of sufficient aggressiveness, feeble gunnery, no night-fighting capability— and a new shortcoming as well, the poor use of radar. But the operation also showed that there had been many improvements, notably an able coordination of submarine, surface, and air units. Operation Mid-June and Operation Mid-August of 1942 showed an even higher level of skill as well as a striking improvement in offensive-mindedness and dash. But August 1942 witnessed the next-to-last major Italian fleet action of World War II. Thereafter, crippling fuel shortages and growing enemy air superiority confined the large surface units of the Regia Marina to their bases until the armistice of September 1943.[35]

Despite its admirable turnaround, the Italian navy already suffered from such serious problems by the summer of 1941 that victory at sea was probably impossible. By then, it had exhausted its slender fuel reserves and depended on what the Germans would dribble out. Given Italy's shortages of skilled industrial manpower and of resources of all kinds, the failure to build sufficient escort ships in peacetime could not be overcome in a timely manner. Lack of even one effective operational aircraft carrier and of any long-range fighter planes left the fleet without the air cover essential to engage the Royal Navy. Still, the success enjoyed by the Regia Marina and its German ally in the first half of 1942 deserves recognition. It also gives some notion of what the Italian navy might have accomplished in 1940 had it entered the war properly led, trained, and equipped.[36]

But that did not happen. Cavagnari let slip the fleeting opportunities presented to the Regia Marina in the five months following Mussolini's declaration of war. Never again would his fuel bunkers be so full, his fleet so powerful, his Royal Navy opponents so weak. Instead, Cavagnari clung to his impossible and archaic vision of engaging in a Mediterranean Jutland, when he was actually operating in the age of Midway.[37] As Mussolini had lamented, Italy was a prisoner in the Mediterranean. But, in this case, it had been due not only to geography but also to the mentality of the Italian naval leadership.

NOTES

1. Benito Mussolini, in a confidential report to the Fascist Grand Council, 4 February 1939, National Archives Microfilm Series T586, Reel 405, frames 39-46, Washington, DC.
2. Giuseppe Fioravanzo, *Le azioni navali*, 2 vols. (Rome: Ufficio Storico della Marina Militare [hereafter USMM], 1959-60), 1:3-10.
3. Ibid., 72-76; Aldo Fraccaroli, *Italian Warships of World War II* (London, 1968), 16-19.
4. Arrigo Petacco, *Le battaglie navali del Mediterraneo nella seconda guerra mondiale* (Milan, 1976), 144.
5. Carlo De Risio and Aldo Cocchia, *I mezzi d'assalto* (Rome: USMM, 1964), 148-70.
6. Fioravanzo, *Le azioni navali*, 2:119-404; Sebastiano Licheri, *L'arma aerea italiana nella seconda guerra mondiale* (Milan, 1976), 163-206.
7. Walter Polastro, "La marina militare nel primo dopoguerra," *Il Risorgimento* 3 (October 1977): 127-33.
8. Giovanni Bernardi, *Il disarmo navale fra le due guerre mondiali* (Rome: USMM, 1975), 41-144.
9. Emilio Canevari, *La guerra italiana*, 2 vols. (Rome, 1948), 1:211-12.
10. Polastro, "La marina militare," 148-49; Giorgio Giorgerini and Augusto Nani, *Almanacco storico delle navi militari italiane* (Rome: USMM, 1978), 104; Romeo Bernotti, *Cinquant'anni nella marina militare* (Milan, 1971), 132-33, 232.
11. Mussolini to Sirianni, 15 August 1927, Archivio Centrale dello Stato, Segretaria Particolare del Duce, Carteggio Riservata, "autografi," box 4, folder V c.
12. Lucio Ceva, *Le forze armate* (Turin, 1981), 201-2, 223-26.
13. Bernardi, *Il disarmo navale*, 188-93, 380-437, 593-97; Giorgerini and Nani, *Almanacco*, 214; Bernotti, *Cinquant'anni*, 250; Romeo Bernotti, *Storia della guerra nel Mediterraneo* (Rome, 1960), 36-40.
14. Giorgio Giorgerini, *La battaglia dei convogli in Mediterraneo* (Milan, 1977), 12.
15. Rosaria Quartararo, *Roma tra Londra e Berlino* (Rome, 1980), 92-93, 113-14; Giorgio Rochat, *Militari e politici nella preparazione della campagna d'Etiopia* (Milan, 1971), 41 n2.
16. Giorgerini and Nani, *Almanacco*, 116; Rochat, *Militari*, 266-68.
17. Emilia Chiavarelli, *L'opera della marina italiana nella guerra italo-etiopica* (Milan, 1969), 60, 71-72.
18. Perth to Eden, 25 October 1937, FO 371/21181, Public Record Office, London.
19. Chiavarelli, *L'opera*, 76-97, 144-53; Giuseppe Fioravanzo, *L'organizzazione della marina durante il conflitto*, 3 vols. (Rome: USMM, 1972-78), 1:42-43; De Risio and Cocchia, *I mezzi d'assalto*, 5-33; Harald Fock, *Fast Fighting Boats, 1870-1945* (Annapolis, 1978), 99; Ceva, *Le forze armate*, 610-11.
20. Bernardi, *Il disarmo navale*, 723; Fortunato Minniti, "Il problema degli armamenti nella preparazione militare italiana dal 1935 al 1943," *Storia contemporanea* 9 (February 1978): 42-43.
21. Ibid., 44-47; Fraccaroli, *Italian Warships*, passim; Domenico Cavagnari, "La marina nella vigilia e nel primo periodo della guerra," *Nuova Antologia* 440 (August 1947): 375.
22. Willard C. Frank, Jr., "Naval Operations in the Spanish Civil War, 1936-1939," *Naval War College Review* 37 (January-February 1984): 33-37, 41-49; Giorgerini, *La battaglia*, 13-14; Fioravanzo, *L'organizzazione*, 1:36-38, 43-51.
23. Lucio Ceva, "Altre notizie sulle conversazioni militari italo-tedesche alla vigilia della seconda guerra mondiale," *Il Risorgimento* 4 (October 1978): 155-59.
24. Fioravanzo, *L'organizzazione*, 1:351-52.
25. *Verbali delle riunioni tenute dal Capo di SM Generale*, 2 vols. (Rome: Stato Maggiore dell'Esercito, Ufficio Storico, 1982-), 1:38.
26. Erminio Bagnasco, *Submarines of World War Two* (Annapolis, 1977), 130, 134; Frank, "Naval Operations," 43.
27. MacGregor Knox, *Mussolini Unleashed* (New York, 1982), 146-47; Petacco, *Le battaglie*, 16; Angelo Iachino, *Tramonto di una grande marina* (Milan, 1959), 68-69.
28. *Verbali*, 1:57, 61, 63; Knox, *Mussolini*, 119-20.
29. Ibid., 149.

30. Fioravanzo, *Le azioni navali*, 2:291-92, 382-504; Arthur Hezlet, *Electronics and Sea Power* (New York, 1975), 203-5.

31. Fioravanzo, *Le azioni navali*, 2:2.

32. Ibid., 2:3-4, 17-30, 119-24; Iachino, *Tramonto*, 262-69.

33. Roger Chesnau, *Aircraft Carriers of the World, 1914 to the Present* (Annapolis, 1984), 153-54; Bagnasco, *Submarines*, 134-35; Fraccaroli, *Italian Warships*, 93-95, 99-105, 141-45; Giorgerini and Nani, *Almanacco*, 218; Licheri, *L'arma aerea*, 118-19; De Risio and Cocchia, *I mezzi d'assalto*, 89-90, 135-37; Iachino, *Tramonto*, 75-76; Fioravanzo, *Le azioni navali*, 2:140-48.

34. Iachino, *Tramonto*, 280-97.

35. Fioravanzo, *Le azioni navali*, 2:152-411, 467.

36. Ceva, "Altre notizie," 158.

37. Knox, *Mussolini*, 21, 147-49.

Erich Raeder and the Coming of the Second World War

CHARLES S. THOMAS

Admiral Erich Raeder's leadership of the German navy early in World War II is well known from operational and strategic studies of the war. Two other features of the admiral's career—his persistent efforts to advance the interests of the Kriegsmarine during the peacetime regime of Hitler and his subsequent role (after his release from Spandau Prison in 1956) as historian/memoirist of the navy—are decidedly less familiar. Professor Thomas explores these features and presents a different picture from those generally drawn of Raeder.

****

In analyzing the collapse of the Imperial Navy in 1918, the German historian Michael Salewski has written: "Seldom has an organization fallen so precipitously from such a lofty position."[1] The repercussions of this sudden descent from glory were traumatic for champions of the navy, and in the grim days that followed the mutinies in the fleet and the signing of the Armistice it must have appeared to many naval officers as if their life's work had been in vain. In view of the crucial role played by the Allied blockade in the eventual defeat of Germany, however, advocates of Germany's naval mission remained as convinced as ever of the righteousness of their cause. In the decade that followed the Imperial Navy's inglorious end, therefore, it became the primary goal of a dedicated coterie of officers to prepare the way for their country's eventual reemergence as a naval power.

This did not promise to be an easy task. Subjected to qualitative and quantitative restrictions by the Treaty of Versailles and discredited in the eyes of innumerable German citizens who, depending upon their political perspectives, chose to see the Service either as a bastion of reaction or a hotbed of revolution, the navy of the Weimar Republic enjoyed only modest growth throughout most of the 1920s.[2] In the summer of 1928, moreover, even these meager accomplishments were jeopardized by revelations of illegal and financially suspect rearmament projects by an active naval officer, Captain Walter Lohmann.[3] Once more the navy appeared to have escaped the control of properly constituted authority, and in the ensuing parliamentary uproar Admiral Adolf Zenker was forced to resign his position as head of the service. In September 1928, Admiral Erich Raeder assumed Zenker's vacated position and began the painful process of rebuilding anew.

Raeder's appointment as head of the navy was the capstone of a distinguished career as a sea officer in the service of the fatherland. Born in 1876, Raeder had entered the Imperial Navy as a midshipman in 1894 and had risen to the rank of captain by the time of the navy's debacle in 1918. As befitted one who had spent almost a quarter of a century in the Imperial Navy, Raeder was and would remain an officer of the old school, whose character revealed both the merits and the shortcomings of the education he had received in the Kaiserliche Marine. Thus his personality was an intriguing mixture of conscientiousness, personal piety, strong authoritarianism, and, with regard to the larger issues of the day, an astonishing political naïveté. Essentially devoid of humor, Raeder was not a brilliant man, but he was ambitious and resourceful. Above all else he was determined to restore Germany to its former position as a naval power of the first rank.[4]

In all of these characteristics Raeder was not markedly different from those who had preceded him in command of the Weimar navy. In two respects, however, he differed significantly from them. For one, as the author of two of the volumes in the Service's lengthy official history of the Great War, Raeder was deeply convinced of the historical importance of Germany's first bid for sea power in the Wilhelmian period and of the equal significance of his own work in rebuilding that power.[5] For another, Raeder was, far more than his predecessors from the early Weimar period, a tenacious and highly capable defender of the interests of the navy. Indeed, although he could boast of no great understanding of the larger issues of politics, as a master of *Interessenpolitik* or *Ressortegoismus* (which translates rather freely as "the defense of one's own turf") Raeder was to have few equals in the late Weimar period or the Third Reich.

These two distinguishing features of Raeder's career—his status as a historian and his mastery of *Interessenpolitik*—in turn raise two basic questions. First, how well did Raeder succeed in representing or defending the interests of the navy under the peacetime regime of Adolf Hitler, that is, during the period from 1933 to 1939? And second, how well did Raeder the historian succeed in his self-imposed task of describing his role in these events? Answers to these questions can be derived by a look at five crucial episodes in the relationship between Raeder and Hitler: the first informal meeting between the two; their formulation of the basis of the Anglo-German Naval Agreement of 18 June 1935; the session of 5 November 1937 (often termed the "Hossbach conference"); and finally, two meetings from the fatal crisis over Poland, one from May and the other from August 1939. In each case there is an account from Raeder's postwar memoirs (which first appeared in Germany in 1956 and 1957 and which were published in translation by the U.S. Naval Institute in 1960).[6] In each case there is also primary evidence from the period, some of which was known to Raeder at the time of writing, some of which was not.[7]

Two caveats are important here. At the time he undertook the memoirs, Raeder was an old and sickly man, and most if not all of the actual job of writing was done by Raeder's former subordinate, Admiral Erich Förste. Raeder's stamp is clearly evident in the memoirs, however, for the chapters were submitted for his comments and approval before going into their final form.[8] Moreover, many of the episodes related in his memoirs are taken almost verbatim from Raeder's testimony at the International Military Tribunal at Nuremberg a decade before, when the developments from the National Socialist era were more freshly implanted in Raeder's mind and when the admiral enjoyed better physical health.[9] In dealing with testimony from the Nuremberg proceedings, one is confronted by a different problem, for Raeder was on trial for his life and was perhaps a little less inclined to respect the canons of historical truth than might otherwise have been the case. Thus the reader is not exactly dealing with a conventional autobiography or, in view of Förste's role as a ghost writer, with an account that is purely Erich Raeder's. Nevertheless, in view of Raeder's significance for the history of National Socialism and the coming of the Second World War, it would seem that an investigation along the lines suggested is appropriate.

During the five years that separated Raeder's appointment as head of the navy in 1928 from Hitler's appointment as Reich Chancellor in early 1933, Raeder was able to put his talents as defender of the navy's interest to considerable use. In 1928 he secured parliamentary approval for the first of three *Panzerschiffe*, the pocket battleship *Deutschland,* which marked the first significant addition to the navy since the end of the Great War. In subsequent years the admiral managed to obtain other increases, still relatively modest to be sure, in the size of the fleet, and in late 1932 he secured the approval of General Kurt von Schleicher, at that time the defense minister in the cabinet of Franz von Papen, for a building program which, had it been carried out, would have given the navy a fleet of six battleships or pocket battleships, six cruisers, six squadrons of destroyers or large torpedo boats, three squadrons of *Schnellboote* (S-boats), three squadrons of U-boats, a fleet air arm, and the necessary personnel to staff such a force.[10] In short, the navy was for the first time planning to expand beyond the limits imposed upon it by the Treaty of Versailles.

Hitler's assumption of power on 30 January 1933 threatened this most recent success of Raeder. To be sure, the new Reich Chancellor was known to be a champion of national defense and an inveterate opponent of the Treaty of Versailles. On the other hand, in his autobiography and in his public addresses Hitler had made a number of disparaging remarks concerning the navy, both past and present. In *Mein Kampf* he had criticized the Imperial Navy's policy of building battleships smaller than those of the British and had even questioned the overall wisdom of building the High Seas Fleet at all. The fleet and the Wilhelmian policy of overseas expansion, Hitler had opined, merely had driven a wedge between Germany and Great Britain; in Hitler's view the Reich would have been better advised to renounce sea power, form an alliance with Britain, and pursue a policy of Continental expansion by acquiring *Lebensraum* in the East.[11] Nor was Hitler overly impressed with the accomplishments of the present navy. In 1928 he had dismissed the Service's cherished pocket battleships as "little ships [*schiffchen*] with which we cannot command the seas."[12] Raeder was well aware of Hitler's view in this regard. As recently as October 1932, Raeder had noticed Hitler's critique of the Papen cabinet's plan to build larger pocket battleships and had exploded that Hitler's views were "among the silliest that he [Hitler] had come up with yet."[13] Accordingly, Raeder must have met Hitler's appointment as Reich Chancellor with a mixture of favorable anticipation and trepidation. Hitler's program for a strong national defense might be made useful for the navy, but he first must be won over to a firm appreciation of the gospel of sea power.

Raeder's first personal meeting with the chancellor occurred four days after the formation of the new cabinet, on 3 February at a birthday celebration in honor of Foreign Minister Konstantin von Neurath.[14] After the dinner Hitler addressed the audience which, with the exception of Neurath, consisted entirely of high-ranking officers from the army and the navy. According to Raeder, Hitler announced that he had three basic goals: he would free the fatherland from the limitations imposed by the Treaty of Versailles, form a true "national community" (*Volksgemeinschaft*), and eliminate unemployment. The armed forces' role in these endeavors was to be an important but at the same time clearly limited one. The army and the navy would not, as in the early days of the Weimar Republic, be used for internal police work but instead would concentrate on their main mission, the defense of the Reich against Germany's external enemies in the event of war. In this latter task, Hitler added, the regular armed forces would know no rivals. They would be the sole bearers of arms. There would be no competition with the National Socialist party's paramilitary forces, the SA or the SS, and there would be no alteration of the existing command structure of the armed forces. (This latter consideration was of special importance given the well-known desire of SA leader Ernst Röhm for a leading role in directing the armed forces of the Third Reich.) Raeder remembers that Hitler's words found a receptive audience that evening.[15] The admiral appears to have been impressed particularly by Hitler's reverential attitude toward the absent Reich President, Field Marshal Paul von Hindenburg.

So much for Raeder's version of his first encounter with Hitler. How well does this account, composed long after the event, square with contemporary evidence concerning the meeting? In a number of respects the admiral's version coincides more closely with the contemporary evidence than in any of the other four examples that will be discussed here. According to two separate and independently prepared accounts of Hitler's speech—one by General Curt Liebmann, the other by a General Mellenthin—the new chancellor did devote most of his comments to domestic affairs and the need for rearmament.[16] This was only natural; on 3 February 1933 the "Thousand Year Reich" was only four days old, and the task of domestic consolidation was uppermost in Hitler's mind at this time. But both Liebmann's and Mellenthin's accounts point out an omission in Raeder's version when they note that, at one time in his address, Hitler did offer a preview of the ultimate aim of his foreign policy. According to Mellenthin the goal was "*Lebensraum* for surplus population"; according to Liebmann's record it was "the conquest of *Lebensraum* and its ruthless Germanization."[17] Thus, through his omission, whether intentional or inadvertent, Raeder imparts a tone of moderation to Hitler's remarks that evidently was not there. As will soon be evident from other examples, important omissions will be a frequently recurring pattern in the Raeder memoirs.

Hitler's comments on 3 February outlined the Reich Chancellor's general views on military policy and economic recovery. They did not, however, include any specific program for the navy, and it was only some time later, possibly as late as March, that Raeder and Hitler had their first official meeting to discuss the particular role for the fleet in National Socialist Germany.[18] According to Raeder, Hitler expressed his desire never to wage war against Great

Britain, Italy, or Japan.[19] The question of future hostilities with the United States—a scenario that Raeder later describes as "entirely utopian," presumably meaning that it was beyond the capabilities of the German navy—appears not to have arisen.[20] Accordingly, the fleet was to be built with the concept of a "European Continental policy" in mind. In view of the current weakness of the Soviet navy, Raeder assumed that this meant that the most likely opponent in a future war would be France and that it was the French Navy that would ultimately serve as the model, in quantitative terms at least, for the growth of the German navy in the immediate future.[21]

Yet if the French navy was the standard for German naval expansion, prior agreement with Great Britain was the key to securing international acceptance of that expansion. And it was here that Hitler's famous notion of a "renunciation of naval power" (*Flottenverzicht*) came into play. According to Raeder, shortly after his first official meeting with Hitler, the Reich Chancellor confided to him that it was his desire to achieve better relations with Great Britain by means of a pledge by Germany to restrict permanently its naval construction to one-third that of the Royal Navy. Raeder responded that, for "practical reasons," it would be better if the figure were raised to an even 35 percent, that is, to the exact percentage allotted to France in capital ships at the Washington Naval Conference of 1921-22. The Führer accepted this addition to his program.[22]

Might British diplomats be receptive to such a proposal? According to Raeder, Britain stood to gain a number of advantages from such a solution. Since German naval rearmament was bound to come "sooner or later," a pledge to limit the fleet to 35 percent of that of the Royal Navy would remove British uncertainty concerning the exact extent of the German building program and would thus quiet British fears of an all-out naval race, such as had poisoned relations between the two nations prior to the First World War. Raeder also reasoned that, in view of the current unwillingness of France, Italy, and Japan to restrict their building programs, a voluntary pledge by Germany to limit its fleet might strengthen British bargaining power at the general naval conference that was to begin in London in late 1935. Finally, Raeder argued, Hitler's 35-percent solution also signified a clear turning toward a Continental policy on the part of the Reich which, in his view, "could not be dangerous for England."[23]

Although one may well doubt whether Raeder's analysis of British estimates of the proposal is entirely correct, British statesmen ultimately did prove willing to accept Hitler's initiative concerning the navy. On 18 June 1935, the 120th anniversary of the Anglo-Prussian victory at Waterloo, Britain and Germany signed an agreement permanently limiting German surface forces to a figure of 35 percent of those of Great Britain and its dominions. Because of the relatively small size of the British submarine fleet, Germany was allowed to build its submarines to 45 percent of those of the British, with the possibility of an increase to 100 percent should Germany deem this necessary at a later date.[24]

When he received the news of the Anglo-German Naval Agreement, a jubilant Hitler is alleged to have exclaimed: "This is the happiest day of my life!"[25] And according to Raeder, Hitler's formula for an understanding with

Britain also met with his complete approval.[26] Interestingly enough, it is here that Raeder concludes the first volume of his memoirs. The choice is a significant one, for it powerfully reinforces the idea that Raeder has been seeking to develop throughout his description of events between 1933 and 1935, namely, of a moderate Führer working closely with his admiral to secure an accommodation with Britain and, presumably, through this to achieve peace and prosperity for Germany. Thus the doubtlessly intended pathos of Raeder's concluding passage:

> The naval agreement led us to hope that the navy would not, as before the World War, be at the center of foreign policy difficulties. I therefore thought I had good reason to look to the future with confidence, especially as the head of the German government, Hitler, declared again and again that a conflict with England was henceforth out of the question.
> It was the tragedy of my life that events took a different course than I had anticipated.[27]

How well does Raeder's account, as touching as it might be, square with contemporary evidence concerning the origins and purpose of the Anglo-German Naval Agreement? A number of questions are likely to remain unanswered. The origin of the one-third or 35-percent solution, for example, and the approximate date of its inception are both a matter of some confusion.[28] Nevertheless, two important clarifications of Raeder's description of what might be termed the "prehistory" of the agreement seem to be warranted. First, Hitler's idea of a *Flottenverzicht* probably originally entailed a greater renunciation of sea power than the figure of 35 percent that was ultimately embodied in the agreement. In other words, the Führer initially would have been content with considerably less in the way of a fleet than the one he ultimately settled for on 18 June 1935. And second, Admiral Raeder clearly sought much more in the way of naval expansion than the 35 percent he ultimately obtained from the negotiations in London. In short, the gap separating Hitler and his admiral vis-à-vis the optimum size of the navy was initially somewhat greater than Raeder's memoirs would seem to suggest.[29]

One of the most intriguing aspects of the period from 1933 to 1935, therefore, is the progressive narrowing of the gap between Hitler's and Raeder's programs for the navy. During this time Raeder immersed himself in the task of apprising the Reich Chancellor of the uses of sea power. In March 1933, for example, he trotted out Alfred von Tirpitz's hoary argument of *Bündnisfähigkeit*, that is, the use that a powerful fleet might play in attracting allies for Germany, for the benefit of the Führer.[30] And in June 1934 the admiral made a rather obvious appeal to Hitler's obsessive concern for German prestige when he elevated naval expansion to an "almost infallible criterion" for Germany's international standing, "for the measure of a nation's importance in the world is a measure of her power at sea."[31]

Once won over to a better appreciation of sea power, Hitler then tried to restrain Raeder's enthusiasm for naval expansion to a point that would still be compatible with Hitler's own long-standing formula of a general accommodation with Britain. For contrary to Raeder's own account, neither he nor his subordinates were entirely satisfied with the 35-percent ratio ultimately chosen by the Führer. To be sure, this figure did give Germany technical parity with France, at least in terms of capital ships, but because of the long-standing French refusal to agree to similar limitations on cruisers and smaller vessels, the overall size of the French navy was actually just over 50 percent of the Royal Navy, rather than the 35 percent represented by capital ships alone. Accordingly, throughout the fall and winter of 1934–35, there were those, including Raeder, who suggested that, when they broached the subject of naval expansion to the British, German negotiators ought to demand a 50-percent ratio for the Reich as well. Hitler's method of dealing with these suggestions was typical of his dealings with his subordinates. When Raeder brought his officers' dissatisfaction with the proposed 35-percent ratio to Hitler's attention in April 1935, the Führer simply refused to consider any alterations in his original plan. His negotiators would demand 35 percent, no more and no less, from the British.[32]

Thus Raeder's account of the "prehistory" of the Anglo-German Naval Agreement seems to obscure a number of the important points of contention that existed between Hitler and his admiral in the period leading up to the agreement. And there is also convincing evidence that Raeder's final assessment of the agreement—namely, that both he and Hitler saw it as the last word in Anglo-German naval relations—is equally misleading. For Hitler it was never more than a means toward an end. It would either open the door toward closer Anglo-German cooperation, perhaps even a firm alliance, that would allow German expansion on the Continent, or it would prove to be a dead end. In the latter case—in other words, if Britain failed to perform its allotted role in Hitler's scheme of things—then the Führer would simply have to use other methods to achieve his ends. Perhaps he could bully the British into a more cooperative attitude, or perhaps he would look elsewhere for support, as indeed he ultimately did, to Italy, Japan, and, for a time, the Soviet Union. Whatever the case, for Hitler the agreement took on a decidedly provisional nature, the utility of which would be confirmed or denied by later developments in the Reich's relationship with Great Britain.[33]

It would appear that Raeder took an equally cavalier attitude toward the supposed permanency of the agreement. To be sure, in the period immediately following its signing, Raeder took steps to silence those officers who persisted in their criticism of the 35-percent ratio by instructing them that the agreement was "entirely satisfactory" to the Kriegsmarine.[34] Yet there are a number of indications that Raeder and his immediate advisers never entertained any illusions that the ratio entered into with Britain was to be anything but temporary. Preliminary studies of the likely effects of the arrangement stressed that the optimum duration of the ratio was about five years. Presumably, by the end of that time the Service's shipyards would be completing the three- to fourfold expansion of the fleet that Germany supposed "renunciation" of sea power had given it, and the concealment of construction beyond the 35-percent limit could no longer be maintained.[35]

Even as the Anglo-German Naval Agreement was being negotiated, moreover, German construction engineers were proceeding with their plans for the battleships *Bismarck* and *Tirpitz*, 52,000-ton behemoths whose size contravened the spirit if not the letter of the agreement.[36] By 1937 the service's planners were projecting a series of battleships beyond the *Bismarck* class whose numbers, in terms of existing or foreseeable British naval construction, were not remotely compatible with the 35-percent limit envisioned in the agreement.[37] Thus one cannot escape the conclusion that, for Raeder as well as for Hitler, the agreement of 18 June 1935, far from establishing a permanent relationship between Britain and Germany, was to be a temporary measure. It would cover the Kriegsmarine during its period of greatest vulnerability. After that, Germany's navy would be sufficiently strong to give potential opponents pause to think, and the cycle of expansion would begin anew—with British approval if possible, without it if necessary.[38]

As it turned out, the two years that followed the signing of the Anglo-German Naval Agreement witnessed the frustration of the hopes that both Hitler and Raeder had derived from it. Despite Hitler's attempts to build on the initial success, by the autumn of 1937 the prospects for a general Anglo-German condominium along the lines suitable to the Führer were as remote as ever. For his part, Raeder soon discovered that the extensive construction program made possible by the agreement faced numerous difficulties, including lengthy delays in the delivery of vessels due to shortages of labor and raw materials, especially steel.[39] In the fall of 1937 the separate concerns of Führer and admiral converged temporarily in the famous Hossbach conference (after the name of Hitler's adjutant, Colonel Friedrich Hossbach) of 5 November.

It was Raeder who apparently provided the impetus for the meeting. On 25 October the admiral described the navy's increasingly difficult position to War Minister Werner von Blomberg and appealed for a "Führer decision" giving the navy a higher priority in the nation's rearmament scheme.[40] Hitler evidently was receptive to the admiral's suggestion, and on 5 November he convened a meeting of his closest military and diplomatic advisers—Blomberg, Raeder, Neurath, Army Chief Werner von Fritsch, Reich Marshal Hermann Göring, and, in addition, Colonel Hossbach, who kept the notes to the meeting.[41]

Before addressing Raeder's request for an increased priority for the navy, Hitler treated his audience to a lengthy preview of his foreign policy aims over the next six to eight years. He began on a serious note, explaining that, in the event of his death, his comments were to be taken as his last will and testament. He then launched into a general analysis of the concept of *Lebensraum*, the general purpose of which was to preserve and enlarge the German nation (*Volksmasse*). In order to accomplish this, Hitler informed his advisers that it was his intention to seize Germany's weaker neighbors, Austria and Czechoslovakia, at the earliest possible moment by means of localized, lightning campaigns. This, however, would provide only a temporary solution for the needs of Germany's growing population. Accordingly, the Führer intended to solve the overall problem of *Lebensraum* by the period 1943–45 at the latest, while Germany still enjoyed an advantage over its potential adversaries in the overall level of armaments. Anglo-French intervention was unlikely on behalf of Austria and Czechoslovakia, he argued; the army and the air force therefore would be sufficient in dealing with these two landlocked countries. But for the larger war for *Lebensraum*, the possibility of hostilities with Britain and France did exist, which meant that the navy would have to be ready for war by the time this was undertaken, by 1943 or 1945 at the latest.

Raeder's response to this bombshell, which represented an almost complete reversal of Hitler's announced policy of accommodation with Great Britain, was to say nothing. The noted American historian, Gerhard Weinberg, has taken this silence to imply consent, arguing that Raeder was "as usual—in general agreement with Hitler."[42] In his memoirs, however, Raeder provides a more elaborate explanation for his silence, namely, that shortly before the meeting Göring had informed him that Hitler's remarks were intended merely to spur the army on to a quicker pace in its rearmament program. Thus, Raeder argues, although he detected the "somewhat sharp tone" in the Führer's pronouncements, he concluded that no major shift in policy was in the offing.[43]

Was Raeder misled by Göring or was he, as Weinberg suggests, in general agreement with Hitler? The former explanation is highly unlikely. By 1937, Raeder and Göring were engaged in a bitter struggle with one another for control of the naval air arm, a struggle which the admiral eventually would lose.[44] Raeder also was disturbed by Göring's confident boast that the Luftwaffe could supplant the navy in many of its traditional tasks. Finally, the admiral was also highly mistrustful of Göring's personal ambitions vis-à-vis the supreme command of the Wehrmacht.[45] Indeed, Raeder claims that later, in 1943, his final advice to Hitler before leaving office was: "Protect my successor and the navy from Göring."[46] For Raeder to argue that he ever believed anything that the Reich Marshal said simply strains credibility.

Professor Weinberg's explanation—that Raeder was in general agreement with Hitler and was simply waiting for the second part of the meeting, when the Führer would take up the difficulties in the navy's construction plan—would seem to be considerably closer to the mark, at least with regard to long-term aims. Nevertheless, it minimizes the apprehension that any talk of a war with France and Britain before the mid-1940s at the earliest was bound to occasion in the admiral's mind. No matter how much the Führer sought to discount such a scenario, it represented a nightmare for the navy, for given the existing building program (and not taking into account the delays in construction that had prompted the very meeting that was then taking place) the Kriegsmarine was not scheduled to reach the 35-percent limit envisioned by the Anglo-German Naval Agreement until sometime in 1942. This was as yet too small a force to confront the combined navies of Britain and France, and even the problematical addition of allied fleets—those of Italy or Japan, perhaps—was unlikely to redress the balance sufficiently in Germany's favor. Although Raeder may well have welcomed the possibility of an eventual confrontation with the Royal Navy, this was to take place only when the Kriegsmarine was fully prepared for such an eventuality, by the mid-1940s at the earliest.[47] Any encounter before that date risked disaster for the navy and the fatherland.

If Raeder neither agreed entirely with Hitler's timetable nor was duped by Göring, how does one explain his silence, alone among Hitler's advisers, on 5 November? The answer would appear to lie in a calculated risk by Raeder. The meeting ostensibly had been called to address the building needs of the navy; it was therefore important for Raeder to save his thunder for the later part of the meeting when Hitler finally would abandon his flights of fancy and get down to brass tacks. To contradict the Führer on matters of foreign policy simply would jeopardize the immediate future of the navy's building plan without promising Raeder any greater influence over more distant developments which, while admittedly highly disturbing to the navy, might in fact never materialize. And in at least one respect, Raeder was correct in his calculations, for during the second part of the 5 November meeting, Hitler decided that the navy would receive a considerably larger quota of steel for its immediate needs. Moreover, additional allocations would go to the Krupp concern to enable it to build a large steel mill at Salzgitter which would increase substantially the navy's supply of that commodity in the future.[48] In this way, it appears, Raeder's *Interessenpolitik* took precedence over matters of *Grosspolitik*. It only remained to be seen if the navy would be given the time to reap the benefits that would accrue to it from the admiral's choice.

The year and one half that followed the Hossbach conference witnessed the dreary deterioration of relations between Great Britain and the Third Reich. The month of March 1938 saw the German *Anschluss* with Austria, followed by the annexation of the Sudetenland that autumn. The spring of 1939 witnessed the German occupation of Bohemia-Moravia, British guarantees to maintain the independence of Poland, and, on 28 April, German repudiation of both the German-Polish Nonaggression Pact of 1934 and the Anglo-German Naval Agreement of 1935. Throughout this period Raeder professes to have admonished Hitler about the dangers of war with Great Britain, but, curiously enough, he also claims to have detected no fundamental change in Germany's relationship with the island kingdom.[49] This latter argument is especially interesting, for if true it would place Raeder virtually alone among his contemporaries in failing to see the increased danger of a war between Germany and Britain.

In reality there would appear to be little truth to Raeder's assertions in this regard. Efforts to adjust the navy's building program by speeding up the construction of submarines in the wake of the Hossbach conference, presumably in order to discourage Western intervention on behalf of Austria or Czechoslovakia, provide indirect evidence that Raeder was well aware of the change that had been wrought in the Reich's foreign policy on 5 November 1937.[50] Even more important, Hitler's and Raeder's adoption of what came to be known as the "Z Plan" in January 1939 bespoke a fundamental shift in policy away from accommodation with Great Britain.[51] Indeed, with the adoption of the Z Plan — which if completed would have given the Reich a mammoth fleet of 10 battleships, 4 aircraft carriers, 15 *Panzerschiffe*, 5 heavy cruisers, 44 smaller cruisers, 68 destroyers, and 249 submarines by the year 1945—the Anglo-German Naval Agreement was dead and buried three months before its formal repudiation by Hitler on 28 April 1939.[52] Finally, there are Raeder's own admonitions to Hitler which, as indicated, the admiral cites both for this period and for the final crisis of the summer of 1939. On numerous occasions, both before and after the adoption of the Z Plan, Raeder asserts that he either advised Hitler of the impossibility of undertaking a war with the forces at hand or else relayed the fears of leading officers that war was imminent.[53] On one occasion he even mentioned the possibility of an alteration in the Kriegsmarine's construction schedule that would give priority to the more rapidly built *Panzerschiffe* and submarines at the expense of battleships. In that way the Service at least would have had something in the event war broke out with Britain.[54] Clearly, Raeder's frantic actions were not those of a man who still believed that the danger of a world war was remote.

So much for what one might term the indirect evidence concerning Raeder's assessment of the international situation during the final two years of peace. Two last examples will indicate the discrepancies between Raeder's autobiographical account and the contemporary record. The first of these concerns Hitler's meeting on 23 May 1939 with a number of high-ranking officers of the army, navy, and air force. Raeder, who was present, remembers that Hitler uttered some "strangely contradictory remarks" concerning Poland and argues that from this he surmised that the basic purpose of the Führer's comments was solely to initiate a small research staff outside the influence of the General Staff. Raeder also notes, quite correctly, that at the end of the meeting Hitler announced that the Z Plan was to be continued and that the completion of some other Wehrmacht armament programs was to be postponed until the years 1943 and 1944. Any kind of change in Hitler's attitude toward Great Britain at this meeting, Raeder adds, was not evident. When Raeder privately expressed his concern over the hostility evident in Hitler's remarks concerning Poland, the Führer allegedly reassured the admiral that matters were well in hand and that the present difficulties over the Polish Corridor would not escalate into a war with Britain.[55]

Very little of Raeder's version agrees with the sole existing contemporary account. According to minutes of the conference kept by Lieutenant Colonel Rudolf Schmundt, Hitler openly stated that his intention in attacking Poland was not, as German propaganda subsequently maintained, to recover Danzig or secure improved transit rights through the Polish Corridor but to acquire *Lebensraum*. Thus the primary goal of the forthcoming campaign was not Poland's defeat but rather its utter destruction. Hitler also was perfectly frank in stating that the possibility of war with France and Britain could not be excluded and that if such a war did break out the major German thrust would come in the West rather than the East. Indeed, as Hitler warmed to his topic, it became clear that, in contrast to his earlier views, Britain now was seen as the main enemy, at least temporarily. Quoting from the Schmundt minutes:

> The Führer doubts the possibility of a peaceful solution with England. It is necessary to prepare for the conflict. England sees in our development the establishment of a hegemony that would weaken England. England is therefore our enemy, and the conflict with England is one of life and death.

And later: "England is the driving force [*Motor*] against Germany"[56]

One could go on with the Schmundt minutes to show other discrepancies. The small research staff that Raeder mentions, for example, was not as harmless as Raeder would like it to appear, for it was intended to ascertain the weaknesses of Germany's most likely enemies in a forthcoming war and was separated from the General Staff to ensure secrecy. Nevertheless, the crucial point is clear. If Raeder could detect no change in Hitler's pronouncements (especially those concerning Great Britain), then this could mean one of three things: perhaps the admiral was daydreaming when Hitler made his comments; perhaps, to put the matter delicately, Raeder's memory failed him when he wrote this account; or perhaps, as the Z Plan would seem to indicate, Hitler's new attitude toward Britain was already so well established that, in this respect at least, there really was nothing new for Raeder to note on 23 May.

One final example will show the difficulties presented by Raeder's account of his dealings with Hitler in the period immediately preceding the outbreak of the Second World War. On 22 August 1939, at the height of the Polish crisis, Hitler ordered the senior officers of the army, navy, and air force to the Obersalzberg for a "Führer briefing" on the existing situation. Although he had forbidden note taking while he spoke, a number of accounts of the meeting were either composed surreptitiously during Hitler's address or else drawn up shortly afterward.[57] In his memoirs, Raeder based his account in part on the notes that were made on the evening of 22 August by his subordinate, Admiral Hermann Boehm.[58] In view of the threatening war situation, Raeder argues, he received the impression that Hitler was seeking to justify his past and present policies to the assembled officers. The Führer conceded that the possibility of war was great, but he sought to convince his audience that Britain and France would not intervene in a conflict with Poland. The Poles were aware of this as well, and for this reason they would eventually negotiate rather than go to the brink.[59]

From these words Raeder concluded that the danger of war was imminent. Nevertheless, the knowledge that Foreign Minister Joachim von Ribbentrop was leaving that very day for Moscow to sign a nonaggression pact with the Soviets led Raeder to hope that Hitler could deliver yet another masterstroke of diplomacy and solve the Polish question peacefully. Just to be sure, however, Raeder approached the Führer after the address and warned him, for the last time it would appear, of the impossibility of the navy's position in the event of war with Great Britain. According to Raeder, Hitler reassured him that he would solve the crisis without resorting to war.[60]

Once again, the contemporary record differs considerably from Raeder's. Taking Admiral Boehm's notes—the account which Raeder used to refresh his memory after the war—one sees that there was precious little in Hitler's address that could have prompted Raeder to conclude that the Führer was confident that the Poles would back down. Indeed, according to Boehm's notes, the aim of the address was to justify Hitler's policy, for "his decision to act was firm." The Führer argued that due in part to the presence of strong personalities on the side of Germany and its potential allies—Hitler modestly included himself along with Benito Mussolini and Francisco Franco in this category—the Reich was currently in a very strong position. Britain and France were in a correspondingly weak position. In a few years, these conditions might alter. It was therefore important to proceed with "the elimination and destruction of Poland's military power, even if conflict with the West results from this."[61]

In addition to Boehm's account there is a second account of Hitler's address, most likely by Admiral Wilhelm Canaris, which also merits attention. It ought to be noted in fairness that Raeder contested the authenticity of this version, but most historians now accept the document as genuine.[62] In any case this account credits Hitler with virtually all of the comments ascribed to him by Boehm—the reliance upon strong personalities such as Mussolini and Franco, for example. Yet in addition to this, Canaris's version recounts one striking passage that, perhaps better than any other, exemplifies the Führer's state of mind at the height of the Polish crisis. Buoyed by the knowledge of the impending nonaggression pact with the Soviet Union, Hitler spoke confidently of the raw materials from the East that would secure Germany against the threat of an Anglo-French blockade. He then added: "[We] have one great goal that demands much effort. My only fear is that at the last moment some *Schweinehund* will come up with another proposal to negotiate." In short, as both Boehm's and Canaris's accounts make clear, the time for negotiations was over; the time for war was at hand.

But what about Raeder's contention that after the address Hitler privately assured him that he would solve the crisis without war? Is it possible that in his general remarks Hitler was simply indulging in bellicose rhetoric—playing at the role of supreme warlord, so to speak—and that, in his heart, the Führer actually expected an eleventh-hour solution to the crisis? It is certainly possible, but it is not very probable, for a third contemporary account of the 22 August meeting, in this case by General Liebmann, casts more than a little doubt on Raeder's version. To be sure, after Hitler's address, Raeder did approach the Führer privately (or rather semiprivately, for Liebmann overheard the conversation), but according to Liebmann the exchange concerned operational matters rather than questions of diplomacy. Acting in accordance with army wishes, Hitler had ordered the aging predreadnought, the *Schleswig-Holstein,* to silence the Polish guns at the Westerplatte during the first hours of the forthcoming campaign. Raeder expressed his concern that the vessel might not survive the pounding that it was likely to receive from the Polish shore batteries, whereupon Hitler responded: "Oh well, if the old barge goes down, it will not really matter." Raeder, Liebmann remembers, was aghast, and he hastened to call Hitler's attention to the presence of 300 officer candidates aboard the *Schleswig-Holstein,* the loss of whom would be a grievous blow to the navy's training program. Hitler merely dismissed Raeder's objection with the wave of a hand.[63]

Liebmann's version of this final exchange between Raeder and Hitler, written just a few weeks after the event, is a frightening example of the Führer's utter lack of concern for the lives of the men under his command. If correctly reported, moreover, the general's account is also a telling commentary on the two main themes under consideration here, namely, Raeder's reliability as a historian and his ability to influence Hitler when the vital interests of the navy were concerned. And if the reasons for Raeder's shortcomings in the first area would seem to be all too evident—the admiral's age and state of health at the time of writing, the difficulty of obtaining primary evidence in the early 1950s, the desire to keep the reputation of the Kriegsmarine unsullied, and, above all, Raeder's determination to justify to posterity his own dealings with Hitler—then the reasons for Raeder's ultimate lack of success in the second area, that of *Interessenpolitik,* would appear to be more complex.

A number of explanations are possible. There was, for example, always a certain tension in the personal relationship between Hitler and Raeder. Part of this doubtless stemmed from the differences in the two men's age, their educational background, and those other indefinable peculiarities in temperament that make the distinction between any two human beings. Whatever the case, Raeder never was able to bridge the gap that separated him from Hitler in the way that many of the Führer's other lieutenants did. It was not that the admiral did not try. Throughout the history of the Third Reich, Raeder strove mightily to stress the connections linking the party with the navy, the Führer with the Admiralität.[64] When the occasion demanded it, Raeder could parrot party jargon in an acceptable if not brilliant fashion. Nevertheless, as his habit of rushing back to naval headquarters as quickly as possible after the completion of a "Führer briefing" suggests, there was always something artificial about the relationship between the admiral and the Führer. Perhaps this was because, unlike Field Marshal Wilhelm Keitel or his own successor, Karl Dönitz, Raeder was not at heart a sycophant.

The second explanation for Raeder's difficulties in dealing with Hitler builds on the first. The tension between the two men severely handicapped the admiral when it came to defending the navy's interests against Göring, the master sycophant of the Third Reich. The reasons for Göring's successes and Raeder's failures varied. The Reich Marshal was aided in his endeavors by the phenomenal advances in the capabilities of the airplane during the interwar years, by his own personal friendship with Hitler (largely a product of his sycophancy), and by his undeniable, if wildly undisciplined, talent. After 1936, moreover, Göring could use his position as head of Germany's Four-Year Plan for economics to the advantage of the Luftwaffe and of himself. Accordingly, throughout most of the 1930s, Göring was able to move from one easy triumph to another, many of which were at the expense of the navy. Prior to the Luftwaffe's debacle in the skies over London in the fall of 1940, whenever Göring talked, Hitler usually listened.

All of which leaves the final explanation for Raeder's ultimate inability to further more successfully the navy's interests, namely, Hitler's own peculiar view of sea power. Despite the Führer's concern for certain aspects of naval technology, and despite his marvelous (and frightening, if one happened to be an ill-informed naval officer) ability to spout forth impressive details about the caliber, penetrating power, and range of particular categories of artillery, Hitler remained an outsider to the navy. Unlike Kaiser Wilhelm II, Hitler was never at home on the sea, and despite Raeder's efforts at naval pedagogy, he never appears to have understood the ultimate role of sea power in warfare.[65] For Hitler, for example, battleships were showpieces, the manifestation of Germany's claim to world power status; and the harmful effects on German morale that might result from their loss in battle were so great as to preclude their use in all but the most vital situations. A similar one-sidedness characterized most of Hitler's understanding of the navy. Accordingly, when alternatives to the use of sea power presented themselves, either in the form of a new strategic weapon (such as the Luftwaffe) or a new land campaign (such as the thrust into the Soviet Union rather than the amphibious invasion of Great Britain, problematical as such an undertaking would have been), he was quick to seize upon them. As a result, the navy inevitably came up short, for even in the Third Reich of Adolf Hitler there was a finite supply of men and materiel.

NOTES

1. Michael Salewski, "Selbstverständnis und historisches Bewusstsein der deutschen Kriegsmarine," *Marine Rundschau* 67 (1970): 66.

2. For the history of the navy in the Weimar Republic see Keith W. Bird, *Weimar, the German Naval Officer Corps, and the Rise of National Socialism* (Amsterdam, 1977); also Werner Rahn, *Reichsmarine und Landesverteidigung 1919-1928: Konzeption und Führung der Marine in der Weimarer Republik* (Munich, 1976).

3. For the Lohmann affair see Bird, *Weimar*, 180-89; Jost Dülffer, *Weimar, Hitler und die Marine: Reichspolitik und Flottenbau 1920-1939* (Düsseldorf, 1973), 90-97; and a report from the year 1937 by a Captain Schüssler, reprinted in International Military Tribunal, *Trial of the Major War Criminals before the International Tribunal* (Nuremberg: U.S. Government Printing Office, 1947-49), 34:552-65 (hereafter IMT).

4. There is a masterful description of Raeder's personality in Michael Salewski, *Die deutsche Seekriegsleitung*, 3 vols. (Munich, 1970-75), 1:108-10.

5. Raeder's contribution to the official history project (Berlin, 1922-37) involved two of the three volumes on cruiser operations. Germany, Marine-Archiv, *Der Kreuzerkrieg in den ausländischen Gewässern*, vol. 1: *Das Kreuzergeschwader*, by Erich Raeder; vol. 2: *Die Tätigkeit der Kleinenkreuzer "Emden," "Königsberg," und "Karlsruhe,"* by Erich Raeder; vol. 3: *Die deutschen Hilfskreuzer*, by Eberhard von Mantey. Raeder was not, however, the only one of the Weimar navy's four commanding admirals with a talent for writing. His predecessor, Admiral Adolf von Trotha, ultimately would undertake a number of works on sea power for Germany's nationalist press, but this was only after his retirement from active duty in 1920. For the official history project as a whole see Keith W. Bird, "The Origins and Role of German Naval History in the Inter-War Period, 1919-1939," *Naval War College Review* 32 (March-April 1979): 42-58.

6. Erich Raeder, *Mein Leben*, 2 vols. (Tubingen, 1956-57), translated as *My Life* (Annapolis, U.S. Naval Institute, 1960). The American edition is slightly abridged and suffers from a rather freewheeling translation.

7. In four of the five examples, a single document or a limited number of documents will serve as the basis of comparison. In dealing with the Anglo-German Naval Agreement, however, use has been made of Dülffer, *Weimar, Hitler und die Marine*, passim; Michael Salewski, "Marineleitung und politische Führung 1931-1935," *Militärgeschichtliche Mitteilungen* 2 (1971): 113-58; and Gerhard L. Weinberg, *The Foreign Policy of Hitler's Germany*, vol. 1: *Diplomatic Revolution in Europe, 1933-36* (Chicago, 1970-80), 210-16.

8. Bird, "German Naval History," 53 n.2.

9. For Raeder's testimony see IMT, 13:595-99, 617-31; 14:1-360.

10. Raeder, *Mein Leben*, 1:274.

11. For Hitler's critique of the Imperial Navy see *Mein Kampf* (Munich, 1940), 151-56, 298-301, 742, 753-55. Useful analyses of Hitler's plans in this regard are provided in Weinberg, *Foreign Policy*, 1:14-16; Klaus Hildebrand, *The Foreign Policy of the Third Reich* (Berkeley and Los Angeles, 1973), 19-23; and Andreas Hillgruber, *Germany and the Two World Wars* (Cambridge, MA, 1981), 49-55. Presumably, after having attained hegemony on the European continent, the Reich would be able to deal with Great Britain as it wished.

12. *Völkischer Beobachter* (Munich ed.), 12 October 1928.

13. Dülffer, *Weimar, Hitler und die Marine*, 224.

14. Raeder's account of the meeting, which he mistakenly identifies as having taken place on 2 February, is in *Mein Leben*, 1:280-81 and 2:106-7.

15. Other officers were more alarmed by Hitler's remarks. For this see Wolfgang Sauer, "Die Mobilmachung der Gewalt," in Karl Dietrich Bracher, Wolfgang Sauer, and Gerhard Schulz, *Die nationalsozialistische Machtergreifung*, 2d ed. (Cologne, 1962), 735.

16. For Liebmann's notes see Thilo Vogelsang, "Neue Dokumente zur Geschichte der Reichswehr 1930-1933," *Vierteljahrshefte für Zeitgeschichte* 2, No. 4 (October 1954): 434-35. For Mellenthin's account see Weinberg, *Foreign Policy*, 1:26-27.

17. Vogelsang, "Neue Dokumente," 435; Weinberg, *Foreign Policy*, 1:27.

18. Raeder's notes for the meeting are reprinted in Salewski, "Marineleitung und politische Führung," 153-57. The exact date of the meeting is uncertain, but internal evidence suggests that it took place after 15 March.

19. Raeder, *Mein Leben*, 1:281.
20. Ibid., 284.
21. Ibid., 281.
22. Ibid., 282. For speculation that matters of prestige stood behind Raeder's "practical reasons" see Dülffer, *Weimar, Hitler and die Marine*, 301.
23. Raeder, *Mein Leben*, 1:283, 299-300.
24. For the text of the agreement see J. A. S. Grenville, *The Major International Treaties, 1914-1973: A History and Guide with Texts* (New York, 1974), 168.
25. IMT, 14:337.
26. Raeder, *Mein Leben*, 1:283.
27. Ibid., 309.
28. The first mention of either of the two ratios within naval circles does not appear to have occurred until the spring of 1934. Salewski, "Marineleitung und politische Führung," 133 n. 107; Dülffer, *Weimar, Hitler und die Marine*, 279.
29. For this see Salewski, "Marineleitung und politische Führung," 129-32.
30. Ibid., 127.
31. Ibid., 139.
32. Dülffer, *Weimar, Hitler und die Marine*, 284, 311-12.
33. Salewski, "Marineleitung und politische Führung," 146.
34. Dülffer, *Weimar, Hitler und die Marine*, 346-47.
35. Ibid., 283-84, 311-12; Salewski, "Marineleitung und politische Führung," 14.
36. On 17 January 1935, Raeder ordered that battleship "F" (the future *Bismarck*) was to be described in public as a 35,000-ton vessel, even though the navy's planners were already envisioning a vessel of 40,000 tons. Dülffer, *Weimar, Hitler und die Marine*, 313.
37. Ibid., 439.
38. Salewski, "Marineleitung und politische Führung," 149.
39. For the navy's problems in this regard see Dülffer, *Weimar, Hitler und die Marine*, 443-46.
40. Ibid., 446-47.
41. The Hossbach memorandum is printed in IMT, 42:220-30. Weinberg provides a thorough analysis of the meeting in *Foreign Policy*, vol. 2: *Starting World War II, 1937-1939*, 35-41.
42. Weinberg, *Foreign Policy*, 2:40.
43. Raeder, *Mein Leben*, 2:149-50.
44. For the navy's conflict with the Luftwaffe see ibid., 91-105.
45. Ibid., 124.
46. Ibid., 119.
47. Later in the memoirs Raeder argues that, even with the optimum use of its resources, the earliest possible date for a successful confrontation with Britain would have been in 1945 or 1946. Ibid., 154.
48. The Hossbach memorandum merely notes that the second part of the conference was concerned with armaments. The particulars of Hitler's decision are given in Dülffer, *Weimar, Hitler und die Marine*, 447.
49. For Raeder's account of what he styles "the critical years," see *Mein Leben*, 2:149-69. For three of Raeder's assertions that he noticed no change vis-à-vis Britain or the danger of war see ibid., 152, 163-64.
50. Dülffer, *Weimar, Hitler und die Marine*, 451-53.
51. For Raeder's account of the Z Plan see *Mein Leben*, 2:159-60. Dülffer provides a thorough account of the deliberations leading to Hitler's approval of the plan in *Weimar, Hitler und die Marine*, 471-512.
52. The figures are taken from Carl Axel Gemzell, *Raeder, Hitler und Skandinavien: Der Kampf für einen maritimen Operationsplan* (Lund, 1965), 94.
53. For these see Raeder, *Mein Leben*, 2:154, 155-56, 158, 161, 163, 164-65, 166-67.
54. Ibid., 155-56.
55. Ibid., 163.
56. Schmundt's minutes are printed in IMT, 37:546-56. Weinberg provides a convincing interpretation of the anti-British nature of Hitler's address in *Foreign Policy*, 2:579-80.
57. An exceedingly thorough analysis of the primary evidence concerning the meeting of 22 August is provided in Winfried Baumgart, "Zur Ansprache Hitlers vor den Führern der Wehrmacht am 22. August 1939," *Vierteljahrshefte für Zeitgeschichte* 16, No. 2 (August 1968): 120-49; 19, No. 3 (July 1971): 294-304.

58. For Boehm's account see IMT, 41:16-25.
59. Raeder, *Mein Leben*, 2:165-66.
60. Ibid., 166.
61. IMT, 41:16-25.
62. The account is printed in two parts in IMT, 26: 338-44, 523-24. For Raeder's doubts concerning the authenticity of the document see *Mein Leben*, 2:166. For the authorship of Canaris see Baumgart, "Hitlers Ansprache am 22. August," 126.
63. Baumgart, "Hitlers Ansprache am 22. August," 147.
64. For this see Charles S. Thomas, "Bluejackets and Brown Shirts: The German Naval Officer Corps in the Era of National Socialism, 1928-1939" (Ph.D. diss., Vanderbilt University, 1983).
65. For this see Raeder, *Mein Leben*, 2:157-58; also Karl Jesko von Puttkamer, *Die unheimliche See: Hitler und die Kriegsmarine* (Vienna and Munich, 1952).

War Plan Orange, 1897-1941: The Blue Thrust through the Pacific

EDWARD S. MILLER

Decades before the Japanese attack upon Pearl Harbor, the U.S. Navy developed a top-secret plan to fight Japan in the event of war. Mr. Miller traces the evolution of the war plans and shows that, although the overall principles were fixed by 1914, some naval strategists urged a swift counterattack across the central Pacific while others advocated a slow, island-hopping campaign. He concludes that World War II strategists hewed to the early principles and drew selectively from campaign plans to fashion victory.

****

In American naval war plans against Japan created in the years before Pearl Harbor, Japan was code-named Orange and the United States was Blue. War Plan Orange took forty years to perfect, but its strategic principles were set long before the war in the Pacific. The focus of this essay is the Blue offensive through the central Pacific. Six periods, from the earliest years through the final days before Pearl Harbor, are discussed. In each of those periods, rivalries existed within the U.S. Navy between advocates of a quick attack and advocates of a cautious advance across the Pacific.

In 1897 the Naval War College drew up a plan to resist Japanese designs against Hawaii.[1] After 1898 and the Spanish-American War, the navy ignored Japan and planned to defend the Philippines against European encroachment; it wanted, but never got, a world-class base there.[2] The real War Plan Orange was born on 14 June 1907 when President Theodore Roosevelt asked for a strategy to fight Japan. Ironically, Roosevelt liked the Japanese; he had won the Nobel Peace Prize for his part in the Treaty of Portsmouth which settled their war with Russia. At the same time, however, he was alarmed by Japan's military strength and the tensions between the two countries over Japanese immigration to the United States.[3]

The Joint Army and Navy Board drew up an analysis,[4] which over the next seven years the navy's General Board refined into the Orange Plan. Both planning boards were chaired by Admiral George Dewey. Although no strategic genius, Dewey lent his immense prestige to the process and picked brilliant subordinates.[5] The basic doctrine evolved: Orange geography determines Blue strategy. Japan's remoteness would allow it easy victories at first, but as a resource-poor island group dependent on imports, it was vulnerable to defeat by naval blockade and bombardment. Blue's problem was how to get its navy over there.[6]

The planners were influenced by epic voyages of two battle fleets. The Russian Baltic Fleet, leaving Europe, crawled seven months to the Far East. With no Russian ports of call and its main base having fallen, the fleet arrived in a decrepit state and was annihilated at Tsushima off Japan in 1905.[7] Three years later America's Great White Fleet left Virginia on a splendid peacetime cruise and circled the world in fourteen months, while serviced by a mobile train in distant ports. It returned in excellent condition and high morale.[8] An earlier voyage by the U.S. Asiatic Fleet under Admiral Robley Evans touched only at American islands from Hawaii to the Philippines.[9]

The first two cruises became symbols of a long-term debate among American naval planners. Some officers, called for convenience "thrusters," were inspired by the self-sufficiency of the Great White Fleet and championed a rapid naval offensive across the Pacific, thus seeking victory by speed and audacity. Others, the "cautionaries," called for a slow campaign with proper bases to avoid a Tsushima-style disaster. Sadly for the modern scholar, war plans were top secret and usually unsigned. The actual names of these men thus are unknown.

First Period, 1906–14

The early plans assumed a three-phase war. In Phase 1, Japan would strike suddenly and powerfully to the south, taking Guam and overrunning the Philippines in three to six months. The Blue Asiatic Squadron would fight briefly and then escape. To the east, Japan would raid or occupy outlying islands and possibly make nuisance raids on Alaska, the West Coast, and Panama.[10] It was feared that Hawaii would fall but, in 1908, Pearl Harbor was selected as Blue's main offshore base. Within a few years all plans assumed that it would be held, for its loss would be "an irretrievable disaster."[11] However, not even the worst pessimist believed that Japan would invade California.[12]

American naval tradition demanded victory, so the thrusters easily dominated the first plans. With Phase 2, they drew a complete blueprint to win the war. The Battle Fleet was in the Atlantic, so it would mobilize and head for the Far East. The route was via the Straits of Magellan or, after 1914, the Panama Canal.[13] The fleet would sail en masse to Manila. It would rescue the troops on the fortress island of Corregidor or, if they had perished, build an advance base in the southern Philippines and retake Luzon. It would start to blockade Japanese trade and, within the area of Guam, Manila, and Okinawa, Blue would sink the Orange battleships in a decisive gunnery battle.[14]

Planners of both schools accepted these principles. Their dispute was about getting to the Philippines quickly and strongly. The thrusters believed in speed, the cautionaries in superior strength; the debate always came down to timing and the route of the attack.

In Phase 3, U.S. forces would move northward to a base within 500 miles of Korea, like Okinawa or on the Chinese coast, and the final siege would begin. A tight blockade would be imposed by ships, mines, and submarines. Ports and industries would be smashed by naval guns and, in later plans, by air attacks. Japan, blasted and starved, then would sue for peace. Never was any invasion of Japan projected.[15]

The next important question was how Blue would cross the Pacific and where would be its bases. As there is no land mass or developed port between Hawaii and Asia, minor islands became very important. Historically, naval battles had been fought near continental shores, but now a fleet action might occur in midocean.

Various attack routes were considered. The northern route, running by way of the Aleutians to Guam and Manila, was favored by Admiral Alfred T. Mahan as the shortest path. It was discarded, however, because of atrocious weather, the lack of facilities, and the dangerous leg near Japan.[16] The southern routes, from Panama and Hawaii, were the longest, but the cautionaries liked them because they were the safest from interception. The fleet could refuel at remote islands and hope their colonial masters would either not know or not care. But these routes also were rejected because of length, poor logistics, and their political complications.[17]

The south central route had distinct advantages. The fleet could steam through Micronesia, an area dense with islands and calm harbors suitable for coaling, like the atolls of Kwajalein or Eniwetok in the Marshall Islands. Admiral Dewey called the latter "the best ... of the group."[18] The Carolines, like Mortlock and Truk, looked even better, and the group extended almost to the Philippines. The islands on this route were German, but there was a quaint belief that the kaiser would wink at the laws of neutrality.[19]

In the end, a north central route was adopted by the thrusters. It was the most direct course from Hawaii and touched only American islands. Midway was the final take-off point, and small ships might pause to coal in the lee of Wake Island. The initial target was Guam.[20] The navy often pleaded for defense forces that might hold out for the fleet, but Guam was never fortified.[21] It was hoped that Guam would be recaptured quickly, and from there the fleet could sail to Manila, perhaps consigning its train to a southern Philippine harbor safely distant from Orange's base in Formosa.[22]

The thrusters believed in speed. They called for a thundering charge across the sea, with only brief stops, a "Through Ticket to Manila." The fleet would weigh anchor the moment war broke out, head for the Pacific, and arrive off Manila one month out of Pearl Harbor.[23] The cautionaries argued for building bases en route to protect the fleet and its supply lines. Their schedule was vague, but a stepwise campaign would need months or a year to reach the Philippines. There would be no troops left to save.[24]

Second Period, 1919–33

World War I interrupted this planning, so the next important period dates from 1919 to 1933. The cautionaries tore up the "Through Ticket" in response to new circumstances. The Battle Fleet moved to California, thus allowing a slower start for the attack. Furthermore, the Washington Naval Treaty of 1922 froze base construction in the western Pacific, making mobile advance bases a necessity. Japan had seized Germany's North Pacific islands. While naval mythology says this was a terrible blow because Orange now could block the sea-lanes to the Far East, in fact Admiral William S. Benson, the first chief of naval operations, advised President Woodrow Wilson to support a Japanese Mandate under the League of Nations. Japan then could not fortify the islands, and thus they would be easy wartime targets.[25]

The War Plans Division was formed, staffed by "capable youngsters with War College training and full of vim and vigor," some fresh from Admiral William Sims's wartime staff in England. Among them were future Fleet Commander Harry Yarnell and William S. Pye.[26] They were cautionaries who applied a sobriety test to the Orange Plan. Given larger fleets and deadly new weapons, they saw a long, bitter war with no room for bravado. They accepted the counterattack but only by the south central route with its many possible bases. By 1921 they outlined a two-step assault on the Mandates. Blue would sail into the Marshalls and seize a lagoon, preparatory to capturing the large island of Truk. It was then on to Guam, reaching the Philippines only a month after the kickoff.[27]

The thrusters rallied. While accepting the Mandates route, they twice tried to salvage the "Through Ticket." In 1924, egged on by Generals Leonard Wood and John J. Pershing to save their troops, they contrived to reaccelerate the timetable. The fleet once again would dash immediately to the Philippines. It would occupy the Mandates, too, but implicitly the seizure of the islands would come later in the war.[28] As this plan jeopardized the supply line, the cautionaries later reinstated the island-hopping campaign. To soothe the army they did so by vague inference rather than forthrightly.[29] Several years later the thrusters tried again. The fleet would make a "Quick Movement" to Manila before the war, and the Mandates would be occupied from there when war began.[30] Wiser heads prevailed. The "Through Ticket" was dead, along with the dream of saving the Philippines.

The cautionaries stamped on the grave. Over time they did make revisions. They delayed the start of the offensive to the fourteenth day of the war, then to the thirtieth day, and then to "as soon as possible."[31] They dropped Guam from the itinerary because the Carolines' harbors were better and because bombers could not yet reach Japan from the Marianas. They definitely headed for a base in the southern Philippines. Although Luzon would be next, operations north of it were omitted, for the slower campaign left time to plan the endgame after the war.[32]

Third Period, 1934–36

The third period extends from 1934 to 1936 when the cautionaries detailed the island-hopping offensive to the southern Philippines. They produced a study called the Royal Road, perhaps after the popular adventure book, *The Royal Road to Romance*. It was adopted as the new Orange Plan. With the main advance, the fleet would grab an anchorage at Wotje, the nearest of the Marshalls. The cautionaries hoped for a naval battle in the Marshalls where the Blue fleet would be closer to its main base than to Japan for the only time in the war. Atolls, occupied as subsidiary air bases, would extend air cover to Truk. From Wotje, the fleet would assault Truk and develop a major base there. A distant blockade of Japan would commence. Blue would take an air station west of Truk, then establish a fleet base at one of two locations in the southwestern Philippines. An aircraft pipeline over this route would replenish losses expected in the Philippines.[33]

The marines were consulted, and they wisely assumed that they would have to invade heavily defended islands, not empty beaches. There were so many islands that they recommended assaulting only a few with overwhelming force and neutralizing the rest by air and sea power.[34]

The campaign now was so prolonged that operations north of Mindanao were omitted. The thrusters had two ideas for speeding it up. The first was to attack Truk promptly, possibly before Japan could fortify it, and pick off the Marshalls later. This idea was rejected because the Marshalls greatly improved the logistics for the Truk operation and because it was still hoped that the Imperial Navy might fight for the Marshalls where Blue aircraft would dominate the skies. The thrusters did win their second point: the Palau Islands were considered nonessential and therefore bypassed. The fleet could double back and capture them later.[35]

Fourth Period, 1937–39

As the late 1930s approached, the Philippines were promised independence; the Washington Naval Treaty expired; and Japan invaded China, grew more bellicose, and was expected to fortify the Mandates. The next planning cycle, 1937–39, was a standoff. The cautionaries further contracted the late stages of the offensive and slowed the timetable. The base at Truk did not need to be completed until a year after war began. Then they deleted specific moves beyond Truk.[36]

This time the thrusters responded realistically. Truk's location in mid-Pacific and the world-class repair and industrial facility to be established there would position the fleet to advance later to the western Pacific.[37] Objectives within range included the Marianas and Bonins, the Philippines, and perhaps even Formosa or Okinawa. It again was decided that Truk had to be taken more quickly.

A way was found serendipitously through Wake, orphan island of a doomed scheme. A special naval board under Admiral Arthur J. Hepburn had resurrected the idea of a major base on Guam to be supported by aircraft fueling stations on Midway and Wake.[38] Pan American Airways already had built flying clipper bases on the atolls with navy encouragement.[39] Isolationists in Washington vetoed Guam, but Admiral Claude Bloch and other thrusters realized that, even so, mid-Pacific air bases would greatly assist the Blue offensive.[40] Naval doctrine required that the waters ahead of an advancing fleet be scouted by flying boats, operating if necessary from tenders in remote lagoons. Planes from Wake could bring the northern Marshalls under surveillance and attack, permitting a descent on an island like Eniwetok. Such a bold move would outflank the entire Marshall group and bring Truk and even the Marianas within aerial range. Eniwetok lay 640 miles from Wake with Truk 785 miles further beyond, whereas the Royal Road's 1,115-mile gap from Wotje to Truk was too wide for most airplanes of the day without intermediate stops.

The thrusters won their point. The choice of "Base One" was delegated to Pacific Fleet Commander in Chief J. O. Richardson, and in the following period he selected Eniwetok.[41]

Fifth Period, 1939–40

The next phase runs from the outbreak of war in 1939 through 1940. It was the heyday for the cautionaries. With Europe engulfed by Hitler, the American army got cold feet about fighting in Asia. It believed that the fleet should stand on the defensive and not venture beyond its air cover. Nevertheless, when the services jointly drafted five multicolored Rainbow Plans, two were offspring of Orange, that is, transpacific wars. In Rainbow Two, the United States fought alone, while in Rainbow Three, the country had allies.[42] But in these plans the opening task of the Pacific Fleet shriveled to a mere diversionary action, in order to distract Orange forces from attacking the allied colonies in the Far East.[43] This suited Commander in Chief Richardson, a cautionary who felt unready to attack even though his fleet was poised at Pearl Harbor.[44]

What could the fleet do? Commander Forrest P. Sherman, Admiral Chester Nimitz's future wartime planner, called Truk a strategic dead end, too distant for blockade while needing continuous defense by the fleet. And if Truk were dropped, why go for the Marshalls?[45] Admiral Harold Stark, chief of naval operations, blew hot and cold. He told the fleet to act aggressively in the Mandates to save Southeast Asia but not to advance to Truk because the ships might be needed in the Atlantic. Truk was not deleted, but its schedule was in limbo.[46]

The thrusters were reduced to desperate schemes. They considered sending the navy to fight from Singapore, as urged by the British, but this was ruled "out of the question."[47] They convinced Stark to rush a carrier and reinforcements to the East Indies on Day 5, but President Franklin D. Roosevelt scratched the mission.[48] The "Through Ticket" stayed in its grave despite an eleventh-hour attempt by the army to hold the Philippines through concentrated air power.

Sixth Period, 1941

The final prewar planning period is 1941. The government adopted Rainbow Five, the plan to beat Germany first. Despite this, the year was a last hurrah for the thrusters, perhaps because cautionaries like Kelly Turner were preoccupied with the Atlantic.[49]

Admiral Husband E. Kimmel, taking charge of the fleet, was eager to distract Japan by waging offensive war in the only place still authorized, the Marshall Islands. He was captivated by the position of Wake for covering the invasion of Eniwetok. He put marines on Wake, hoping they might act as bait for a Japanese expedition and enable the United States "to get at naval forces with naval forces."[50]

Kimmel's final prewar version of Plan O-1 of Rainbow Five, updated on

26 November 1941, called for a cancellation of an earlier pet project, a cruiser sweep into the Philippine Sea to catch enemy convoys en route to take Guam or reinforce the Mandates.[51] The plan projected a four-day raid into the Marshalls. Carriers would depart from Pearl Harbor on the first day of the war, refuel at a point covered by three American islands, and then at high speed bombard and reconnoiter the Marshalls. Aircraft staging from Wake would cover and guard against intervention. (This is why no PBYs were on long-range patrol at Pearl Harbor on 7 December; they were being readied for this deployment.) The battleships would stand by at sea. The raid was to precede the invasion of Eniwetok, date unspecified, and of Truk, some day.[52] Liberation of the Philippines lay perhaps two or three years in the future.

An epilogue is needed on the prewar story of War Plan Orange. With the outbreak of war, Corregidor held out for six months, with no naval rescue attempted. The raid on Pearl Harbor canceled Plan O-1 and terminated Kimmel's career just as he tried to save Wake.[53] Nimitz took over, and his first offensive act was to raid the Marshalls.

In comparing the American counterattacks with some older plans, the advance from the Southwest Pacific resembled the southern routes rejected in the old days. General Douglas MacArthur used the Admiralties and improvised a base in the southern Philippines, at Leyte, before retaking Luzon. Admiral Ernest J. King, chief of the wartime navy and a thruster by nature, had played the Orange game at the Naval War College many years before the war. He believed in the strategy, especially the long-ago emphasis on the Marianas.[54] When the navy was ready he persuaded the Joint Chiefs to strike in the central Pacific, to the disgust of MacArthur.[55]

By examining how the war was conducted in the Pacific, it can be compared to running a film backward. The fleet did strike deep into the Marshalls, bypassing many islands. Nimitz covered the fleet with air power from the Gilberts, not from fallen Wake. Japan had a major base at Truk and, until early 1944, the navy intended to follow the Royal Road of the 1930s.[56] But success permitted Truk and later Mindanao to be neutralized and bypassed. Instead, King shifted north to the favorite target of Dewey's time, the Marianas. From there, aerial bombardment of Japan began. As predicted back at the beginning, Blue moved on to Luzon and Okinawa and drew the final noose of blockade and bombardment, including atomic, and the war ended without an invasion of Japan's home islands.

One may ponder why the services concluded late in the war that Japan must be invaded. Even granting the fanatical resistance of the enemy, the decision contradicted forty years of planning and came just when Phase 2 of the Orange Plan had been brilliantly executed. King later said that he went along because of the time needed to prepare an invasion, but in his heart he believed that sea and air power could win the war.[57] President Harry Truman said he dropped the bomb to avoid horrendous invasion casualties. No evidence has yet been found to show that he was informed of the long prewar history of the Phase 3 siege, whereas Roosevelt was familiar with the concept since his days in the Navy Department during the Wilson administration. In any event, dropping the bomb was just as consistent with the traditional strategy of blockade and bombardment as with preempting an invasion.

How, then, is War Plan Orange to be judged? It was one of the longest thought-out plans of the war and the most successful. Some critics have called it a fantasy; the army's top planner said a rapid naval offensive in the 1930s "would be literally an act of madness."[58] Other critics have seen the plan as a gimmick for the navy to justify itself and to win appropriations.[59] Neither view holds much water. The "Through Ticket" may have been wishful thinking, but the strategies of counterattack and siege were sound and the central Pacific island-hopping route was excellent. War Plan Orange persevered for forty years and eventually won the war. What more can one ask of a great plan?

NOTES

1. Ronald H. Spector, "Professors of War: The Naval War College and the Modern American Navy" (Ph.D. diss., Yale University, 1967), 197.

2. Rear Admiral Henry C. Taylor, "Memorandum Read to the General Board," 10 June 1904, File 325, Record Group 225, Records of Joint Army and Navy Boards and Committees, National Archives, Washington, DC (hereafter RG 225, NA); William R. Braisted, *The United States Navy in the Pacific, 1897-1909* (Austin, 1958; reprint ed., New York, 1969), 191-239.

3. Raymond A. Esthus, *Theodore Roosevelt and Japan* (Seattle, 1966), 182.

4. Joint Board to Secretary of Navy, 18 June 1907, File 325, RG 225, NA.

5. Ronald H. Spector, *Admiral of the New Empire, The Life and Career of George Dewey* (Baton Rouge, 1974), 122.

6. The principal strategic documents of the pre-World War I era are: "Naval War College to General Board, Strategic Campaign of Blue against Orange, 14 March 1911" (hereafter 1911 Plan), and "Orange War Plan, Strategic Section for War in the Pacific Ocean, Approved by the General Board, 14 March 1914" (hereafter 1914 Plan), both located in Records of the General Board, Operational Archives, Naval History Division, Washington Navy Yard, Washington, DC (hereafter GB, OA-NHD).

7. J. N. Westwood, *The Illustrated History of the Russo-Japanese War* (London, 1973), chap. 11.

8. Robert A. Hart, *The Great White Fleet* (Boston, 1965), passim.

9. Edwin A. Falk, *Fighting Bob Evans* (New York, 1931), 390-92.

10. 1911 Plan; 1914 Plan.

11. Braisted, *United States Navy, 1897-1909*, 222; 1914 Plan, App. "C," 146.

12. Captain W. R. Shoemaker, "Strategy of the Pacific: An Exposition of the Orange Plan," lecture to Naval War College Conference, 25 August 1914, Microfilm reel #1, "Strategic Planning in the U.S. Navy, Its Evolution and Execution, 1891-1945" (Wilmington, DE, 1977), 44, 53.

13. 1914 Plan, 7. Alternative voyages through the Atlantic and Indian oceans were studied, but every Orange Plan rejected them. The Suez was too shallow for battleships and might be barred; after all, Britain and Japan were allies. The big ships might sail around Africa, but there were few major ports and perhaps no friendly ones. Ibid., App. "D," 154-55.

14. The battle locale is the author's generalization based on Orange plans from their inception to World War II and from the list of Orange war games later played at the Naval War College as cited in Michael Vlahos, *The Blue Sword: The Naval War College and the American Mission, 1919-1941* (Newport, 1980), App. 3.

15. 1911 Plan, 56-57; "Navy Basic Plan Orange, Approved by Secretary of the Navy, 1 March 1929" (hereafter 1929 Plan), Records of the Strategic Plans Division, Office of the Chief of Naval Operations, and Predecessor Organizations, 1912-47 (hereafter CNOPO Records), OA-NHD, Section 3, Miscellaneous File, 1917-47, vol. 1, chap. 2, 18.

16. Robert Seager II, *Alfred Thayer Mahan: The Man and His Letters* (Annapolis, 1977), 485-86.

17. 1914 Plan, "Transfer of Blue Naval Forces to Pacific and Thence to Hostile Area," 66-67 (hereafter 1914 Plan, Transfer).

18. 1914 Plan, App. "C," Routes 1 through 3; U.S. Navy, General Board, Table of Islands, 1907, GB, OA-NHD, Folder 142, OP 29, File 6.

19. 1914 Plan, Transfer, 66-67; Shoemaker, "Strategy of the Pacific," 67.

20. 1914 Plan, 27, 55-56.

21. Earl S. Pomeroy, *Pacific Outpost: American Strategy in Guam and Micronesia* (New York, 1951), chap. 2.

22. 1914 Plan, 72, 77; Shoemaker, "Strategy of the Pacific," 70.

23. 1914 Plan, 16.

24. Louis B. Morton, "War Plan ORANGE: Evolution of a Strategy," *World Politics* 11 (January 1959): 228.

25. William R. Braisted, *The United States Navy in the Pacific, 1909-1922* (Austin, 1971), 446, 452-53.

26. Told by Admiral Harry Yarnell, cited in Robert G. Albion, *Makers of Naval Policy, 1798-1947* (Annapolis, 1980), 90.

27. "Director of War Plans to General Board, 19 October 1921," GB, OA-NHD.

28. "Joint Board to Secretary of War, Defense of the Philippines, 7 July 1923," Joint Board, No. 305, Ser. 208, RG 225, NA; "Joint Planning Committee to Joint Board, Joint Army and Navy Basic War Plan Orange, 12 March 1924," Joint Board, No. 325, Ser. 290, RG 225, NA.

29. 1929 Plan, chap. 2, 21-25.

30. "Battle Problem—Special Study, BLUE vs. ORANGE, Quick Movement," Miscellaneous Subject File, 1917-47, CNOPO Records.

31. Admiral James O. Richardson, *On the Treadmill to Pearl Harbor* (Washington, 1973), 263, 268-69.

32. 1929 Plan, The Logistics Plan, 136.

33. Commander Cary W. Magruder, "Orange-'Royal Road'-Plan O-1 Orange, U.S. Joint Asiatic Force Operating Plan Orange, 21 July 1934," File Orange-Royal Road, Box 64, CNOPO Records (hereafter Royal Road).

34. T. Holcomb, "Memorandum for Director, War Plans Division, Denial of a Base to the Enemy in the MARSHALL-CAROLINES, 31 March 1933," monographs of attack and defense plans for specific islands by Headquarters, Fleet Marine Force for NWPD, 1934-37, boxes 56, 69, 77, CNOPO Records.

35. Royal Road, Section 5, Course 1.

36. WPL 13, Navy Basic War Plan Orange, vol. 1 (March 1939), Registered Document #22, OA-NHD.

37. Memorandum, Chief of Naval Operations to Secretary of the Navy, 12 November 1940, 14175-15, 11, Record Group 165, NA. Known as the Plan Dog memo (hereafter Plan Dog), it was forwarded to Roosevelt and became the basis of the Rainbow Five Plan.

38. U.S. Congress, House, Commission headed by Rear Admiral A. J. Hepburn to Secretary of the Navy, "Report on Need of Additional Naval Bases," House Doc. 65, 27 December 1938, 76th Cong., 1st sess., 1938, 26-28.

39. Francis X. Holbrook, "United States National Defense and Trans-Pacific Commercial Air Routes, 1933-1941" (Ph.D. diss., Fordham University, 1969), chap. 3.

40. Commander-in-Chief, United States Fleet, to Chief of Naval Operations, "Development of MIDWAY, WAKE and GUAM, 28 February 1938," Record Group 80, "General Records of the Department of the Navy," NB/ND 14, NA.

41. Change No. to WPL-16, April 1938, and WPL-13 of 1939 defined "Base One" only as "a typical atoll in the Marshall Islands." Eniwetok was a possible target in "Commander Minecraft, Battle Force to CinCUS, 22 July 1939," Enclosure H BASE ONE, box 236, File A-16-1/EG 12-1, CNO Secret and Confidential Files, RG 80, NA. It was not firmly designated until Plan O-1 of Rainbow Five. See below.

42. Louis B. Morton, *Strategy and Command: The First Two Years*, United States Army in World War II Series, *The War in the Pacific* (Washington, 1962), 41-42, 68ff, 71-72.

43. U.S. Navy, Rainbow Plan No. III (WPL-44), December 1940, CNOPO Records, cited on Reel #5, Scholarly Microfilm (hereafter Rainbow No. III).

44. Richardson, *On the Treadmill*, 278-79, 288-92.

45. Memorandum, Commander F. P. Sherman to Director, WPD, CinCUS's Operating Plan O-1, 30 April 1940, Box 91, File A16-3/FF, Warfare U.S. Fleet, RG 80, NA.

46. Commander-in-Chief to Chief of Naval Operations, 28 January 1941; Chief of Naval Operations to CinCUS, 10 February 1941, both with Rainbow No. III.

47. Plan Dog, 16.

48. WPL 44, Initial U.S. Strategic Deployment, Rainbow No. III; Memorandum, Chief of Staff for War Plans Division of War Department, General Staff, 17 January 1941, White House Conference of 16 January 1941, WPL 4175-18, cited in Morton, *Strategy and Command*, 85; Stark to Richardson, dispatch 212155, 22 January 1941, cited in ibid., 299.

49. Vice Admiral George Carroll Dyer, *The Amphibians Came to Conquer: The Story of Admiral Richmond Kelly Turner*, 2 vols. (Washington, 1971), 1: chap. 5, passim. Admiral R. E. Ingersoll told Dyer that Turner had written Rainbow Three and the first supporting draft of Rainbow Five.

50. Commander-in-Chief, U.S. Pacific Fleet, to Chief of Naval Operations, "WAKE ISLAND—Policy in regard to construction on and protection of, 18 April 1941," CNOPO Records, Ser. 029W, Box 91, File A16-3/FF Warfare U.S. Fleet.

51. Commander-in-Chief, U.S. Pacific Fleet, to Chief of Naval Operations, "Initial Deployment, U.S. Pacific Fleet under Plan Dog," ibid.

52. U.S. Congress, Hearings before the Joint Committee on the Investigation of the Pearl Harbor Attack, Commander-in-Chief, Pacific Fleet, "Plan O-1, Rainbow Five," 79th Cong. (Washington, 1946), Part 17, 2578-79; Annex II, "Marshall Reconnaissance and Raiding Plan," ibid., 2595-98.

53. Samuel Eliot Morison, *History of United States Naval Operations in World War II*, 15 vols. (Boston, 1950), 3:249.

54. Ernest J. King and Walter Muir Whitehill, *Fleet Admiral King: A Naval Record* (New York, 1952), 239.

55. Grace Person Hayes, *The History of the Joint Chiefs of Staff in World War II: The War against Japan* (Annapolis, 1982), 431.

56. Ibid., 546, 553-60.

57. King and Whitehill, *Fleet Admiral King*, 605.

58. Stanley D. Embick for Commanding General, Philippine Department, 19 April 1933, WPD 3251-15, cited in Ronald Schaffer, "General Stanley D. Embick: Military Dissenter," *Military Affairs* 37 (October 1973): 90.

59. Richardson, *On the Treadmill*, 262-63, 275-77.

Portrait of an Intelligence Officer: James McHugh in China, 1937-42

WILLIAM M. LEARY

James M. McHugh played a significant, if unappreciated, role as a naval intelligence officer in Sino-American relations between 1937 and 1942. Professor Leary shows how McHugh, with access to the highest levels of the Chinese government during the Sino-Japanese War, served as a channel of confidential communications between China and the United States and thus helped to arrange American economic and military assistance for Chiang Kai-shek.

****

The lot of military intelligence officers has never been particularly happy. They are expected to report with ruthless honesty even when faced with the tendency of superiors to associate bad news with the bearer. Convinced that most of their reports—compiled only after the greatest effort—are filed without ever having been read, they usually feel isolated and unappreciated. Obscurity is often the hallmark of success. While their peers sport decorations, they must be content with discrete praise for a job well done. A commitment to intelligence work usually means a truncated career: few intelligence officers reach senior rank. But there are rewards. At times, intelligence officers can serve their country in special ways, even exerting an influence on the course of history. The career of James Marshall McHugh (1899–1966), while hardly typical, illustrates the joys and frustrations of the intelligence calling.

McHugh graduated from Annapolis in the top third of his class, that of 1922. Opting for the Marine Corps, he spent fifteen months at Quantico, Virginia, and then was ordered to the Legation Guard at Peking. This was a choice assignment, and McHugh enjoyed the less-than-arduous duty in China's old imperial capital. He especially enjoyed the company of American Minister Jacob Gould Schurman's youngest daughter. The two were married in 1926. As McHugh later wrote, he now had "a professional gold spoon in my mouth."[1]

The young officer returned to the United States in June 1926 and joined the Engineer Battalion of the Expeditionary Force at Quantico, a far cry from the heady life of Peking. In December, however, McHugh was called to Marine Corps headquarters and asked if he would like to return to China as a language student. He accepted "with alacrity."

McHugh took up residence in Peking in February 1927, the first U.S. naval language student of Chinese since World War I. He reported to the naval attaché, Captain George Pettingill, a gruff wartime destroyer skipper who had a reputation as a formidable drinker. McHugh, who had known Pettingill from his earlier tour in China, recalled that when he went into the office, the captain looked up and said: "Well, if I have to have a Marine around here, I'm glad it's you." Pettingill then ordered McHugh to arrange his language lessons so that he would have every afternoon free to play golf. It turned out that Pettingill had gone on the wagon and played golf every afternoon as a way to let off steam, so they played through the summer and into the winter. Snow failed to intimidate the determined captain; he simply painted the golf balls red so that they could be seen more clearly.

Golf did pay one important dividend that later would have a significant impact on McHugh's career. It was on the links that he came to know W. H. Donald, an Australian journalist and sometime employee of the Chinese government. Down on his luck, Donald supplied information to Pettingill on local politics for a small monthly retainer. He often joined Pettingill and McHugh on the golf course, regaling them with tales of his long career in China that went back to the first years of the twentieth century. A friend of Sun Yat-sen, Donald had played an important role in the Revolution of 1911 that overthrew the Manchu government. He knew Charlie Soong and his pig-tailed daughter Mei-ling, soon to marry Chiang Kai-shek. Although McHugh at first took Donald's stories "with a good deal of salt," he later discovered that there was "more truth than poetry" in most of them.[2]

McHugh also developed a wide range of Chinese contacts. For twenty-eight years his father-in-law, Dr. Schurman, had been president of Cornell University, where many prominent Chinese, including philosopher Hu Shih, had been educated. McHugh's marital connection afforded him entry into Chinese circles that normally would not have been open to a junior officer, and he was able to meet these former students of Dr. Schurman's "under auspicious circumstances."

McHugh lived for a time with Military Attaché John Magruder, who had married his wife's sister. In many ways, Magruder came to serve as McHugh's model for the ideal intelligence officer. He read the attaché's reports, which he considered "models of keen perception," and expressed admiration for his integrity and honesty. Magruder took an unsentimental view of the Nationalist movement that was sweeping China. Emphasizing the need to keep American interests firmly in mind, he decried the tendency of many officials to see events in terms of their hopes for the country's regeneration rather than the reality of the situation. He also called attention to the problem that would cause honest observers of the Chinese scene no end of trouble in the years to come. "There have been times," Magruder wrote in 1929, "when to tell the facts about the situation in China one consciously has to lay himself open to the charge at home of being unsympathetic to the aspirations of the Chinese people." And, he warned, "when official intelligence agencies develop too much emotion, Lord help statesmen!"[3]

McHugh spent four happy years in China, developing a wide range of contacts, learning a good deal about the country and its people from lengthy trips into the interior, and honing his language skills. In his final year he served as assistant Chinese secretary in the American legation and helped to translate official communications between the Washington and Nanking governments. He also wrote a textbook for beginning students of Chinese that would be widely used until the Japanese burned down the printing plant in Hong Kong in 1942.

In July 1931, McHugh reported to Commander Hartwell C. Davis, in charge of the Far Eastern section of the Office of Naval Intelligence (ONI) in Washington. Davis, who was interested mainly in Japanese codes, ran the section himself, a not uncommon situation during a time of severe budgetary restraint. He welcomed the appearance of an extra hand and arranged for another desk to be placed in the office. McHugh organized ONI's first China section just as the Japanese army unleashed an attack in Manchuria that threatened the postwar treaty structure. He watched the situation deteriorate in East Asia and kept his superiors informed on the background of events through a series of monographs on such topics as the strategic and economic importance of the Chinese Eastern Railway.

Less than two years later, McHugh was back in China as intelligence officer for the 4th Marines—on occupation duty in Shanghai since 1927—and shore intelligence officer for the U.S. Asiatic Fleet. He made frequent trips to the Nationalist capital of Nanking where he reestablished contact with Donald, now a trusted adviser to Madame Chiang. Through Donald, he met her and Generalissimo Chiang. McHugh reported on the latter's attempt to consolidate his power by destroying Communist opponents and subjugating regional warlords. At one point, he obtained Chiang's permission to observe Nationalist military operations in Fukien Province against T'sai Ting-kai's 19th Route Army.

Although Chiang made significant progress in dealing with domestic opposition, he did little to check Japanese expansionism. By the summer of 1935, McHugh noted, Japan had established control over most of North China. Ignoring a growing popular demand for action and rejecting the advice of his wife, Chiang continued to do nothing, believing that outright war would only play into Japanese hands. "Whether his policy will prove best for China in the long run," McHugh wrote to Dr. Schurman, "only time will tell."[4]

The demands of career training brought McHugh back to the United States at the end of 1935 to attend the Marine Corps school at Quantico, but he kept in touch with events in China through correspondence with Donald. In the spring of 1937, Donald predicted that full-scale war would soon break out with Japan, and he suggested that McHugh return to China. Shortly thereafter, the Japanese provoked an incident at the Marco Polo Bridge outside of Peking. Chiang at last decided that the time had come to take a stand, and the conflict quickly expanded to the Shanghai area. Donald again wrote to McHugh and urged him to come out and observe events. Accordingly, McHugh showed the letter to Commander John M. Creighton, then head of ONI's Far Eastern section. Creighton asked McHugh if he was willing to go back to China. McHugh assured him that he was. Two weeks later, orders were issued for McHugh to take up the assignment of assistant naval attaché in Nanking.

McHugh reached the Nationalist capital on 8 November 1937. Reporting to Ambassador Nelson T. Johnson, he learned that the war was not going well for the Chinese. In August Chiang had sought a decisive victory in the south by initiating action in Shanghai against the Japanese navy garrison. He also hoped to draw the Japanese away from northern China, where his forces were weak, and face them on more favorable ground. After nearly three months of bitter fighting, however, Chiang had lost 300,000 of his best troops and was about to order the battered survivors to retreat along the Shanghai-Nanking Railway.[5]

American policy, Johnson explained, was to protect the lives of U.S. citizens while carefully avoiding any involvement in the conflict. This hands-off policy was creating a communications problem: Johnson could not maintain close contact with Nationalist leaders lest this be construed by the Japanese as official American support for China. The ambassador hoped that McHugh, through his association with Donald, might improve the situation. Johnson then asked the new attaché if he would like to move in with him. "I accepted," McHugh recalled, "because the quarters were scarce and [because] living with the Ambassador was an important advantage [in dealing with the Chinese]."[6]

When McHugh contacted Donald, he found that the Australian journalist's influence had increased greatly since 1937. The Chiangs now considered him the elder statesman and treated him with great respect. He was especially close to Madame Chiang; he called her "Missimo," and she called him "Gran." Madame Chiang relied on Donald to draft most of her extensive correspondence and to prepare public statements issued by the generalissimo. McHugh judged Donald to be "a very shrewd and powerful figure."[7]

McHugh visited Donald nearly every morning. The two men would walk in the park east of the city, near the Ming tombs, or climb Purple Mountain to watch the Japanese air raids. McHugh often stayed for a private lunch with Donald and the Chiangs. The relationship between the confidential adviser and the intelligence officer grew ever closer. McHugh reported to ONI:

> It slowly dawned on me during my daily visits that he expected me to accept as master to pupil, without argument or question, his version of events in China. In fact he irritably rebuked me on more than one occasion when I attempted to cross-examine him or suggest that any conditions other than those which he was describing might exist. I therefore gradually assumed the role of meek listener.[8]

As Ambassador Johnson had hoped, McHugh became an important conduit for informal communications between the Chinese and American governments. Donald and the Chiangs spoke frankly to McHugh on a variety of issues, knowing that their remarks would be passed on to Washington through the ambassador. They stressed that Japan was succeeding because the world's greatest powers had failed to heed China's cry for help. At one point, Donald told McHugh that peace negotiations were likely. These two themes— the need for assistance and the possibility of a peace settlement with Japan— would be heard often in the years to come.[9]

McHugh's easy access to the highest levels of the Chinese government facilitated the collection of technical intelligence, although his first major project came to an unfortunate end. In early December, as the Japanese army approached Nanking, he learned that the Chinese had recovered the latest model bombsight from a downed Japanese aircraft. Madame Chiang, who was serving as head of the Commission on Aeronautical Affairs, gave him permission to send the bombsight to the United States for examination. McHugh turned it over to the commanding officer of the gunboat *Panay*, which was preparing to evacuate American personnel from the area. However, it never reached its destination. On 12 December 1937, Japanese aircraft attacked and sank the *Panay*. Divers later tried but failed to recover the bombsight. McHugh always wondered if the Japanese had broken the U.S. naval code, learned of the *Panay*'s cargo, and decided to keep the bombsight out of the hands of American technical experts.[10]

On 7 December the Japanese army reached Tangshan, twenty miles east of Nanking. Driving Madame Chiang's personal car, McHugh left the doomed city at 5:30 that morning. He reached Hankow four days later, suffering from a severe case of conjunctivitis caused by the dusty roads, and promptly reestablished his routine.[11] He took an apartment in the APC Building, two floors above the American embassy, shared meals with the ambassador, and worked at a desk in Johnson's office. McHugh liked the gregarious diplomat, who had a good sense of humor and a fondness for cheap Chinese cigarettes, and he considered Johnson "wise in the ways of this part of the world." Above all, he shared Johnson's view that the fundamental goal of U.S. policy in China was to promote American self-interest. As Johnson's biographer notes, the ambassador, although sympathetic toward the Chinese, remained "an American nationalist first and foremost." The same could be said about McHugh.[12]

McHugh played nine holes of golf with Donald on most mornings, during which the Australian discussed the previous day's events in the Chiang household. He placed the American in contact with all important government agencies, and he introduced him to Chiang's German military advisers and to U.S. aviation adviser Claire L. Chennault. "I can usually keep in pretty direct touch with what is happening," McHugh remarked.[13]

The danger existed, as it always does in such situations, that McHugh would get too close to his sources, that he would become (as accused by some historians) a mouthpiece for the Nationalists.[14] But this did not happen. Indeed, his memoranda reflected an exceedingly unsentimental view of events in China. For example, on 20 January 1938 he reported to ONI in detail about the bitter family feuds among the Soong clan—Madame Chiang, her sister Madame Kung, and her brother T. V. Soong. He termed Finance Minister H. H. Kung "a mere figure-head and puppet in the hands of his wife," who was "a woman insane with lust for power." Most people correctly saw his ministry as "a venal and corrupt organization." T. V. Soong, although far more capable and honest, was vain, stubborn, domineering, and dictatorial; he had an "attitude toward his family, particularly the Generalissimo, with whom he had never gotten along, of contempt, bitterness and aloofness."[15]

McHugh reserved his most critical comments for Chiang, terming the Chinese leader "a dictator" who ruled "by fear and not by confidence." His military judgment left a good deal to be desired; in particular, his decision to defend Nanking had been a major blunder. Yet, despite Chiang's failure to move against the corruption that was pervading his regime, he had become "a symbol of unity and resistance against Japanese aggression."[16]

Besides the reports to ONI (which were passed on to senior naval officers, the General Board, the War College, and the Military Intelligence Division[17]), McHugh also opened other channels of communication. By invitation, he began to correspond with Major General Thomas Holcomb, commandant of the Marine Corps and a former Chinese language student who retained a keen interest in the Far East. In April 1938, McHugh informed Holcomb that the military situation was turning against Japan. The Chinese had lured their enemy into an attritional fight, and the Japanese were paying an increasingly high price for their success. "They were involved on a tremendous front," he observed, "and are faced by masses of Chinese in every sector who are constantly interrupting their communications. I think the Japs are walking into a swamp.... They cannot go far ahead and they cannot turn back."[18]

Holcomb thanked McHugh for a "most interesting letter," which he forwarded to Rear Admiral Ralston Holmes, director of Naval Intelligence, and to Stanley K. Hornbeck, head of the State Department's Far Eastern office. Also, Holcomb continued, "I showed [it] to Admiral [William D.] Leahy, who took it to the White House and read several passages to the President, who expressed himself as much interested."[19]

As the Japanese advanced toward Hankow during the summer of 1938, McHugh became an advocate of American economic support for China. The Nationalist government, he informed General Holcomb in September, had exhausted its financial reserves and needed additional funds to continue the fight against Japan. "I think it very much to our interest not to permit the breakdown of the present Chinese resistance," he counseled. "Whatever we spend now will save the expenditure of vastly greater sums later on if we permit the Japs to get away with their present project." In November he told Ambassador Johnson that the United States "should do something besides defend Chinese principles." Johnson agreed; he forwarded McHugh's memorandum to Washington and endorsed the attaché's recommendations for economic assistance. The following month the United States granted China a commodity credit of $25,000,000, marking the end of benign neglect and the beginning of a new policy that emphasized economic help to the Chinese as a way to thwart Japanese expansionism.[20]

McHugh, who had played only a small role in bringing about the change in policy, welcomed the new attitude. He wanted American aid for China not because he had developed pro-Nationalist sympathies; rather, he had become militantly anti-Japanese during 1938. The Japanese army, he believed, "was just a bunch of savages and the sooner the rest of the world realizes this the better." The interests of the United States and Japan were bound to clash. As Japan would not listen to reason, the only alternative was a policy of "uncompromising firmness."[21]

The war entered a new phase in 1939. The Japanese now controlled China's most important centers of commerce and industry, leaving the Nationalists to fight on from the isolated new capital of Chungking. Beginning in May, Japan initiated a massive air campaign against Chungking, aimed at demoralizing the government and crushing its will to resist.

During this period McHugh continued to serve as a vital communications link between the Chinese and American governments. He shared a house with

Ambassador Johnson on the south bank of the Yangtze River. Johnson was content to allow McHugh to make the arduous trip across the river to Chiang's headquarters on the other side. Every morning McHugh boarded a sampan that had to fight the Yangtze's strong current with only a stern oar; usually he ended up a half-mile downriver from where he wanted to land. After reaching the intended landing point, McHugh then had to climb 367 slippery steps to get to the city's outer limits. However, Johnson appreciated McHugh's work. "Major McHugh has been indefatigable in maintaining contacts with important people throughout the Chinese Government," he informed Secretary of State Cordell Hull, "and in keeping his Department and this Mission informed of developments in a situation where high qualities of tact and patience have been demanded."[22]

In addition to his liaison duties, McHugh also spent a good deal of time collecting technical intelligence. He acquired and sent to Washington bomb fragments, aircraft parts, and other Japanese military equipment. After the Chinese tested a captured Type 97 fighter plane, McHugh secured a detailed analysis of its performance. Perhaps his most important contribution came with the recovery of code books that were used by the navy cryptanalyst Laurence W. Safford to help crack some of the more difficult Japanese cyphers.[23]

McHugh—and everyone else—found life in Chungking far from pleasant. The winter of 1938–39 seemed an endless procession of cold, damp, foggy days. Then, the heat and humidity began in May, with temperatures often rising above 100 degrees. Clearing skies brought the Japanese bombers; Ambassador Johnson estimated that between May and July 1939 planes dropped 12,900 tons of bombs on the city.[24]

The isolation and constant tension took its toll on McHugh. His wife filed for divorce, which he blamed at least in part on the long separation that his duties demanded, and his two sons were growing up without him. "I have sacrificed my family in my fervor over this job," McHugh wrote in November 1939 to Major Ronald A. Boone, a fellow marine intelligence officer; yet ONI seemed not to appreciate what he was accomplishing in China. He rarely heard from his superiors in Washington. In fact, he began to doubt that they even read the reports that he was sending back. Was the work for ONI, he wondered, having an adverse impact on his professional career? "The point of the whole matter," he told Commander Harvey E. Overesch, naval attaché in Peking, "and incidentally a question vital to my whole life both professionally and personal, is: Do they [ONI] really find what I have been doing useful and do they want it continued?"[25]

McHugh received assurances about the value of his work. "I know definitely that your work has been highly praised," General Holcomb wrote, "and highly appreciated by all hands who know of it, especially by the navy. You must believe this, and avoid getting in a frame of mind that would lessen your value in this work." Also, Holcomb reminded McHugh that he was making an important contribution to the Marine Corps's effort to be fully accepted by the navy in intelligence work. "With a Marine [Lt. Col. Maurice G. Holmes] in charge of the Lat. Am. desk in ONI, and with Nav. Atts. to four missions in the same field, it appears that the ancient prejudice is waning, at least temporarily. It is up to us to prove we can do this work, as we can."[26]

Despite these encouraging words, it was difficult to maintain a positive attitude in China's wartime capital. As Ambassador Johnson's biographer has written, the hardships that he experienced in Chungking were "probably unexceeded in the annals of American diplomacy." McHugh shared these hardships in full measure.[27]

In August 1940, McHugh returned home after nearly three years in China. He no sooner had begun the advanced course at Marine Corps school at Quantico when Japan occupied northern Indochina and signed a treaty of alliance with Germany and Italy. Secretary of the Navy Frank Knox sent for McHugh and asked him to return to China as his special representative to Chiang. Also, he would become naval attaché as well as naval attaché for air, the first marine to hold these posts. McHugh accepted. He was back in Chungking by Christmas.[28]

As the United States began to provide substantial aid to the Nationalist government, McHugh's liaison duties became more important than ever. In late January 1941, Presidential Special Assistant Lauchlin Currie visited China to examine the military and economic situations. He carried a handwritten letter of introduction from Knox to McHugh that also expressed the secretary's delight "with the way you are handling the mission with which you are charged."[29]

McHugh accompanied Currie on his visits to various governmental agencies and installations. The Chinese, Currie learned, were especially interested in funds for currency stabilization and equipment and in advisers to create a modern air force. Currie returned to the United States in March and reported the results of his survey to the president. Sympathetic to China's requests, Franklin Roosevelt gave Currie the task of expediting aid to China under the new Lend-Lease program.[30]

McHugh welcomed Roosevelt's decision to aid China, but he saw American assistance as useful more for psychological than for military purposes. American national interest, he wrote to Currie in April, should govern the aid program. At present, it was essential to boost the morale of the Chinese in order to keep them active against the Japanese.

> If you could dump a hundred planes and the fifty million dollars in their laps tomorrow ... it would come far closer to serving our own ends through the boost in their morale, even though it went down the drain in actual use, than to work out a carefully established scheme and send out a well trained force to fly their planes. The latter can follow in due course, but I firmly believe we ought to give them planes to crack up *immediately*, ask no questions, and merely say "we are with you to the bitter end." We cannot run their country for them, and we cannot fight their war for them, but we can keep their heads up and let them do the job in their own way.[31]

This letter from McHugh to Currie of 14 April 1941, enclosing a memorandum of a conversation with Chiang "which I am giving only to the Ambassador and to you, and which will not be forwarded officially," marked the beginning of an extensive "Dear Lauch"-"Dear Mac" correspondence. Currie sometimes used McHugh to bypass normal diplomatic channels and communicate directly with Chiang. McHugh, in turn, provided information about events in high Nationalist circles. "I can't tell you how much I have appreciated your frequent letters," Currie acknowledged. "They have been most helpful in keeping me informed, and a few things I passed along verbally to my boss."[32]

The period between Currie's departure in March and the arrival of the U.S. Military Mission under General Magruder in October 1941 marked the high point of McHugh's service as confidential channel of communications between the highest levels of the Chinese and American governments. He corresponded not only with Currie but also with Secretary Knox, passing along his comments on men and events, and he enjoyed direct access to Generalissimo and Madame Chiang. The War and Navy departments considered his reports so authoritative, McHugh learned, that rumors began to circulate in Washington "about me being on the inside out here because I was Madame Chiang's paramour."[33]

In addition to conveying information, McHugh played a key role in assisting Chennault with his American Volunteer Group (AVG). When McHugh first had been introduced to him by Donald in 1937, Chennault was living in secrecy at the deserted Nanking Golf Club; officials of the State Department had charged that he had violated U.S. law by working for a foreign government, and they were threatening to cancel his passport. McHugh spoke to Ambassador Johnson about the situation, and Johnson managed to fend off the passport office. "Thereafter," McHugh recalled, "Chennault and I were unusually close and he confided in me completely about all his activities. He is a very effective operator and a wonderful leader of men. Everyone who worked for him in China swore by him."[34]

In 1940, just before McHugh left Washington for Chungking, he introduced Chennault to Secretary Knox. Chennault and General P. T. Mow had come to the United States in search of American aircraft and crews. McHugh recommended to Knox that American officers on active duty be allowed to join the projected volunteer force without losing their military seniority or citizenship. The secretary later secured President Roosevelt's approval of this plan.[35]

After the first AVG contingent arrived in Burma in June 1941, McHugh worked closely with Chennault to remedy the many problems that arose. At Chennault's request, McHugh wrote to Secretary Knox in August and asked him to seek presidential assistance in obtaining .50-caliber machine gun ammunition from the reluctant army. Later, McHugh sought Knox's help in getting MacArthur to release badly needed spare parts for Chennault's P-40s. Knox not only secured the materiel but also ordered four Navy PBYs to fly from Manila to Singapore.[36]

These efforts on behalf of the AVG paid rich dividends in the weeks following Pearl Harbor. At a time when American forces in the Pacific were suffering defeat after defeat, the success of Chennault's young pilots provided a rare glimmer of hope. The work of the AVG, McHugh wrote to Currie on 10 January 1942, "has exceeded our fondest hopes and, among other points, demonstrates beyond a doubt that our boys are more than a match for the Japs." Japanese victories elsewhere, he continued, were not because the enemy had suddenly realized a hidden strength; instead, they showed that the United States was weaker than had been realized. "I am completely confident that once we get our forces built up we can take their measure very decisively."[37]

While optimistic about the eventual outcome of the war, McHugh was not happy with U.S. diplomatic representation in China. Ambassador Charles E. Gauss, who had replaced Johnson in mid-1941, did not impress McHugh. "His controlling passion," he noted, "appears to be one of personal vanity and precedence coupled with an ill-disguised vindictiveness." Gauss had opposed the AVG, and he was against unrestricted Lend-Lease aid for China. While professing friendliness toward the Chinese, he failed "to conceal his hostility and contempt" toward them. McHugh advised Currie:

> If we are seeking to retain the goodwill of the Chinese and keep them with us (for our own selfish interests, admittedly) during the war, then we certainly have a misfit as a representative. If, on the contrary, we feel that we must watch our step at every turn to keep from being cheated and if we wish to ensure a post war return on our present financial and material investments, then we probably have the right man. Personally, I am of the former school and I think it will pay off in the end.[38]

McHugh was even less happy with Joseph W. Stilwell, selected in February to replace Magruder as senior American military representative in China. McHugh considered Stilwell "a small, mean-minded, sarcastic man"[39] who not only lacked diplomatic skills but also left a good deal to be desired as a military leader. McHugh believed that his conduct of the Burma campaign had been inept. Stilwell, McHugh informed Secretary Knox, "got himself out on a limb in Burma which the Japanese chopped off on him." Although Stilwell blamed the disaster on the Chinese 55th Division, which broke and ran while holding the eastern flank, McHugh disagreed. "I can only say," he told Knox,

> that I think one who professes to be an "Old China Hand" should not have put so much trust in the Chinese to start with, not have permitted himself to be drawn so far over to the west in an attempt to help the British cover Malay when by his own admission he did not know the location and strength of the Japanese moving in from Thailand against his left flank. He not only left that flank guarded by an untried Chinese division, but actually had no reserve available behind it to cover his vital route of communications to the rear through Lashio.[40]

Developing Chinese attitudes toward the British and their attempts to manipulate American Lend-Lease assistance also troubled McHugh. "I feel that there is a studied campaign of slander against the British," he reported in March, "and because they are our allies and are white men, I resent it." He saw the current flattery of Americans at the expense of the British as part of the Chinese tendency to play off one group of foreigners against another. This lavish praise of the United States "has a mercenary, opportunistic, and undependable ring to it," and he was convinced "that when we have ceased to be useful, we will be discarded." McHugh hastened to assure Currie that he was masking his true feelings when dealing with the Chinese. "I fully appreciate and feel very deeply the urgency of keeping them sweet and getting the maximum effort out of them for our cause," he wrote, "but only a fool would close his eyes to the realities of the situation."[41]

Chinese threats to make peace with Japan as a lever to obtain increased American aid left McHugh unimpressed. "I believe that China like Russia is fighting primarily because she has to," he informed Secretary Knox, "because it is in defense of her soil and I think that in each case they will go on fighting irrespective of the degree of help they get." However, McHugh supported "reasonable assistance" for China as a way to maintain morale. Logistical difficulties made it impossible to provide the supplies necessary for a large-scale offensive by the Chinese army, even if the army was psychologically capable of mounting such an offensive, which McHugh doubted. The best military strategy under the circumstances would be to use air power against the Japanese.[42]

Prospects for air power in China suffered a severe setback when Brigadier General Clayton L. Bissell, Stilwell's air officer, took a heavy-handed and unsuccessful approach to inducting the AVG into the army air forces. Bissell and his superiors, McHugh believed, "were out to get Chennault," who had disproved the widely accepted Douhet theory that bombers would prevail against fighters. McHugh considered Chennault "an outstanding aviation leader and strategist," and he wanted to see him placed in charge of air operations in China.[43]

Frustrated with the trend of events, McHugh asked to be relieved of his assignment. "My usefulness here as a medium of special contact with the Chinese has largely disappeared," he advised Knox in August 1942. His contacts with Chiang had ended with the arrival of the Magruder mission in October 1941. Magruder, he pointed out, "represented in the flesh the promise of assistance which I had been holding out." Also, he was not on cordial terms with either Ambassador Gauss or General Stilwell.

McHugh further expressed concern that his confidential reports were being leaked to the Chinese. "As you know," he wrote, "my reports have by no means been paeans of praise for China, and the Chinese resent any kind of criticism." The most recent incident had occurred in late July. Based on information received from Commander Milton E. Miles, who was working with the Chinese secret police, McHugh informed the ambassador and wrote to ONI about a Chinese general who recently had surrendered to the Japanese, without firing a shot, on orders from Chungking. Four days later, Miles came to see McHugh "in great alarm." One of Miles's friends in the secret police had left him an anonymous note which read: "McHugh reported to the Ambassador that Miles had informed him that a certain general had surrendered Li Shui without firing a shot, and the Ambassador is about to send this to Washington in his lousy codes." "My candid opinion," McHugh concluded, "is that the time has come for me to do a quiet fade-out from here." While disclaiming any ulterior motives in the request for relief, he pointed out to Knox "that I have not had Xmas with my youngsters since 1936 and that it would be undeniably pleasant if I could be back there for December 25, 1942."[44]

Secretary Knox, after discussing the matter with the director of Naval Intelligence, agreed that McHugh's usefulness had come to an end. Formal orders would follow in due course, he informed McHugh. "I cannot conclude this letter," Knox went on, "without expressing my great admiration of the manner in which you have discharged your duties on this assignment. The information with which you have supplied me has been of the greatest value and I am greatly in your debt therefor."[45]

Unfortunately for his career, McHugh's departure turned out to be anything but a "quiet fade-out." In October McHugh met presidential emissary Wendell Willkie in Chinese Turkestan and accompanied him during his visit to Chungking and tour of the war front. At one point, Willkie interviewed General Chennault, who took the opportunity to pour out his accumulated anger and frustration. Instead of building on the success of the AVG, the army seemed intent on fighting a pointless ground war in China. This was a great mistake, Chennault told Willkie, because with only a minimum of resources he could inflict a major defeat upon Japan. Willkie asked the general to put his ideas in writing so that he could carry them back to Washington. However, due to a change in schedule, Chennault was not able to complete his letter before Willkie left China. A few days later, he gave the letter to McHugh to forward to the United States, together with a copy to use as he saw fit.[46]

Chennault's letter to Willkie was destined to become the focal point for debate over U.S. strategy in China. In it, he promised to defeat Japan with 105 fighters, 30 medium bombers, 12 heavy bombers, and suitable spares. He planned an air offensive in China that would draw the Japanese air force into "the best air warning net of its kind in the Far East." Using tactics that the AVG had employed so effectively, Chennault envisioned the destruction of Japanese aircraft at the ratio of 10–20:1. After all, he argued, the AVG had destroyed over 300 Japanese aircraft at a cost of only twelve pilots killed by enemy action.

After winning air superiority in China, Chennault then would use his medium bomber force against enemy sea supply lines in the Southwest Pacific. This would bring out Japan's last air reserves and enable him to complete the destruction of the enemy's air force: thus the U.S. Navy would operate in the Pacific "with freedom," while MacArthur could push his offensive "at will." At the same time, Chennault would employ his twelve heavy bombers to devastate the industrial center of Japan.

And there was more. "I am confident," Chennault informed Willkie, "that given full authority as American military commander in China that I can not only bring about the downfall of Japan but that I can make the Chinese lasting friends of the United States. I am confident that I can create such good will that China will be a great and friendly market for generations."[47] The surprise about Chennault's wildly unrealistic scheme for winning the war in the Pacific is that so many otherwise sensible people, like McHugh, took it seriously. "General Chennault 'draws a pretty long bow' in his claims as to what he can accomplish," McHugh informed Knox, "but I personally believe he can come very close to achieving all he claims *if* he receives regular supplies and whole-hearted support."[48]

If McHugh merely had sent copies of Chennault's letter, together with a brief covering letter, to Secretary Knox and Rear Admiral H. C. Train, director of Naval Intelligence, it seems unlikely that he would have been drawn into the subsequent controversy between Chennault and Stilwell that so troubled America's wartime policy in China. But McHugh went much further and appended his own estimate of the situation. Deeply unhappy with the course of events in 1942, he decided that the time had come "to call a spade a spade . . . and name individuals," even though such honesty might violate "service etiquette." Ignoring logistical considerations, McHugh warmly endorsed Chennault's proposal to use China primarily as a base for air operations against Japan. He then attacked Stilwell's plans for the recapture of Burma as "essentially fallacious," more the result of injured pride than sound military strategy. Finally, McHugh dropped his bombshell: "I firmly believe—and I report this without the slightest personal rancor or feeling—that the war in this theater would be materially aided by the removal of both Generals Stilwell and Bissell and their huge staffs."[49]

Secretary Knox passed on McHugh's letter to President Roosevelt and to Secretary of War Henry L. Stimson. It subsequently reached Stilwell, who protested to Chief of Staff George C. Marshall. The chief of staff complained to Admiral Ernest J. King, chief of Naval Operations. King in turn telephoned Captain E. M. Zacharias, deputy director of Naval Intelligence, and wanted to know just who was this McHugh. King told Zacharias that McHugh would not be permitted to return to China under any circumstances.[50]

McHugh returned to the United States in December 1942. After two months in the hospital, recovering from malaria and dysentery, he attended Marine Corps school at Quantico, worked for a time in the Office of Strategic Services (OSS), and then was assigned in 1944 to headquarters of the 5th Marine Amphibious Corps on Guam. But McHugh could not settle into the ordinary service career. "I do my work mechanically most of the time," he wrote in November 1944 to Currie, "and with my mind still on the problems of China and the future."[51] Through Currie and General William Donovan, McHugh arranged a transfer back to OSS. Donovan wanted to send McHugh to China—and he very much wanted to go—but the War Department opposed the assignment. In an effort to overcome this opposition, McHugh sought an interview with Stilwell, who had been recalled from China. After expressing regret for "certain passages" in his critical letter to Knox and Train of October 1942, McHugh asked Stilwell if he would speak to General Marshall about the situation. Stilwell replied that he was a "damned fool" for wanting to go back to China, but that he would talk to Marshall. Although Stilwell was prepared to forgive and forget, Marshall was not. In March 1945 the Navy Department informed McHugh "that objection to your assignment to China has not been withdrawn."[52]

McHugh retired from the Marine Corps in 1946 and faded into private life. He continued to appraise events in China with an unsentimental eye, and he even hoped for a time to write a book about Chiang. While crediting the generalissimo with placing China on the road to becoming a modern nation, McHugh believed that the Nationalist leader had sowed the seeds of disaffection among the Chinese people whom the Communists were able to exploit so effectively. Chiang had lost China "for the simple reason that he never understood his own people, their wants and their needs." Together with his "worthless political generals" and secret police, he had "ground [them] down... by merciless taxation, torture and violation of their women until they finally revolted." The United States could not have saved Chiang after World War II. "Had we made the attempt," McHugh argued, "we would have been sucked down into that swamp which is China and would have lost."

Ironically, Chiang's influence in Washington grew "in geometric progression" as his fortunes at home declined. After his exile to Taiwan, the generalissimo held the United States under his sway "with all the force of a snake-charmer." McHugh concluded: "He would like to have us declare war on Communist China and invade the country, carrying him on our backs but letting him dictate strategy." Continued support of Chiang, McHugh warned, was against "the dictates of sound American policy."[53] McHugh never found a publisher for his book.

During the summer of 1964, McHugh and Vice Admiral Paul S. Foster (then a member of the Atomic Energy Commission) had a casual conversation about the former's wartime service in China. Foster was surprised to learn that McHugh never had received any recognition for his assignment. The admiral contacted General Holcomb about the situation, and the eighty-five-year-old former commandant prepared a recommendation for a decoration. In January 1965, General Wallace M. Greene presented McHugh with the Legion of Merit. McHugh died the next year.[54]

Notes

1. Biographical information from taped reminiscences and the draft of a memoir are in the James M. McHugh Papers, Cornell University Library, Ithaca, New York (hereafter McHugh Papers). For sketches on the life of marines in China during the 1920s see Allan R. Millett, *Semper Fidelis: The History of the United States Marine Corps* (New York, 1980), 216-28.
2. On Donald's career see Earl Albert Selle, *Donald of China* (New York, 1948).
3. Magruder to Schurman, 15 May 1929, Jacob Gould Schurman Papers, Cornell University Library, Ithaca, New York (hereafter Schurman Papers).
4. McHugh to Schurman, 19 June, 12, 17 July 1935, Schurman Papers.
5. On the Sino-Japanese War see Ch'i Hsi-sheng, *Nationalist China at War* (Ann Arbor, 1982); Hu Pu-yu, *A Brief History of the Sino-Japanese War* (Taipei, 1974); and Dick Wilson, *When Tigers Fight* (London, 1982).
6. Dorothy Borg, *The United States and the Far Eastern Crisis of 1933-1938* (Cambridge, 1964), is best for American policy.
7. McHugh, Memorandum for the Publisher, n.d. [c. 1963], McHugh Papers.
8. McHugh, Report No. 1-38: Present Political Situation in China, 20 January 1938, McHugh Papers.
9. McHugh, Notes on Conversation with Donald, 6 December 1937, McHugh Papers.
10. See Jeffrey M. Dorwart, *Conflict of Duty: The U.S. Navy's Intelligence Dilemma, 1919-1938* (Annapolis, 1983), 93; and Hamilton Darby Perry, *The Panay Incident: Prelude to Pearl Harbor* (New York, 1969).
11. McHugh to Major General Thomas Holcomb, 12 April 1938, McHugh Papers.
12. Ibid.; Russell D. Buhite, *Nelson T. Johnson and American Policy toward China, 1925-1941* (East Lansing, 1968), 16.
13. McHugh to Holcomb, 12 April 1938, McHugh Papers.
14. See Barbara W. Tuchman, *Stilwell and the American Experience in China, 1911-45* (New York, 1970); Michael Schaller, *The U.S. Crusade in China, 1938-1945* (New York, 1979), 44, 51.
15. McHugh, Report No. 1-38.
16. Ibid.
17. Commander Harvey E. Overesch to McHugh, 25 June 1938, McHugh Papers.
18. McHugh to Holcomb, 12 April 1938, McHugh Papers.
19. Holcomb to McHugh, 19 July 1938, McHugh Papers.
20. McHugh to Holcomb, 30 September 1938, McHugh Papers; McHugh to Johnson, 24 November 1938, quoted in Buhite, *Nelson T. Johnson*, 139-40; Warren I. Cohen, *America's Response to China: An Interpretive History* (New York, 1971), 145-50.
21. McHugh to Holcomb, 4 June 1939, McHugh Papers.
22. Johnson to Hull, 24 June 1940, quoted in Dorwart, *Conflict of Duty*, 133.

23. McHugh to ONI, 26 May 1938, ONI General Correspondence, 1929–42, File Op-16-B-11, Record Group 38, National Archives, Washington, DC; McHugh, Report No. 4-39: Japanese Aviation, 27 September 1940, McHugh Papers; Dorwart, *Conflict of Duty*, 90–93.

24. Buhite, *Nelson T. Johnson*, 145–46.

25. McHugh to Overesch, 15 November 1939; McHugh to Boone, 18 November 1939; McHugh to Holcomb, 20 November 1939, all in McHugh Papers.

26. Holcomb to McHugh, 10 December 1939, McHugh Papers.

27. Buhite, *Nelson T. Johnson*, 145–46.

28. McHugh, Memorandum for the Publisher.

29. Knox to McHugh, 25 January 1941, McHugh Papers.

30. Charles F. Romanus and Riley Sunderland, *Stilwell's Mission to China* (Washington, DC, 1953), 14–15; Schaller, *U.S. Crusade*, 47–51.

31. McHugh to Currie, 14 April 1941, McHugh Papers.

32. Currie to McHugh, 17 May 1941, McHugh Papers.

33. McHugh to Knox, 27 June 1941; McHugh to Madame Chiang, 30 May 1941; Madame Chiang to McHugh, 31 May 1941; McHugh to Currie, 25 August 1941; all in McHugh Papers.

34. McHugh Memorandum, "Chennault," n.d., McHugh Papers.

35. McHugh, Memorandum for the Publisher; Romanus and Sunderland, *Stilwell's Mission*, 10–11, 17–18.

36. McHugh to Currie, 6 August 1941, McHugh Papers; McHugh, Memorandum for the Publisher.

37. McHugh to Currie, 10 January 1942, McHugh Papers.

38. Ibid.

39. McHugh Memorandum, "Chiang Kai-shek and Stilwell," n.d., McHugh Papers.

40. McHugh to Knox, 9 July 1942, McHugh Papers.

41. McHugh to Currie, 16 March 1942, McHugh Papers.

42. McHugh to Knox, 9 July 1942, McHugh Papers.

43. McHugh to Currie, 16 March, 13 July 1942, McHugh Papers.

44. McHugh to Knox, 1 August 1942, McHugh Papers.

45. Knox to McHugh, 28 August 1942, McHugh Papers.

46. McHugh to Captain Paul E. Pihl, 13 October 1942, McHugh Papers.

47. Chennault to Willkie, 8 October 1942, McHugh Papers.

48. McHugh to Knox, 13 October 1942, McHugh Papers.

49. McHugh to Knox and Train, Estimate of Situation in China, n.d. [October 1942], McHugh Papers.

50. McHugh, Memorandum for Mr. Cheston, 26 January 1945, McHugh Papers; Tuchman, *Stilwell*, 338–39.

51. McHugh to Currie, 2 November 1944, McHugh Papers.

52. McHugh, Memorandum for General Donovan, 16 February 1945, and R. S. Edwards to McHugh, 14 March 1945, both in McHugh Papers.

53. McHugh, Memorandum for the Publisher. Among the many books about Chiang Kai-shek and Nationalist China, Lloyd E. Eastman's, *Seeds of Destruction: Nationalist China in War and Revolution, 1937–1949* (Stanford, 1984) stands out as a model of lucid, dispassionate scholarship.

54. Undated newspaper clipping, McHugh Papers.

The Distorted Danger: Winston Churchill and the French Dreadnoughts

CALVIN W. HINES

Much controversy surrounds Winston Churchill and the bombardment of the French naval squadron at Mers-el-Kébir in July 1940. However, little attention has focused on the disposition of the two French dreadnoughts, *Richelieu* and *Jean Bart.* Dr. Hines traces the course of Churchill's alarm over these two warships and evaluates the reasons behind the wartime prime minister's decisions concerning them.

****

In the history of World War II one subject, despite its tragic dimensions, has received less attention than is deserved. This is the matter of the French navy and Great Britain's relationship to it in the summer of 1940. Out of this linkage would come one of the most controversial, if not the most difficult, of all the personal decisions Winston Churchill would make as Britain's wartime prime minister. By the time the drama of Mers-el-Kébir had ended, an enduring and acrimonious debate would begin which would not only wreck careers but also poison the public relations of the two former allies for years to come. Questions were raised at that time which have not, and may never, come to enjoy a consensus answer. Among these are whether or not the prime minister acted with wrongful impetuosity or proceeded toward his fateful decision to attack the French navy along deliberate and methodical paths; whether he exhausted all avenues and options toward securing peacefully the neutralization of the French warships before ordering the Royal Navy's surgical strike; whether either by the allowance of further time for contemplation or through a slight modification of the terms presented to the honor-bound French admirals involved, a common ground could have been found which would have avoided the ensuing bloodshed; and finally, perhaps ultimately, was the menace Churchill saw in a possible surrender of France's fleet to Germany genuine or distorted?[1]

Almost every study heretofore has argued that Churchill was of two minds concerning the French navy at the time of France's surrender in June 1940: that the composite fleet was the principal danger to be removed and that he formulated plans toward its elimination with a rashness bordering on frenzy. A closer examination validates only a portion of these contentions. Initially, Churchill viewed the entire French navy as a threat should it be delivered intact to Germany, and his own efforts as well as those of his colleagues looked to encouraging France to remove its fleet to English ports in advance of any cease-fire, so as to thwart the presumed German claim for its surrender. As it became apparent, however, that most of France's operational warships were outside of metropolitan waters, at least until the conclusion of the armistice, Churchill shifted his gaze to those units remaining which, in his opinion, would have contributed decisively to the naval balance should they become part of the German battle fleet, either through capture or capitulation. As his own priorities changed, his actions remained constant. The road to, through, and beyond "Operation Catapult" was marked not only by the exploration of every practical option consistent with Britain's self-interest but also was notable for the extended nature of such efforts.[2]

The chronology of the French debacle is well known. Between 15 and 16 June 1940, as France's last defenses crumbled before overwhelming German armor and the fugitive government of Paul Reynaud groped for any alternative to surrender, deliberate measures were being taken in the country's endangered ports to remove all shipping before the arrival of the onrushing invaders. By 17 June, the day Reynaud's administration gave way to the defeatist regime of Marshal Henri Philippe Pétain, hundreds of vessels had fled their anchorages along the English Channel, steaming either to Britain or to French North Africa. This exodus accelerated on 18 June when a cease-fire became more likely and when Admiral François Darlan, commander in chief of the French navy, decided to move his warships beyond Germany's grasp so as to retain some leverage in any peace negotiations.[3]

Churchill approached this crisis with three disturbing considerations. Could French resistance be maintained or continued overseas? What would be the status of the French colonial empire under any cease-fire? And, in a similar vein, what would become of the French fleet? As all efforts toward ensuring continued resistance either on the European continent or in North Africa faded in the face of Reynaud's despair and Pétain's defeatism, attention turned to the parallel objectives of either retaining or somehow neutralizing France's overseas possessions and navy. Although in many respects these were related goals, the greatest concern revolved around the latter. The addition of all, or a significant part, of France's battle line to Hitler's Kriegsmarine could become the instrument by which Britain's dominance of the North Atlantic, superiority in the Mediterranean, and control of the Channel might be imperiled or permanently removed.[4]

Confronting the prospect of a sudden tilt in the naval balance, Churchill could not view with disinterest the circumstances and conditions of France's capitulation. In the last hours of the Reynaud government a succession of British representatives crossed the Channel in an attempt to achieve a wholesale transfer of the French navy to British-controlled ports. In the first moments of the Pétain regime an inaccurate assumption was made that such was about to occur. Churchill's stipulation that France remove its fleet to England before it would be released from its obligations under the Anglo-French alliance seemed to have been accepted. Indeed, in his last meeting with Marshal Pétain and Admiral Darlan, the latter had promised that his warships never would be surrendered. Yet this pledge was merely a reiteration of earlier assurances and not an acknowledgment that any agreement assumed to have been reached with the outgoing government either existed or had been transferred, or that a new understanding was in place. By that time, however, lesser French warships had arrived in English ports, among them the elderly battleships *Paris* and *Courbet*. Although Churchill obviously read more into the statements from the new French leaders than existed, he evidently took encouragement at the outset from news of the arrival of those elements of the French Channel Squadron and reports that a general sortie had begun from Brest and Bordeaux.[5]

It was the presence in Brest of the French navy's largest dreadnought, the *Richelieu*, that captivated Churchill's interest almost from the moment a surrender seemed imminent. The *Richelieu* displaced 35,000 tons and mounted a main battery of eight 15-inch guns. The warship recently had completed sea trials and lacked only some secondary armament to be considered fully operational. Its sister ship, the *Jean Bart*, rode at anchor at Saint-Nazaire, its status less threatening owing to the placement of only one 15-inch turret and the absence of considerable internal machinery. Of the two, only the *Richelieu* seemed capable of escape, as it did on the afternoon of 18 June.[6]

While the news of the *Richelieu*'s sortie caused great relief in London, it was the misplaced expectation of its impending arrival in a British port that contributed to Churchill's earliest thoughts on the possible use of force to deny Germany any chance of ever securing any French warship, this one in particular. How much he had counted on the *Richelieu* steaming to England can be measured through the multitude of signals to British patrols in the Channel, advising them to stand ready to escort the dreadnought into port. Similar orders were flashed to the British squadron standing off Saint-Nazaire, where a frantic effort was under way to dredge a channel through which the *Jean Bart* might sail. When, in the early hours of 19 June, it was learned that the *Richelieu* had altered course to the south following its escape, subsequent reports announced that it had broken contact and vanished. Anxiety mounted when word came from Saint-Nazaire that the *Jean Bart*, following its miraculous escape that same day, also was steaming south. A collection of supplementary alarms now arrived reporting the disappearance of France's lone aircraft carrier, the *Béarn*, and one of the fastest cruisers in the world, the *Emile Bertin*.[7]

It was in the midst of this fog that the terms of the Franco-German armistice were revealed. From the beginning of the French collapse Churchill had warned of a disastrous protocol. Now, in the draft of Article VIII, his worst fears appeared to be confirmed: the scattered and demoralized French navy would be returned to home ports for "demilitarization" under Axis supervision.[8]

Since Churchill always had dismissed any German disclaimers toward France's navy, he now ordered plans formulated to exorcise this threat by whatever means were required. Over the next four days his mood remained dark. As the intelligence picture clarified, however, he grew less irritable. Even his belligerency diminished as he saw some hope that the French warships might remain beyond Hitler's grasp and that some outposts of empire might declare resistance.[9]

When Churchill learned on 21 June that the *Richelieu* had passed Casablanca bound for Dakar, he began to speak soberly of the consequences of the

Richelieu being seized or surrendered, becoming hostile, or, in his worst-case scenario, being joined to a German navy that counted the *Bismarck* in the equation. He therefore decided that the neutralization of the *Richelieu* took precedence over all other French warships. The first step toward that end, however, would be diplomacy. Accordingly, Admiral G. H. D. Lyon, commander in chief of the South Atlantic Station, was ordered to depart Freetown, Sierra Leone, for Dakar to try and negotiate that port's continuance in the war and to encourage his French counterparts to do likewise. Concurrently Churchill announced that other remedies should be prepared as contingencies. These would include plans for mining Dakar's harbor, attacking the dreadnought with torpedo aircraft, or, in what would have been an unequal encounter unless some major British warships could be employed, immobilizing the *Richelieu* by means of naval shellfire.[10]

These plans were well under way when Churchill learned that the *Jean Bart* had managed to reach Casablanca. Shortly thereafter, signals were received from the American and West Indian Stations that both the *Béarn* and the *Emile Bertin*, which had been scheduled originally to return to France following the completion of their respective missions to Canada, were observed en route to Martinique. This information forced Churchill to speculate on which of the remaining French warships could or would attempt to comply with the pending armistice, which by process of elimination reduced the list to "Force X" in Alexandria, the "Force de Rade" at Oran, those French units already anchored in British home waters, and the *Richelieu*.

The prime minister was confident that the French warships in home ports could be secured. He seemed not to appreciate at that time that Force X was in a similar position, that is, confined to a British port and unable to maneuver without permission. Consequently, he retained it among the unreliables. To this he added the Force de Rade, which consisted of two modern battle cruisers, the *Strasbourg* and the *Dunkerque*, with the *Jean Bart*, which scarcely qualified owing to its incomplete state, and the *Richelieu*. These, he thought, constituted the clear and present danger should they obey the stipulations of Article VIII and return to French metropolitan ports.[11]

In his sorting of the dangers, Churchill's obvious choice of the highest risk should have rested on the more numerous and collectively more powerful Force de Rade, yet he placed the initial priority on the *Richelieu*. Part of his decision evidently hinged on what to him was the frightening prospect of the *Richelieu* and the *Bismarck* operating jointly in the near future. Another element in his thinking emerged out of the *Richelieu*'s isolated and exposed situation as it made its way down the West Africa coast toward Dakar. Finally, should the dreadnought become belligerent, it alone, he reasoned, could menace all shipping lanes in the South Atlantic from the roadstead at Dakar. With the exception of the *Emile Bertin*, he saw no other reflagged French warship capable of inflicting damage to Britain's merchant marine in that section of the Atlantic.[12]

Yet the *Richelieu*, though holding a higher priority at that moment than either Force X or the Force de Rade, did not exist in a vacuum. Churchill regarded all of these units, excepting the antiquated *Béarn*, as uncertain. This outlook translated into common action along several routes, all leading toward a single goal—the effective denial of France's major warships to Germany. One such path lay through on-site diplomacy conducted by either Royal Navy officers or diplomats residing at certain ports in which French warships were located. Thus, in the forty-eight hours following the delivery of the German terms at Compiègne, British officers, diplomats, and colonial agents waited upon their former comrades in Martinique, Casablanca, Oran, Alexandria, Dakar, and Saigon, encouraging them to rally their colonies and their warships to resistance. Most French officials initially expressed defiance of the cease-fire, reports of which created undue optimism in London. Soon it appeared that these were only understandable and temporary human reactions to the humiliation of defeat. A closer study of the various statements arriving from the scattered French colonies, especially those coming from the French admirals commanding in Alexandria and Oran, suggested that they merely had vowed to prevent the outright surrender of their respective flotillas. They had not categorically refused to obey a recall order from the new Pétain government. By 23 June the early proclamations of belligerence were dissolving into fatalistic acquiescence.[13]

While allowing these efforts to proceed and perhaps anticipating their eventual failure, Churchill's doubts about French compliance with his misconstrued understanding concerning their warships merged with his mounting suspicion that they could ever honor their pledge to scuttle their fleet rather than permit Germany's seizure of it. The diversion of the *Richelieu* and the *Jean Bart* to Africa certainly influenced the prime minister's planning. He likewise noticed the Italian navy lurking ominously near the vital Mediterranean supply lines, and he frequently was reminded of the increased and multiplying obligations on his own warships as a result of the French defection. It is this last consideration that helps explain Churchill's preference for—and the diplomatic activity toward—securing as much of the French fleet as possible for continued service alongside the Royal Navy. Lacking any specific signals of German intentions beyond the cryptic klaxon sounded in Article VIII of the armistice, Churchill acted on the direst assumptions. The options outlined in the event diplomacy failed reveal this all too clearly: internment of French warships in British, American, or French West Indian ports; on-site demobilization and demilitarization incapable of being corrected in those ports in which the ships were berthed; interception en route of any French vessel which attempted to comply with the armistice; attacks on any French warships found in home ports on the effective date of the armistice; or confrontations with the various French units where they lay outside of France and compelling them to scuttle and sink their ships if they refused to do so.[14]

Between 23 and 30 June, extensive discussions on these choices took place in the British War Cabinet. It was during these conversations that Churchill's fixation on the *Richelieu* and the *Jean Bart* was most apparent. Although the latter could manage only half-speed and lacked most of its firepower, its presence in Casablanca warranted regular surveillance lest it attempt to return to France. Considering that up to that point in the war Britain had lost the battleship *Royal Oak*, the aircraft carriers *Glorious* and *Courageous*, and dozens of supporting vessels in the Norwegian and Dunkirk operations, the thought of Germany's gaining the *Jean Bart*, completing its fitting out, and introducing it into the conflict was disturbing. Allowing that the *Richelieu* was virtually battle-ready all but made it an obsession. Churchill voiced strong arguments that these ships be eliminated first, a stance opposed by a majority of his ministers. They countered that the Force de Rade, based on its proximity to French metropolitan ports, its combined strength, and its firepower warranted higher concern. Their most telling point—that the sparseness of British naval forces in the Mediterranean would not allow for an indefinite surveillance of either of the two French squadrons situated there—dovetailed with the Mediterranean Fleet commander's own assessments. Admiral Andrew B. Cunningham's situation, as he put it, was "precarious." He could not, he said, fulfill five roles simultaneously: watching Force X, guarding the sea-lanes, supporting British operations in Egypt, waiting for the Italian navy to sortie, and observing the Force de Rade.[15]

These revelations took the edge off of Churchill's position. He conceded the immediacy of danger in the Force de Rade and likewise admitted the burdens placed on Cunningham. Dealing with the French squadron would require the creation of a special task group, "Force H," to avoid additional weight on Cunningham's command. This would require a temporary drain on both the Home Fleet and the North Atlantic Station but would release Cunningham to deal with Force X alone. The *Richelieu*, however, remained in the right corner of Churchill's eye. As orders were cut creating Force H and outlining Operation Catapult, the dreadnought's place on the target list dropped behind the Force de Rade. Once that matter was resolved, Churchill intended for Force H to steam en masse to Dakar to deal with the *Richelieu* as well.[16]

Concurrent with these deliberations several different negotiations were taking place in Dakar. On 24 June Captain Richard Onslow, commanding the aircraft carrier *Hermes*, received instructions from Admiral Lyon to open talks with port authorities pending the latter's arrival from Freetown. It quickly became apparent that neither Onslow nor the resident British diplomats enjoyed much chance of winning any of their opposite numbers to resistance. With the *Richelieu* expected to reach Dakar by 25 June, Churchill authorized Onslow to make a direct appeal to the *Richelieu*'s commander, Captain René Marzin, on the latter's arrival in port. The motive for this démarche, which was attempted unsuccessfully elsewhere, was a curious interpretation of the terms of the Franco-German armistice. Though lacking any real foundation, the War Cabinet had concluded that any French vessel (including merchant shipping) not actually anchored in a French port, be it metropolitan or colonial, on 25 June 1940, the official date of the cease-fire, would be free from its diktat. Onslow therefore was empowered to offer to escort the *Richelieu* to Freetown, thus keeping it at sea on 25 June and thereby releasing Marzin from his obligation to honor the terms of the armistice.[17]

On the *Richelieu*'s arrival Captain Onslow presented this project to Captain Marzin, who refused. Then, shortly before Admiral Lyon arrived in his flagship, the *Albatross*, the *Richelieu* raised steam and dashed out to sea. Lyon's initial reaction, as reported to London, suggested that the *Richelieu* intended to make for Casablanca. Considering that Marzin may have acted independently, perhaps intending to be at sea when the armistice became official, Lyon hastily attempted to achieve what Onslow and others could not: to rally Dakar or else encourage a similar escape by other French warships lying there. None of these efforts succeeded, however. On the morning of 26 June Lyon learned that the *Richelieu*, having evaded detection by the *Hermes* and the *Dorsetshire*, which had shadowed it since it passed Gibraltar, had been observed steaming north. Then, just as abruptly, he heard that the *Richelieu* had turned about and was returning toward Dakar. Lyon's last resort, a second appeal to Marzin, was frustrated when he was ordered by the harbor commander to leave port. Exchange visits were prohibited, and he was forbidden even to communicate with the *Richelieu* as it returned.[18]

It appears now that the twenty-four hours following the *Richelieu*'s hasty exit from Dakar were as anxious for Admiral Darlan as they were for Churchill. Each man, however, drew an opposite conclusion as to the cause of the *Richelieu*'s departure, as well as to its probable destination. Churchill accepted the Admiralty's assessment that the *Richelieu* would try to join the *Jean Bart* at Casablanca, though to what purpose none could say. Darlan, on the other hand, evidently suspected that Marzin intended to put into Gibraltar. Thus, each individual took simultaneous though dissimilar steps to thwart the expected move.[19]

In this naval chess game the British moved first. A blocking force comprising the *Hood* and the *Ark Royal* was positioned near the Canary Islands. Concurrently, the *Dorsetshire* and the *Hermes* were readied for action once contact was regained with the *Richelieu*. The wording of the orders to these units suggests that the risk of a clash was implied, understood, and anticipated. Once contact was made, they read, the *Richelieu* was to be shadowed, conducted to a British port, or captured "by force if absolutely necessary." The *Richelieu*'s sortie had caused such alarm that Churchill and his associates, some of whom had earlier opposed his installation of the dreadnought as a menace greater than any other, were prepared to compromise any surprise value Operation Catapult may have possessed. Indeed, they appear to have accepted the possibility of endangering the entire operation and jeopardizing Britain's fragile position in the Mediterranean, rather than to allow the *Richelieu* to reach another port. As a footnote, however, they left the option of allowing the *Richelieu* to return to Dakar. But a stop line to any further movement northward had been drawn and units disposed to enforce it.[20]

The failure of the *Dorsetshire* to locate the *Richelieu* at midnight on the night of 25–26 June made a bloody engagement more likely. Unknown in London, however, were Admiral Darlan's orders to Captain Marzin to return to Dakar. That morning, almost as the *Richelieu* turned about in compliance, one of the *Dorsetshire*'s scout planes spotted it and reported the reversal in course. After working up to full speed the *Dorsetshire* raised its quarry in the mid-afternoon of 26 June.[21]

Strenuous efforts now began either to delay or deter the *Richelieu*'s return to Dakar. At first Captain Marzin was asked to heave to and receive a personal message from the *Ark Royal*'s commander, Captain C. S. Holland, inviting him to join Britain against "the common enemy." When this was refused a request was then flashed asking him to assist in searching for the *Dorsetshire*'s scout plane which had force-landed shortly after radioing the *Richelieu*'s position. Legitimate as these efforts may have been, both were rejected. News of this abortive ploy presented Churchill with two options: allow the *Richelieu* to return to Dakar, or apply force to prevent it. The imbalance of firepower between the two warships made a compelling argument for restraint, despite the fact that the *Hood* and the *Ark Royal* were rushing south and the *Hermes* was closing. With some reluctance Churchill rescinded the earlier orders and allowed the *Dorsetshire* merely to continue a surveillance as the *Richelieu* steamed south. Later that afternoon, following repeated requests from the *Dorsetshire*'s captain, Churchill released the cruiser from this assignment so that it might search for its as yet unlocated scout plane.[22]

Almost as quickly as it had peaked, the crisis abated. The *Hermes* was permitted to join the *Dorsetshire* in searching for the downed pilot while the Canary Islands blocking force turned about toward Gibraltar, destined to become part of Force H. Just as Churchill grudgingly had reconciled himself to allowing the *Richelieu*'s second escape to succeed, the dreadnought suddenly altered course again to the north. Suspecting that this maneuver had been timed to catch their forces unaware, the War Cabinet instantly ordered the *Hood* and the *Ark Royal* to return to their previous station while directing the *Dorsetshire* and the *Hermes* to close on the *Richelieu*. Whether or not a battle would have resulted is still uncertain. The French admiral commanding at Dakar must have thought so, because he quickly sought out Admiral Lyon and explained that the *Richelieu* had been diverted at the last minute to escort a convoy of merchant ships bound for that port. The next day the *Dorsetshire* resumed surveillance of the *Richelieu* and reported that, as predicted, the dreadnought was screening a small group of merchantmen steaming toward Dakar. On the evening of 28 June, after three tension-filled days, the *Richelieu* dropped anchor in the outer roads of Dakar, its captain oblivious to the fact that his recent actions, whether sanctioned or not, had guaranteed that his ship would remain a high-priority target once the Mediterranean phase of Operation Catapult was concluded.[23]

The historiography of the tragedy of Mers-el-Kébir finds a common thread in the speculation that the bombardment of 3 July 1940 could have been avoided had any one of several actions been taken. Most cite as evidence the timely and somewhat unorthodox measures employed by Admiral Cunningham in his peaceful and successful neutralization of Force X in Alexandria. On balance, however, one must admit that both the conditions and circumstances were as different in Oran and Alexandria that fateful day as were the two respective British commanders, who were given what both later considered the most unpleasant tasks of their careers. What is ignored, however, is that Churchill's decision to dispose of the *Richelieu* following the battle of Mers-el-Kébir all but guaranteed that the only option available to its conclusion was the use of force. Although Force H was to have been the instrument for the *Richelieu*'s scourging, Churchill suddenly perceived a higher degree of danger from the Italian navy than previously assigned. Rather than weaken the British Mediterranean flotilla to dispose of the *Richelieu*, as detaching the *Hood*, the *Resolution*, the *Renown*, and the *Ark Royal* would have done, it was decided that a smaller unit consisting of the cruisers *Dorsetshire* and *Australia*, the aircraft carrier *Hermes*, and the sloop *Milford* would complete the task.[24]

An ultimatum was drafted for delivery to Captain Marzin that varied only slightly from those presented to the French admirals commanding Force X and the Force de Rade. On 7 July this ultimatum was flashed to the *Richelieu*, but Marzin gave no reply. Taking this silence as rejection, Captain Onslow ordered two distinctly different attacks against the *Richelieu*. The first, a commando-style raid designed to wreck its propellers with depth charges, had little if any success. The second, an equally hazardous aerial torpedo attack, produced better results and damaged the *Richelieu* sufficiently to prevent its making a sortie until February 1943, when the dreadnought and its consorts rallied to the resistance following the American invasion of French North Africa.[25]

The *Richelieu*'s later role in World War II is episodic at best. Following the immobilizing attacks on 8 July 1940, it became a target a second time in the following September during the abortive Anglo-Free French assault on Dakar, code-named "Operation Menace." Afterward the *Richelieu* languished under a tropical sun until it steamed to New York in the spring of 1943 for extensive repair and refitting. It concluded its wartime service in the Far East as part of Britain's Pacific Fleet, plying those same waters where two of its earliest adversaries, the *Dorsetshire* and the *Hermes*, had been sunk by the Japanese in 1942.[26]

The question remains whether there actually existed an imminent threat of the transfer of the *Richelieu* and other elements of the French navy to Germany in the summer of 1940 or, for that matter, at any other time. That the transfer would never take place seems to be substantiated with the mass suicide of the Toulon squadron in November 1942, as Admiral Darlan had promised. Within a year the long-dormant Force X would join the *Richelieu* in advancing the day of victory. So too, in time, would the last holdouts in Martinique. If one places a premium on hindsight, the events of 1942–43 dilute the imagined danger seen in the summer of 1940. The fact remains, however, that a danger was seen and, as is so often the case, what was believed quickly eclipsed other, more rational, impressions. In the minds of the British leaders menace existed, though less with the intractable personalities of the French admirals than in the size and location of their squadrons, combined with the precarious nature of British strength in the Mediterranean at a time when German power seemed omnipotent and Italian ambitions capable of fulfillment. There, in those two separate French flotillas, is where the first and correct priority came to rest, though not without a strenuous opposition from the prime minister. Churchill never lost sight of the *Richelieu*. Even had the Force de Rade been neutralized in a fashion similar to that afforded Force X, the *Richelieu* would have retained the high profile Churchill had awarded it.

A peaceful resolution at Oran might have been duplicated at Dakar, but the evidence shows that Churchill, on two occasions previous to 3 July 1940, was prepared to pull the trigger against the *Richelieu* even at the expense of Operation Catapult's chances in the Mediterranean. It may be that the dreadnought became his earliest symbol of perfidious France, or that the South Atlantic was so open and vulnerable to another battering such as the *Graf Spee* had administered, or that the balance of power was far too delicate to hazard the *Richelieu*'s fate in the hands of an unscrupulous enemy that caused Churchill to evaluate the *Richelieu* to a plateau of concern that was, owing to its peculiar circumstance, undeserved. Its range, while impressive, was not without limits. Lacking facilities for refueling outside of Dakar, had it quit that port its only resource in the absence of a supply ship would have been to steam to the French West Indies. Such a voyage undoubtedly would have caused the United States to assume the role of watchdog and may have drawn down on Martinique the storm that was only barely avoided over the presence of the *Béarn* and the *Emile Bertin* adjacent to the outer approaches of a vital American domain. Had the *Richelieu* become a commerce raider, as Churchill imagined it might, its base at Dakar would have been as vulnerable as it was convenient. Even this, however, could have been accomplished only through the complete replacement of the dreadnought's original crew with willing collaborators or, in the wildest fantasy, German sailors. As the suicide of the Toulon squadron illustrates, not even the bloodshed at Oran two years earlier outraged France's sailors to the point where they would sanction, much less cooperate in perpetuating, the enslavement of their nation.[27]

At a distance now of almost fifty years it is astonishing that, if a priority on danger was required, any British official could advocate placing any other French warships, with the obvious exceptions, above the *Richelieu*. Yet for over a week the prime minister maintained exactly this stance. Even after surrendering to logic Churchill returned to the earlier argument when it appeared that the *Richelieu* might be the first warship to comply with the armistice. That he was able to carry along the majority of his cabinet in reversing the priorities suggests that they were never that far from accepting his initial estimates of the peril which that warship presented. In the final analysis the known capabilities and unknown intentions of the *Richelieu* counted more than detached and dispassionate evaluations. Nor can one ignore the possibility that Churchill saw symbolic value in the eradication of all of France's battle line. If so, then the *Richelieu*, despite all the countervailing points disproving its presumed danger, may have become part of a hand that was being played out. From our vantage point the threat of the French dreadnoughts appears to have been exaggerated, if not manufactured. Yet such was the environment and the temperament of the individual that any danger, however distorted, demanded not only attention but action. As a student of British history, Churchill often quoted Horatio Nelson, frequently citing his role in fending off Napoleon's threatened invasion in another war. Although it was a point of critics to compare Mers-el-Kébir to Copenhagen, it also would be argued that the latter may have guaranteed no less than did Aboukir Bay or Trafalgar that there would be a British history of the Napoleonic Wars. Knowing this, Churchill hardly could have expected to act otherwise in confronting the French navy in 1940. Failure to do so might not only ensure that the principal history of World War II would be written in German but also that few other than Germans would read it.[28]

NOTES

1. Among the studies which range across this subject the reader should consider Admiral Paul Auphan and Jacques Mordal, *The French Navy in World War II* (Annapolis, 1959); Arthur J. Marder, *From the Dardanelles to Oran: Studies of the Royal Navy in War and Peace*

(London, 1974); Albert Vulliez, *Mers-el-Kébir* (Paris, 1975); Albert Kammerer's *La passion de la flotte française* (Paris, 1951) and his *La tragédie de Mers-el-Kébir: L'Angleterre et la flotte française* (Paris, 1945); Warren Tute, *The Deadly Stroke* (New York, 1973); and Stephen W. Roskill, *The War at Sea: 1939–1945* (London, 1954).

2. The most recent scholarship on this subject is Martin Gilbert's *Winston S. Churchill: Finest Hour: 1939–1941* (Boston, 1983), 589, 627–34.

3. Winston S. Churchill, *The Second World War: Their Finest Hour* (Boston, 1949), 100–223 passim, 229–31; William L. Shirer, *The Collapse of the Third Republic: An Inquiry into the Fall of France in 1940* (New York, 1969), 807–900 passim; Eleanor M. Gates, *End of the Affair: The Collapse of the Anglo-French Alliance, 1939–1940* (Berkeley, 1981), 222; Geoffrey Warner, *Pierre Laval and the Eclipse of France: 1931–1945* (New York, 1968), 169–76.

4. London, Public Record Office (hereafter PRO), Cabinet Papers, CAB 65/13, WM (40) 168th Conclusions, Confidential Annex; PRO, CAB 65/7, WM (40) 173d Conclusions; Churchill, *Their Finest Hour*, 200–31 passim. See also Sir Ernest Llewelleyn Woodward, *British Foreign Policy in the Second World War* (London, 1970), 1:289–311 passim; Roger Parkinson, *Blood, Toil, Tears and Sweat: The War History from Dunkirk to Alamein, Based on the War Cabinet Papers of 1940 to 1942* (London, 1973), 21–53 passim; and P. M. H. Bell, *A Certain Eventuality: Britain and the Fall of France* (London, 1974), 71–76, 81–95 passim.

5. PRO, Chiefs of Staffs Papers (1940), "Plans to Meet a Certain Eventuality," CAB 80/16; Churchill, *Their Finest Hour*, 231–33; Parkinson, *Blood, Toil, Tears and Sweat*, 54–55; Sir Edward Spears, *Assignment to Catastrophe: The Fall of France: June, 1940* (London, 1954), 282–83; Adolphe Lepotier, *Les derniers cuirassés* (Paris, 1967), 45–50; Georges Blond, *L'épopée silencieuse: Service à la mer: 1939–1940* (Paris, 1942), 181–95.

6. Auphan and Mordal, *French Navy in World War II*, 106–21 passim; Lepotier, *Les derniers cuirassés*, 48–50; Gilbert, *Winston S. Churchill*, 589.

7. PRO, CAB 65/13, WM (40) 176th Conclusions, Confidential Annex; PRO, Admiralty Papers, ADM 199/821, "Out" Signals; PRO, ADM 199/826, "In" Signals; "Selection of Signals, Etc., Relating to the Disposal of the French Fleet, 1940," Andrew B. Cunningham Papers, British Library, London (hereafter Cunningham Papers).

8. Gilbert, *Winston S. Churchill*, 589; Churchill, *Their Finest Hour*, 233–36; PRO, CAB 65/13, WM (40) 180th Conclusions, Confidential Annex.

9. Ibid.; Note by A. V. Alexander, 20 June 1940, Alexander Papers, Roskill Library, Churchill College, Cambridge.

10. PRO, "Out" Messages (20–24 June 1940) and "Situation at Dakar on Collapse of France," ADM 1/11165; Note by A. V. Alexander, 22 June 1940; PRO, CAB 65/12, WM (40) 176th Conclusions, Confidential Annex.

11. PRO, "In" Signals from Flag Officer Commanding, North Atlantic (Gibraltar), ADM 1/11165; PRO, "Collapse of France—Situation in the West Indies," ADM 199/367; PRO, "Situation at Dakar"; PRO, CAB 65/12, WM (40) 176th, 178th Conclusions, Confidential Annex.

12. PRO, CAB 65/13, WM (40) 176th, 179th Conclusions, Confidential Annex.

13. Andrew B. Cunningham, *A Sailor's Odyssey* (New York, 1951), 239–45; PRO, "Collapse of France—Situation in the West Indies"; PRO, "Situation at Dakar"; Jacques Mordal, *La bataille de Dakar* (Paris, 1956), 39–41; René Godfroy, *L'aventure de la force 'X' à Alexandrie: 1940–1943* (Paris, 1950), 47–48; Daniel Chenet, *Qui a Sauvé l'Afrique* (Paris, 1949), 77.

14. "Signals File," Cunningham Papers; Cunningham, *A Sailor's Odyssey*, 241; PRO, CAB 65/13, WM (40) 177th Conclusions, Confidential Annex.

15. "Signals File," Cunningham Papers; Andrew B. Cunningham to Admiral Sir Howard Kelly, 16 July 1942, Kelly Papers, National Maritime Museum, Greenwich; PRO, CAB 65/13, WM (40) 178th, 179th, 189th Conclusions, Confidential Annex.

16. Ibid.

17. Ibid.; PRO, "Situation at Dakar"; Lepotier, *Les derniers cuirassés*, 51–54; Kammerer, *La tragédie de Mers-el-Kébir*, 90–100.

18. Lepotier, *Les derniers cuirassés*, 53–54; PRO, "Situation at Dakar." Lyon inserted a scathing indictment of the British consul in Dakar, accusing him of dereliction of duty. Lyon emphasized that on Sunday and Monday, 17 and 18 June—two days he considered vital in any negotiation—the consul was absent from his post on a fishing trip. For an alternate view see PRO, Victor Cusden to the Secretary of State for Foreign Affairs, 22 July 1940, "Summary of Events Leading to the Expulsion of His Majesty's Representative in Dakar" 199–824 (Copy of

FO K9876/9432/217). See also Kammerer, *La passion de la flotte française*, 243-44, for an account of the erosion of the spirit of resistance in Dakar; and Vice-Admiral Jules Docteur's *La verité sur les amiraux* (Paris, 1949), 103, for a denial of the argument that a strong British force in Dakar on 23 June would have rallied that port.

19. PRO, CAB 65/13, WM (40) 178th, 179th, 180th Conclusions, Confidential Annex. See also Lepotier, *Les derniers cuirassés*, 56-58; Mordal, *La bataille de Dakar*, 43-45; and PRO, "Situation at Dakar," for the French version of this incident and for the contemporary information and rumors on which the Admiralty based their speculations.

20. PRO, "Out" Messages to HMS *Hood* and HMS *Ark Royal* (25 June 1940), ADM 1/11165; PRO, Log of HMS *Hood*, ADM 112449; PRO, Log of HMS *Ark Royal*, ADM 11435; Log of HMS *Hermes*, ADM 112435; PRO, Log of HMS *Dorsetshire*, ADM 112037.

21. Lepotier, *Les derniers cuirassés*, 55, for the Darlan signal; PRO, "Situation at Dakar," Enclosure 1—"Operations with French Battleship Richelieu, June 25-28, 1940."

22. Ibid.; Lepotier, *Les derniers cuirassés*, 57-59; PRO, Log of HMS *Dorsetshire*, 26 June 1940.

23. Adolphe Lepotier, *La bataille de l'Or* (Paris, 1957), 189-92, 210-11; Lepotier, *Les derniers cuirassés*, 61-62; PRO, "Situation at Dakar"—"Operations with French Battleship Richelieu."

24. See Stephen W. Roskill, *Churchill and the Admirals* (New York, 1978), 158, for an assessment of the attitudes of the British commanders involved in implementing Operation Catapult. See also PRO, CAB 65/13, WM (40) 188th Conclusions, Confidential Annex; PRO, "Report of Proceedings of Force H for the Attack on the 'Force de Rade,'" PREM 3/159/4 CIC MED SIGNALS/Admiralty Signals, 3 July 1940.

25. PRO, CAB 65/14, WM (40) 196th Conclusions, Confidential Annex; PRO, "Ultimatum to French Naval Authorities in Dakar," Appendix 3 to "Report of Rear Admiral Commanding," ADM 199/826. This document reveals that the French officers in Dakar were not invited to join their ships with those of the Royal Navy or to sail to the United States for internment. All other terms duplicated those given to the French admiral commanding the Force de Rade in Oran. For the particulars on the attacks on the *Richelieu* see ibid., "Report of Attack against Richelieu," Appendix 4 to "Report of Rear Admiral Commanding" and also in the same "Report of Vice-Admiral G. H. D. Lyon on Attack on French Battleship Richelieu," 27 July 1940. For French accounts see Mordal, *La bataille de Dakar*, 56-58, and Lepotier, *Les derniers cuirassés*, 71-74. For information on the damage inflicted and its source see "Report of the Glassford Mission," 17 January 1943, Combined Chiefs of Staff 358, Appendix A, National Archives, Washington, DC.

26. Auphan and Mordal, *French Navy in World War II*, 378.

27. Author's interview with Admiral John H. Hoover, 19 February 1968.

28. Gilbert, *Winston S. Churchill*, 778, 1151.

RCN-USN, 1939-45: Some Reflections on the Origins of a New Alliance

MARC MILNER

Few historians give the Royal Canadian Navy of 1939-45 more than a passing nod, while those who mention its enormous contribution do so in a British Commonwealth setting. Much of its actions in the early years of the war, however, was influenced by and in turn influenced the interests and operations of the U.S. Navy. Professor Milner explores some of the highlights of the unexplored Canadian-American naval partnership during the desperate days of World War II.

****

In March 1943 the commanding officer of the Canadian corvette *Trillium*, Lieutenant Paul Evans, RCNVR, an American and former U.S. Coast Guardsman, submitted an article for publication in an American journal. It argued that the campaign in the Atlantic to that date should properly be called the "Battle of Canada," the title chosen for his article. As Evans explained, early 1943 marked the end of a chapter for the Royal Canadian Navy (RCN) — perhaps the most important period in Canadian naval history. In a somewhat flowery and melodramatic style, Evans wrote:

> Soon—but oh, make haste!—the vast resources of the United States will be hurled into the North Atlantic to turn the tide.... But until that happy day—and long after...remember the Canadian corvettes—those far flung, storm tossed little ships on which the German Fuhrer has never looked and yet which have, since 1940, stood between him and the conquest of the world.[1]

What Evans and his Canadian colleagues sensed in early 1943 was the fulfillment of American potential and the key role played by the RCN in allowing that to happen. In 1943 alone, more destroyer escorts were completed in American yards than there were warships in the entire Canadian navy by 1945. In time the RCN too went to bigger and better vessels: to cruisers and aircraft carriers. Never again would Canada's contribution to the margin of victory and defeat be as important as it was before 1943. And although the RCN's wartime effort has been perceived as supportive of the Royal Navy, it was actually in aid of the U.S. Navy that the early Canadian effort was most crucial.

Evans was concerned with quantity and quality of ships, but the softening of American entry into the war went well beyond filling gaps in escort groups. Undoubtedly, the most important early contacts between the RCN and the U.S. Navy concerned Naval Control of Shipping (NCS) and naval intelligence.

From 1939 to 1942 both of these duties fell to a single officer at Naval Service Headquarters (NSHQ) in Ottawa, Captain Eric S. Brand, RN, director of Naval Intelligence and Trade (a post invariably held by a British officer on loan). From August 1939 onward Brand's office was a major clearinghouse for North American and world shipping intelligence. Ottawa was, in fact, the North American regional center of the Commonwealth's global NCS and intelligence network. It was linked directly with other regional centers (such as Jamaica, Cape Town, and Singapore) and with the master world plots at the Admiralty in London. Information on shipping movements was passed to and fro within this network through a regular system of signals known as VESCA.[2]

Ottawa's jurisdiction extended as well to ports along the Pacific and Atlantic coasts of the continental United States. By 1939, the NSHQ's contacts with British consulates on those coasts already were long established, having been the source of intelligence on U.S. Navy and Axis merchant ship movements throughout the interwar years. When war broke out each consulate was accredited a consular shipping agent, actually a retired Royal Navy officer who kept his uniform in the closet and his eyes on the waterfront. His duty was to regulate the movement of Commonwealth registered and leased shipping and to report on Axis vessels as well. Brand's network therefore extended to twenty major U.S. ports. The consular shipping agents passed and received their information through diplomatic pouches or by writing directly to Mr. Ernest Lamb, Brand's alias, at the Canadian National Steamship Company in Ottawa. Not all the correspondence passed quickly or easily across the border, and on at least a couple of occasions coded letters to Mr. Lamb were intercepted and detained by zealous Canadian postal employees.[3]

The RCN was instrumental from the outset in the organization and dispatch of convoys, and much of the work of the consular shipping agents was directed at getting ships to Halifax or Sydney, Nova Scotia, in order to meet convoy sailings. Perhaps not surprisingly, then, the American navy took an immediate interest in Ottawa's trade efforts. The first U.S. naval attaché accredited to Canada in the summer of 1940 paid particular attention to Brand's operations. Closer contacts developed in early 1941, just after the announcement of Lend-Lease. A Canadian naval trade liaison officer was sent to Washington in the spring, and in June a U.S. Navy observer was appointed to Halifax to oversee trade matters. Later in the summer the observer at Halifax took charge of the pool of U.S. flag shipping maintained at that port to provide a token U.S. presence in "American" convoys to Iceland.[4]

It was in the role as middleman between the British and the American navies that the RCN played its most important part in the quiet bureaucratic war before 1943. In the last year of Washington's neutrality the consular shipping agents throughout the United States began to work even closer with American naval authorities. Direct liaison between the agents and the newly appointed U.S. Navy port directors began in early 1941 and included the provision of confidential books and special publications on trade matters by the Naval Distributing Authority of the NSHQ.[5] Canadian annual reports, at least, maintain that the tasks of NCS were passed on to the U.S. Navy through this means. After Pearl Harbor the network continued to operate as the consular shipping agents donned their uniforms, changed their title to British routing liaison officers (BRLO), and kept up their trying duties of supervising use of American ports by Commonwealth shipping. This task was greatly facilitated by the overwhelming acceptance of the agents by their American naval counterparts, to the point of finding the new BRLOs office space as close as possible to the port directors.[6]

While much of the groundwork linking the Americans to the Commonwealth's NCS system was laid in 1941, the precipitous U.S. entry into the war on 7 December cast an enormous burden on the NSHQ. Over the next seven months, as the American navy made the transition to full wartime status, Ottawa's trade sections served as the direct link between Washington and the Admiralty's global NCS system. Until July 1942 all trade intelligence, including daily VESCA summaries from London and from concerned regional centers, passed through Ottawa. It fell to Brand's staff to sift through this mass of data and provide Washington with a summary of pertinent information. Known as the CHATFOLD system, this link was dropped when direct contact between Washington and the rest of the Commonwealth's NCS system was in place.[7]

The efficiency of the Canadian navy's NCS and intelligence operation also allowed the NSHQ to take over all diversions of merchant shipping in the western Atlantic north of the equator from December 1941 until July 1942. This experience, and that in providing the U.S. Navy trade summaries, stood the Canadian navy in good stead in 1943 when it made a case for a separate Canadian theater in the northwest Atlantic. At that time the RCN made up the bulk of escorts operating in the area, but they were weak and ill trained. It was the undisputed efficacy of the Canadian navy's NCS and intelligence establishments that decided the issue.[8]

Canadians took great pride during the war in the work they did to educate the U.S. Navy in NCS. Thanks largely to the efforts of Captain Brand and his bright young reservists, Canada's role in the bureaucratic side of trade defense is an unsung success story. Unfortunately, at present virtually nothing is known of how the U.S. Navy reacted to, or employed the benefits of, the Anglo-Canadian NCS organization. The British always have maintained that the Americans learned nothing from several years of shared experience and had to suffer six months of dreadful—and avoidable—losses off the eastern seaboard to learn the obvious. It is clear that the American delay in introducing convoys owed nothing to lack of up-to-the-minute trade intelligence. Further, by early 1941 the U.S. Navy had enjoyed a full year of close liaison with Ottawa's trade network, including access to all relevant publications—and yet no convoys until driven to the brink. Perhaps what made the British particularly upset was the knowledge that through Brand's extensive network they actually had the skeleton of an effective system already in place; it just lacked an act of will and a little help from the locals.

An ounce of experience, however, was clearly worth a ton of paper, and it is here that the Canadians offered the U.S. Navy an erroneous view of just what the operational side of trade defense had actually been. What exposure the American navy had had in the Battle of the Atlantic by 1942 had been alongside the struggling RCN. Indeed, as it turned out, the brief spell of shared responsibility in the northwest Atlantic in the last months of 1941 would have lasting and negative consequences for both navies.

The Canadian navy was drawn into defense of convoys in the mid-Atlantic partly by accident. By early 1941, as the main thrust of trade defense shifted from cruisers and battleships to small antisubmarine escorts, the RCN found itself with a multitude of auxiliary vessels—corvettes and minesweepers. Their rate of construction had been determined by modest needs and a hope that many could be bartered in the United Kingdom for *Tribal*-class destroyers, which were to be the primary thrust of Canadian naval expansion. The government was, in any event, intent on using the war to develop Canadian industry, and shipbuilding was an important part of that scheme. When the barter scheme fell through in March 1940, the orders for small ships were allowed to stand. Indeed, more were ordered in the summer of 1940 simply to maintain steady rates of construction. The Canadian navy had specific plans for some of these ships. Under the terms of "Plan Black," a worst-case scenario worked out by the new American-Canadian Permanent Joint Board of Defence in late 1940, most of the corvettes were tied to Ottawa's system of defended ports. Those beyond the RCN's immediate needs were to be sent to serve with the Royal Navy in European waters. *Tribal*s would be built to Canadian accounts in domestic and British yards and would not enter the war before 1943.[9]

The Canadian navy's burgeoning fleet of corvettes (seventy-nine in commission or building by early 1941) finally found a meaningful role in May 1941, when the Newfoundland Escort Force (NEF) was formed. Its task was to close the link in end-to-end antisubmarine escort of convoys between Newfoundland and Iceland, at least until the U.S. Navy could assume responsibility. The tentative nature of the NEF was confirmed in August when Winston Churchill and Franklin Roosevelt met at Argentia, Newfoundland, to divide the world between them. Under the terms of the ABC-1 agreement hammered out the previous winter, the NEF and the rest of the Canadian navy passed under the American navy's "Support Force," soon designated Task Force Four and later still Task Force Twenty-Four. An American admiral was placed in charge of convoy operations in the western Atlantic, and fifty American destroyers were assigned to escort fast trade convoys in the NEF's area. By agreement the slower, predominantly corvette, Canadian navy escort groups took charge of slow convoys as a temporary measure until this duty too could be passed to the U.S. Navy. It was expected that the bulk of the RCN soon would be serving overseas in the war zone around Britain.

Despite direct U.S. Navy participation in escort duties and the promise of a full American takeover west of Iceland, the NEF grew through the fall of 1941 until it contained fully three-quarters of all the Canadian navy's oceangoing escort forces: about seventy ships. Virtually all of them had been hastily commissioned with green crews and were thrown into operations without many basic stores and without essential training. Such were the luxuries of building a navy in a declared "nonwar zone" under the aegis of a neutral admiral. But problems of severe weather, increased enemy activity, and difficult operational cycles complicated the RCN's modest attempts to build the expansion fleet into a credible force in late 1941. Canada's corvettes did well to survive the North Atlantic, and their convoys fared very badly indeed when attacked. Slow, weakly escorted Canadian convoys frequently fell afoul of prowling U-boats in the latter half of the year. SC 42 lost fifteen ships in early

September; SC 48 lost nine ships and two Royal Navy relief escorts (and the USS *Kearny* was torpedoed) a month later; and SC 52 was driven back by a U-boat pack off Newfoundland at the end of October, after losing four ships.[10]

Significantly, this brief but trying period in Canadian naval expansion was the only time when Canadian and American naval forces served side by side in the same theater on something like equal terms. Thus, the U.S. Navy obtained firsthand a devastating lesson in the problems of adequately defending convoys in the face of determined attackers. Perhaps not surprisingly then, when the American navy's Board on the Organization of East Coast Convoys reported in March 1942, its conclusions stood in the face of the doctrine of convoy and escort which the British had for so long impressed on the Americans. The board observed "that effective convoying depends on the escort being in sufficient strength to permit their taking offensive action against attacking submarines."[11] And so it did, at least in midocean. Unfortunately, the same conditions did not obtain inshore, where the real problem of early 1942 lay.

Service alongside the U.S. Navy in the fall of 1941 also had repercussions for the Canadian navy. Like its larger British and American counterparts, the RCN had professed an offensive antisubmarine doctrine at the outset of the war. The Royal Navy finally abandoned offensive escorting tactics in the spring of 1941 when *Western Approaches Convoy Instructions* (*WACI*) were introduced. Although the Canadians had adopted *WACI* as the basis for escort operations until the end of 1942, their escorts frequently failed to adhere to *WACI*'s most fundamental tenet: the primacy of safe and timely arrival of the convoy.[12]

The adoption of *WACI* by the Canadian navy closely coincided with its passing under American navy operational direction. U.S. *Escort-of-Convoy Instructions* (Lantflt 9A) placed "conduct of the convoy clear of the enemy" dead last on its list of priorities.[13] Thus, in the fall of 1941, Canadian navy escort forces were not only out of reach of the Royal Navy's purveyors of doctrine, but also they were actually operating alongside a fleet which professed a Mahanist view of escort's role. Worse still, perhaps, was the absence of any firm Canadian leadership in the area of escort doctrine. Caught in a doctrinal limbo, unfettered and poorly led, the Canadians followed their natural tendency to pursue even the most tenuous contacts with zeal. The British attempted, in January 1942, to reassert their operational control over Canadian escorts east of Newfoundland in order to permit continuity in Anglo-Canadian tactics and doctrine, but the American navy refused.[14] A few months later, however, changes in the escort arrangements effectively brought the Canadian navy back into the fold. Nonetheless, it took until the end of 1942 for the demagogues of orthodoxy to sort out the Canadian navy, and not before the Canadians got into more difficulty.

It was not just in the hard-to-measure areas of doctrine that the wartime relationships between the Canadian and American navies had an impact on Ottawa. The entry of the United States into the war cast an enormous burden on existing forces as it opened vast new theaters for enemy attack. Attempts to sort out the difficulties for the Canadian navy's early expansion were among the first casualties of the wider war. In late November 1941, Commodore L. W. Murray, the commander of the NEF, developed a plan to introduce badly needed operational training for his ships. He intended to establish one additional escort group to allow such groups to slip out of their cycle for instruction. He also hoped to build a training program around Commander J. D. Prentice, an energetic and somewhat eccentric Canadian veteran of the Royal Navy, and his corvette, the *Chambly*. Murray outlined his scheme in a lengthy memo to the Naval Board which he dispatched on 7 December.[15]

For all intents and purposes Murray's operational training establishment at Newfoundland was sunk by Japanese bombs. It was evident that American naval forces would be needed elsewhere, and the Naval Board refused permission for the necessary additional group. In some measure the loss was compensated for by the switch of the eastern terminus of Newfoundland-based escort groups from Iceland to Ireland and the combining of all trans-Atlantic escorts into a new Mid-Ocean Escort Force (MOEF) in February 1942. The Canadian navy now enjoyed—and would for the balance of the war—the full support of the U.S. Navy's NOB Londonderry and access to Royal Navy training facilities. But the situation at the Canadian base at St. John's, Newfoundland, would remain, as one senior officer described it, a "beggar's portion" until 1943.[16] In the meantime, American escort of North Atlantic trade convoys declined sharply. By April only a token U.S. escort group, A.3., remained on the North Atlantic run. Even its composition was nominally American: usually the *Treasury*-class cutters, or four-stacker destroyers. The balance of group strength usually was made up of Canadian and British corvettes. Four other groups in MOEF were nominally RCN and six were "B" groups, largely British but with a healthy smattering of European navies in exile.

The real scramble in early 1942 was off the eastern seaboard of North America. The Canadian zone, protected by a coastal convoy system and extremes of weather, proved a poor hunting ground for the Germans. But off the United States, they enjoyed their second "happy time." In due course the RCN was drawn southward to help stem the tide and to secure Canada's own oil supplies from the West Indies. By September, when the assembly points for trans-Atlantic convoys switched from Halifax to New York, the Canadian navy's Halifax-based Western Local Escort Force was responsible for the main trade routes for fully one-third of their passage, while about one-third of escort forces of MOEF were also Canadian. Although the American admiral at Argentia retained control of escort operations in the northwest Atlantic, his forces north of New York were overwhelmingly Canadian. In fact, about half of all the escorts along the main trade routes were RCN, about 2 to 3 percent were U.S. Navy, and the balance were Royal Navy (including various European navies in exile).

The Canadian navy finally was stretched to the limit by the fall of 1942. The NSHQ estimated that it had only half of the 212 escorts it needed to meet all commitments and to leave room for refits and training.[17] The Canadians chose to concentrate on operations, allowing all but essential maintenance and the barest of training to lapse. The RCN made no complaint about its extended commitments and seemed content to be doing essential, if colorless, work. But the operational emergency of 1942 cost the Canadian navy the chance to make good on the lessons of 1941. Its concentration on the elementary defense of inshore convoys was successful, but it robbed the mid-Atlantic groups of the time, training, and resources needed to master their more deadly enemy: the U-boat wolf packs. During 1942 the Canadian navy's MOEF groups still escorted the bulk of slow convoys—the legacy of an earlier RCN-U.S. Navy agreement—and perhaps for this reason were intercepted at about twice the rate of their British counterparts. They also still lacked cohesion in the face of the enemy and up-to-date equipment, both signs of poor senior direction. Consequently, the terrible battles of 1941 were repeated in late 1942, when sixty of the eighty ships sunk in North Atlantic convoys went down while under Canadian escort.[18]

Canadian midocean groups underwent a period of retraining and reequipping in early 1943 and were on the sidelines when the Battle of the Atlantic reached its climax in the spring. It was during this period of recuperation that Lieutenant Evans, whose *Trillium* was active in the mid-Atlantic with A.3., penned his plea to remember the Canadian corvettes. The RCN's holding action during 1942 earned for it one American's now forgotten epithet, the Battle of Canada. The friction of war and the vicissitudes of partnership in an alliance conspired to elevate the Canadian contribution to importance and yet soften the impact of this contribution on the cutting edge of the battle. Perhaps Vice-Admiral P. W. Nelles, the chief of the Naval Staff, summed it up best at the end of 1943, when he observed that had it not been for the Royal Canadian Navy there might not have been efficient escorts in anyone's navy by 1943.[19] Certainly, without them the shape of the war would have been markedly different.

If the Canadian record in operations prior to 1943 left something to be desired, the same cannot be said of its unqualified success in NCS and naval intelligence. Unfortunately, since historians and their readers prefer action-oriented accounts, these latter activities garner little attention. It makes for undramatic reading to describe how evasive routing of convoys was the decisive element in the Battle of the Atlantic until the final crisis of 1943, and how intense and protracted actions between escorts and wolf packs were really only the last resort in a sophisticated battle of boffins and bureaucrats.

On both counts—at sea and ashore—the RCN made a remarkable contribution to the Atlantic campaign, much of it directed toward easing the U.S. Navy into the war. Ironically, the professional Canadian navy, aping the Royal Navy, maintained a cautious attitude toward the American navy during and after the war. In contrast, the reserves in what one Canadian writer has called the "Sheepdog Navy" found Royal Navy establishments stuffy and inhibited and much preferred the casual North American camaraderie of NOB Londonderry and other American bases.[20] Even after the war the Canadian navy's lower deck reacted strongly in a series of mutinies to attempts by the officer corps to revert to the good old prewar days when the navy was more "Royal" than Canadian.[21] Perhaps the final legacy of those early contacts with the U.S. Navy and the Canadian navy's discovery of its North American roots is to be found in the "new" Canadian navy. Now in the process of shunning the dark ages of unification green, the new uniform for the seagoing element of Maritime Command owes less to the plush, old-world charm of Gieves—long the clothier for the navies of the Empire—than it does to the clothing stores at Newport News, Virginia.

Notes

1. P. E. Evans, "Battle of Canada, March 1943," Washington, DC, Naval Historical Center, Operational Archives Branch (hereafter OAB), Heineman Papers, Box 4, ONS 166, additional information.

2. "Notes of the Vesca System for Dealing with Mercantile Movements as Developed by August 1941," 14 August 1941, Ottawa, National Defence Headquarters, Directorate of History (hereafter DHist), Captain E. S. Brand Papers, 81/145.

3. Correspondence between naval intelligence in Ottawa and British consular agents in the United States can be found in Public Archives Canada (hereafter PAC), RG 24, 3816, 3817, NS 1012-11-1, General Correspondence.

4. "Director of Naval Intelligence's Annual Report, 1941," DHist, Brand Papers; "Outline History of Trade Division, 1939–1945," DHist NS 8280B, vol. 2, 27–32.

5. Ibid., 21.

6. See correspondence in PAC, RG 24, 3816, NS 1012-11-1, vol. 1.

7. "Naval Staff Minutes, 11 June 1942," DHist; "History of Anti-Submarine Measures Division of the Tenth Fleet," OAB, Chronology.

8. Marc Milner, *North Atlantic Run: The Royal Canadian Navy and the Battle for the Convoys* (Annapolis, 1985), chap. 8, passim. Thanks are given to Dr. W. A. B. Douglas for pointing out the importance of the intelligence and trade work in the struggle for a Canadian theater.

9. Ibid., chap. 1, passim.

10. Ibid., chap. 3, passim.

11. "Board on the Organization of East Coast Convoys, Report to CinC, U.S. Fleet," n.d., London, Public Record Office, ADM 205/19.

12. *Western Approaches Convoy Instructions*, DHist Operations Section, Article 101, "General Instructions for Escorts," 83/761.

13. *Escort-of-Convoy Instructions*, Part 5, "Primary Duties of Escorts, as Amended to 17 November 1941," OAB.

14. "Admiralty to OPNAV, 29 January 1942," OAB, CNO-COMINCH Papers, Box 51, COMNAVEU-Admiralty Dispatches.

15. "Flag Officer, Newfoundland to Naval Secretary, 7 December 1941," PAC, RG 24, 11929, MSOO 220-3-6.

16. "Captain (D), Newfoundland to Commodore Commanding Newfoundland, 2 September 1941," PAC, RG 24, 3892, NSS 1033-6-1.

17. "Director, Operations Division to Naval Minister, 19 June 1942," PAC, RG 24, 3842, NSS 1017-10-22.

18. Milner, *North Atlantic Run*, 129.

19. Ibid., 268.

20. "'Personal Appreciation of Situation for R.C.N. Ships in United Kingdom,' Lieutenant Commander W. E. S. Briggs, RCNR to Captain Commanding Canadian Ships, London, 12 April 1943," PAC, RG 24, 11960, CS 34.

21. L. C. Audette, "The Lower Deck and the Mainguy Report of 1949," in J. A. Boutilier, ed., *RCN in Retrospect* (Vancouver, 1982), 235–49.

An Antediluvian Monstrosity: The Battleship Revisited

LAWRENCE C. ALLIN

Examining the uses and misuses of the battleship by various navies from the nineteenth century to the present, Professor Allin traces just what was expected of the vessel and whether it has lived up to these expectations. He concludes with a look at the recent reemergence of the battleship in the U.S. Navy and how it is seen in present maritime strategic thinking.

****

The residents of Allin Street in Long Beach, California, enjoy the proximity and view of the roadstead of the Los Angeles-Long Beach Harbor. During 1940 they saw the battle force of the Pacific Fleet riding majestically at anchor. In 1969 the low, sleek *New Jersey* cut quietly across their harbor with the Arnheiter Affair behind it and the mothballs of deactivation before it. During 1985 the few residents of the short street saw the *Missouri* come to the Long Beach Naval Shipyard for reactivation. They later saw it sail to join its sister ships of the *Iowa* class as a mainstay of one of the controversial battle groups of the U.S. Navy. That one naval officer called such a battleship "an antediluvian monstrosity" should make sailors and scholars search their memories and records to determine what the battleship was and did before 1945 and what it since has become and done.[1]

Such recollections must be clear and true, as Anne Firor Scott held in her presidential address to the Organization of American Historians. "It is a truism," she reminded her audience, "yet one easy to forget, that people most easily see the things they are prepared to see and overlook those they are not prepared to encounter." Professor Scott tempered the battleship quarrel with a caveat: "Historians, looking at the past," she explained, "do not see all that is there. There is no truth-in-labeling law that requires us to admit on our title pages that our 'history' is not the whole story but just so much of it as our own preparation enables us to see and understand."[2]

Even a modest concession to historical truth in labeling would make most officers and historians admit that they dismissed the leviathans as fighting craft and saw them as magnificent noncombatant shrines. Then, in 1982, after the hostage crisis in Iran and the Soviet invasion of Afghanistan, David Woodward published his popular and anglocentric monograph, *Sunk! How the Great Battleships Were Lost.* Bringing a great deal of information and offering several conclusions, Woodward said that the age of the battleship lasted eighty-five years, from the American Civil War to the last stages of World War II. With the resurrection of the *Iowa* class, the battleship now spans 120 years, during which 545 ironclads came down the ways and 130 of them sank.[3]

And how they sank! Woodward told how when he began his book with an account of the sinking by an avalanche of aerial bombs and torpedoes of the last armorclad, Japan's *Yamato*, the largest and possibly the best battleship ever built. Much has been written of its ritual sacrifice. Perhaps Yoshida Mitsuru honored the ship best when he wrote how it wore the Imperial Chrysanthemum.[4] The claim that the *Yamato* was the best has been challenged, probably correctly, by Thomas Hone and Norman Friedman, who believe that superior fire control and electronics rather than big guns would have made an *Iowa* the winner.[5]

The lesser equipped, the unlucky, and the losers of other encounters appear in Woodward's lists. Statistically, its own crew has been the battleship's worst enemy. Scuttling sank twenty-one of them, more than any other cause. Submarine-launched torpedoes claimed fourteen, surface-launched torpedoes thirteen, seaborne guns thirteen, and shore guns four. The latter four were Russian battleships trapped in Port Arthur by the ineptitude of their commander. Only eight of the capital ships went under because of aerial torpedoes. Mines caused thirteen sinkings as did internal explosions.[6] Groundings fatally damaged six armorclads and jinxed the *Missouri* (because of its encounter with Thimble Shoals in the Chesapeake Bay in January 1950, rumor persists that it can make only fifteen knots). Clumsy collisions claimed three of the craft. Sabotage took two. Turning turtle, or capsizing, took one. A fire sank one battleship, as did a glide bomb.[7] Such is the ironclad's tally.

That history should teach caution and humility and perhaps give wisdom is shown in the first sinking of a battleship: the *Re d'Italia*, rammed in 1866. The ram tactic was an answer to the problems of the gun. The difficulty of loading, aiming, and firing the early great guns, as much as twelve minutes between rounds, made naval officers despair. They needed a weapon to make naval combat decisive. The best they could do was to advocate chasing, ramming, holing, and, hopefully, driving their enemy to the bottom.

The sinking of the *Re d'Italia* and the ramming tactics and technology helped to confuse naval thinking for forty years. Perhaps the concept and existence of the battleship has done so even longer. For perspective one must ask: "What did those 545 monuments to bright-work polish, holystones, and the bosun's macramé achieve? Did they become the great arbiters of world power after Alfred Thayer Mahan? Were they before? Were they ever?"[8] The arguments can be honest—and endless.

Only once did the battleship live up to its billing as the greatest weapon and final arbiter in war. Only once did nearly equal battle fleets engage in the classic decisive big-gun duel. This was on 26–27 May 1905 in the Straits of Tsushima when the Japanese sank six Russian armorclads and most of the rest of the czarist fleet.[9] After Tsushima the era of the ram was over. The rifled, breech-loading cannon came to supremacy when the British and the Americans launched the *Dreadnought* and *Michigan*, respectively, to carry even larger guns at greater speed. These types of ships had their test at Jutland. It was inconclusive.

After Jutland the airplane went to sea. Aircraft and their carriers were neither fully developed nor understood during the interwar period. By 1938 the major powers had built more heavily armed and armored battleships. The Japanese brought the type to its big-gunned epitome in the *Yamato* and its sister, the *Musashi*. The Germans built light, fast pocket battleships as well as the magnificent heavyweights, the *Bismarck* and the *Tirpitz*. The Americans had the *Iowa* class, and the French and Italians continued the expensive and prestigious competition.

By 1939 the airplane, the aircraft carrier, and the battleship were misunderstood and expensive. The drains made by the battleship on national monies, natural resources, and skilled personnel were, and are, great. As there had been since its creation, there was great debate during the 1930s and 1940s concerning how the armorclad should be built and used. A 1943 example makes the point.[10] Two young designers, Walmer Elton Stroppe and Stanley J. Dwyer, offered to make the battleship smaller and less expensive. They proposed a 470 × 83-foot vessel with a 21-knot speed to carry six 14-inch guns in two turrets and six 5-inch 38-caliber guns in single turrets. Stroppe and Dwyer believed their design would help clarify the problem of battleship size, enable moderate-size yards to build moderate-size battleships, and allow several Latin American nations to build the type to aid in hemispheric defense.[11]

Stroppe and Dwyer's design took an intellectual pounding, which only reinforces Professor Scott's cautions about historical preceptions. Naval engineers and Captain W. D. Puleston, a naval historian, sank the design with verbal blasts and were prepared only to see large battleships.[12] Perhaps Puleston and the engineers had the 1939 funeral pyre of the *Graf Spee* in mind when they spoke against building small, middlingly capable vessels. A pocket battleship, Germany's *Graf Spee* could fight any vessel except a full-sized battleship. It met its end when it could neither outrun nor outgun a flotilla of British cruisers. The *Graf Spee*'s example makes it plain that, in the world of battleships, big and bigger do not matter, only biggest.[13]

But the biggest had a difficult time being best, so Malcolm Muir, Jr., contended. In his essay on the "Misuse of the Fast Battleship in World War II," Muir claimed that the actions at Taranto, Pearl Harbor, and in the South China Sea discredited the battleship. In those fights aerial bombs and torpedoes sank ten of the leviathans.[14]

During 1943, as American war production grew, as the airplane became comprehensible, and as the men who fought became wiser, the battleship returned to grace in the U.S. Navy. It had proven that it could survive air attack, sustain heavy damage, sink armorclads, bombard enemy troops, and shoot aircraft out of the sky. Still, there were two flaws in the use of the battleships. They were seldom fought after dark because the training of their officers and crews was inadequate for night maneuvering, and the Americans would not risk piecemeal destruction of their battle line. As a consequence, the vessels were often held back from engaging parts of the Japanese battle force. This was, apparently, because their commanders awaited the great surface action, the opportunity to fight another Tsushima.[15]

Perhaps another Tsushima will never be fought. The roles and perceptions of the battleship and of naval warfare changed in August 1945. The atomic weapon forced new technical and intellectual circumstances upon the naval world. Many historians and officers still carry a heavy coat of allegorical battleship barnacles from the preatomic era. Santiago, Tsushima, Jutland, and Surigao Strait are difficult shibboleths to unlearn. Younger scholars who do not remember the battle line will have a different perspective.

Scuttling, scrapping, or effective use in their traditional roles seemed beyond the young *Iowa*s when the atomic bomb changed the naval equations but not all of the naval problems. One can revisit the era before the bomb by looking into Peter Padfield's neatly done work, *The Battleship Era*. In it, some of the technological, tactical, and strategic changes that affected the capital ship can be reexamined. Padfield offered intellectual solace from the era gone by and gave insights into the new circumstances of naval warfare attained in 1945. He demonstrated that the basic questions of "What is a battleship? Why is it built, and how can it be used?" are still problems. They have not been answered because technological and strategic innovations both endanger and enhance the type.[16]

Since Padfield wrote, four chapters have been added to the battleship's technological and strategic history. These are the Korean War, the gun line in Vietnam, the Phase I resurrection, and the Phase II fantasy of conversion. The battleship shot well but was almost unopposed during the peculiar Korean War. With sanctuary for friend and foe and tacit limitations on combat, the type bombarded the shore and met little opposition on the surface or from the air. The Korean War showed that change had come to naval warfare but gave little instruction on the place of the battleship in the fleet.

In the dark days between Korea and the *New Jersey*'s Vietnam activation, many changes in battleship usage were proposed. During 1953, Admiral Robert Carney, chief of naval operations, said that the ironclads could carry missiles.[17] During 1955 the *Kentucky*, the 72 percent complete fifth ship of the *Iowa* class, and its four sisters were seen as supply ships, as intermediate-range ballistic missile ships, and as antiaircraft guided missile carriers. But the *Kentucky* was never completed, and its sisters went into mothballs.[18] In 1957 using the behemoths as electronics-laden command ships was discussed. During the next year some pundits saw the *Iowa*s as cruise missile ships, as antiaircraft guided missile ships, and as antisubmarine warfare ships.[19] Polaris missiles would have been fitted to the beasts in 1959 to make them into yet another version of the guided missile ship.[20] And, if as nothing else, the *Iowa*s could be used as target ships, wrote John Milsop, who also said that the vessels could be utilized as tactical command craft, heavy repair ships, experimental rocket test ships, guided missile dreadnoughts, and landing support ships.[21]

Such ideas became kerosene thrown on the hot coals of controversy as Paul Stillwell showed in his discussion of "The Battleship Battle, 1964–1967." He told of the fight to reactivate the *New Jersey* for service in Vietnam while also rehearsing many of the arguments on the vessel type that continue today.[22] Stillwell said that reactivating the *Iowa*s was seen as a cure for the gun gap, the absence of large-caliber artillery from the navy's ships. The lack was evident in the Cuban Missile Crisis and acute in Vietnam. It was most evident to the marines who wanted the 16-inch guns for shore bombardment and for covering amphibious landings. The 5-inch 38-caliber guns of the *Iowa*s would be used against small enemy surface craft. The accuracy, lethality, and range of their guns and their invulnerability called for the battleships to be reactivated. They could fight in all conditions of weather and interdict the Vietnamese coastal supply routes. Their aft 16-inch gun turrets also could be removed to provide space for a marine assault unit and helicopters.

Several objections to the plan were voiced and still are heard today. The battleships cost too many dollars and too many people. They take money from other naval programs. They fail to provide continuous gunfire support because the vessels and crews need periodic rest, repair, and replenishment. And they demand other units to give them antiaircraft protection.[23]

Regardless, Senator Richard B. Russell, a politically powerful proponent of the type, had his way. The *New Jersey* was pulled out of mothballs and sailed to spend but 120 days on the firing line and serve as it had in Korea. It bombarded enemy shore positions and then went into mothballs a second time. Within the context of Professor Scott's advice, this chapter of post-1945 battleship history appears neither economically, politically, nor militarily rational.

During the *New Jersey*'s Vietnam gunship era, suggestions for the type's conversion were mercifully few and its sisters were left to their slumber. In 1973 it was proposed that they be given the Aegis missile. By 1975 it was plain that Sea Sparrow, Harpoon, and Aegis weapons could be hung from them like Christmas tree ornaments and thus, once more, the craft could become missile ships.[24]

These prescriptions led to the Phase II conversions, and they reinforce Dr. Scott's caution that accurate perceptions of the historical [naval] world are needed. It is a world in which ships must be prepared to fight and to fight with many purposes. Various versions of those purposes have appeared in published lists. As Dr. Scott would point out, those lists reflect the viewpoints and understandings of the men who write them. Some of the lists obfuscate the purposes of a navy and the purposes of a vessel type. One officer's catalog holds that the navy's roles are power projection ashore (invasion?), destruction of seagoing commerce (guerre de course?), and antinaval strikes (sinking the enemy fleet?).[25] This limited American proposal can be considered in light of the traditional European uses of the battleship: sinking the enemy's battle line and gaining command of the sea, protecting the carriers, protecting convoys, destroying enemy merchant vessels, and supporting amphibious landings.[26]

Current American policy will use the *Iowa*s and their great guns with a carrier task force, on the surface as the kingpin of a harassing force, as a battering ram for amphibious landings, as a bludgeon against shoreside targets, and as a jackstaff for showing the flag.[27] They also can use their newly fitted and long-range Harpoon and Tomahawk missiles against other vessels and shore targets.[28]

With the same mystique that keeps the *Titanic* Historical Society afloat, three of the antediluvian monsters are returning to active service for two major reasons. One is strategic; that is, the "prestige factor," or showing the flag. The other is tactical, that is, the "punching factor," or shooting the big guns. The United States has used the *New Jersey* to uphold its prestige against technologically backward Vietnam and the chaotic hills of Lebanon. The benefits are a long time coming.[29]

The U.S. Marine Corps wants the *Iowa*s to punch with their gunfire during "forcible entry" or amphibious invasion. There are no better tools for the task.[30] But the dustbin of history, wherein lie the naval dreams of Winston Churchill, gives a warning. The admonition comes with the viewing of photographs of the *New Jersey* standing immediately off Beirut. The photographs caution the viewer to recall Churchill's Dardanelles Campaign of 1915. Six battleships went down in those narrow waters, three the victims of fortuitously placed mines.[31]

The photographs and memories of the Dardanelles inspire fears of close shore bombardment, the ten-fathom curve, and mines. Those three linked concerns constitute a hiatus in the reactivation literature of the *Iowa*s. The gap must be closed as mines constitute a danger to the *Iowa*s and to their Surface Action Groups during inshore firing, the task they are most likely to perform.[32]

There is another omission from the literature: the lack of an open discussion of the potential for losing one or all of the *Iowa*s in action. They were made to fight. Even if they are fought hard and well, they may be sunk. The probability should be openly entertained. There is no gain of prestige if the battleships are kept from harm's way.

With the *New Jersey, Iowa,* and *Missouri* in commission, the Phase II chapter in the new life of the battleship has been opened. Phase II has been espoused by Secretary of the Navy John Lehman and his supporters. Involving further refitting and improvement of the armorclad, their Phase II rebuilding would use modernization ideas already advanced and would dramatically change the battleships' capabilities and costs. The plans most often put forward include removing the after main-battery turrets and sowing the fantail with the dragon's teeth of 300 vertical-launch missiles. Additionally, two "ski-jump" V/STOL ramps could be placed aft with a hangar deck for an aviation component. The unused space below decks of the Phase I vessels could be modified to carry a 700-man marine contingent for quick assaults.[33] However, politics have ended the Phase II chapter and made it nothing more than a quaint collection of ideas, so testimony of Vice-Admiral Robert L. Walters seems to say.[34]

While the Phase I *New Jersey, Iowa,* and *Missouri* are in commission, the future of the fourth sister, the *Wisconsin,* is greatly debated. Professor Scott probably would say that many different eyes view the *Wisconsin* in many different ways.[35]

Woodward told how the battleships sank. In his final paragraph, Padfield told of the accumulating reality attained throughout the battleship era. That reality should affect thinking on the fleet's composition today. The battleship

> is no longer in command. The conflict in both European and Pacific Theatres had been won and lost by all arms, submarines, torpedoes, mines, aircraft and bombs. Surface ships had played their part, but the great gunned ships, although more powerful than ever, had lost their major role at sea.[36]

The battleship is many things to many eyes. It deserves truth in labeling. It must be seen as and used for what it is: a weapon of high cost and great power and one of discrete and limited abilities.[37]

NOTES

1. Robert Debs Heinl, "Instant Sea Control Ships," *Proceedings of the U.S. Naval Institute* 99 (September 1972): 88 (hereafter *Proceedings*). On the *New Jersey's* arrival on the gun line in Vietnam see Heinl, "Welcome to the War," *Proceedings* 89 (March 1969): 58-62.
2. Anne Firor Scott, "On Seeing and Not Seeing: A Case of Historical Invisibility," *Journal of American History* 77 (June 1984): 7-8.
3. David Woodward, *Sunk! How the Great Battleships Were Lost* (London, 1982), 143-46.
4. Yoshida Mitsuru, *Requiem for Battleship Yamato*, trans. Richard H. Minear (Seattle, 1985), passim.
5. Thomas Hone and Norman Friedman, "*Iowa* vs. *Yamato*: The Ultimate Gunnery Duel," *Proceedings* 109 (July 1983): 122-23.
6. Woodward, *Sunk!*, passim; for technical data, a wealth of plans, and some history of the type see Siegfried Breyer, *Battleships and Battle Cruisers, 1905-1970* (Garden City, 1973).
7. F. J. Koch, Jr., "A Sea-based Interdiction System for Power Projection," *Proceedings* 106 (June 1980): 85. For the grounding of the *Missouri* see Terry W. Jackson, "A Sea-based Interdiction System for Power Projection," *Proceedings* 106 (February 1980): 75.
8. Samuel S. Robison and Mary Robison, *A History of Naval Tactics from 1530 to 1930* (Annapolis, 1942), 660-90. See also Alfred Thayer Mahan, *Naval Strategy* (Boston, 1911). This is the matured version of his strategic thought and is more tempered than his classic work, *The Influence of Sea Power upon History, 1660-1783* (Boston, 1890).
9. For insights into the effects of Tsushima on American battleship thinkers see Elting Morison, *Admiral Sims and the Modern American Navy* (Boston, 1942), chap. 11.
10. Mitsuru, *Requiem*, passim; R. O. Dulin, Jr., and W. H. Garzke, Jr., stated: "Without question the *Iowa*-class battleships were the best ever built"; further, that the *Iowa*s were never designed to fight the *Yamato*s but were designed to fight a new class of four 16-inch gunned battleships that Japan was thought to be building during 1938-39. Dulin and Garzke, "Welcome to the War," *Proceedings* 105 (August 1979): 111-12; Dulin and Garzke, *Battleships: United States Battleships in World War II* (Annapolis, 1976), 107.
11. Walmer Elton Stroppe and Stanley J. Dwyer, "Reinvestigation of the Practicability of the Small Displacement Capital Ship," *Marine Engineering* 48 (January 1943): 156-58.
12. Ibid., 158-59. Gene Anderson proposed to create "the light battleship," taking his inspiration from the Phase II conversion scheme for the *Iowa*s. In the proposed Phase II the vessels would lose their after main-battery turrets. Anderson wanted to use the turrets as the keystone of a vessel similar to Stroppe and Dwyer's. Gene Anderson, "The Light Battleship (BBL)," *Proceedings* 108 (November 1982): 116-17. Lieutenant Commander M. C. West applauded Anderson's idea but said that his design would be too slow. M. C. West, "The Light Battleship (BBL)," *Proceedings* 109 (January 1983): 12. The West German naval writer, Stefan Terzibaschitsch, suggested that something between a British monitor and a German pocket battleship be created in place of the *Iowa*s to give gunfire support to the marines. His design is much like Stroppe and Dwyer's and like Anderson's. Stefan Terzibaschitsch, "Reactivation of the Battleship *New Jersey*," *Proceedings* 89 (February 1969): 107-8. Such "doing it on the cheap" designs are a subset of problems within the historical battleship controversy. These as yet academically unexplored problems constitute the battleship/small-ship quandary.
13. Arthur Marder, *From the Dardanelles to Oran* (Oxford, 1974), 137-39.
14. Malcolm Muir, Jr., "Misuse of the Fast Battleship in World War II," *Proceedings* 105 (February 1979): 57-62.
15. Ibid., 59-62. Both Muir and Clark Reynolds's works are pertinent in understanding the change from a battleship mentality to a carrier mentality in the U.S. Navy. Clark G. Reynolds, *The Fast Carriers* (New York, 1968), 156-253.
16. Peter Padfield, *The Battleship Era* (New York, 1972), passim.
17. Howard W. Serig, Jr., "The *Iowa* Class: Needed Once Again," *Proceedings* 108, Naval Review Issue (May 1982): 136. For further discussion on the subject by Serig see his "Update on the *Iowa* Class," *Proceedings* 108 (December 1982): 108-10, and his "Where Are the Battleships?" *Proceedings* 109 (July 1983): 119-22.
18. Serig, "*Iowa* Class," 136. The man who may be responsible for the 1980s reactivation of the *Iowa*s is Charles F. Meyers, Jr., "A Sea-based Interdiction System for Power Projection,"

Proceedings 105 (November 1979): 103-5. Meyers made the same plea, this time using the Salerno landings to buttress his point. Charles F. Meyers, Jr., "The *Iowa*s: A Legacy to Be Exploited," *Marine Corps Gazette* 65 (August 1981): 48-53. For the importance of Meyers's argument see William H. Honan's two-part article, *New York Times Magazine*, 4 April 1982, 27; ibid., 11 April 1982, 24. Terry W. Jackson contended that the last three *Iowa*s were unfit for sea when he stated that the *Missouri* was too slow because of its grounding, that the *Wisconsin* had suffered a devastating fire in its electronics suite, and that the *Iowa* had been cannibalized to put the *New Jersey* back on the line. Terry W. Jackson, "A Sea-based Interdiction System for Power Projection," *Proceedings* 106 (February 1980): 75.

19. Anthony Harrigan, "Missile Battleships," *Proceedings* 78 (October 1958): 123-25.

20. Serig, "*Iowa* Class," 136.

21. John Milsop, "Let's Use Our Battleships," *Proceedings* 82 (August 1962): 110.

22. Paul Stillwell, "The Battleship Battle, 1964-1967," *Marine Corps Gazette* 65 (August 1981): 38-46; Paul Stillwell, "The New/Old Dreadnoughts," *Sea Power* (October 1983): 11-18.

23. Stillwell, "The Battleship Battle," 39-40. Recent objections to the *Iowa*s are found in L. Edgar Prina, "The Battle for the Battleships," *Sea Power* (September 1981): 55. James Exon, senator for Nebraska, has been critical of the battleships as seen with his statement of 22 May 1985, *Congressional Record*, 99th Cong., 1st sess., 6766-80.

24. Norman Polmar, *Ships and Aircraft of the U.S. Fleet*, 13th ed. (Annapolis, 1984), 102-5; Serig, "*Iowa* Class," 137.

25. T. J. McKearney, "The Offensive Surface Ship," *Proceedings* 109 (December 1983): 65-69.

26. Terzibaschitsch, "Reactivation of the Battleship *New Jersey*," 107-8.

27. A. M. Bowen, E. J. Gannon, and Steven Morrison, *Battleship Reactivation Brief* (Washington, DC, 1985), 6-7.

28. Ronald O'Rourke, analyst in national defense, Congressional Service, to Olympia J. Snowe, M.C., 27 August 1985, deals briefly with the battleship's missiles. The Tomahawks are new weapons in their first operational use aboard the *New Jersey*. There are three versions: the TASM, TALM/C, and TALM/N, for antiship, conventional land attack, and nuclear land attack. The *Iowa*s can carry thirty-two of these missiles in any mix. The entire question of the armament of the *Iowa*s, or what it should be, is confused by the richness of opportunities. For concise descriptions of the *Iowa*s' weapons see Norman Friedman, *U.S. Naval Weapons* (Annapolis, 1982), passim.

29. M. C. Franklin, "A Sea-based Interdiction System for Power Projection," *Proceedings* 106 (January 1980): 23-24; Interview with John F. Lehman, Jr., Secretary of the Navy, in *U.S. News and World Report*, 4 May 1981, 31.

30. Anthony Gurnee, "The BB(V)," *Proceedings* 108 (August 1982): 90.

31. William E. Smith, "Familiar Fingerprints," *Time* 122 (26 December 1983): 18-19. The *New Jersey* fired 290 16-inch rounds into Beirut on 8 February 1984. U.S. Navy, Office of Information, *Lebanon Ops* (revised ed.: 23 February 1984), 4.

32. R. D. M. Furlong, "U.S. Navy Bringing Back the Battleships?" *International Defense Review* (14 June 1981): 744 passim.

33. Walter T. Piotti, Jr., *Reactivation of Battleships, Hearings before the House of Representatives Seapower and Strategic and Critical Materials Subcommittee* (Washington, DC, 1983), 5, 7. See also Robert L. Walters, "Bigger Punch for BBs: *New Jersey* Gets Tomahawk and Harpoon," *Surface Warfare* (October 1981): 4.

34. The temporary retreat from Phase II modifications is revealed in the testimony of Vice-Admiral R. L. Vaughn, deputy chief of naval operations for surface warfare, before the Subcommittee on the Department of Defense of the Senate Appropriations Committee, 29 March, 8 May 1984, and before the Seapower and Force Projection Subcommittee of the Senate Armed Services Committee, 22 March 1984. The testimony is in typescripts furnished by committees in a letter to O. J. Snowe, M.C., 12 April 1985.

35. Dudley Glendinen, "Cities Compete to Be Home for *Iowa*," *Maine Sunday Telegram*, 15 May 1983. The battleships are seen as economic boons by some cities and by others as "nuclear lightning rods" which would attract Soviet missiles. If it is activated, the *Wisconsin* may be home ported at Corpus Christi, Texas. James J. Kilpatrick, *Washington Post*, 13 August 1985.

36. Padfield, *Battleship Era*, 290; Archer Jones and Andrew J. Keough, "The Dreadnought Revolution: Another Look," *Military Affairs* 49 (July 1985): 124-31. Although he published his work in 1972, Padfield ignored the *Iowa*s, excepting a single-page entry for the class. He also

totally ignored the reactivation of the *New Jersey*. Jones and Keough reflect on the creation of the HMS *Dreadnought,* a major event in the continuing technological and economic revolutions that have made the battleship a focus of national pride, energy, and controversy. They deal with the question of technological obsolescence and its impact upon lesser craft.

37. A logical target for the *Iowa*s' antiship missiles is the *Kirov*s. The heaviest surface units in the Soviet fleet, they are not analogous to the *Iowa*s and carry fewer missiles than the American craft. "Soviets Testing Battle Cruiser in Baltic Sea," *Aviation Week and Space Technology,* 26 January 1981.

General Louis H. Wilson: 26th Commandant of the Marine Corps, 1975-79

DAVID H. WHITE, JR.*

During his tenure as commandant, General Louis H. Wilson led the Marine Corps through the difficult post-Vietnam transition which proved to be a test of the ability of the Corps to adapt during peacetime. Professor White shows how General Wilson confronted, fought, and won a host of military and political challenges; revitalized the traditional Marine Corps; and thus ensured its adaptation to the U.S. defense evolution which followed the Vietnam War.

****

Our Corps is the gift of over two and a half million Marines who have gone before us. What we do with it, as we enter our third century, will be our gift to future generations.[1]

—General Louis H. Wilson
Commandant, Marine Corps
November 1975

A forceful leader with a sense of history, General Louis H. Wilson, the 26th commandant of the Marine Corps, from 1975 to 1979, guided the corps from the shadowy post-Vietnam purgatory into its third century of existence as a fighting force. The last marine commandant to have fought in the Pacific island-hopping campaign during World War II and a Medal of Honor winner in the last war that the United States clearly won, Wilson distinguished himself as a combat infantryman. As commandant, his military professionalism, leadership style, tremendous capacity for involvement with people, and political finesse combined to create a veritable *deus ex machina* who would retrieve the Marine Corps from its Vietnam legacy and carry it on to victory in the ultimate test of organizational survival in the 1970s.[2]

Vietnam—both the costly war and the fragmenting historical phenomenon it represents—confronted the Marine Corps with unprecedented criticism of its mission, personnel policies, and force structure and therefore diminished the prestige of this elite service. With the collapse of a global containment consensus during the Nixon and Ford administrations, the Marine Corps adjusted to a strategy of global flexibility while U.S. defense planners shifted from Southeast Asia to a more Europe-oriented, NATO defense posture. Amid lingering polarization between the American people and the armed forces and

*The author gratefully acknowledges research support from the Citadel Development Foundation which made possible preparation of this essay on General Louis H. Wilson, USMC. Appreciation is also expressed for the research assistance provided by the staff of the History and Museums Division, Headquarters Marine Corps, Washington, DC.

with inflation gnawing at the defense budget, critics within the defense establishment and think tanks labeled the corps's amphibious mission and capability obsolete and questioned its independent existence as a special force in readiness. Indeed, the challenging half-decade from 1975 to 1979 is a crucial chapter in the continuum of Marine Corps history, a recent episode in what historian Allan Millett has described as a "story of institutional adaptation in both peace and war."[3]

Wilson's selection as commandant following a publicized intracorps struggle for the post and an attempted purge of senior lieutenant generals, including Wilson himself, by the incumbent commandant, General Robert E. Cushman, can be attributed largely to the evolution of American national security policy in the wake of the Vietnam War. In the spring of 1975, Cushman recommended the appointment of his assistant commandant, General Earl E. Anderson, but Secretary of the Navy J. William Middendorf II and Secretary of Defense James R. Schlesinger pressed instead for Wilson.[4]

During the interview process, Schlesinger and Middendorf found Wilson, then commanding general, Fleet Marine Force–Pacific, an innovative and responsive officer who favored reorientation of the Marine Corps for commitments worldwide, with attention to Western Europe and NATO. Moreover, his rhetorical preview matched the Defense Department's evolving concept of marine deployment in the event of war in Western Europe. Impressed by Wilson's adaptability and his credentials, Schlesinger obtained President Gerald Ford's approval of the nomination by telephone in April 1975 with Wilson still sitting in the secretary's Pentagon outer office. In early May the Senate Armed Services Committee, chaired by Senator John C. Stennis, a staunch supporter of Wilson and a fellow Mississippian, unanimously and with dispatch confirmed the appointment.[5]

After a six-week interim stint as special assistant to the commandant—a somewhat distant four wings down from Cushman's office at Headquarters Marine Corps in Washington—Wilson was promoted to general and embarked upon his command. At the outset, he demanded organization obedience to bring the corps's performance up to his standards and to meet Schlesinger's expectations of flexibility. At the change of command ceremony at Marine Barracks in Washington on 30 June 1975, Wilson laid out his job philosophy in a very short sentence: "I call upon all Marines to get in step, and to do it smartly." Two days later, at the Pentagon swearing-in ceremony, Secretary Schlesinger called upon the Marine Corps to retain its special competence in amphibious operations while broadening its capabilities as a "general purpose" force. During the next four years, Commandant Wilson aimed to prepare the corps for global missions and to restore its elitist image.[6]

At first, Wilson faced a barrage of external criticism about the Marine Corps's mission and force structure, all of which led up to a crescendo in January 1976 with publication of the Brookings Institution's study on the future of the corps. Declaring that the end of the age of amphibious warfare had arrived, the authors warned that the corps had to shift its focus to a more relevant mission, such as the defense of Korea or Central Europe, or be diminished to a costly amphibious anachronism.[7] The passage of a decade makes the Brookings study appear jaded, especially after the Falklands War, but it did contribute to institutional self-examination which psychohistorians will, no doubt, one day applaud.

When defense and media analysts questioned the survival of his corps, Wilson struck back with the earnestness of a Scots Presbyterian and the incisiveness of a cobra. While interviewing the commandant for a Marine Corps birthday feature in 1975, CBS newsman Ike Pappas observed that the amphibious assault mission appeared to be out of date. Wilson responded that the "critics had said that before. They were wrong then and just as wrong now." As for searching for a mission, Wilson reported to Congress at the end of 1975 that as a ready, mobile, general purpose force with amphibious expertise, the corps had a mission—a global force in readiness.[8] The ability to project combat power over the seas and onto a hostile shore was, in Wilson's mind, a building block of American strategy in the 1970s. In this sense, Wilson was to the core a traditionalist.

After disengagement from Southeast Asia, however, Wilson broadened his own vision of a Marine Corps poised for deployment in low- or high-intensity combat around the globe. While he opposed specialized restructuring for combat in Europe only, he prepared the marine forces as a strategic reserve for deployment in Europe to support a NATO war contingency. Wilson's best-use northern flank scenario, based on advance notice of an enemy threat, held that the Marine Corps could send one Marine Amphibious Force (MAF) to Denmark and one brigade to Norway to protect the Baltic approaches and to provide air support against an enemy threat in Iceland. Wilson theorized that the marines could establish a defensive position between the North Sea and the Baltic—along the Kiel Canal—in case of Soviet movement across the north German plain, and attack from the flank if Soviet forces penetrated West Germany.[9]

Convinced that the corps should not be typecast as exclusively an amphibious force, Wilson directed a Headquarters Marine Corps staff board, headed by Major General Fred Haynes, to analyze the corps's structure and mission in order to mold it as a viable force with combat credibility in all types of future wars. From the Haynes study grew an emphasis on imaginative task organization to provide flexibility rather than a radical departure to new technology. On the ground, the M-60 tanks replaced the M-48, the TOW and Dragon missiles increased the infantry's antiarmor capability, and the M-198 155mm howitzer was selected to become the primary direct-support artillery weapon. Basic infantry weapons remained the M-16, M-60, and mortars. By 1979 the streamlined marine division boasted centralized logistics and increased firepower.[10]

Structural refinements and the twin principles of task organization and intensive training created the traditional foundation upon which Wilson's Marine Corps prepared for future combat. For that purpose, Wilson established the Air-Ground Combat Center at Twenty-nine Palms, California, to practice combined arms training, desert maneuver warfare, and mechanized and antimechanized operations.[11] Amphibious operations and maneuvers in northern Europe, the Caribbean, the Mediterranean, and East Asia ensured global training for a Marine Corps with a global mission. Wilson delivered what he had promised Schlesinger.

Determined to recapture the public admiration lost during the Nixon-Cushman years, Wilson also attacked the problem of quality in the Marine Corps as a priority military and political imperative. On his first day as commandant, he ordered action on grooming and weight control for all personnel, and he broadcast to the ranks an absolute insistence on quality all the way from the recruiting effort, through the training pipeline, into the operating and support forces. Said Wilson, "The battlefield is no place to find out that our standards should have been higher." But he had more in mind than operational readiness. In striving for the highest moral, mental, and physical standards, he intended to restore in the American people the traditional conviction that the marines truly represent the epitome of elitism.[12]

Wilson did not shrink from the challenge of maintaining the quality of the Marine Corps in a competitive, all-volunteer environment with manpower costs consuming seventy to eighty cents of every budget dollar. What has been dubbed the Great Personnel Campaign, 1973–77, became Wilson's inheritance from the Cushman-Anderson regime. In 1973 and 1974 unacceptably high rates of courts-martial, nonjudicial punishment, confinement, unauthorized absence, and desertions threatened combat readiness. Making matters worse, the Cushman assumption that mental aptitude (IQ) was the best indicator of quality caused the percentage of high-school graduate enlistees to drop from 54 percent in 1973 to 51 percent in 1974, despite a congressional order to enlist 55 percent in high-school graduates in Fiscal Year (FY) 1974.[13]

To combat the recruiting problem, Wilson called upon the expertise of newly promoted and newly appointed Lieutenant General Robert Barrow, deputy chief of staff for manpower at Headquarters. Barrow, who had just arrived from a tour as commanding general, Marine Corps Recruiting Depot, Parris Island, South Carolina, held strong convictions about recruiting and recruit training and therefore proved to be an able adviser to the commandant, who had never himself been stationed at a recruit depot. The Wilson-Barrow reform initiatives in late 1975 grew out of Wilson's willingness to accept a corps below its budget-authorized strength of 196,000, thus opening the way for an offensive on substandard marines through disciplinary action and an expedited discharge program.

In the recruiting arena, the main enlistment criterion shifted from IQ test score to high-school diploma as the most reliable indicator of quality in terms of retention, trainability, and acceptance of discipline. Wilson also set the new enlistment standard at 67 percent in high-school graduates for FY 1976 and 75 percent for FY 1977. In the fall of 1975, Headquarters in Washington began to shift responsibility for recruiting from the six Marine Corps district headquarters to the commanding generals of the recruit depots at Parris Island and San Diego, in order to give control of recruit input to the two commanders who were responsible for boot camp production of quality marines.[14]

These key recruiting reforms, along with increased budget outlays for the recruiting service, coincided with Headquarters's comprehensive review of recruit training beginning during the closing months of 1975. The thrust of policymaking was to reduce recruit training stress and eliminate abuse of authority by training personnel. However, a gulf existed between policy and drill instructor practice during the winter of 1975–76. When drill instructors increased pressure on recruits of 1975 vintage quality—what the late Colonel Robert Heinl described as the effort to make silk purses out of sows' ears—attrition rates rose along with complaints of recruit abuse.[15]

Early in 1976, before Wilson could either implement reforms or fine-tune the system, allegations and several notorious cases of recruit abuse prompted ranking leaders in the Senate and House to call for congressional investigations into Marine Corps recruiting and recruit training. The case of Private Harry Hiscock, who was shot in the hand by a drill instructor at Parris Island, and the death of Private Lynn McClure as the result of head injuries sustained in mock bayonet practice with pugil sticks at San Diego generated critical press reports and aroused doubts among politicians that the corps could cope with All-Volunteer Force manpower problems. The Hiscock and McClure cases also resurrected the ghost of Ribbon Creek, where six recruits drowned during a march into a tidal creek at Parris Island in 1956. As Wilson recalls the specter: "The American public remembrance of Marine training is very long and the Ribbon Creek affair... was constantly brought up as if it happened yesterday."[16]

Hearings before the House Armed Services Committee accelerated the pace and broadened the scope of change in recruit training. In their testimony and statements from May to August 1976, Wilson and Barrow outlined specific changes and practices to curb abuses of authority and made four general commitments to Congress:

1. To reduce the level of stress on both recruits and drill instructors by eliminating the "motivation platoons," shortening the training syllabus, and permitting recruits a limited amount of free time daily and on weekends.

2. To strengthen and improve supervision of recruit training at all levels by doubling the number of officers assigned to recruit companies and platoon series and by assigning a brigadier general to each depot to reinforce the supervisory program.

3. To review and improve the processes of screening, selection, and training of drill instructors to include psychiatric evaluation and counseling instruction.

4. To provide the recruits with a protected, confidential channel through which to report abuses (personal interviews with officers).[17]

Wilson expected drill instructors at the depots to rise up en masse against the changes, but senior noncommissioned officers at Parris Island and San Diego rallied to support the commandant's order that training abuses would not be tolerated. However, changes at the highly structured depots did produce discontent among drill instructors whose authority was eroded, and Wilson could foresee dissatisfaction among young officers who would rather lead in the Fleet Marine Force than supervise at the depots. Nevertheless, on his watch, Wilson honored the mandate of Congress to implement rigorous reforms and guarantee their enforcement. And when Barrow was selected as 27th commandant in June 1979, Wilson was confident that the reforms would remain in place for at least four more years. Even now, the conduct of training is in compliance with the 1976 reforms. Wilson's vigilance preserved the integrity of recruit training and protected its ultimate purpose: to produce marines to fight, survive, and win in any future combat.[18]

Wilson's performance under fire during the 1976 hearings proved a successful test of his ability to represent the Marine Corps before Congress. A critical advantage during his command was his past experience from 1967 to 1968 when he served as legislative assistant to Commandants Wallace M. Green, Jr., and Leonard F. Chapman, Jr., both of whom enjoyed the respect of Congress. In that staff assignment, unique among the services, then Brigadier General Wilson had developed close working relationships with senators, House members, and staff assistants who would prove to be influential contacts when he became commandant in 1975.[19]

Supporters included senior Southern Democrats, conservative Republicans, former marines in Congress, and defense-oriented congressmen. A longtime friend and political ally was Senator Stennis (D-MS), chairman of the Senate Armed Services Committee. Other staunch supporters on that committee included Senator John Tower (R-TX), who provided backing especially on Marine Corps aviation issues; Senator Stuart Symington (D-MO), who retired from the Senate but remained a powerful figure in the Democratic party when Wilson was commandant; Senator Dewey F. Bartlett (R-OK), ranking minority member and former marine lieutenant-colonel aviator; and Senator Daniel Inouye (D-HI), a former member of the committee. On the Senate Appropriations Committee, Wilson depended on Stennis again and upon Senator Milton R. Young (R-ND), the ranking minority member. Wilson assiduously courted his friends on the Armed Services Committee and paid courtesy calls on many during his first month in office. Although they were not on that particular committee, several other senators offered support on major issues; James Eastland (D-MS), chairman of the Judiciary Committee; John Glenn (D-OH), the marine aviator and astronaut who vigorously supported Wilson's efforts to acquire the AV-8B *Harrier* aircraft; and John Warner (R-VA), a "great booster" of the Marine Corps.[20]

On the House side, Wilson's network included many personal and official friends, especially members of the House Armed Services Committee. A primary adviser and Basic School classmate of Wilson's, Major General John R. Blandford, had for many years served as chief counsel for that committee under its late chairman Mendel Rivers (D-SC). Blandford had worked closely with Wilson when the latter was legislative assistant to the commandant, and even though Blandford was phasing out as chief counsel in 1975, he continued to be an important point of contact and general adviser. Wilson was a constituent and close personal friend of Congressman G. V. "Sonny" Montgomery (D-MS) who, as a member of the Armed Services Committee, had participated in the 1976 hearings on recruit training. Congressman George H. Mahon (D-TX), Wilson's golf partner and longtime friend, chaired the House Appropriations Committee. One notable congressman with whom Wilson had no contact was Thomas P. "Tip" O'Neill (D-MA).[21]

Because it afforded him opportunities to deal personally with congressmen and thus establish his credibility, the legislative assistant's job was Wilson's best preparation for the position of commandant. The job also taught him the legislative process, since he accompanied Greene and Chapman in all their appearances before the House and Senate Authorization and Appropriations committees. From Greene, a meticulous organizer of data, Wilson learned and perfected for his own use a flash card system for the annual hearings on the Marine Corps budget. A military assistant would pass to the commandant—

"very much like a surgeon is handed his instruments"—a card bearing information requested during the hearings.[22] In this fashion, Wilson could respond flawlessly to any query related to the budget request. Surely, he cherished his relationship with Congress.

Wilson's budgetary knowledge and mastery of the legislative process carried the Marine Corps through three of President Jimmy Carter's lead defense budgets. With personal costs skyrocketing due to 10 percent-plus inflation, Carter and Secretary of Defense Harold Brown authorized Wilson to save money through manpower reductions in order to fund operations, maintenance, and procurement. This management flexibility, for example, permitted Wilson to plan a reduction of 10,000 marines in FY 1981 ($10,000 per marine per year) and thereby save $100 million for procurement, operations, and maintenance.[23] Manpower shrinkage had to be tolerated as a necessary evil.

Along with manpower, amphibious shipping and aviation posed serious budget problems throughout the Carter years. The Carter budgets from 1977 to 1979 and the navy's efforts to maintain a balanced fleet forced a continual reduction in MAF amphibious lift capability, thus a reduction in strategic mobility. Wilson and his former National War College classmate, Chief of Naval Operations Admiral James L. Holloway III, compromised on a 1.33 MAF lift goal for the 1970s, which was overly ambitious. Wilson also hoped for the navy's replacement by the 1980s of the aging LSD-28s on a one-for-one basis with the LSD-41s that would carry the futuristic LCAC (landing craft air cushion).[24]

This modernization of Marine Corps aviation resulted in nothing short of bureaucratic warfare. In July 1975, Wilson canceled Cushman's earlier plan to purchase the Grumman F-14, despite the objections of senior marine aviators who wanted the high-technology fighter with its Phoenix missile and sophisticated tracking system. Opting for greater versatility, Wilson decided to retain the F-4 *Phantoms* and await development of the McDonnell Douglas F-18 with its attack/fighter capability. The corps pulled four F-14 squadrons from Naval Air Station Miramar in order to transfer those aircraft to the navy, saving the chief of naval operations (CNO) blue-water aviation dollars. Wilson's military decision yielded political benefit because the navy badly needed the F-14s. Admiral Holloway in return promised Wilson in writing that the marines would be first to receive the F-18s.[25]

At the same time Wilson insisted that, while waiting for the F-18, the Marine Corps would go forward with plans to acquire the new *Harrier*, the AV-8B, to replace the AV-8A. The commandant demanded both the F-18 and the AV-8B, a V/STOL (vertical short take off and landing) aircraft. To be built by McDonnell Douglas, the AV-8B was considered vital to assure land-based, fixed-wing, close air support in amphibious operations without having to rely on existing airfields.

Wilson fought the Department of Defense (DOD) and the navy for the new *Harrier*. His chief opponent in the DOD, Russell Murray, assistant secretary of defense for program analysis and evaluation, had great influence with Secretary Brown. In 1978 the DOD blocked continued development and procurement. Wilson then appealed directly to his friends and allies in Congress. Senator Glenn, a strong supporter of the AV-8B and respected by his Senate colleagues for his aviation knowledge, may have been a key player, among others, in the struggle. In any case, Congress in early 1979 authorized $180 million for the AV-8B program for 1980, but in the spring Wilson faced opposition from the new CNO, Admiral Thomas B. Hayward. In Navy Department Program Objective Memorandum FY 1981-85 (POM-81), Hayward questioned the affordability of the AV-8B. Disappointed and furious over what he perceived as a "carefully woven tapestry of truths, half-truths, and innuendos," Wilson reacted in a blistering confidential letter to Hayward and dismissed "affordability" as a smoke screen for the real issue—navy opposition to the AV-8B because it represented a significant threat to the large aircraft carrier. Wilson, refusing to be pressured into a decision unfavorable to marine interests, outflanked the CNO and mobilized support for the *Harrier* from Navy Secretary W. Graham Claytor and Under Secretary R. James Woolsey. In the end, Wilson felt confident that Congress, "which has always been our friend in time of need," would appropriate funds in the 1981 budget for the follow-on *Harrier*. Time would tell that Wilson and his allies had won the bureaucratic battle for the AV-8B.[26]

The crowning achievement of Wilson's stewardship of the Marine Corps came in 1978 when the commandant became for the first time a permanent member of the Joint Chiefs of Staff (JCS). Technically limited by law to discussions of Marine Corps interest, the commandant's position had evolved by the 1970s to the point where Wilson participated in practically all JCS decisions. Wilson's strategy all along had been to wait until his fourth year in office to try to get the law changed, to make it clear that he was acting on behalf of the corps and his successors, not himself. A catalyst that prompted Wilson to press for statutory change was the recent past behavior of General George Brown, USAF, chairman of the JCS. Brown tolerated the commandant's collaboration in JCS decision making as appeasement of Congress, and by his attitude he made Wilson aware that the marine commandant was not actually a JCS member.[27]

Sensitive of the status issue and caught in an Orwellian position—the other service chiefs more equal than the commandant—Wilson girded himself for a major political drive. He consulted over a dozen close allies on how best to legislate the change and followed a course of action suggested by Congressman Bob Wilson (R-CA), the ranking minority member of the House Armed Services Committee. Congressman Wilson recommended the addition of a clause to the Senate Defense Authorization Bill for 1979 to make the corps commandant a full JCS member. Desiring to "have it happen on my watch," Commandant Wilson asked Senator Stennis to intercede on his behalf, to grant a favor. Said Stennis, "I'll do it for you." Tactical assistance came from Senator Bartlett, a member of the Senate Armed Services Committee. The World War II marine dive-bomber pilot proposed an amendment to the bill making the commandant a permanent member of the JCS. With the support of Stennis, Tower, and other loyalists, the resolution passed unanimously, a tribute to the incumbent commandant and to Bartlett, who was serving his last term in the Senate because of lung cancer. The commandant kept his strategy a well-guarded secret from the DOD and JCS members until after the Senate voted, telling only Secretary of the Navy Claytor what he was doing twenty-four hours in advance of the vote. The next morning Secretary of Defense

Brown was reported to be surprised and appalled—and he knew that the commandant was behind the strategy.[28]

Ranking members of the House Armed Services Committee held the key to passage in that chamber, and General Wilson lobbied hard and heavy among committee members. The commandant had secured secret pledges of support from Congressman Melvin Price (D-IL), Samuel S. Stratton (D-NY), Bob Wilson, and others if the Senate passed the resolution without controversy, which it had done. Despite ruffled feathers at the Pentagon, no one openly criticized the commandant's full membership on the JCS and no organized opposition materialized to delete the enabling amendment from the Defense Authorization Bill, which breezed through the House Conference Committee without dissent. After a Carter veto and a revision of the bill to remove a nuclear carrier that the president opposed, Carter finally signed the Appropriations Authorization Act of 1979 and presented Commandant Wilson with a plaque welcoming him as a full member of the JCS. Even reluctant Defense Secretary Brown "congratulated the Marine Corps for the high prestige it has in Congress which permitted such a potentially controversial bill to [go] through in such a smooth manner."[29]

Wilson had mobilized his political capital and engineered the triumph to raise the corps commandant to his rightful place as a full JCS member, to benefit future generations of marines. Marines and friends of the Marine Corps alike looked upon the JCS battle as a righteous crusade. Symbolically, it ended the marines' desperate thirty-five-year struggle for survival as a corps, for recognition as a separate military service, and for fair treatment by the Pentagon, the three larger services, and an often hostile defense bureaucracy. Cast in the phraseology of the late Colonel Heinl, the Marine Corps had come to the end of a long march to the top.[30]

The JCS victory marked the high point of Wilson's command and of his distinguished Marine Corps career. When he retired to Mississippi in 1979 after thirty-eight years of active duty, Wilson could look to the distant past with personal pride as a Medal of Honor winner during the golden age of amphibious warfare, the Second World War. As custodian of the Marine Corps as an institution for four years, he could recall the recent past with proud confidence that his corps had adapted successfully to the American defense evolution that came hard on the heels of the Vietnam War. With a curious blend of egotism and humility, Wilson remarked from retirement: "I leave [it] to future historians to judge my watch in comparison to the many fine commandants who were my predecessors and that long line who will be my successors."[31]

The Wilson era was both a test of institutional survival for the Marine Corps and a test of the commandant's force. Wilson proved to be a consummate politician, an accumulator and user of political capital, ideally suited to negotiate the politico-military terrain of Headquarters Marine Corps, the Pentagon, and Congress. The Wilson legacy was a revitalized yet traditionally elite corps, more versatile and more independent, esteemed by the public and Congress. Those same characteristics apply to Wilson the leader—traditional but adaptable and politically adept. In many ways, the 26th commandant owed his successful "watch" to the fact that he personified the best institutional characteristics of the corps.

NOTES

1. Quoted in Gen. Louis H. Wilson, "Looking Around," *Leatherneck* (November 1975): 27.
2. Allan R. Millett, *Semper Fidelis: The History of the U.S. Marine Corps* (New York, 1980), 560; Allan R. Millett, "The United States Marine Corps: Adaptation in the Post-Vietnam Era," *Armed Forces and Society* (Spring 1983): 363–92.
3. Millett, *Semper Fidelis*, xiv.
4. Transcript of oral history interviews with Gen. Robert E. Cushman, 405–520, Oral History Collection (hereafter OHC), History and Museums Division (hereafter H&MD), Headquarters Marine Corps, Washington, DC; see also newsclippings from the *Washington Star*, 27 April 1975, and 6 May 1975, and the *Washington Post*, 1 July 1975, in Wilson Files, Reference Branch, H&MD.
5. Transcript of oral history interviews with Gen. Louis H. Wilson, 5, OHC, H&MD; Wilson to Middendorf, 8 April 1975, and newsclipping from the *St. Louis Post Dispatch*, 30 June 1975, Wilson Files; *Hearings before the Committee on Armed Services*, U.S. Senate, 94th Cong., 1st sess., on Nomination of Lt. Gen. Louis H. Wilson to Become Commandant of the Marine Corps, 6 May 1975 (Washington, DC, 1975), 3.
6. Wilson interview transcript, 23, 38, OHC; newsclipping from the *Washington Post*, 1 July 1975, and remarks by Secretary of Defense James R. Schlesinger at swearing-in ceremony, Pentagon, 2 July 1975, Wilson Files; Millett, "The United States Marine Corps," 389.
7. Martin Binkin and Jeffrey Record, *Where Does the Marine Corps Go from Here?* (Washington, DC, 1976), 88.
8. Memorandum, 24 October 1975, and Wilson to Sen. Sam Nunn, 31 December 1975, Wilson Files.
9. Wilson interview transcript, 205–6, OHC.
10. Headquarters Marine Corps News Release, 24 October 1975, Wilson Files; Wilson interview transcript, 405, OHC; Millett, *Semper Fidelis*, 615–17.
11. Millett, "The United States Marine Corps," 386.
12. Wilson interview transcript, 43, 57, quoted in "A Message from the Commandant," *Leatherneck* (July 1975): 16.
13. Notes, Plans and Operations Department, Headquarters Marine Corps, October–November 1975, Wilson Files; Cushman interview transcript, 424–25; Millett, *Semper Fidelis*, 619–20.
14. Wilson, "Spirit of '76," *Marine Corps Gazette* (March 1976): 16; Wilson interview transcript, 43, OHC.
15. Excerpt from Robert D. Heinl, "The DI Mystique, Sows' Ears and a Delicate Imponderable," *Sea Power* (June 1976), Wilson Files; Millett, *Semper Fidelis*, 621.
16. Wilson interview transcript, 177, OHC.
17. *Hearings on Marine Corps Recruit Training and Recruiting Programs*, Subcommittee on Military Personnel, Committee on Armed Services, House of Representatives, 94th Cong., 24–26 May, 2–29 June, 9 August 1976 (Washington, DC, 1976), 126–30, 161–76, 192, 215–16.
18. Wilson interview transcript, 176–77, OHC.
19. Ibid., 139, 583.
20. Ibid., 21–22, 49, 74.
21. Ibid., 12, 16, 20–21.
22. Ibid., 582–83.
23. Ibid., 164.
24. Ibid., 47.
25. Millett, *Semper Fidelis*, 612; Wilson interview transcript, 68–69, OHC.
26. Wilson interview transcript, 22, 69, 277, 281, OHC; Millett, *Semper Fidelis*, 612; memorandum, Wilson to Chief of Naval Operations, 18 May 1979, Wilson Files; Millett, "The United States Marine Corps," 384.
27. Wilson interview transcript, 50, 473, OHC.
28. Ibid., 474–76.
29. CMC White Letter, "CMC Status as a Member of the Joint Chiefs of Staff," No. 12-78, 24 October 1978, Wilson Files; Wilson interview transcript, 476–80, OHC.
30. Wilson interview transcript, 480, OHC; copy of news release, Robert D. Heinl, "Marine Corps Comes to End of a Long March to the Top," 4 August 1978, Wilson Files.
31. Wilson interview transcript, 609, OHC.